The Origins of Object Knowledge

The Origins of Object Knowledge

Edited by

Bruce M. Hood

Bristol Cognitive Development Centre,
Department of Experimental Psychology,
University of Bristol,
Bristol, UK

Laurie R. Santos

Department of Psychology,
Yale University,
New Haven, USA

OXFORD
UNIVERSITY PRESS

OXFORD
UNIVERSITY PRESS

Great Clarendon Street, Oxford, OX2 6DP,
United Kingdom

Oxford University Press is a department of the University of Oxford.
It furthers the University's objective of excellence in research, scholarship,
and education by publishing worldwide. Oxford is a registered trade mark of
Oxford University Press in the UK and in certain other countries

© Oxford University Press 2009

The moral rights of the authors have been asserted

First published by Oxford University Press 2009

Published in the United States of America by Oxford University Press
198 Madison Avenue, New York, NY 10016, United States of America

British Library Cataloguing in Publication Data

Data available

Library of Congress Cataloging in Publication Data

Data available

ISBN 978-0-19-921689-5

Oxford University Press makes no representation, express or implied, that the
drug dosages in this book are correct. Readers must therefore always check
the product information and clinical procedures with the most up-to-date
published product information and data sheets provided by the manufacturers
and the most recent codes of conduct and safety regulations. The authors and
the publishers do not accept responsibility or legal liability for any errors in the
text or for the misuse or misapplication of material in this work. Except where
otherwise stated, drug dosages and recommendations are for the non-pregnant
adult who is not breast-feeding

Preface

This edited volume grew out of a meeting in April 2005 funded by the Economic and Social Research Council (ESRC) of Great Britain. The goal of the meeting was to bring together psychologists studying the origins of object knowledge from a variety of different perspectives. The question of how organisms come to represent and understand objects is one that has concerned psychologists for some time, but recent years have seen an explosion of empirical work on this topic across a number of different areas in the cognitive sciences. The goal of the ESRC Symposium on Object Knowledge was to bring these different perspectives together and to highlight the new work done in this classic area.

We decided to hold the meeting at Yale University, as many of the leading researchers in this area were based on the east coast of the United States. We designed the meeting differently than the typical conference workshop in two critical ways. First, the meeting was not intended to represent all the work being done in the area of object knowledge. Instead, we intended the meeting to be a small intimate gathering of a select group of researchers, one that enabled a dialogue of ideas that is all too absent from larger meetings. For this reason, we intentionally kept the meeting quite small—it was limited to only thirty researchers whose work directly addressed issues related to the origins of object knowledge. Second, we wanted to design a meeting that explicitly promoted student involvement. More specifically, we wanted to showcase up-and-coming graduate students rather than more established researchers. Most of the senior researchers who attended already knew each other's work fairly well and so we wanted to address recent advances in the development of object representation from a collegiate view. In this way, it gave our students a rare opportunity to present their work in a context that was conducive to discussion but at a level that was much higher than commonly found in graduate school classes.

The meeting itself over three days worked extremely well. Mentors took a backseat while the graduate students gave most of the presentations. Together, the talks presented provided a diverse multifaceted approach to the question of object knowledge origins. The different researchers used a variety of different techniques and populations to address how the mind comes to represent physical objects. As the meeting continued, it became increasingly evident that the interdisciplinary approach to the puzzle of the object representation delivered at the meeting was likely to yield more insight into this classic problem. The discussions after invited talks often spilled over into the coffee breaks, with established researchers debating the relevant issues with graduate student colleagues. As expected, the level of collaboration and discussion was outstanding, so much so that we decided to approach Oxford University Press with a proposal for an edited volume.

When we came to submitting a proposal for an edited volume, we recognized that there were some conspicuous absences in interdisciplinary perspectives, undoubtedly due to the small size of the Yale meeting. In an attempt to redress this issue, we have invited key researchers who were not at the meeting to add their perspectives to the mix. The following edited volume represents the fruits of all these labors. The final collection is not all inclusive of the field, but it does show that the question of object knowledge origins is incredibly broad, one that spans a variety of subject populations, experimental techniques, and theoretical perspectives.

As a testament to the secondary goal of the Yale meeting, we are happy to report that all of the graduate students who took part in our meeting have graduated and moved on to the next step in their academic careers—some have moved on to postdoctoral positions, whereas many more have secured faculty positions. The success of any one individual researcher should be considered in light of not only personal contributions to the field but also the extent to which they have nurtured, encouraged, and supported the next generation of researchers. We would like to believe that an early exposure to high-level presentation, dialogue, and discussion with other senior academics at a relatively early stage in their careers, three years ago, helped our students in some way to pursue their own research careers.

Bruce M. Hood & Laurie R. Santos
August 2008

Contents

List of contributors   *ix*

1 Object representation as a central issue in cognitive science   *1*
Laurie R. Santos & Bruce M. Hood

2 Beyond 'what' and 'how many': Capacity, complexity, and resolution of infants' object representations   *25*
Jennifer M. Zosh & Lisa Feigenson

3 A comparative approach to understanding human numerical cognition   *53*
Kerry E. Jordan & Elizabeth M. Brannon

4 Multiple object tracking in infants: Four (or so) ways of being discrete   *85*
Marian L. Chen & Alan M. Leslie

5 Do the same principles constrain persisting object representations in infant cognition and adult perception?: The cases of continuity and cohesion   *107*
Erik W. Cheries, Stephen R. Mitroff, Karen Wynn, & Brian J. Scholl

6 Spatiotemporal priority as a fundamental principle of object persistence   *135*
Jonathan I. Flombaum, Brian J. Scholl, & Laurie R. Santos

7 Infants' representations of material entities   *165*
Rebecca D. Rosenberg & Susan Carey

8 The developmental origins of animal and artifact concepts   *189*
Kristin Shutts, Lori Markson, & Elizabeth S. Spelke

9 Building object knowledge from perceptual input   *211*
Dima Amso & Scott P. Johnson

10 Modeling the origins of object knowledge   *227*
Denis Mareschal & Andrew J. Bremner

11 Induction, overhypotheses, and the shape bias: Some arguments and evidence for rational constructivism   *263*
Fei Xu, Kathryn Dewar, & Amy Perfors

12 Young infants' expectations about self-propelled objects *285*
Renée Baillargeon, Di Wu, Sylvia Yuan, Jie Li, & Yuyan Luo

13 Clever eyes and stupid hands: Current thoughts on why
dissociations of apparent knowledge occur on solidity tasks *353*
Nathalia L. Gjersoe & Bruce M. Hood

Index *373*

Contributors

Dima Amso
Sackler Institute for
Developmental Psychobiology,
Weill Medical College of
Cornell University,
New York,
USA

Renée Baillargeon
Department of Psychology,
University of Illinois,
Urbana-Champaign,
USA

Elizabeth M. Brannon
Department of Psychology and
Neuroscience and Center for
Cognitive Neuroscience,
Duke University,
Durham,
USA

Andrew J. Bremner
Department of Psychology,
Goldsmiths College,
University of London,
London,
UK

Susan Carey
Harvard University,
William James Hall,
Cambridge,
USA

Marian L. Chen
Department of Psychology,
Northwestern University,
Evanston IL,
USA

Erik W. Cheries
Harvard University,
William James Hall,
Cambridge,
USA

Kathryn Dewar
Department of Psychology,
University of British Columbia,
Vancouver, B.C.,
Canada

Lisa Feigenson
Department of Psychological and
Brain Sciences,
Johns Hopkins University,
Baltimore, MD,
USA

Jonathan I. Flombaum
Department of Psychology,
Yale University,
New Haven,
USA

Nathalia L. Gjersoe
Bristol Cognitive Development
Centre,
Department of Experimental
Psychology,
University of Bristol,
Bristol,
UK

Bruce M. Hood
Bristol Cognitive Development
Centre,
Department of Experimental
Psychology,
University of Bristol,
Bristol,
UK

Scott P. Johnson
Department of Psychology,
University of California,
Los Angeles,
USA

Kerry E. Jordan
Department of Psychology,
Utah State University,
Logan,
USA

Alan M. Leslie
Department of Psychology and
Center for Cognitive Science,
Rutgers University,
Busch Campus,
Piscataway,
USA

Jie Li
Department of Psychology,
University of Illinois,
Urbana-Champaign,
USA

Yuyan Luo
Department of Psychological
Sciences,
University of Missouri,
Columbia,
USA

Denis Mareschal
Centre for Brain and Cognitive
Development,
School of Psychology,
Birkbeck College,
University of London,
London,
UK

Lori Markson
Department of Psychology,
Washington University,
One Brookings Drive,
St Louis,
USA

Stephen R. Mitroff
Department of Psychology and
Neuroscience,
Duke University,
Durham, USA

Amy Perfors
Department of Psychology,
University of British
Columbia,
Vancouver, B.C.,
Canada

Rebecca D. Rosenberg
Harvard University,
William James Hall,
Cambridge,
USA

Laurie R. Santos
Department of Psychology,
Yale University,
New Haven, USA

Brian J. Scholl
Department of Psychology,
Yale University,
New Haven,
USA

Kristin Shutts
Department of Psychology,
Harvard University,
William James Hall,
Cambridge,
USA

Elizabeth S. Spelke
Department of Psychology,
Harvard University,
William James Hall,
Cambridge,
USA

Di Wu
Department of Psychology,
University of Illinois,
Urbana-Champaign,
USA

Karen Wynn
Department of Psychology,
Yale University,
New Haven,
USA

Fei Xu
Department of Psychology,
West Mall,
University of British Columbia,
Vancouver, B.C.,
Canada

Sylvia Yuan
Department of Psychology,
University of Illinois,
Urbana-Champaign,
USA

Jennifer M. Zosh
Department of Psychological and
Brain Sciences,
Johns Hopkins University,
Ames Hall
Baltimore,
USA

Chapter 1

Object representation as a central issue in cognitive science

Laurie R. Santos & Bruce M. Hood

1.1 Knowing objects

Philosophers of mind make a distinction between knowledge that is derived or mediated and knowledge that is immediate. Mortals must derive mediated knowledge whereas divine knowledge is immediate. Oddly enough, cognitive scientists interested in the nature of human object knowledge have their fair share of arguments about a rather similar distinction. Indeed, the question of where knowledge comes from has pervaded debates in object cognition since the field's inception. Do humans begin life privileged with the capacity to immediately detect and represent objects? Or is our object knowledge instead derived only as the result of prolonged experience in the external world? Are we simply able to perceive objects by watching their actions in the world, or do we have to act on objects ourselves in order to learn about their behavior? Finally, do we come to know all aspects of objects in the same way, or are some aspects of our object understanding more epistemologically privileged than others?

Thankfully, over the past few decades, psychologists interested in the development of object knowledge have made remarkable empirical headway even in the face of this philosophical controversy. Such empirical headway is in large part due to a growing interest in the origins of object knowledge among psychologists outside the developmental sphere. Indeed, researchers in disciplines as varied as vision science, comparative cognition, and cognitive neuroscience have added to the investigational furor surrounding the origins of human object knowledge. The result is a veritable explosion of work in this area, with each field taking on the classic problem of object representation from different but often equally important perspectives.

This volume aims to provide a snapshot of the current state of this comparative research explosion, with an emphasis on the current results shaping our theories of the origins of human object understanding. In particular, the goal of the book is to have researchers in each field pause, take a step back, and theoretically reflect on what new results from these intersecting perspectives on object knowledge origins have taught us to date. The goal of this chapter, however, is to take a few more steps back, and to provide some theoretical and historical background for the issues to be discussed in later chapters.

In this chapter, we draw attention to some of the most relevant historical work on object representation to have emerged from developmental and comparative research. Our focus, unfortunately, will have to be rather narrow, as any summary chapter on a topic as central to cognitive science as object representation could potentially occupy volumes. Nonetheless, there are several characteristic questions about the nature of object representation that have historically had a rather important bearing on the course of research in developmental psychology, and thus will likely be areas where a comparative approach can have its greatest impact. With this in mind, we will focus on three specific areas here:

1 The question of objects as permanent entities

2 The question of objects as entities with properties

3 The question of objects as entities to be manipulated

1.1.1 Objects as permanent entities

Historically, one of the most important questions facing developmental psychologists has concerned the question is when infants come to represent objects as permanent entities, ones that persist across time, space, and occlusion. Of course, the concept of object permanence itself is really a misnomer, as all objects comprise energy in continuous states of change. Nervous systems, however, are not built to be metaphysical realists. Their job is not to represent objects as a quantum physicist might. Instead, nervous systems were developed via natural selection to represent objects so that organisms may interact with the external world in an adaptive way, and thus, brains are built to capture what is functionally relevant about objects.

One of the most functionally relevant aspects of physical objects is the fact that they persist—standardly speaking, objects do not go in and out of existence and, thus, it is important that an organism be able to represent their continued presence even when they cannot be directly perceived or apprehended. Consequently, most human adults are, at least implicitly, committed to the notion that objects are external entities that exist independently of the observer and that—all things being equal—they will continue to exist as they move across time and space.

So how do we come to know that objects are permanent entities? This seemingly simple question is one of the oldest and perhaps the most controversial issues in both philosophy and in the field of developmental psychology. For example, Idealist philosophers such as George Berkeley argued with Realists such as John Locke about the priority of the mind over matter. In short, how was the experience of an external physical reality generated? Did the mind create objects or did objects impose themselves on the mind? Such philosophical considerations about the origin of perceiving objects as enduring entities led to the first empirical investigations of what infants—who lack experience in interacting with objects—actually know about the external physical world. These metaphysical issues motivated investigations by the Swiss psychologist Jean Piaget who was primarily interested in how biological systems could represent and adapt to their physical environments. Piaget's approach to the problem of investigating infant knowledge involved allowing infants to act on the world and observing what they did and did not seem to know about the world based on these active behaviors. Through a long series of painstaking observational studies on his own children, Piaget was able to develop hypotheses about how the youngest infants ultimately come to represent their world in more adult-like ways (see Piaget, 1955).

Based on his observations, Piaget theorized that infants gain more adult-like knowledge of the physical world by constructing it themselves through their actions on the world. He hypothesized that preverbal infants experience their world in a way that is radically different than adults do—without the capacity to act on the external world, infants have no way of knowing about it and, more specifically, no way to recognize that objects are tangible, permanent entities. In one famous example of this phenomenon, Piaget hid his daughter's beloved toy duck under a sheet and observed how she reacted. Surprisingly, the young infant did not continue searching for the missing toy. Observations such as this led Piaget to his famous notion that infants lack 'object permanence', the understanding that objects continue to exist when one is not in perceptual contact with them. In this sense, 'out of sight' (and similarly, 'out of hand') literally meant 'out of mind'.

As Piaget noted, it is only around 6–8 months of age that infants begin to search for hidden objects. Prior to this, he argued, infants have no enduring representation of objects when they are out of sight. Moreover, even when infants do begin to search for hidden objects, their early representations of the missing objects do not correspond to separate entities, ones that are independent of the infants' own actions with their own spatial temporal coordinates. For example, Piaget observed that when infants successfully find an object, if the object is then moved to a new location 'B', the infant returns to search in the original location 'A'. Even though the infant saw the object moved in full view to a new position, it is as if the act of searching would recreate the object at the original location. This became known as the A not B error. Based on errors such as these, Piaget hypothesized that infants only come to represent objects in any meaningful way after they have had substantial experience acting on objects in a coordinated way and internalizing the consequences of such action. This achievement, which Piaget hypothesized occurred at around 18 months of life, was thought to represent a major conceptual change for the developing child, one in which mere sensory–motor information was somehow transformed into more adult-like representational thought.

Although he was one of the first to empirically investigate the origins of object knowledge, Piaget's study of and hypotheses about object permanence highlight several of the major themes still at work in the study of object representation today—ones that will be debated in detail in the chapters that follow. The first issue concerns *the role of perceptual and motor experience in the development of adult-like object understanding.* Piaget, of course, championed that sensory–motor experience is essential for the development of object permanence as well as any concrete object understanding. Although, as we will discuss in the following sections, more recent methods have called Piaget's evidence into question, the issue of what motor experience provides the developing child is one that is still unsettled in the field today. The second issue highlighted by Piaget's initial work concerns *the role of conceptual changes in the development of our adult-like object understanding.* Here, Piaget came down on the side of the conceptual change theorists, arguing that the developing child undergoes major and stage-like conceptual shifts in the understanding of the permanence of objects. But as many of the chapters in this volume will attest, the question of how (and even whether) conceptual change is relevant to our object knowledge is one that drives much current empirical work.

From constructivist piagetianism to nativist core knowledge theories

Although Piaget was the first to look at these issues, in the decades that followed his pivotal observations, many of his textbook conclusions have come to be questioned. Although he did an impressive job of chronicling the development of infants' early object manipulation skills,[1] most of his observations involved the use of infants' reaching behavior as a proxy for what the developing child

---

[1] As the psychologist Steven Pinker allegedly once put it, 'for a guy who just played with his three kids, his observations have stood the test of time astonishingly well' (*New Yorker*, September 4, 2006).

knows about the physical world. In the decades since his initial work, many researchers have begun doubting the extent to which his reaching measures indeed provide a valid measure of infants' object competence. First, researchers have observed that young infants reach for objects that are out of sight. Filming with infrared cameras in total darkness, Hood and Willatts (1986) observed that infants reach more to the correct side for a previously seen object when the room lights go out, suggesting that infants are able to represent objects with which they have no direct perceptual access (for similar findings, see Clifton et al., 1991; Clifton et al., 1999; Goubet & Clifton, 1998; Shinskey & Munakata, 2003). These studies indicate that search rather than representation is problematic. In particular, the use of other objects to occlude the target presents a means-end problem wherein the infant has to coordinate a means (remove cover) to achieve the goal (retrieve toy). Means-end coordination taxes the problem-solving capacity of young infants (for review, see Willatts, 1989) and occluders can themselves become the focus of interest thereby disrupting the original goal. Such response biases present a difficulty that affects infants' performance on any reaching measures designed to illustrate their competence (e.g., Diamond, 1991; Munakata et al., 1997).

The problems with reaching measures led infancy researchers to seek out an alternative method for examining infant object competencies. In the 1980s, experimental psychologists turned to a response that young infants had more control over than their reaching—their looking. Indeed, other researchers had previously used infants' looking responses as a measure of discrimination. For example, Fantz and collegues (Fantz, 1965; Fantz & Fagan, 1975) presented infants with different visual displays and observed that the infants preferred to look at more complicated over less complicated patterns. The researchers were then able to use this preferential looking method to explore whether infants were able to discriminate some patterns and not others.

Using insight from these early habituation and discrimination looking procedures, developmental psychologists were able to establish a method for using infants' looking to get at their expectations. In a now-renowned example, Baillargeon et al. (1985) presented five-month-old infants with an event in which an opaque drawbridge-like screen occluded a box and then began rotating toward it. They found that infants expected the drawbridge to stop rotating when it hit the box, looking reliably longer at unexpected events in which the drawbridge completed a full rotation as though the box had disappeared. This technique of looking time afforded the possibility to investigate all sorts of knowledge that could be contextualized as a violation. These early results and others (e.g., Baillargeon, 1987, 1993; Baillargeon & Graber, 1987; Baillargeon et al., 1990; Leslie, 1984; Leslie & Keeble, 1987; Spelke, 1988;

Spelke & van de Walle, 1993; Spelke et al., 1992; Spelke et al., 1995; Wynn, 1992) directly contradicted Piaget's hypotheses about infants' object understanding. Not only was the idea that there was no representation of the unseen object untenable, but infants also had expectations about the nature of unseen objects' properties as well.

In the 1990s, Spelke and colleagues (Spelke et al., 1994; see also Spelke et al., 1992) synthesized findings from these new looking method studies and proposed three principles that govern infants' reasoning about objects as permanent entities: cohesion, continuity, and contact. The first of these principles—cohesion—is the idea that moving objects maintain their boundaries and connectedness. Infants appear to recognize that objects are cohesive and have been shown to look longer at events in which an individual object violates its connectedness (e.g., Spelke et al., 1989; Spelke et al., 1993). Second, infants recognize that objects move on *continuous* paths through time and space. Infants look longer at violations of continuity, ones in which two solid objects appear to move through each another (Baillargeon et al., 1985; Spelke et al., 1992) and ones in which a single object appears to have moved through space in a discontinuous manner (see Spelke et al., 1994; Spelke et al., 1995; Xu & Carey, 1996). Finally, infants appear to recognize that inanimate objects move if and only if they are *contacted* by another object (e.g., Leslie, 1984; Leslie & Keeble, 1987).

Interestingly, although infants appear to reason about objects in terms of cohesion, continuity, and contact, they do not appear to understand *all* the aspects of inanimate object motion that adults do. Spelke and colleagues, for example, observed that infants fail to use the principles of inertia and gravity to predict how objects will move in space (see Spelke et al., 1992; Spelke et al., 1994). Similarly, although young infants represent objects as having coherent boundaries over motion, they fail to represent them as having coherent properties until almost at one year of age (see Simon et al., 1995; Leslie et al., 1998; Xu & Carey, 1996). Infant therefore appear to possess some but not all of adults' intuitions about the nature of objects. Indeed, infants' patterns of successes and failures on looking time tests of object knowledge suggest that infants are built to recognize the most fundamental properties of objects (see Spelke, 1994, for a similar argument).

These results and others led Elizabeth Spelke and her colleagues to propose what is now a dominant theory of the origins of object knowledge, the *core knowledge hypothesis* (see Spelke, 2000; Spelke et al., 1994). The core knowledge (hereafter, CK) hypothesis argues that our adult human knowledge of the physical world stems from experience-independent, innate principles for reasoning about entities within the domain of inanimate physical objects.

Under this view, adults possess their basic intuitions about objects and motion from birth. The CK hypothesis, thus, differs in two critical ways from the constructivist theories of Piaget that preceded it. First, CK proposes that our knowledge of objects has many of the properties of a Fodorian module: our knowledge of objects is specific to the domain of objects and encapsulates itself from other kinds of inputs (Fodor, 1983). Therefore, our knowledge of objects is unlikely to require much motor experience to get off the ground developmentally. In this way, the CK hypothesis differs radically from all constructivist approaches in that it argues not only that experience plays little role in getting our object knowledge off the ground to begin with, but also that experience plays little role in shaping our basic object understanding through the life course. Second, because experience plays little role, the CK hypothesis argues for continuity across development, rejecting the Piagetian notion of drastic conceptual change. According to the CK hypothesis, our basic understanding of objects and their motion is not subject to change—the principles that underlie our understanding of objects are with us from cradle to grave.

Although the CK hypothesis was originally proposed to account for the development of human understanding of objects, the theory made interesting predictions about the evolutionary history of these principles. Even in some of their earlier inceptions (e.g., Carey & Spelke, 1996; Spelke, 1994), the principles that make up our CK of objects were meant to be adaptive responses to constraints on the physical world that had been present throughout a long evolutionary history. Therefore, it would make sense that other species facing similar physical constraints may have developed similar, or even homologous, systems for representing objects. If the CK hypothesis is correct, one might expect that humans share their innately specified object representation mechanisms with other animals, particularly other closely related primates.

Using this logic, comparative researchers have used expectancy violation looking methods such as those used with human infants to demonstrate that a variety of nonhuman primates appear to represent objects according to the three principles originally outlined by Spelke and colleagues (see Santos, 2004, for review). Adult rhesus monkeys (*Macaca mulatta*), for example, appear to represent objects as *cohesive* entities: similar to human infants, rhesus macaques look longer at events in which an object appears to break apart as it moves in space (Munakata et al., 2001). Similarly, adult primates appear to reason about objects in terms of their *continuity*: a number of primate species tested with looking measures successfully tracked objects behind occluders (Flombaum et al., 2005; Hauser & Carey, 2003; Hauser et al., 1996; Santos et al., 2005;

Uller et al., 2001) and look longer when the objects violate *solidity* by appearing to move through each another (Santos & Hauser, 2002; Santos et al., 2006). Finally, there is some evidence that primates also utilize the principle of *contact*: monkeys look longer when inanimate objects appear to move on their own (Hauser, 1997). These observations have led to the view that infants share their core principles of objects with closely related species, and thus, that our core ideas of objects as permanent entities are both developmentally and evolutionarily central.

Since its original articulation, the CK hypothesis has generated considerable controversy (see, for example, Bogartz et al., 1997; Haith, 1998, 1999; Melkman & Rabinovitch, 1998; Smith, 1999). Some of the controversy surrounding the hypothesis had to do with its experience-independent nativist take on infant object knowledge. Others have criticized the CK hypothesis with the view that infants' performance on looking tasks reflects their *perceptual* processing of the displays rather that a *conceptual* knowledge of objects (e.g., Bogartz et al., 1997; Haith, 1998). Perceptual representations, under this view, are transient and tied to the immediate input-processing stream in contrast to the conceptual representations proposed by the CK hypothesis. Critics have argued that the earlier competencies revealed in these violation of expectancy studies are perceptually grounded discriminations that are emergent from the nature of the way infants extract information over the course of testing (Bogartz et al., 1997; see also, Amso & Johnson, Chapter 9).

In their analysis of the dichotomy between perception and cognition of object knowledge, Scholl and Leslie (1999) advocate a middle ground as neither polarized position is sufficient to account for observable phenomena. Three arguments have been raised against a purely perceptual account: (1) input to the perceptual system is inherently continuous and cannot individuate objects, (2) objects can be represented over considerable amounts of occlusion that cannot be accounted for by sensory decay, and (3) perceptual illusions reveal that the system is susceptible to conceptual hypotheses that tell the observer what to experience (Gregory, 1966). However, the weakness of a purely perceptual account of object knowledge does not necessitate abdication to the conceptual position.

In order to resolve these two views, Scholl and Leslie proposed a different account of infants' successful performance on object cognition tasks. They argued that the infants' object principles are best characterized as the operation of object-based attentional mechanisms. Drawing upon several models of object-based attention (e.g., Kahneman, Triesman, & Gibbs, 1992; Pylyshyn, 1994), Scholl and Leslie described how the principles of cohesion and continuity could emerge epiphenomenally from the actions of object indexing mechanisms of the visual system. These object-based indexes are not considered to be either solely perceptual or conceptual entities but rather have properties from both representational perspectives. Object indexes, for example, have the capacity to survive occlusion, indicating that they are entities that can be represented and so are not transient perceptions. Nevertheless, although the operation of object indexes is constrained by features such as cohesion and spatiotemporal continuity, they do not embody these principles in any explicit or 'theory-like' way, as a rich conceptual account of infant cognition such as the CK hypothesis might suggest.

Object permanence and persistence: the current controversies and questions

Since the time of Piaget, developmental psychologists have gained much insight into how infants come to represent objects as permanent entities. Even today, however, researchers debate over the exact nature of the development of this capacity and the mechanisms that drive it. For example, although much empirical evidence suggests that infants can represent objects from an extremely young age, there is growing evidence that this capacity shows some improvement even in the first few months of life. Johnson and colleagues have observed that infants' capacity to represent objects as permanent, spatiotemporally continuous entities depends on low-level perceptual features and gradually improves early in the first year of life (see Amso & Johnson, Chapter 9). How this early improvement in object tracking translates into infants' object concept is a topic of much debate (see Amso & Johnson, Chapter 9). A second topic of much current work concerns the extent to which adult humans' object cognition also possesses some of the limitations present in infants' early processing. Mitroff and colleagues (Chapter 5) have explored the extent to which adults' object processing can be interrupted by the same limitations that prevent infants from tracking hidden objects. Finally, developmental research focusing on older infants and toddlers has demonstrated that early infants' object knowledge does not always translate into the knowledge that older infants use to act on the world. The issue of what such developmental dissociations in performance really reveal is a topic to which we will return in subsection 1.1.3.

1.1.2 Features to objects

As reviewed in the preceding, there is a growing body of work suggesting that even very young infants conceive of objects as permanent entities, ones that persist across occlusion with coherent boundaries and consistent motion constraints. How then do infants go from recognizing objects merely as objects to recognizing them as individuals? After all, the infant's world is typically filled with numerous different bounded cohesive objects, and infants must quickly learn to deal with these different objects in different ways. How and when do infants go from thinking of the object feeding them as merely a 'coherent bounded entity' to an 'object with female, mother-looking properties' to '*my mother*'?

A growing body of empirical work has come to address how infants come to track objects as particular individuals with particular features that are members of particular kinds. In going through this work, however, it is important to distinguish between the different component processes that infants must use to ultimately track different individual objects over time. Borrowing from Leslie et al. (1998), we here distinguish between *individuation*, the process of locating distinct individual objects that are in a scene, and *identification*, determining whether a previously individuated object is the same as has been seen previously. Note that individuation is a process that is required for *enumeration*, the process of determining how many individual objects are present.

There is much evidence to suggest that infants are able to individuate objects, namely tack particular individuals over time and occlusion, from a very early age. Spelke and colleagues (1995) presented infants with events in which a bar moved behind two separate screens. When the bar appeared to move between the two screens, infants expected a single individual bar to be present in the test displays. In contrast, when the bar did not appear to move between the two screens, infants expected more than one individual to be present in the test displays, suggesting that discontinous motion cues trigger the individuation of a new object. These results and others (e.g., Leslie et al., 1998; Needham, 1998, 1999; Needham & Baillargeon, 1997, 1998; Van de Walle et al., 2000; Needham et al., 2005; Wilcox, 1999; Wilcox & Baillargeon, 1998a,b; Xu & Carey, 1996) suggest that infants can successfully use spatiotemporal and other motion cues to individuate occluded objects. Moreover, infants are able to enumerate objects delineated by spatiotemporal cues so long as the number of objects to be enumerated is less than three or four individuals. (e.g., Feigenson, Dehaene, & Spelke, 2004; Simon et al., 1995; Wynn, 1992; Xu, 2003.)

Property/Kind individuation and the role of language

Although the capacity to use spatiotemporal information to individuate objects comes on quite early, the capacity to use other relevant features, such as an object's properties or its kind, appears to develop quite late in infancy. In a landmark study, Xu and Carey (1996) presented infants with events in which a duck and a truck alternatively moved from behind an occluding screen. When the two objects were presented simultaneously, ten-month-old infants successfully predicted that there should be exactly two objects behind the screen. In contrast, when the two objects were presented sequentially, such that the infants were no longer able to use spatiotemporal cues for individuation, ten-month-old infants were unable to individuate the objects, showing no expectation about the number of objects behind the screen. This study and a number of clever follow-ups (see Xu, 2003; Xu & Carey, 1996; Xu et al. 1999; Xu et al., 2004) indicate that infants undergo a major shift in their capacity to use a combination of property and kind information (hereafter, property/kind information) to individuate objects. Moreover, this shift seems to correspond to the time when infants are first learning the word for new objects (see review in Xu, in press). In one impressive demonstration, Xu et al. (2005) allowed twelve-month-olds to reach into a box to find hidden objects, but not to see the box's contents ahead of time. Before reaching into the box, infants heard an adult say either two different words or the same word twice after looking at the box's contents. Infants who heard two different words expected two distinct individual objects, whereas those who heard the single word repeated expected only one object (for similar findings, see Xu, in press).

For these reasons, Xu and colleagues have hypothesized that infants are able to individuate objects using property/kind information only after they have begun learning words for these objects. According to Xu (1999), language may play a critical role in 'reorganizing' infants' object concepts: rather than thinking about objects merely as bounded entities, linguistically saavy infants come to think of objects in terms of their kind. In support of this view, Xu et al. (2004) observed that twelve-month-old infants succeed in individuating objects using property/kind information when the kind of objects (and thus, their labels) differs, but not when their properties and not kind differ. Similarly, Xu (2002) observed that younger infants are able to succeed on the Xu and Carey (1996) property/kind individuation tests when they are trained with labels for the toys to be enumerated (see Xu, in press, for review).

Although Xu and colleagues have presented a compelling case for the role of language in human infants' kind individuation, work with nonlinguistic animals suggests that language, although important, is not necessary for property/kind individuation. Uller et al. (1997), for example, presented adult rhesus macaques with the original Xu and Carey (1996) property/kind individuation test and observed that they perform similar to older infants, successfully using a combination of property/kind information to individuate food objects placed behind a screen. Rhesus monkeys have exhibited similar successes in property/kind individuation when tested by using other looking methods (e.g., Munakata et al., 2001) as well as searching tasks (Phillips & Santos, 2007; Santos et al., 2002). These findings in primates demonstrate that language is not necessary for property/kind individuation. In addition, they raise the question of how language in fact allows young infants to succeed on these tasks.

Object tracking and enumeration: evidence for developmental continuity?

Young infants' performance on different types of object individuation tasks leads to the view that spatiotemporal information is the primary means by which they locate individual objects in the world. Indeed, this view of infants' object individuation fits with a growing body of work in adult visual attention. Vision scientists working in the area of mid-level vision have devoted much empirical attention to the question of how and when the visual system is able to focus on and attentionally track a particular individual object. Interestingly, research in this area suggests that the visual system is limited in the same way as infants' object individuation capacities: it is bound to spatiotemporally distinct objects, and appears to ignore other featural information (e.g., Kahneman & Treisman, 1984; Kahneman et al., 1992; Scholl, 2001; Scholl & Pylyshyn, 1999; Yantis, 1995; see Cheries et al., Chapter 5, for review). In addition, similar to infants, adults appear to show deficits on visual tracking tasks in which objects do not cohere across time and space (van Marle & Scholl, 2003, see also Mitroff, Scholl, & Wynn, 2005). These similarities have led to the view that adult attentional mechanisms may underlie infants' performance on object individuation tasks (Carey & Xu, 2001; Chiang & Wynn, 2000; Leslie et al., 1998; Scholl, 2001; Scholl & Leslie, 1999; Simon, 1997; Wynn & Chiang, 1998).

Such a view has been bolstered by another similar limit on infant and adult object individuation: the fact that it is limited in number. Work using the multiple-object tracking (MOT) paradigm has demonstrated that adults are limited in the number of objects that they can simultaneously attend to at any one time (see Pylyshyn, 2001; Pylyshyn & Storm, 1988; Trick & Pylyshyn, 1994), with a limit of around four objects (see Intrilligator & Cavanagh, 2001). The numerical set-size limitation that plagues the adult attentional system appears to be mirrored in young infants' enumeration performance. A growing body of work suggests that young infants are limited in the number of occluded objects they can enumerate (see Feigenson et al., 2004, for review). Infants can successfully discriminate exact quantities of objects up to four individuals, but their performance falls to chance when the number of individuals exceeds four (e.g., Feigenson et al., 2004). This set-size limit also appears in adult nonhuman primate subjects, who can also enumerate exact quantities up to about four individuals (Hauser & Carey, 2003; Hauser et al. 1996; Hauser et al., 2000; Santos et al., 2005; Uller et al., 2001). Therefore, the set-size limit on exact enumeration is a signature that seems to be continuous both across development and across phylogeny (Hauser & Spelke, 2004?; Spelke, 2000).

A question currently facing researchers, and one that will be discussed in detail in this volume, concerns what information infants have about the objects they have enumerated. A central assumption of researchers today is that enumerated objects are those that are currently being attended to (e.g., Scholl & Leslie, 1999; Xu & Carey, 2000). As several researchers will address in the chapters that follow (see Zosh & Feigenson, Chapter 2; Chen & Leslie, Chapter 4; Cheries et al., Chapter 5; Flombaum et al., Chapter 6), much present work is aimed at exploring the limits on infants' object representations. In particular, much of the research in this volume will examine how human infants, human adults, and nonhuman animals can and cannot use the representations that they have for individuated objects.

A further question concerns how infants' individuation and enumeration processes connect with the other mechanisms they possess for quantity estimation (see Zosh & Feigenson, Chapter 2; Jordan & Brannon, Chapter 3). Although infants cannot exactly enumerate large numbers of objects, much research suggests that infants are able to correctly approximate large numbers of individuals (see Feigenson et al., 2004; McKrinck & Wynn, 2004; Xu, 2003; Xu & Spelke, 2000). Similarly, although some animals appear to have a set-size limit when enumerating small numbers of individuals exactly (Hauser et al., 2000), animals also possess a system for approximately estimating large numbers of objects (see Brannon & Terrace, 1998; Flombaum et al., 2006; Feigenson et al., 2004; Hauser et al., 2003). A central topic in comparative developmental psychology today is how these two systems interact, and how the limits of one system might affect processing in another system.

1.1.3 Objects as entities to be acted upon

As the computational motor theorist Daniel Wolpert has pointed out, metabolically hungry brains are only found in organisms that actually move around and negotiate their environments. Other, more stationary living things that do not need to move around do not develop nervous systems. Indeed, one organism, the sea cucumber, has a central nervous system during one phase of its life when it is seeking a suitable rock upon which to attach itself; having found the best place to settle, it proceeds to the second phase of its life and digests its own nervous system, no longer having any use for a function that requires metabolic resources.[2] Even in basic organisms, there seems to be a critical link

---

[2] The late Francis Crick used to liken this peculiar neuronal self-absorption to academics who finally achieve tenure and then settle into a period of nonproductivity.

between action and nervous tissue, or as a cognitive scientist might put it, between action and complex cognitive capacities.

How then is action connected with the capacity to represent and reason about objects? As reviewed earlier, Piaget famously argued that infants lack complex, constructed representations of the material world precisely because they are unable to act on objects (Piaget, 1955). But in emphasizing the need for competent action, Piaget curtailed the opportunity for infants to reveal object knowledge that was demonstrated in the looking time studies. Although the CK revolution that followed the use of these looking tasks rejected many of Piaget's claims about the role of experience, even the staunchest CK theorist would have to agree that one of the fundamental purposes of object representations is to support action. The mental machinery that evolves to represent objects is inevitably in the service of actions and behaviors that could benefit the survival of the individual. Nature does not select for a good idea alone (Hood, 2004). So, performance limitations may mask true representational capacity in the infant, but they are neither trivial nor irrelevant in terms of functionality. If infants have such consistent problems in retrieving hidden objects that are not due to a failure of object permanence, then there is arguably an equally important question as to why their search is so poor.

One attitude is to consider infants' failures in reaching measures as uninteresting performance errors. After all, there are a multitude of ways to fail on tasks but relatively much fewer ways to succeed (Leslie et al., 2005). But the flexibility to apply object knowledge across different tasks is as important as the capacity for representation. The world is not set up as a large habituation study and so the onus is on psychologists to explain both the success of looking and the failure of reaching. With this in mind, others have begun to look at the demands that each type of task bears upon the infant with a view to elucidating the nature of domain-general capacities that could operate across tasks. Diamond and colleagues (Diamond, 1991; Diamond & Gilbert, 1989; Diamond & Goldman-Rakic, 1989), for example, have championed the view that success in reaching for hidden objects requires both the working memory capacity to represent objects over time and the inhibitory control to overcome prepotent responses that disrupt search. This theory has been notably successful in the analysis of Piaget's famous A not B error described earlier, in which infants search at a previously correct location 'A' despite observing the hiding of the object at a new location 'B'. Such errors, however, are only characteristic of infants' reaching performance, not their looking behavior. Indeed, even Piaget noted that infants failing his A not B search task occasionally reached to the wrong location but looked at the correct B position, indicating that infants' eyes were correctly oriented to the goal but the action retrieval system had failed. (see also, Hofstadler & Reznick, 1996; Ahmed & Ruffman, 1998).

Diamond and colleagues (e.g., Diamond, 1988) have hypothesized that young infants' poor inhibitory control selectively affects their reaching but not their eye movements in an object retrieval task (Diamond, 1988, 1989, 1990). To explore this possibility, she examined the role of the dorsal lateral prefrontal cortex (DLPFC)—an area involved both in holding representations of working memory and in inhibiting behavior. Notably, the DLPFC is an area that is still fairly underdeveloped at the age where infants typically fail A not B and other object retrieval tests (Huttenlocher, 1979). Diamond and colleagues presented monkeys with an object retrieval task that was a direct analogue of Piaget's A not B paradigm. Diamond and Goldman-Rakic (1989) demonstrated that the DLPFC is essential for updating the last seen position of a target object in a delayed response task where the animal had to remember in which of two wells an object had just been hidden. Mature monkeys with lesions in the DLPFC and young monkeys with immature DLPFC performed poorly in comparison with controls. The proposed role of the DLPFC in maintaining a representation of the last seen location of an object has been supported by human electrophysiological studies showing a relationship between the coherence of infant prefrontal neuronal activity and their ability to retrieve objects in search tasks (Bell & Fox, 1992). Likewise, increasing the delay between hiding the object at location B and allowing the infant to search comprises this coherent representation as such a manipulation can reinstate the A not B error in older children (Diamond, 1985).

Damage to the DLPFC also impairs inhibitory control, which as explained previously is a crucial capacity for successful object retrieval. For example, on nonmemory tasks such as detour reaching, individuals have to avoid a direct reach to a potent target object in a transparent box by detouring to the side opening of the container. Both animals with lesions in the DLPFC and young infants repeatedly reach directly at the target, failing to suppress this response in order to execute the correct detour reach. The sight of the goal is so potent that it elicits a direct reach even though the individual is thwarted repeatedly in the attempts. This suggests that in addition to maintaining an active representation of the new object location the DLPFC is also responsible for a corresponding inhibition of previously correct responses (Diamond, 1998).

Because they lack a full mature DLPFC, it seems plausible that infants might fail reaching tasks because of domain-general inhibitory control demands rather than problems with their knowledge of objects. Armed with this neural evidence, many developmental psychologists have dismissed infants' reaching failures as the result of the demands of domain-general tasks.

Unfortunately, however, infants' problems in searching tasks do not fully disappear in early infancy as one might expect. A growing body of work suggests that some of infants' reaching failures and search errors persist well into the first few years of life (Berthier et al., 2000; Butler et al., 2002; Hood, 1994; Hood et al., 2000; Hood et al., 2003).

Hood and colleagues (1994, 2000) purposefully designed a search analogue of one of the CK sequences that had been used to demonstrate the solidity principle in infants (Spelke et al., 1992) and showed that search is random at 2 years of age. In this task, children had to search correctly for an object dropped onto a shelf and not underneath it. A similar solidity principle was addressed in a horizontal version where children had to understand that an object could not pass through a solid wall. Berthier and colleagues (2000) found that toddlers fail to use solidity information even at three years of age, a finding replicated in other laboratories (Hood et al., 2003). However, knowledge based on looking is still evidenced in toddlers on these tasks (Hood et al., 2003); so, the underlying core solidity principle is present but does not constrain correct search. Why do infants look so smart and toddlers look so dumb on these object retrieval tasks (Keen, 2003)?

There are a number of plausible alternatives that warrant further investigation. One class of explanations appeals to weak representations of the occluded object and/or wall (Munakata, 2001). The interpretation is that although a weak representation can produce sufficient output for a looking measure, a stronger representation is required to support search behavior (Morton & Munakata, 2002; Munakata et al., 1997). Similarly, but with a neurological flavour, one intriguing hypothesis argues that various dissociations can be understood in light of the functional distinction that is believed to exist between object recognition in the ventral processing stream ('what') as opposed to the dorsal action system ('how') of the cortex (Milner & Goodale, 1995). Objects that are graspable activate the dorsal stream whereas stationary large objects activate the ventral stream (Kaufman et al., 2003; see Mareschal & Bremner, Chapter 10), producing dissociation between looking and reaching.

Another explanation also endorses a representational interpretation but focuses on the spatial layout of unseen critical components of the tasks. In the case of search involving shelves and walls, the children know that walls, shelves, and objects continue to exist behind the occluders but are uncertain as to the spatial relationship between them (Keen & Berthier, 2005;). Another recent interpretation motivated by models of developing executive function argues that all search tasks present children with a multitude of competing demands and that these are most problematic when the correct response involves coordinating actions (see Gjersoe & Hood, Chapter 13). In this approach, success could reflect the ability to reject or inhibit all other potentially competing responses in favour of the one that is required to retrieve the object.

Curiously, human infants are not the only organisms to show search errors late into life. Hauser, Santos and colleagues have demonstrated that a number of different nonhuman primates perform poorly on search tasks involving object motion even as adults. For example, adult rhesus monkeys search incorrectly for objects that are dropped onto a stage (Hauser, 2001), despite the fact that they look longer at such violations (Santos & Hauser, 2002). Similarly, adult cotton-top tamarins look longer at objects that appear to roll through a solid barrier, but search incorrectly when asked to look for the same object (Santos et al., 2006). Importantly, to date, adult primates' failures on search tasks appear to exactly mirror the cases in which human toddlers perform poorly (see Santos, 2004, for review). The fact that these are found in adult animals and not in adult humans begs the question as to whether the development observed over human childhood reflects an evolutionarily significant departure between the species. A tantalizing prospect is that there was a leap that made some forms of object representation and not others available to drive the action system selectively in humans but not other primates.

1.2 Objects in cognitive science

Clearly, we have come a long way over the past 30 years in our understanding of the development of object knowledge. What was once pondered from the comfort of the philosopher's armchair is now under investigation in laboratories around the world. Rather than settling the issues surrounding the origins of object knowledge, the discoveries of extremely early object representation in infants have spurred many more researchers on to try and understand how such competencies emerge and how they come to support and underpin later abilities in a variety of species.

Piaget's seminal account of infant object knowledge may no longer be true in terms of how object representation comes about, but his focus on knowledge-based action still remains a theoretically legimate concern. As we have come to appreciate the fractionation of object knowledge in the developing mind, we have arrived at a better understanding of the underlying architecture of the mature mind. Cognitive scientists who previously focused on object representation in the human adult have come to recognize that developmental findings combined with a comparative perspective can contribute to a richer explanation. Ultimately, a more comprehensive understanding of any complex biological system that has evolved will need to reconcile the evidence from developmental and comparative perspectives. Object representation is arguably uniquely positioned in this respect as it is essential to most species, which explains why the issues have been successfully pursued from a diverse range of populations, methodologies, and perspectives summarized in this book.

References

Aguiar, A., & Baillargeon, R. (2002). Developments in young infants' reasoning about occluded objects. *Cognitive Psychology, 45*, 267–336.

Ahmed, A., & Ruffman, T. (1998). Why do infants make A not B errors in a search task, yet show memory for location of hidden objects in a non-search task? *Developmental Psychology, 34*, 441–445.

Baillargeon, R. (1987). Object permanence in 31/2- and 41/2-month-old infants. *Developmental Psychology, 23*, 655–664.

Baillargeon, R. (1993). The object concept revisited: new directions in the investigation of infants' physical knowledge. In C. E. Granrud (Ed.), Carnegie-Mellon Symposia on Cognition: Vol. 23. *Visual Perception and Cognition in Infancy* (pp. 265–315). Hillsdale, NJ: Erlbaum.

Baillargeon, R. (2002). The acquisition of physical knowledge in infancy: a summary in eight lessons. In U. Goswami (Ed.), *Blackwell Handbook of Child Cognitive Development* (pp. 47–83). Oxford: Blackwell.

Baillargeon, R., & Graber, M., (1987). Where's the rabbit? 5.5-month-old infants' representation of the height of a hidden object. *Cognitive Development, 2*, 375–392.

Baillargeon, R., Graber, M., DeVos, J., & Black, J. (1990). Why do young infants fail to search for hidden objects? *Cognition, 36*, 255–284.

Baillargeon, R., Spelke, E. S., & Wasserman, S. (1985). Object permanence in 5-month-old infants. *Cognition, 20*, 191–208.

Bell, M.A. & Fox, N. A. (1992). The Relations between Frontal Brain Electrical Activity and Cognitive Development during Infancy, *Child Development, 63*, 1142–1163.

Berthier, N., DeBlois, S., Poirier, C., Novak, M., & Clifton, R. (2000). Where's the ball? Two- and three-year-olds reason about unseen events. *Developmental Psychology, 36*, 394–401.

Bogartz, R., Shinskey, J., & Speaker, C. (1997). Interpreting infant looking: the event set × event set design. *Developmental Psychology, 33*, 408–422.

Brannon, E. M., & Terrace, H. S. (1998) Ordering of the numerosities 1–9 by monkeys. *Science, 282*, 746–749.

Carey, S., & Spelke, E. S. (1994). Domain-specific knowledge and conceptual change. In L. Hirschfeld & S. Gelman (Eds.), *Mapping the Mind: Domain Specificity in Cognition and Culture* (pp. 169–200). Cambridge, UK: Cambridge University Press.

Carey, S., & Xu, F. (2001). Infant knowledge of objects: beyond object files and object tracking. *Cognition, 80*, 179–213.

Chiang, W-C., & Wynn, K. (2000). Infants' representation and tracking of multiple objects. *Cognition, 77*, 169–195.

Clifton, R.K., Perris, E., & Bullinger, A. (1991). Infants' perception of auditory space. *Developmental Psychology, 27*, 187–197.

Clifton, R. K., Perris, E. E., & McCall, D. D. (1999). Does reaching in the dark for unseen objects reflect representation in infants? *Infant Behavior and Development, 22,* 297–302.

Clifton, R. K., Rochat, P., Litovsky, R. Y., Perris, E. E. (1991). Object representation guides infants' reaching in the dark. *Journal of Experimental Psychology, 17,* 323–329.

Diamond, A. (1985). The development of the ability to use recall to guide action, as indicated by infants' performance on A not B. *Child Development, 56,* 868–883.

Diamond, A. (1991). Neuropsychological insights into the meaning of object concept development. In S. Carey, & R. Gelman (Eds.), *The Epigenesis of Mind: Essays on Biology and Cognition* (pp. 67–110). Hillsdale, NJ: Erlbaum.

Diamond, A. (1988). Differences between adult and infant cognition: Is the crucial variable presence or absence of language? In L. Weiskrantz (Ed.), *Thought without Language* (pp. 337–370). Oxford: Oxford U. Press.

Diamond, A. (1998). Understanding the A-not-B error: working memory vs. reinforced response, or active vs. latent trace. *Developmental Science, 1,* 185–189.

Diamond, A., & Gilbert, J. (1989). Development as progressive inhibitory control of action: retrieval of a contiguous object. *Cognitive Development, 4,* 223–249.

Diamond, A., & Goldman-Rakic, P. (1989). Comparison of human infants and rhesus monkeys on Piaget's A-not-B task: evidence for dependence on dorsolateral prefrontal cortex. *Experimental Brain Research, 74,* 24–40.

Fantz, R. L. (1965). Visual perception from birth as shown by pattern selectivity. In H. E. Whipple (Ed.), New issues in infant development. *Annals of New York Academy of Science, 118,* 793–814.

Fantz, R. L., & Fagan, J. F. (1975). Visual attention to size and number of pattern details by term and preterm infants during the first six months. *Child Development, 46,* 3–18.

Feigenson, L., Dehaene, S. & Spelke, E. S. (2004). *Core systems of number. Trends in Cognitive Sciences, 8,* 307–314.

Flombaum, J., Junge, J. A., & Hauser, M. D. (2005). Rhesus monkeys (*Macaca mulatta*) spontaneously compute addition operations over large numbers. *Cognition, 97,* 315–325.

Fodor, J. A. (1983). *Modularity of Mind.* Cambridge, MA: MIT Press.

Goubet, N., & Clifton, R. K. (1998). Object and event representation in 6-and-a-half-month-old infants. *Developmental Psychology, 34,* 63–76.

Gregory, R. L. (1966). *Eye and Brain.* London: Weidenfeld & Nicolson.

Haith, M. M. (1998). Who put the cog in infant cognition: Is rich interpretation too costly? *Infant Behavior and Development, 21,* 167–179.

Haith, M. M. (1999). Some thoughts about claims for innate knowledge and infant physical reasoning. *Developmental Science, 2,* 153–156.

Hauser, M. D. (2001). Searching for food in the wild: a nonhuman primate's expectations about invisible displacement. *Developmental Science, 4,* 84–93.

Hauser, M. D., & Carey, S. (2003). Spontaneous representations of small numbers of objects by rhesus macaques: examinations of content and format. *Cognitive Psychology, 47,* 367–401.

Hauser, M. D., Carey, S., & Hauser, L. B. (2000). Spontaneous number representation in semi-free-ranging rhesus monkeys. *Proceedings of the Royal Society of London, Part B: Biological Sciences, 267,* 829–833.

Hauser, M. D., MacNeilage, P., & Ware, M. (1996). Numerical representations in primates. *Proceedings of the National Academy of Sciences, 93*, 1514–1517.

Hauser, M. D., & Spelke, E. S. (2004). Evolutionary and developmental foundations of human knowledge: a case study of mathematics. In M. Gazzaniga (Ed.), *The Cognitive Neurosciences III*. Cambridge, MA: MIT Press.

Hauser, M. D., Tsao, F., Garcia, P., & Spelke, E. S. (2003). Evolutionary foundations of number: spontaneous representation of numerical magnitudes by cotton-top tamarins. *Proceedings of the Royal Society of London, Part B: Biological Sciences, 270*, 1441–1446.

Hofstadter, M., & Reznick, J. S. (1996). Response modality affects human infant delayed-response performance. *Child Development, 67*, 646–658.

Hood, B., & Willatts, P. (1986). Reaching in the dark to an object's remembered position: evidence for object permanence in 5-month-old infants. *British Journal of Developmental Psychology, 4*, 57–65.

Hood, B. M. (1994). Searching for falling objects in 2-year-olds is different from watching them fall in 4-month-olds. Poster presented at the 9th biennial International Conference for Infant Studies, Paris, France.

Hood, B. M. (2004). Is looking good enough or does it beggar belief? Invited commentary on Baillargeon. *Developmental Science, 9*, 415–417.

Hood, B. M., Carey, S., & Prasada, S. (2000). Predicting the outcomes of physical events: two-year-olds fail to reveal knowledge of solidity and support. *Child Development, 71*, 1540–1554.

Hood, B. M., Cole-Davis, V., & Dias, M. (2003). Looking and search measures of object knowledge in preschool children. *Developmental Psychology, 39*, 61–70.

Huttenlocher, P.R. (1979). Synaptic density in human frontal cortex – developmental changes and effects of aging. *Brain Research, 163*, 195–205.

Intriligator, J., & Cavanagh, P. (2001). The spatial resolution of visual attention. *Cognitive Psychology, 43*, 171–216.

Kahneman, D., & Treisman, A., 1984. Changing views of attention and automaticity. In R. Parasuraman & R. Davies (Eds.) *Varieties of Attention* (pp.29–61). New York: Academic Press.

Kahneman, D., Treisman, A., & Gibbs, B. (1992). The reviewing of object files: Object-specific integration of information. *Cognitive Psychology, 24*, 175–219.

Kaufman, J., Mareschal, D., & Johnson, M. H. (2003). Graspability and object processing in infants. *Infant Behavior and Development, 26*, 516–528.

Keen, R. (2003). Representation of objects and events: Why do infants look so smart and toddlers look so dumb? *Current Directions in Psychological Science, 12*, 79–83.

Keen, R. E. & Berthier, N. E. (2005). Continuities and discontinuities in infants' representation of objects and events. In R. Kail (Ed.) *Advances in Child Development and Behavior* (pp 243–279), New York: Elsevier.

Leslie, A. M. (1984). Spatiotemporal continuity and the perception of causality in infants. *Perception, 13*, 287–305.

Leslie, A. M., German, T. P., & Polizzi, P. (2005). Belief-desire reasoning as a process of selection. *Cognitive Psychology, 50*, 45–85.

Leslie, A. M., & Keeble, S. (1987). Do six-month-old infants perceive causality? *Cognition, 25*, 265–288.

Leslie, A. M., Xu, F., Tremoulet, P., & Scholl, B. (1998). Indexing and the object concept: developing 'what' and 'where' systems. *Trends in Cognitive Sciences, 2*, 10–18.

McCrink, K., & Wynn, K. (2004). Large-number addition and subtraction in infants. *Psychological Science, 15*, 776–781.

Melkman, R. & Rabinovitch, L. (1998) Children's perception of continuous and discontinuous movement. *Developmental Psychology, 34*, 258–263.

Milner, A. D., & Goodale, M. A. (1995). *The Visual Brain in Action*. New York. Oxford University Press.

Mitroff, S. R., Scholl, B. J., & Wynn, K. (2005). The relationship between object files and conscious perception. *Cognition, 96*, 67–92.

Morton, J. B., & Munakata, Y. (2002). Active versus latent representations: a neural network model of perseveration, dissociation, and decalage. *Developmental Psychobiology, 40*, 255–265.

Munakata, Y. (2001). Graded representations in behavioral dissociations. *Trends in Cognitive Sciences, 5*, 309–315.

Munakata, Y., McClelland, J. L., Johnson, M. H., & Siegler, R. S. (1997). Rethinking infant knowledge: toward an adaptive processing account of successes and failures in object permanence tasks. *Psychological Review, 104*, 686–713.

Munakata, Y., Santos, L., O'Reilly, R., Hauser, M. D., & Spelke, E. S. (2001). Visual representation in the wild: how rhesus monkeys parse objects. *Journal of Cognitive Neuroscience, 13*, 44–58.

Needham, A. (1998). Infants' use of featural information in the segregation of stationary objects. *Infant Behavior and Development, 21*, 47–76.

Needham, A. (1999). The role of shape in 4-month-old infants' segregation of adjacent objects. *Infant Behavior and Development, 22*, 161–178.

Needham, A., & Baillargeon, R. (1997). Object segregation in 8-month-old infants. *Cognition, 62*, 121–148.

Needham, A., & Baillargeon, R. (1998). Effects of prior experience in 4.5-month-old infants' object segregation. *Infant Behavior and Development, 21*, 1–24.

Needham, A., Dueker, G. L., & Lockhead, G. (2005). Infants' formation and use of categories to segregate objects. *Cognition, 94*, 215–240.

Piaget, J. (1955). *The Child's Construction of Reality*. London: Routledge & Kegan Paul.

Phillips, W. & Santos, L. R. (2007). Evidence for kind representations in the absence of language: Experiments with rhesus monkeys (*Macaca mulatta*). *Cognition, 102*, 455–463.

Pylyshyn, Z. W. (2001). Visual indexes, preconceptual objects, and situated vision. *Cognition, 80*, 127–158.

Pylyshyn, Z. W., & Storm, R. W. (1988). Tracking multiple independent targets: Evidence for a parallel tracking mechanism. *Spatial Vision, 3*, 179–197.

Santos, L. R. (2004). Core knowledges: a dissociation between spatiotemporal knowledge and contact-mechanics in a non-human primate? *Developmental Science, 7*, 167–174.

Santos, L. R., Barnes, J., & Mahajan, N. (2005). Expectations about numerical events in four lemur species (*Eulemur fulvus, Eulemur mongoz, Lemur catta and Varecia rubra*). *Animal Cognition, 8*, 253–262.

Santos, L. R., & Hauser, M. D. (2002). A non-human primate's understanding of solidity: dissociations between seeing and acting. *Developmental Science*, 5, F1–F7.

Santos, L. R., Seelig, D., & Hauser, M. D. (2006). Cotton-top tamarins' (*Saguinus oedipus*) expectations about occluded objects: a dissociation between looking and reaching tasks. *Infancy*, 9(2), 147–171.

Santos, L. R., Sulkowski, G., Spaepen, G. M., & Hauser, M. D. (2002). Object individuation using property/kind information in rhesus macaques (*Macaca mulatta*). *Cognition*, 83, 241–264.

Scholl, B. J. (2001). Objects and attention: the state of the art. *Cognition*, 80(1/2), 1–46.

Scholl, B. J., & Leslie, A. M. (1999). Explaining the infant's object concept: beyond the perception/cognition dichotomy. In E. Lepore, & Z. Pylyshyn (Eds.), *What is Cognitive Science?* (pp. 26–73). Oxford: Blackwell.

Scholl, B. J., & Pylyshyn, Z. W. (1999). Tracking multiple items through occlusion: clues to visual objecthood. *Cognitive Psychology*, 38, 259–290.

Scholl, B. J., Pylyshyn, Z. W., & Feldman, J. (2001). What is a visual object? Evidence from target merging in multiple-object tracking. *Cognition*, 80(1/2), 159–177.

Shinskey, J. L., & Munakata, Y. (2003). Are infants in the dark about hidden objects? *Developmental Science*, 6, 273–282.

Simon, T., Hespos, S., & Rochat, P. (1995). Do infants understand simple arithmetic? A replication of Wynn (1992). *Cognitive Development*, 10, 253–269.

Smith, L. B. (1999). Do infants possess innate knowledge structures: the con side. *Developmental Science*, 2, 133–144.

Spelke, E., Breinlinger, K., Jacobson, K., & Phillips, A. (1993). Gestalt relations and object perception: a developmental study. *Perception*, 22, 1483–1501.

Spelke, E., Kestenbaum, R., Simons, D. J., & Wein, D. (1995). Spatiotemporal continuity, smoothness of motion and object identity in infancy. *British Journal of Developmental Psychology*, 13, 113–142.

Spelke, E. S. (1988). Where perceiving ends and thinking begins: the apprehension of objects in infancy. In A. Yonas (Ed.), *Perceptual Development in Infancy: Minnesota Symposia on Child Psychology, Vol. 20*. Hillsdale, NJ: Erlbaum.

Spelke, E.S. (1994). Initial knowledge: Six suggestions. *Cognition*, 50, 431–445.

Spelke, E. S. (2000). Core knowledge. *American Psychologist*, 55, 1233–1243.

Spelke, E. S., Breinlinger, K., Macomber, J., & Jacobson, K. (1992). Origins of knowledge. *Psychological Review*, 99, 605–632.

Spelke, E. S., Katz, G., Purcell, S. E., Ehrlich, S. M., & Breinlinger, K. (1994). Early knowledge of object motion: continuity and inertia. *Cognition*, 51, 131–176.

Spelke, E. S., & van de Walle, G. (1993). Perceiving and reasoning about objects: insights from infants. In N. Eilan, R. McCarthy, & W. Brewer (Eds.), *Spatial Representation* (pp. 132–161). Oxford, UK: Basil Blackwell.

Spelke, E. S., von Hofsten, C., & Kestenbaum, R. (1989). Object perception in infancy: interaction of spatial and kinetic information for object boundaries. *Developmental Psychology*, 25, 185–196.

Trick, L. M., & Pylyshyn, Z. W. (1994). Why are small and large numbers enumerated differently? A limited capacity preattentive stage in vision. *Psychological Review*, 101(1), 80-102.

Uller, C., Hauser, M., & Carey, S. (2001). Spontaneous representation of number in cotton-top tamarins (*Saguinus oedipus*). *Journal of Comparative Psychology, 115,* 248–257.

Uller, C., Xu, F., Carey, S., & Hauser, M. D. (1997). Is language needed for constructing sortal concepts? A study with nonhuman primates. *Proceedings of the 21st Annual Boston University Conference on Language Development, 21,* 665–677.

Van de Walle, G., Carey, S., & Prevor, M. (2000). Bases for object individuation in infancy: evidence from manual search. *Journal of Cognition and Development, 1,* 249–280.

Van Marle, K., & Scholl, B. J. (2003). Attentive tracking of objects vs. substances. *Psychological Science, 14*(5), 498–504.

Wilcox, T. (1999). Object individuation: infants' use of shape, size, pattern, and color. *Cognition, 72,* 125–166.

Wilcox, T., & Baillargeon, R. (1998a). Object individuation in infancy: the use of featural information in reasoning about occlusion events. *Cognitive Psychology, 37,* 97–155.

Wilcox, T., & Baillargeon, R. (1998b). Object individuation in young infants: Further evidence with an event-monitoring paradigm. *Developmental Science, 1,* 127–142.

Wilcox, T., & Chapa, C. (2002). Infants' reasoning about opaque and transparent occluders in an individuation task. *Cognition, 85,* B1–B10.

Wilcox, T., & Chapa, C. (2004). Priming infants to attend to color and pattern information in an individuation task. *Cognition, 90,* 265–302.

Willatts, P. (1989). Development of problem solving in infants. In A. Slater, & G. Bremner (Eds), *Infant Development.* Hove, UK: Lawrence Erlbaum Associates.

Wynn, K. (1992). Addition and subtraction by human infants. *Nature, 358,* 749–750.

Wynn, K., & Chiang, W. (1998). Limits to infants' knowledge of objects: the case of magical appearance. *Psychological Science, 9,* 448–455.

Xu, F. (1999). Object individuation and object identity in infancy: the role of spatiotemporal information, object property information, and language. *Acta Psychologica, 102,* 113–136.

Xu, F. (2003). The development of object individuation in infancy. In H. Hayne, & J. Fagen (Eds.), *Progress in Infancy Research*, Vol. 3 (pp. 159–192). Mahwah, NJ: Lawrence Erlbaum.

Xu, F. (2007). Sortal concepts, object individuation, and language. *Trends in Cognitive Sciences, 11,* 400–406.

Xu, F., & Carey, S. (1996). Infants' metaphysics: the case of numerical identity. *Cognitive Psychology, 30,* 111–153.

Xu, F., Carey, S., & Quint, N. (2004). The emergence of kind-based object individuation in infancy. *Cognitive Psychology, 49,* 155–190.

Xu, F., Carey, S., & Welch, J. (1999). Infants' ability to use object kind information for object individuation. *Cognition, 70,* 137–166.

Xu, F., Cote, M., & Baker, A. (2005). Labeling guides object individuation in 12-month-old infants. *Psychological Science, 16,* 372–377.

Xu, F., & Spelke, E. S. (2000). Large number discrimination in 6-month-old infants. *Cognition, 74,* B1–B11.

Yantis, S. (1995). Perceived continuity of occluded visual objects. *Psychological Science, 6,* 182–186.

Chapter 2

Beyond 'what' and 'how many': Capacity, complexity, and resolution of infants' object representations

Jennifer M. Zosh & Lisa Feigenson

Memory is a must for thinking about objects. We frequently reason about objects even when we lack direct perceptual evidence of their existence, as when we saccade from one visual location to another, experience darkness, or observe occlusion. In all of these cases, object representations must be stored in memory in order to support even the most basic of computations—computations such as deciding whether an object is the same as one seen a moment earlier, or determining whether a hidden object can still be obtained. The richness of object representations as a case study in cognitive science is revealed by the diversity of chapters in this book. Our co-authors explore issues ranging from cross-species comparisons of object representations (Jordan & Brannon, Chapter 3) to implicit versus explicit knowledge of objects (Gjersoe & Hood, Chapter 13), to the representational consequences when tenets of object-hood are violated (Baillargeon et al., Chapter 12; Rosenberg & Carey, Chapter 7). Here, we offer the suggestion that none of these inquiries into the nature of object representations would be possible in the absence of working memory.

In what follows, we explore the architecture of the working memory system that supports object representation throughout development. Specifically, we suggest that although recent research has addressed the question of *how many* objects working memory can represent—both in adults and in infants—much less work has asked how this memory capacity is affected by the nature of the object representations themselves. The question of how the *quantity* and the *quality* of object representations interact has been particularly underexplored from a developmental perspective.

Here, we offer some data from our work with infants that may serve as a first step toward filling this gap. We proceed in three parts. First, we review evidence that, across development, constraints on working memory capacity abruptly limit the number of objects that can be represented at any given time. Then, we consider two cases in which the content of object representations affects capacity—cases in which *what* is remembered affects *how many* are remembered. Our first case concerns the nature of the object representations that are successfully stored in working memory: this work suggests that, for both adults and infants, there is a trade-off between the featural resolution of object representations and the number of objects that can be simultaneously represented. Our second case concerns what happens when working memory capacity is exceeded: this work suggests that exceeding the limits of working memory can have different consequences for infants' object representations than for adults'. Furthermore, the particular features of the objects being represented determine whether or not infants show adult-like performance. Together, these two cases illustrate ways in which the architecture of working memory affects object representation, and how in turn object representations affect working memory.

2.1 How many items does working memory hold?

2.1.1 Working memory capacity in adults

We are continuously barraged by an enormity of environmental information—this presents us with a processing problem. Take, for example, the information surrounding you at this very moment. You might be thinking about the words on this page, or about the feel of the paper in your hand (for those who do not prefer learning about object representation electronically). You might be thinking about the cup of coffee you are about to sip, or about the voices you hear in the background. You might be thinking about the chair that is supporting you, or about the clock ticking on the wall. The list goes on.

How is it possible to represent all of this information at once? The answer is that it isn't. We avoid this problem of information overload by effectively ignoring the vast majority of what is available at any given moment in time. Instead, we selectively attend to and store in memory only a tiny fraction of the sights and sounds surrounding us. Research in both attention and working memory has identified discrete items, such as individual objects,[1] as the essential units of this processing, such that we are limited to storing a finite number of object representations at once (Alvarez & Cavanagh, 2004; Broadbent, 1975; Cowan, 2001, 2005; Luck & Vogel, 1997; Song & Jiang, 2006; Sperling, 1960;

---

[1] See Feigenson (2008) and Halberda et al. (2006) for evidence that *collections of objects* can also function as individuals for the purposes of attention and working memory.

Todd & Marois, 2004; Xu & Chun, 2006). This capacity limit on working memory representations has been in evidence for some time. For example, Sperling (1960) showed adult observers 3×4 grids of letters and digits, presented too briefly for all 12 items to enter into memory. On whole-report trials, when asked to report the names of all of the items they could remember, observers averaged 4 items. On partial-report trials, when asked to report only the items from one of the grid's three rows, as specified by an experimenter-presented cue, observers reported an average of 1.3 of the 4 items in the cued row.[2] Multiplied by the number of rows in the grid, this again yielded approximately 4 as the upper limit on working memory capacity.

Convergent evidence for this capacity limit has been obtained through more recent work, exemplified by a now-classic study by Luck and Vogel (1997). Adults saw briefly flashed arrays of 1–12 objects, each containing 1–4 features, and were instructed to respond if any of the objects changed their features from one flash to the next. For example, one of the objects might have changed from a short line segment to a longer line segment while the other objects maintained their properties. Adults' performance in this change detection task was excellent when 1, 2, 3, or 4 objects were presented; but with more than 4 objects, performance suffered. This provides further support for the 4-item limit observed some 30 years earlier, extending the result to objects that could not as easily be verbally labeled as the letters and digits in Sperling's study. Furthermore, the neural substrate supporting this storage of objects in working memory has begun to be identified (McCollough et al., 2007; Todd & Marois, 2004; Xu & Chun, 2006). The inferior intraparietal sulcus (IPS) is a cortical region that has been associated with attention and numerical processing in both adults and young children (Cantlon et al., 2006; Canton et al., in press; Jordan & Brannon, Chapter 3). It exhibits monotonically increasing activity when 1, 2, 3, or 4 objects are remembered, regardless of object complexity or location. Critically, IPS activity reaches an asymptote at 4, providing a physiological correlate to the behavioral pattern whereby capacity reaches its maximum at 4 (Xu & Chun, 2006; see also Vogel & Machizawa, 2004).

2.1.2 Working memory capacity in infants

This item-based capacity limit remains surprisingly consistent across development, starting in infancy. Earlier work in developmental psychology focused

---

[2] Presenting the cue for less than 1 second after the disappearance of the letter grid resulted in much higher capacity limits, which Sperling took as evidence for the existence of a very short-lived, iconic memory store. Iconic memory, which endures for less than a second, is distinct from the working memory that is our focus here.

on demonstrating that infants could represent a single object in the absence of immediate perceptual input, such as under conditions of occlusion (e.g., Baillargeon, 1987; Luo et al., 2003) or darkness (Shinskey & Munakata, 2003). Other studies have extended these results to show that as early as 5 months of age, infants represent *multiple* hidden objects. For example, Wynn (1992) showed 5-month-old infants an object placed atop a puppet stage. Infants watched as the object was occluded by a screen, then saw a hand pass behind the screen carrying a second object, and finally saw the hand exit the stage empty. After seeing this sequence, infants looked longer when the screen was removed to reveal unexpected outcomes of 1 or 3 objects, relative to their looking at the expected outcome of 2 objects. Success in this task depends on forming a working memory representation of the sequentially presented objects and then comparing that mental representation to the revealed outcome. Without the ability to form and maintain 2 distinct object representations in working memory, infants would have failed to differentiate the correct from incorrect outcomes. Following Wynn, other studies have used similar methods to confirm infants' ability to track at least 2 hidden objects at once (Berger et al., 2006; Koechlin et al., 1997; Simon et al., 1995; Uller et al., 1999).[3]

Thus, infants can remember at least 2 hidden objects—Can they also remember more? The item-based capacity limit of infants' working memory has been examined in work that parametrically varied the number of hidden objects infants were asked to track. In one investigation, 10- and 12-month-old infants participated in a single trial of a modified foraging task. Infants watched an experimenter sequentially place a number of crackers into one bucket and a different number of crackers into another bucket. Infants were then allowed to walk or crawl to either bucket, with the dependent measure being which bucket they approached first. Infants successfully chose the bucket containing the greater quantity when 1, 2, or 3 crackers were hidden in either of the buckets (i.e., with choices between 1 vs. 2 or 2 vs. 3 crackers). But when the experimenter hid more than 3 crackers in either bucket (i.e., with choices of 2 vs. 4, 3 vs. 4, 3 vs. 6, and even 1 vs. 4), infants chose randomly

---

[3] Infants in some versions of this task have been shown to base their expectations on the total continuous extent (e.g., total area) of the array rather than on the number of individual objects in the array (Feigenson, Carey, & Spelke, 2002). However, infants can also form expectations based on a discrete number (Cheries et al., 2003). For further discussion of infants' ability to represent both discrete and continuous properties of object arrays, see Feigenson (2005) and Feigenson et al. (2004). Regardless of when infants base their expectations on total object number and when they base them on total object extent, working memory is required to store the object representations that can then support either discrete or continuous computation.

(Feigenson & Carey, 2005; Feigenson, Carey, & Hauser, 2002). Various control conditions ruled out the possibility that duration or presentation complexity determined infants' performance. This pattern of success and failure suggests that infants can remember up to 3 hidden objects per location, but no more.[4]

Infants also remember a maximum of 3 objects when presented with single arrays in which the entire array is simultaneously visible (as opposed to two sets of sequentially presented objects, as in the cracker choice studies described in the preceding). Twelve- to 14-month-old infants saw an experimenter hide varying numbers of identical objects in an opaque box, and then were allowed to retrieve all or just a subset of them (Feigenson & Carey, 2003, 2005). On key trials, the experimenter surreptitiously withheld some of the objects. The dependent measure was whether infants continued searching for the 'missing' objects. Specifically, comparing the duration of infants' searching when more objects were expected in the box with that when the box was expected to be empty provided a measure of how many objects infants were able to remember.

For example, because infants searched the box longer when 2 objects had been hidden and only 1 had been retrieved, relative to when 2 objects had been hidden and both had been retrieved, infants demonstrated that they had successfully formed 2 object representations, stored these in working memory, and used them to determine whether any more objects remained in the box. This method reveals that 12- to 14-month-old infants searched appropriately when 1, 2, or 3 objects were hidden (see Fig. 2.1). For example, after seeing 3 objects hidden and retrieving just 2 of them, infants continued searching the box for the missing object. However, when infants saw 4 objects hidden and only retrieved 1 or 2 of them, they failed to search for any remaining objects (Feigenson & Carey, 2003, 2005): that is, after seeing 4 objects hidden and retrieving any subset of them, infants searched the box no longer than they did on trials when the box was expected to be empty. This suggests that infants cannot represent 4 objects in working memory.

Infants' dramatic failure to remember 4 objects in both the cracker choice task (Feigenson & Carey, 2005; Feigenson, Carey & Hauser, 2002) and the

---

[4] Importantly, infants' working memory in this task was *locally limited*, in that infants could remember up to 3 objects per hiding location rather than up to 3 objects totally. Other work in our laboratory has extended this finding to show that infants can use spatial cues (e.g., the spatially separated hiding locations in this cracker choice task) or conceptual cues (e.g., familiar semantic categories) to group objects into sets (Feigenson & Halberda, 2004, 2008). Parsing, or chunking, an array in this way appears to enable both infants (Feigenson & Halberda, 2004, 2008) and adults (Chase & Simon, 1973; Ericsson et al., 1980; Miller, 1956; Simon, 1974) to exceed the 3-item limit of working memory under certain conditions.

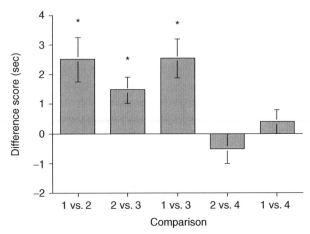

Fig. 2.1 Difference scores (searching when the box contained more objects minus searching when the box was empty) (±SEM) reflect 12- to 14-month-old infants' success-ful searching when 1, 2, or 3 objects were hidden, and their failure with 4 (Feigenson & Carey, 2003, 2005). Difference scores significantly greater than chance are indicated by * (p < .05).

manual search task (Feigenson & Carey, 2003, 2005) is striking, in that infants could have simply ignored the objects that exceeded their memory capacity, or could have remembered only the 3 most recently hidden objects. Instead, infants presented with more than 3 objects exhibited a catastrophic memory failure, such that they appeared to remember *none* of the objects in the array. This failure is surprisingly persistent, with infants as old as 20 months failing to search for remaining objects after seeing 4 objects hidden and retrieving only 1 of them (Barner et al., 2007).

In summary, working memory capacity exhibits remarkable developmental continuity.[5] A variety of tasks reveal that adults can store up to 3 or 4 items in working memory. Similarly, a variety of tasks reveal that by about 10 months infants can store up to 3 items in working memory. On the other hand, adults' working memory and infants' working memory do seem to differ in at least one important way: when faced with arrays that exceed their working memory capacity, adults appear to store only as many items as working memory can hold (e.g., Luck & Vogel, 1997). In contrast, infants faced with such arrays seem to experience a catastrophic memory failure, whereby none of the items in the array are successfully remembered. But, although the consequences of

---

[5] Several studies suggest that working memory also exhibits continuity across species. Monkeys engaging in tasks similar to those used with human infants also show an abrupt limit to the number of individual items they can represent (Hauser et al., 2000; Wood et al., 2008).

exceeding working memory capacity seem to differ in infants versus adults, the fundamental capacity of working memory appears to be quite stable across development.

2.2 Do the *contents* of working memory affect the *capacity* of working memory?

2.2.1 Capacity and complexity in adults

The earlier-mentioned studies suggest that adults can store up to 3 or 4 objects in working memory at any given time. What are the contents of those object representations? The change detection task employed by Luck and Vogel (1997) reveals that adults' object representations can contain a variety of featural information about the remembered objects, including their color, spatial orientation, and size. Moreover, Luck and Vogel suggested that once an object is represented in working memory, binding features to that object representation imposes no additional cost. This conclusion comes from the finding that adults were as good at detecting a change to a scene containing 4 objects, each with 4 separate features (16 total features), as they were at detecting a change to a scene containing 4 objects, each with just one feature (4 total features). Hence, in Luck and Vogel's study, adults' object representations contained information about multiple features bound to each object. The authors interpreted their results as suggesting that working memory capacity is determined solely by the number of objects that could be stored, and not by informational load (i.e., by the total number of object features being stored).

However, subsequent work has questioned Luck and Vogel's 'fixed capacity' view, suggesting that there may instead be a trade-off between the capacity of working memory and the featural complexity of the object representations that are stored. Alvarez and Cavanagh (2004) used a change detection task similar to that of Luck and Vogel, but systematically manipulated the complexity of the stimulus objects. They found that as the complexity of the objects increased (e.g., from colored squares to Chinese characters to shaded cubes), the number of objects that could be accurately remembered decreased monotonically—when objects became complex, adults remembered fewer of them. This contradicts Luck and Vogel's suggestion that object features are automatically represented when an object representation is stored in working memory. However, Alvarez and Cavanagh's results seemed to confirm Luck and Vogel's claim that working memory can never store more than 4 items. Even with the simplest (i.e., least visually complex) objects, adults' working memory capacity reached its asymptote at about 4 (Alvarez & Cavanagh, 2004; Eng et al., 2005; Xu & Chun, 2006; but see Awh et al., 2007). Thus, on Alvarez and Cavanagh's 'flexible capacity' view, working memory can store no more than 4 items but may store fewer if the items impose a heavy informational load.

Neuropsychological data appear consistent with this view. Xu and Chun (2006) and Todd and Marois (2004) used functional magnetic resonance imaging (fMRI) to image cerebral activation for arrays of different numbers of objects, where the objects varied in their complexity in ways similar to those in Alvarez and Cavanagh's task. They found that the inferior IPS showed differential activation depending on whether 1, 2, 3, or 4 objects were remembered, regardless of object complexity or spatial location. In contrast, activity in the superior IPS and posterior parietal cortex reflected not only the number of objects presented but also the complexity of those objects (Song & Jiang, 2006; Xu & Chun, 2006).

Subsequent studies more directly addressed the relationship between these two brain areas. This work found that, as predicted, cues that led observers to visually group individual objects together reduced the number of items observers stored in working memory. This, in turn, led to reduced activation of the inferior IPS. But this grouping came at a cost. Although grouping reduced the number of individual objects in the scene, representations of the grouped objects necessarily became more internally complex. This increase in objects' perceived complexity was reflected by an increase in the activity of the superior IPS, the region thought to track object complexity (Xu & Chun, 2007): that is, grouping caused a trade-off in activity between the inferior and superior IPS. This result is consistent with the view that working memory capacity decreases as object complexity increases.

2.2.2 Capacity and complexity in infants

Is there evidence of a similar trade-off between working memory capacity and complexity earlier in development? Evidence from several paradigms suggests that infants, similar to adults, are constrained to storing about 3 items in working memory at a time, as reviewed earlier in this chapter. Other research has shown that the object representations that infants store in working memory can have features such as color or spatial location bound to them (e.g., Kaldy & Leslie, 2003; Oakes et al., 2006; Ross-Sheehy et al., 2003). However, to date, the question of whether working memory capacity is affected by the complexity of object representations has not yet been asked from a developmental perspective. Developmental data have not yet been brought to bear on the debate over whether working memory capacity is better characterized as fixed or as flexible. One reason that developmental data may be relevant is that methodological issues have complicated the debate. Some researchers have suggested that the apparent trade-off between adults' capacity and the resolution of their object representations is an artifact of the change detection paradigm typically used to measure adults' working memory capacity (Awh et al., 2007). Are trade-offs between capacity and complexity observed in tasks other than change detection? Here, we describe data from a very different paradigm with infants that seem to support the flexible capacity view.

We examined the interaction between working memory capacity and information load by asking whether infants can successfully *individuate* objects when shown arrays containing varying numbers of objects. Individuation refers to the ability to detect whether a currently seen object is the *same one* as viewed earlier, or is instead a different object (see also Tremoulet et al., 2000; van de Walle et al., 2000; Wilcox, 1999; Xu, 1999; Xu & Carey, 1996; Xu et al., 1999; Xu et al., 2004; Xu et al., 2005). Imagine seeing a cat enter the kitchen, and a moment later seeing a dog walk out. In order to know that two numerically distinct animals took part in this scene, one had to have stored in memory a representation of the first animal (e.g., that it had pointy ears and whiskers), then have compared it to a representation of the second animal (e.g., that it had floppy ears and lacked whiskers). Because the features bound to the two representations do not match, and because we have a commitment that one animal cannot magically change its properties, we can conclude that two animals were seen—a cat and a dog. If we had not been able to store a representation of the first animal in memory, or if we had not bound specific features to the object representation (e.g., if we had simply remembered that 'an animal entered the kitchen'), no mismatch would have been computed and we would not have been able to individuate. Instead, we either would have concluded that we had seen just a single animal or would have been ambivalent as to how many animals there had been. Because working memory is required for successful individuation, individuation can be thought of as an index of which features were stored in working memory.

To date, no studies have asked whether infants' individuation abilities interact with working memory load. Answering this question can bear on the debate over whether working memory capacity is better thought of as fixed or as flexible. Alvarez & Cavanagh (2004) and Eng et al. (2005) found that, for adults, representing the features of complex objects meant that fewer object representations were stored in memory, relative to representing the features of simple objects. The flip side of this coin predicts that as the number of objects stored in memory increases, the featural resolution of those object representations should correspondingly decrease. We tested infants' memory for object features as a function of the number of objects in the presented array, using individuation as our dependent measure. We predicted that infants would be able to individuate objects from arrays containing small numbers of objects; but when faced with larger arrays (even arrays within the 3-item limit of infants' working memory capacity), we predicted that infants would fail to individuate because they had not stored enough of the objects' features to do so.

We tested 18-month-old infants in a modified manual search paradigm in which they saw 1, 2, or 3 objects hidden in a box and then were allowed to search for them. There were two methodological differences distinguishing this study from our previous uses of the manual search paradigm. First, in previous studies, we always hid arrays of identical objects (e.g., 3 identical ping-pong balls; Feigenson & Carey, 2003, 2005; Feigenson & Halberda, 2004). In the present study, we hid heterogeneous arrays of small toys that contrasted in their perceptual features and in their category membership (e.g., a cat, a car, and a shoe). Second, in previous studies, we always manipulated the number of objects infants were able to retrieve from the box, relative to the number they had seen hidden. In the present study, we always let infants retrieve the same *number* of objects as they had seen hidden, and instead manipulated the *identities* of the retrieved objects relative to the hidden objects. Thus, we did not ask infants to compute a numerical match between the hidden array and the retrieved array (because our previous work shows that infants can reliably do so for 1-, 2-, and 3-object arrays by 12 months of age, much younger than the infants we tested here). Instead, we asked whether infants could compute a match or a mismatch in object identities for arrays containing varying numbers of objects.

Infants watched 1, 2, or 3 objects being hidden in the box. For each of these array sizes, on half of the trials, infants were then allowed to reach into the box and retrieve exactly the same objects they had just seen hidden.[6] These were called *No Switch* trials because all of the objects retrieved from the box were identical to those just hidden (they were the same objects). Almost immediately after these objects had been retrieved, the experimenter took them away, and a 10-second measurement period followed during which the box remained in place and infants were able to further search the box if they chose to do so. On these No Switch trials, the box was expected to be empty during this measurement period, because infants had already retrieved all of the objects they had seen hidden.

---

[6] In order to equate the duration over which objects remained hidden across the 1-, 2-, and 3-object trials, immediately after infants had retrieved the first object, the experimenter reached into the box, retrieved any remaining objects (on the 2- and 3-object trials), and gave them to infants to play with briefly. The experimenter then took the object(s) away and the critical measurement period began. Hence, the time elapsed between the point when infants saw objects hidden and the time when the critical measurement period began was equated across all array sizes.

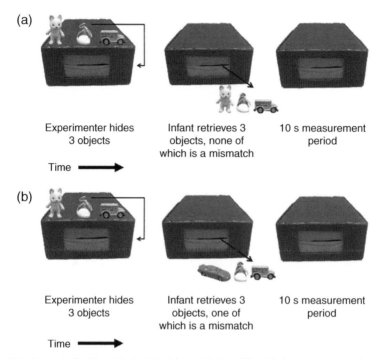

Fig. 2.2 Example 3-object No Switch (a) and Switch (b) trials from the manual search experiment by Zosh and Feigenson (submitted).

The other half of the trials were *Switch* trials in which one of the objects retrieved from the box was different from those that infants had seen hidden.[7] As in the No Switch trials, a 10-second measurement period then followed during which any searching was measured. If on these Switch trials infants had successfully remembered the objects' properties and used them to individuate, they should have expected one object remaining in the box. For example, on a 3-object Switch trial, infants saw a cat, a shoe, and a bus hidden, but retrieved a *car*, a shoe, and a bus (see Fig. 2.2). Successful individuation of the objects would have led infants to expect that the cat was still remaining in the box (although in fact during the measurement periods the experimenter always

---

[7] On Switch trials, we changed the identity of only a single object, regardless of the number of objects comprising the initial array. We did this to equate the extent of change across the different array sizes. Controlling for the number of 'switched' objects across the different array sizes avoided the possibility that any differential searching behavior observed for the arrays containing more objects was due to infants being overwhelmed by the much greater amount of total change on Switch trials (e.g., if a cat, a brush, and a bus had been hidden and a car, a duck, and a spoon were retrieved).

secretly held any remaining object out of the infants' reach in the rear of the box). Overall, we wanted to know (1) whether after having retrieved the same number of objects as they had initially seen hidden, infants would use matches and mismatches in object features to search the box longer on Switch trials than on No Switch trials, and (2) whether this effect would vary as a function of the number of objects in the initial stimulus array.

We found that infants successfully individuated when 1 or 2 objects had been hidden. This is shown by infants' longer searching when one of the objects had 'magically' changed its properties (Switch trials) relative to searching when all of the objects retrieved matched those seen hidden (No Switch trials; Fig. 2.2). This means that when 1 or 2 objects were hidden, infants remembered both how many objects there had been and what their properties were. However, when we hid 3 objects, infants failed to individuate—they searched the box equally long on Switch and No Switch trials (Zosh & Feigenson, submitted): that is, infants showed no evidence of detecting that 1 of the 3 objects had radically changed its properties (i.e., had turned from a cat into a car). It is important to note that previous studies in our laboratory have shown that 3-object arrays are within the 3-item working memory capacity of infants much younger than those tested here (Feigenson & Carey, 2003, 2005). Furthermore, we have previously found that infants search for the correct number of objects when presented with heterogeneous arrays of objects with contrasting properties (small toys similar to those used here), as well as when presented with homogeneous arrays of identical objects (Zosh & Feigenson, in preparation). Therefore, infants' failure to differentiate Switch from No Switch trials when presented with 3 objects was not due to a general failure to remember arrays of this size, nor due to an inability to remember 3 objects with contrasting properties.

Instead, we suggest that infants in our task stored the correct number of object representations in working memory, regardless of whether 1, 2, or 3 objects had been presented. With the smaller arrays containing only 1 or 2 objects, infants were also able to store property information about each object (i.e., that a *cat* and a *brush* had been hidden). Storing this information allowed infants to individuate the objects by detecting a mismatch on Switch trials, such that they then continued searching the box for the missing object. But when faced with arrays containing 3 objects, infants were not able to store as much information about the represented objects, and in this sense formed object representations with a coarser degree of resolution (i.e., they may have remembered just that *an object* and *another object* had been hidden [see Xu & Carey, 1996]). This coarser resolution did not contain enough featural detail to support object individuation.

Our results suggest that infants, similar to adults, experience a trade-off between the number of objects stored in working memory and the resolution of those object representations. In adults, this trade-off is revealed by the change detection task. Adults' aim in this task is to remember objects' features so that they can report whether any of those features differed between the target array and test array. Because the change detection task focuses subjects on object features, adults' performance decrement is manifested in capacity—they do not store as many objects in working memory when those objects are featurally complex rather than simple. Our manual search task reveals this same trade-off in infants. Infants' aim in this task is to retrieve individual objects from inside the box and to decide when the box is empty versus when it contains more. Because the manual search task focuses subjects on discrete objects (see Feigenson & Carey, 2003), the observed performance decrement is manifested in the resolution with which object are represented—not in capacity.

Because these forms of the trade-off between capacity and resolution can be viewed as opposite sides of the same coin, our results add convergent evidence to the debate between fixed and flexible capacity. Infants' performance in our manual search task is consistent with the view that working memory can store no more than 3 or 4 items (3 items for infants, 3–4 items for adults), but that fewer items will be stored if the items impose a high informational load. Alternatively, as in our task, 3 items can be stored with less informational resolution. Our findings shed light on the origins of this trade-off. Rather than being a strategy formed by the working memory system in response to years of experience, the balancing act between capacity and resolution is already being performed in infancy. *What* is stored in working memory affects *how many* object representations can be maintained (Alvarez & Cavanagh, 2004), and *how many* objects are remembered affects *what* features are bound to the resulting representations (Zosh & Feigenson, submitted).

2.3 Do the *contents* of working memory affect the format of forgetting?

2.3.1 Exceeding adults' working memory capacity

Many studies show that adults can store 3 or 4 items in working memory (Alvarez & Cavanagh, 2004; Broadbent, 1975; Cowan, 2001; Luck & Vogel, 1997; Song & Jiang, 2006; Sperling, 1960; Todd & Marois, 2004; Xu & Chun, 2006). But, what happens when working memory capacity is exceeded, as is the case when 5 or 6 objects are presented? When faced with displays containing more items than they can remember, adults appear to represent 3 or 4 of them and to ignore or forget the items that exceed this limit.[8] This is reflected by the smooth decline in adults' performance with increasingly large arrays containing numbers of items greater than capacity (Eng et al., 2005; Luck & Vogel, 1997; Vogel & Machizawa, 2004).

For example, when faced with arrays containing 6 objects, adults' performance at detecting a change to any one of those objects is still above chance, although far from perfect (Luck & Vogel, 1997). This suggests that adults successfully represented 3 or 4 out of the 6 total objects. In the change detection task, if one of those 3 or 4 stored objects happened to change its properties, adults detected this. If instead one of the unremembered objects changed its properties, adults simply guessed whether there had been a change or not, and were therefore at chance. Across trials, this led to above-chance performance with supracapacity arrays. Thus, adults' working memory capacity is not diminished when they are shown arrays containing large numbers of items, relative to when they are shown only 3 or 4 items. In both cases, they store 3 or 4 items in working memory.

2.3.2 Exceeding infants' working memory capacity

Infants exhibit an entirely different pattern of performance. When shown arrays containing numbers of items exceeding their 3-item capacity, infants experience 'catastrophic forgetting': that is, they seem to forget all of the presented items rather than simply storing a subset as adults do. For example, infants who have seen 4 objects hidden in a box do not continue searching after retrieving only 1 of the 4 (Feigenson & Carey, 2005), a failure which persists until 20 months of age (Barner et al., 2007). Had infants remembered 3 of the 4, they would have continued to search for the missing objects. Similarly, given a choice between 4 crackers hidden in one location and 1 cracker hidden in another location, infants chose randomly, again suggesting that they do not represent 4 as '3' or even as 'more than 1' (Feigenson & Carey, 2005).

Why do infants experience catastrophic working memory failure for supracapacity arrays, whereas adults do not? One possibility is that once infants have stored the maximum of 3 items in memory, they have difficulty inhibiting any other items from attempting to enter memory and therefore suffer interference effects leading to memory breakdown, whereas adults do not experience this interference effect. A different possibility is that methodological differences

---

[8] But see Feigenson (2008) for an exception. When shown serially presented collections of objects, where each collections contained many tokens of a single object type and where collections were temporally interleaved, adults exhibited complete failure of working memory once the number of presented collections exceeded capacity. With 4 or 5 collections, adults failed to store any of the presented collections in memory—a parallel pattern to the failure observed in infants.

between studies with infants and studies with adults contribute to the performance divergence. Specifically, studies with infants have typically measured working memory capacity using displays of visually identical objects, such as ping-pong balls (Barner et al., 2007; Feigenson & Carey, 2003, 2005; Feigenson & Halberda, 2004). In contrast, studies with adults have typically measured capacity using displays of visually contrasting objects, such as differently colored squares or different alphanumeric characters (Alvarez & Cavanagh, 2004; Broadbent, 1975; Cowan, 2001; Luck & Vogel, 1997; Song & Jiang, 2006; Sperling, 1960; Todd & Marois, 2004; Xu & Chun, 2006). Do infants perform differently than adults when presented with supracapacity arrays because of developmental differences, or because of stimulus differences?

If stimulus differences contribute, this might be revealed by presenting infants with stimulus arrays that are more similar to those used with adults: that is, infants might show better working memory performance with heterogeneous object arrays (e.g., cat, bottle, shoe, bus) than with homogeneous arrays (e.g., ball, ball, ball, ball). A small amount of existing evidence suggests that array heterogeneity can indeed affect infants' working memory. When habituated to 2-object arrays containing objects that contrasted in color, pattern, and texture, 7-month-old infants responded to a change in the number of objects present; but when habituated to 2-object arrays containing objects that were perceptually identical, infants failed to respond to a change in the number of objects present and instead responded on the basis of the objects' combined surface area (Feigenson, 2005). This suggests that heterogeneity might help to preserve representations of individual items in working memory.

Alternatively, the opposite prediction (that infants might show worse performance with heterogeneous arrays than they do with homogeneous arrays) also seems reasonable, in light of previous findings that, for adults, the complexity of individual stimulus items appears to reduce working memory capacity (Alvarez & Cavanagh, 2004; Eng et al., 2005). An array containing a cat, a bottle, a shoe, and a bus contains objects that are each *individually* more complex than an array containing 4 balls. Additionally, the array as a whole is *globally* more complex. Furthermore, some studies have found that children have greater difficulty abstracting numerical information or making numerical matches with sets of heterogeneous objects than sets of homogeneous objects (Cantlon et al., 2007; Klahr & Wallace, 1976; Siegel, 1974). These findings suggest that perhaps infants will remember fewer objects from heterogeneous than homogeneous arrays.

So, when presented with arrays that exceed capacity, does *what* infants store affect *how many* they remember? We tested the effects of array heterogeneity on infants' representations of supracapacity arrays by comparing their performance in the manual search task when shown heterogeneous arrays (the present experiments) with their performance when shown homogeneous arrays (previous experiments). To recapitulate, in previous experiments, infants were able to remember 1, 2, or 3 identical hidden objects, but not 4 (Barner et al., 2007; Feigenson & Carey, 2003, 2005). Infants successfully continued searching the box after seeing 2 objects hidden and retrieving just 1 of them (a 1 vs. 2 comparison), after seeing 3 objects hidden and retrieving just 1 of them (a 1 vs. 3 comparison), and after seeing 3 objects hidden and retrieving just 2 of them (a 2 vs. 3 comparison). However, infants failed to keep searching after seeing 4 objects hidden and retrieving either 1 or 2 of them. In these experiments, the arrays always comprised visually identical objects (e.g., 4 orange ping-pong balls), and infants always heard 4 identical verbal labels (e.g., 'Look at this. Look at this. Look at this. Look at this.') We asked whether conceptual, lexical, or perceptual heterogeneity would allow 12-month-old infants to succeed with 4-object arrays in the face of their previous failures.

In our first experiment, we examined the effects of conceptual and lexical heterogeneity. In contrast to previous studies, here we presented infants with conceptually heterogeneous arrays containing objects from contrasting categories known to be familiar to infants of this age (e.g., brush, cat, spoon, duck). Second, we manipulated infants' knowledge of contrasting lexical labels for the objects in two ways. For infants in the Heterogeneous Labels condition, we presented only objects for which each infant was reported by parents to know the label. For infants in the Homogeneous Labels condition, we presented only objects for which parents reported the infant did not know the label. In addition, infants in the Heterogeneous Labels condition heard the experimenter refer to objects using contrasting labels prior to hiding them in the box (e.g., 'Look a brush! Look, a cat!'). Infants in the Homogeneous Labels condition heard the experimenter refer to objects using noncontrasting labels ('Look at that! Look at that!').

Each infant was tested with two kinds of numerical comparisons: 1 versus 2 (Fig. 2.3) and 2 versus 4 objects (Fig. 2.4). On 1 versus 2 comparisons, we compared the duration of infants' searching after they had seen 2 objects hidden and retrieved just 1 of them (and therefore, the box was expected to contain another object) with their searching after they had seen 1 object hidden and retrieved 1 (and therefore, the box was expected to be empty). If infants successfully searched longer when the box was expected to contain another object relative to when it was expected to be empty, we can conclude that infants successfully represented 2 objects in working memory, replicating results from our previous experiments (Feigenson & Carey, 2003, 2005).

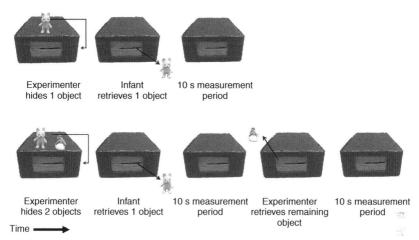

Experimenter hides 1 object   Infant retrieves 1 object   10 s measurement period

Experimenter hides 2 objects   Infant retrieves 1 object   10 s measurement period   Experimenter retrieves remaining object   10 s measurement period

Time ➡

Fig. 2.3 Sequence of presentation events comprising a 1 vs. 2 object comparison (Zosh & Feigenson, in preparation) In the top row, infants' searching is measured after they see 1 object hidden and have retrieved 1 object—the box is expected to be empty. In the bottom row, infants' searching is measured after they see 2 objects hidden and have retrieved just 1 object—the box is expected to contain more objects.

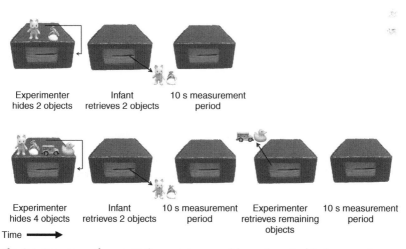

Experimenter hides 2 objects   Infant retrieves 2 objects   10 s measurement period

Experimenter hides 4 objects   Infant retrieves 2 objects   10 s measurement period   Experimenter retrieves remaining objects   10 s measurement period

Time ➡

Fig. 2.4 Sequence of presentation events comprising a 2 vs. 4 object comparison (Zosh & Feigenson, in preparation) In the top row, infants' searching is measured after they see 2 objects hidden and have retrieved 2—the box is expected to be empty. In the bottom row, infants' searching is measured after they see 4 objects hidden and have retrieved just 2 of them—the box is expected to contain more objects.

On 2 versus 4 object comparisons, we compared the duration of infants' searching after they had seen 4 objects hidden and retrieved just 2 of them (and therefore, the box was expected to contain more objects) with their searching after they had seen 2 objects hidden and retrieved 2 (and therefore, the box was expected to be empty). If infants successfully searched longer when the box was expected to contain more objects relative to when it was empty, we can conclude that infants were able to represent 4 objects in working memory (or could at least discriminate 4 from 2). Overall, we wanted to know (1) whether infants presented with our new heterogeneous object arrays would succeed on 2 versus 4 object comparisons, in the face of their previous failures with 2 versus 4 comparisons using identical objects (Feigenson & Carey, 2003, 2005), and (2) whether this success was affected by the presence or absence of lexical cues to heterogeneity.

First, we predicted that infants in both conditions would succeed with 1 versus 2 object comparisons, because 1 and 2 objects are well within infants' working memory capacity. Our results confirmed this. Regardless of whether they knew and heard contrasting labels for objects, infants successfully searched longer on trials when 2 objects had been hidden and only 1 had been retrieved, relative to trials when 1 object had been hidden and it had already been retrieved (see Fig. 2.5). Infants in previous studies using homogeneous

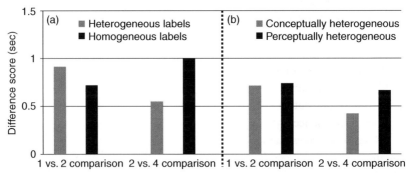

Fig. 2.5 Difference scores (searching when the box contained more objects minus searching when the box was empty) for 1 vs. 2 and 2 vs. 4 object comparisons in the heterogeneity experiments of Zosh and Feigenson (in preparation). Difference scores above zero indicate infants' successful differentiation of 1 from 2 or 2 from 4. In panel (a), objects were conceptually and perceptually heterogeneous, and contrasting lexical labels were used to refer to them. Infants succeeded in all conditions. In panel (b), objects were perceptually heterogeneous, and conceptual heterogeneity was manipulated. Infants again succeeded in all conditions. These successes show that perceptual heterogeneity was sufficient to allow infants to successfully discriminate 2 from 4, in the face of their previous failures to do so (Barner et al., 2007; Feigenson & Carey, 2003).

arrays of identical objects also demonstrated success with such 1 versus 2 object comparisons; therefore, this finding simply confirms that infants in our task were able to store representations of 2 visually contrasting objects in working memory.

Second, we predicted that infants would succeed on 2 versus 4 object comparisons with our conceptually heterogeneous object arrays, but only in the Heterogeneous Labels condition where they both knew and heard contrasting labels for the presented objects. Surprisingly, we found that infants in *both* the Heterogeneous and Homogeneous Labels conditions succeeded on 2 versus 4 comparisons (Fig. 2.5). When shown arrays of familiar objects that contrasted with one another, infants who saw 4 objects hidden and only retrieved 2 of them successfully continued to search the box for the missing objects. This success is striking given infants' multiple previous failures with 2 versus 4 comparisons involving identical objects (Barner et al., 2007; Feigenson & Carey, 2003, 2005). However, this improvement in infants' working memory performance did not require lexical heterogeneity (Zosh & Feigenson, in preparation). Even when they did not know the objects' labels and did not hear them labeled by the experimenter, infants successfully continued searching after seeing 4 contrasting objects hidden and retrieving only 2 of them.

Our findings demonstrate infants' improved working memory performance with heterogeneous arrays relative to homogeneous arrays. What type of heterogeneity was responsible for this effect? Our stimulus objects were from familiar categories that contrasted with one another conceptually (e.g., brush, cat, car, duck). However, the objects also contrasted with one another on the basis of perceptual features (e.g., blue brush, white cat, red car, yellow duck). Therefore, the results of our first experiment do not reveal whether conceptual or perceptual heterogeneity was responsible for infants' improved memory performance. We addressed this issue by next presenting 12-month-old infants with arrays that were always perceptually heterogeneous, but either contained conceptually familiar or conceptually novel objects.

In the Conceptually Heterogeneous condition, the experimenter hid the same familiar objects as were used in our first experiment (e.g., brush, cat, car, duck). In the Perceptually Heterogeneous condition, the experimenter hid contrasting novel objects that were chosen to be unfamiliar to infants (e.g., a plastic crab claw, a piece of a hair clip, a plastic towel holder, and a plastic skirt from a doll set). These novel objects contrasted in visual features such as color and shape, but were reported by parents to be entirely unfamiliar.

As in the previous heterogeneity experiment, both the Conceptually Heterogeneous and the Perceptually Heterogeneous conditions involved

1 versus 2 object comparisons and 2 versus 4 object comparisons, again forming a 2 × 2 design. We predicted that infants in both the Conceptually Heterogeneous and the Perceptually Heterogeneous conditions would succeed with 1 versus 2 object comparisons, because arrays of 1 and 2 objects are well within infants' working memory capacity (Feigenson & Carey, 2003, 2005; Feigenson, Carey & Hauser, 2002). Our results confirmed this. Regardless of whether they had seen familiar or novel objects hidden, infants successfully searched longer on trials when 2 objects had been hidden and only 1 had been retrieved, compared with trials when 1 object had been hidden and it had already been retrieved (Fig. 2.5).

Second, we predicted that infants might only succeed on 2 versus 4 object comparisons in the Conceptually Heterogeneous condition, when they saw objects from contrasting familiar categories. But surprisingly, we found that infants in both the Conceptually Heterogeneous and Perceptually Heterogeneous conditions succeeded on 2 versus 4 comparisons (Fig. 2.5). When 4 conceptually unfamiliar, perceptually dissimilar objects were hidden and infants had retrieved just 2 of them, infants continued searching the box for the missing objects. This success contrasts with the several other failures of infants of this age to represent 4 objects in this same paradigm (Barner et al., 2007; Feigenson & Carey, 2003, 2005). The sole difference is that here we used perceptually heterogeneous object arrays instead of perceptually homogeneous arrays. This means that seeing arrays of objects that contrasted in their early visual features was sufficient for infants to experience a working memory benefit.

This pattern of results raises a puzzle: What was the difference in the way that infants represented the heterogeneous object arrays relative to the homogeneous arrays? One possibility is that heterogeneity actually *expanded* infants' working memory capacity, allowing them to store representations of 4 individual objects in memory. Alternatively, heterogeneity might have acted to prevent the catastrophic memory failure observed in previous studies (Barner et al., 2007; Feigenson & Carey, 2003, 2005), thereby allowing infants to perform in a way similar to that of adults. According to this second possibility, infants presented with heterogeneous object arrays might have been able to store up to (but not beyond) their usual 3-item working memory capacity, and would therefore have represented a 4-object array as containing 3 objects. Doing so would have led to success on 2 versus 4 object comparisons because infants who saw 4 objects hidden would have represented them as '3'—after retrieving just 2 of them, they would have continued searching for the missing third object. Representing just a manageable subset of supracapacity arrays is exactly what adults do when presented with heterogeneous arrays (Eng et al., 2005; Luck & Vogel, 1997; Vogel & Machizawa, 2004).

We tested these two possible benefits of heterogeneity by presenting infants with heterogeneous 4-object arrays, and allowing them to retrieve either 2 of the 4 objects (a 2 vs. 4 comparison, just as in our previous studies) or 3 of the 4 objects (a 3 vs. 4 comparison). If heterogeneity increases memory capacity such that infants can successfully remember 4 individual objects, they should succeed with both the 2 versus 4 and 3 versus 4 comparisons. Alternatively, if heterogeneity does not alter capacity but instead prevents catastrophic memory failure, infants should succeed with 2 versus 4 object comparisons but fail with 3 versus 4 object comparisons because they represented 4 as 3.

We found evidence for this second account. After seeing 4 contrasting objects hidden and retrieving just 2 of them, infants continued to search the box (replicating the results of the previous two experiments); but after seeing 4 contrasting objects hidden and retrieving 3 of them, infants stopped searching (Fig. 2.6). Thus, infants appeared to represent 4 heterogeneous objects as 3 (Zosh & Feigenson, in preparation). This means that they did not experience the usual pattern of catastrophic memory failure in which all of the presented objects were forgotten (Barner et al., 2007; Feigenson & Carey, 2003, 2005). Instead, they appeared to fill working memory to capacity without storing any information about the remaining object that exceeded capacity.

Taken together, these three experiments suggest that infants remember heterogeneous object arrays differently than homogeneous arrays. When shown homogeneous arrays of identical objects that exceed their 3-item working memory capacity (e.g., 4-object arrays), infants experience catastrophic failure

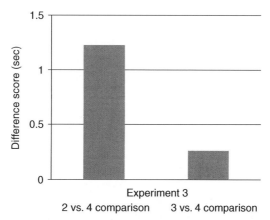

Fig. 2.6 Difference scores (searching when the box contained more objects minus searching when the box was empty) reflect infants' searching after 4 objects had been hidden and 2 of them retrieved, versus when 4 objects had been hidden and 3 of them had been retrieved.

and seem to forget *all* of the presented objects; but when presented with heterogeneous arrays of perceptually contrasting objects, infants remember 3 of the objects and ignore or forget any others. Our results also show that perceptual heterogeneity is sufficient to obtain this effect—when conceptual and lexical heterogeneity were removed from the arrays, infants still succeeded with 2 versus 4 object comparisons. It remains unknown whether perceptual heterogeneity is *required* for this effect, or whether, for example, infants might also succeed when presented with 4 visually identical objects referred to with contrasting verbal labels (e.g., 'Look, a blicket. Look, a pizer. Look, a dax. Look, a toma.'). Future studies will be needed to identify the various sources of array heterogeneity from which infants can benefit.

Another open issue is the mechanism underlying the observed heterogeneity effect. In adults, heterogeneity can help working memory by decreasing interference between stored items. For example, Bunting (2006) found that when adults performed a working memory task with stimulus items from different categories (e.g., words and digits), they were less susceptible to proactive interference than when items were from the same category or had similar features (see also Conlin et al., 2005; Oberauer & Kliegl, 2006; Wickelgren, 1965). Bunting suggested that when items within or across memory lists differed in identity, proactive interference was released. Infants' difficulty in representing subsets of arrays containing 4 identical objects might have been due to such interference effects.

The heterogeneity effect we observed might also be related to the phenomenon of repetition blindness, in which adults are better at reporting features of briefly presented items when the items have contrasting features (e.g., a yellow S and a blue O) rather than identical features (e.g., two blue O's; Kanwisher et al., 1995). It is possible that infants too have difficulty encoding 4 identical objects into memory (although this would not provide an obvious explanation for why they successfully encode and remember 2 or 3 identical objects). Future studies will be needed to test these possibilities. Surprisingly, little research has examined the effects of heterogeneity versus homogeneity on adults' working memory capacity. Our finding that heterogeneity clearly improves infants' performance opens the door to conducting similar investigations with adults.

2.4 Concluding remarks

In this chapter, we have suggested that in order to understand object representations, one must come to understand the working memory system that supports their storage and maintenance. In particular, we offered a developmental perspective to this approach. Infants' object representations have been elegantly investigated for the past several decades. One of the most controversial and exciting revelations of this work has been that, starting quite early in the first year of life, infants can think about objects in the absence of direct perceptual evidence of their existence (e.g., Amso & Johnson, Chapter 9; Baillargeon, 1987; Flombaum et al., Chapter 6; Luo et al., 2003; Shinskey & Munakata, 2003; Spelke et al., 1992; Wynn, 1992). More recent work has demonstrated that the same holds true for nonhuman species—monkeys too can represent and reason about unseen objects (Cheries et al., 2006; Flombaum et al., Chapter 6; Hauser & Carey, 2003; Munakata et al., 2001; Santos et al., 2006).

Importantly, thinking and reasoning about hidden objects requires memory. Without a mental storage system in which object representations can be maintained and processed, infants (and monkeys) would not be able to expect hidden objects to be solid, continuous, or cohesive—instead, out of sight would truly be out of mind (Piaget, 1954). In this way, the architecture that constrains working memory in turn constrains how and when we can think about objects. Because working memory can be thought of as constrained by both discrete and continuous limits (i.e., by limits on how many individual items can be stored, and by limits on how much total information can be stored), thinking about objects will be influenced by both discrete and continuous properties of the scenes in which those objects appear. Here, we have attempted to bring together investigations of these two types of constraints, uniting studies of working memory capacity (*how many* objects can be remembered) with studies of the information that is bound to object representations (*what* features of objects are remembered). We have tried to show that for both infants and adults, the quantity and quality of object representations interact in some surprising ways. First, we saw that working memory computes a trade-off between the number of items stored and the resolution of the resulting representations. Second, we saw that the features bound to object representations can determine the nature of forgetting when working memory capacity is exceeded.

A lesson from this work is that the architecture of working memory shapes our reasoning about objects—this is true throughout the lifespan. We suspect that future investigations that continue to explore the alignment of infants' working memory with adults' working memory will be fruitful. Such work will add detail to the emerging portrait of how working memory supports thinking about things unseen.

References

Alvarez, G. A., & Cavanagh, P. (2004). The capacity of visual short-term memory is set both by visual information load and by number of objects. *Psychological Science, 15*(2), 106–111.

Awh, E., Barton, B., & Vogel, E. K. (2007). Visual working memory represents a fixed number of items regardless of complexity. *Psychological Science, 18*(7), 622–628.

Baillargeon, R. (1987). Object permanence in 3 1/2-month-old and 4 1/2-month-old infants. *Developmental Psychology, 23*(5), 655–664.

Barner, D., Thalwitz, D., Wood, J., Yang, S. J., & Carey, S. (2007). On the relation between the acquisition of singular-plural morpho-syntax and the conceptual distinction between one and more than one. *Developmental Science, 10*(3), 365–373.

Berger, A., Tzur, G., & Posner, M. I. (2006). Infant brains detect arithmetic errors. *Proceedings of the National Academy of Sciences of the United States of America, 103*(33), 12649–12653.

Broadbent, D. E. (1975). The magic number seven after fifteen years. In A. Kennedy, & A. Wilkes (Eds.), *Studies in Long-Term Memory* (pp. 3–18). John Wiley & Sons.

Bunting, M. (2006). Proactive interference and item similarity in working memory. *Journal of Experimental Psychology-Learning Memory and Cognition, 32*(2), 183–196.

Cantlon, J. F., Brannon, E. M., Carter, E. J., & Pelphrey, K. A. (2006). Functional imaging of numerical processing in adults and four-year-old children. *Proceedings of London Society Biology, 4*, e125.

Cantlon, J. F., Fink, R., Safford, K. E., & Brannon, E. M. (2007). Heterogeneity impairs numerical matching but not numerical ordering in preschool children. *Developmental Science, 10*, 431–440.

Canton, J. F., Platt, M. L., & Brannon, E. M. (in press). Common constraints on quantities in cognition and cortex. *Trends in Cognitive Sciences.*

Chase, W. G., & Simon, H. A. (1973). Perception in chess. *Cognitive Psychology, 4*, 55–81.

Cheries, E. W., DeCoste, C., & Wynn, K. (2003). Number not area: infants use property contrasts for quantifying objects. Poster presented at the Society for Research in Child Development, Tampa, FL.

Cheries, E. W., Newman, G. E., Santos, L. R., & Scholl, B. J. (2006). Units of visual individuation in rhesus macaques: objects or unbound features? *Perception, 35*(8), 1057–1071.

Conlin, J. A., Gathercole, S. E., & Adams, J. W. (2005). Stimulus similarity decrements in children's working memory span. *The Quarterly Journal of Experimental Psychology, 58A*, 1434–1446.

Cowan, N. (2001). The magical number 4 in short-term memory: a reconsideration of mental storage capacity. *Behavioral and Brain Sciences, 24*(1), 87–114.

Cowan, N. (2005). *Working Memory Capacity.* Hove, UK: Psychology Press.

Eng, H. Y., Chen, D., & Jiang, Y. (2005). Visual working memory for simple and complex visual stimuli. *Psychonomic Bulletin and Review, 12*(6), 1127–1133.

Ericsson, K. A., Chase, W. G., & Faloon, S. (1980). Acquisition of a memory skill. *Science, 208*, 1181–1182.

Feigenson, L. (2005). A double-dissociation in infants' representations of object arrays. *Cognition, 95*(3), B37–48.

Feigenson, L. (2008). Parallel non-verbal enumeration is constrained by a set-based limit. *Cognition, 107*, 1–18.

Feigenson, L., & Carey, S. (2003). Tracking individuals via object-files: evidence from infants' manual search. *Developmental Science, 6*(5), 568–584.

Feigenson, L., & Carey, S. (2005). On the limits of infants' quantification of small object arrays. *Cognition, 97*(3), 295–313.

Feigenson, L., Carey, S., & Hauser, M. (2002). The representations underlying infants' choice of more: object files versus analog magnitudes. *Psychological Science, 13*(2), 150–156.

Feigenson, L., Carey, S., & Spelke, E. S. (2002). Infants' discrimination of number vs. continuous extent. *Cognitive Psychology, 44*, 33–66.

Feigenson, L., Dehaene, S., & Spelke, E. S. (2004). Core systems of number. *Trends in Cognitive Sciences, 8*(7), 307–314.

Feigenson, L., & Halberda, J. (2004). Infants chunk object arrays into sets of individuals. *Cognition, 91*(2), 173–190.

Feigenson, L., & Halberda, J. (2008). Conceptual knowledge increases infants' memory capacity. *Proceedings of the National Academy of Sciences.*

Halberda, J., Sires, S. F., & Feigenson, L. (2006). Multiple spatially overlapped sets can be enumerated in parallel. *Psychological Science, 17*(7), 572–576.

Hauser, M. D., & Carey, S. (2003). Spontaneous representations of small numbers of objects by rhesus macaques: examinations of content and format. *Cognitive Psychology, 47*(4), 367–401.

Hauser, M. D., Carey, S., & Hauser, L. B. (2000). Spontaneous number representation in semi-free-ranging rhesus monkeys. *Proceedings of the Royal Society of London, Series B, 267*, 829–833.

Kaldy, Z., & Leslie, A. M. (2003). Identification of objects in 9-month-old infants: integrating 'what' and 'where' information. *Developmental Science, 6*(3), 360–373.

Kanwisher, N., Driver, J., & Macado, L. (1995). Spatial repetition blindness is modulated by selective attention to color or shape. *Cognitive Psychology, 29*, 303–337.

Klahr, D., & Wallace, J. G. (1976). *Cognitive Development: An Information-Processing View.* Hillsdale, NJ: Erlbaum.

Koechlin, E., Dehaene, S., & Mehler, J. (1997). Numerical transformations in five-month-old human infants. *Mathematical Cognition, 3*, 89–104.

Luck, S. J., & Vogel, E. K. (1997). The capacity of visual working memory for features and conjunctions. *Nature, 390*(6657), 279–281.

Luo, Y., Baillargeon, R., Brueckner, L., & Munakata, Y. (2003). Reasoning about a hidden object after a delay: evidence for robust representations in 5-month-old infants. *Cognition, 88*, B23–B32.

McCollough, A. W., Machizawa, M. G., & Vogel, E. K. (2007). Electrophysiological measures of maintaining representations in visual working memory. *Cortex, 43*(1), 77–94.

Miller, G. A. (1956). The magical number seven, plus or minus two: some limitations on our capacity for processing information. *The Psychological Review, 63*(2), 81–97.

Munakata, Y., Santos, L. R., Spelke, E. S., Hauser, M. D., & O'Reilly, R. C. (2001). Visual representation in the wild: how rhesus monkeys parse objects. *Journal of Cognitive Neuroscience, 13*(1), 44–58.

Oakes, L. M., Ross-Sheehy, S., & Luck, S. J. (2006). Rapid development of feature binding in visual short-term memory. *Psychological Science, 17*(9), 781–787.

Oberauer, K., & Kliegl, R. (2006). A formal model of capacity limits in working memory. *Journal of Memory and Language, 55*, 601–626.

Piaget, J. (1954). *The Origins of Intelligence in Children*. New York: International University Press.

Ross-Sheehy, S., Oakes, L. M., & Luck, S. J. (2003). The development of visual short-term memory capacity in infants. *Child Development, 74*(6), 1807–1822.

Santos, L. R., Seelig, D., & Hauser, M. D. (2006). Cotton-top tamarins' (*Saguinus oedipus*) expectations about occluded objects: a dissociation between looking and reaching tasks. *Infancy, 9*(2), 147–171.

Shinskey, J. L., & Munakata, Y. (2003). Are infants in the dark about hidden objects? *Developmental Science, 6*(3), 273–282.

Siegel, L. (1974). Heterogeneity and spatial factors as determinants of numeration ability. *Child Development, 45*, 532–534.

Simon, H. A. (1974). How big is a chunk? *Science, 183*, 482–488.

Simon, T. J., Hespos, S. J., & Rochat, P. (1995). Do infants understand simple arithmetic—a replication of Wynn (1992). *Cognitive Development, 10*(2), 253–269.

Song, J-H., & Jiang, Y. (2006). Visual working memory for simple and complex features: an fMRI study. *Neuroimage, 30*, 963–972.

Sperling, G. (1960). The information available in brief visual presentations. *Psychological Monographs, 74*.

Spelke, E. S., Breinlinger, K., Macomber, J., & Jacobson, K. (1992). Origins of knowledge. *Psychological Review, 99*, 605–632.

Todd, J. J., & Marois, R. (2004). Capacity limit of visual short-term memory in human posterior parietal cortex. *Nature, 428*(6984), 751–754.

Tremoulet, P. D., Leslie, A. M., & Hall, D. G. (2000). Infant individuation and identification of objects. *Cognitive Development, 15*(4), 499–522.

Uller, C., Carey, S., Huntley-Fenner, G., & Klatt, L. (1999). What representations might underlie infant numerical knowledge? *Cognitive Development, 14*(1), 1–36.

Van de Walle, G. A., Carey, S., & Prevor, M. (2000). Bases for object individuation in infancy: evidence from manual search. *Journal of Cognition and Development, 1*(3), 249–280.

Vogel, E. K., & Machizawa, M. G. (2004). Neural activity predicts individual differences in visual working memory capacity. *Nature, 428*(6984), 748–751.

Vogel, E. K., McCollough, A. W., & Machizawa, M. G. (2005). Neural measures reveal individual differences in controlling access to working memory. *Nature, 438*(7067), 500–503.

Wickelgren, W. A. (1965). Acoustic similarity and retroactive interference in short-term memory. *Journal of Verbal Learning and Verbal Behavior, 4*, 53–61.

Wilcox, T. (1999). Object individuation: infants' use of shape, size, pattern, and color. *Cognition, 72*, 125–166.

Wood, J. N., Hauser, M. D., Glynn, D. D., & Barner, D. (2008). Free-ranging rhesus monkeys spontaneously individuate and enumerate small numbers of non-solid portions. *Cognition, 106*, 207–221.

Wynn, K. (1992). Addition and subtraction by human infants. *Nature, 358*(6389), 749–750.

Xu, F. (1999). Object individuation and object identity in infancy: the role of spatiotemporal information, object property information, and language. *Acta Psychologica, 102*(2/3), 113–136.

Xu, F., & Carey, S. (1996). Infants' metaphysics: the case of numerical identity. *Cognitive Psychology, 30*(2), 111–153.

Xu, F., Carey, S., & Quint, N. (2004). The emergence of kind-based object individuation in infancy. *Cognitive Psychology, 49*(2), 155–190.

Xu, F., Carey, S., & Welch, J. (1999). Infants' ability to use object kind information for object individuation. *Cognition, 70*(2), 137–166.

Xu, F., Cote, M., & Baker, A. (2005). Labeling guides object individuation in 12-month-old infants. *Psychological Science, 16*(5), 372–377.

Xu, Y., & Chun, M. M. (2007). Visual grouping in human parietal cortex. *Proceedings of the National Academy of Sciences, 104*(47), 18766–18771.

Xu, Y., & Chun, M. M. (2006). Dissociable neural mechanisms supporting visual short-term memory for objects. *Nature, 440*(7080), 91–95.

Zosh, J. M. & Feigenson, L. (submitted). A capacity-resolution tradeoff in infant working memory.

Zosh, J. M. & Feigenson, L. (in preparation). Effects of array heterogeneity on infants' working memory for hidden objects.

Chapter 3

A comparative approach to understanding human numerical cognition

Kerry E. Jordan & Elizabeth M. Brannon

3.1 Introduction

The field of animal cognition endeavors to identify similarities and differences between human and animal cognition. Recent foci for research are as varied as tool use, communication systems, categorization, cultural traditions, object concepts, metacognition, and precursors of a theory of mind (e.g., Beck, 1980; Boesch, 1995; Hare et al., 2000; Hauser, 1997, 2006; Kornell et al., 2007; Santos et al., 2002; Tomasello et al., 2003; van Schaik et al., 2003; Whiten et al., 1999). Animal cognition research has asked whether the cognitive feats that seem to exemplify the complexity of human cognition are actually unique to humans or, alternatively, have a more ancient evolutionary origin. The comparative approach has also been used to directly compare nonverbal animals and preverbal human infants to provide convergent insight into the relationship between thought and language. This approach has made great strides at integrating the once disparate disciplines of animal behavior and developmental psychology, providing a more comprehensive view of the factors that influence nonlinguistic thought. In this chapter, we illustrate how the comparative approach has been used in the domain of number to identify the origins of mathematical thinking.

3.2 Do animals really represent number?

Where would we be without numbers? How would we quantify money, ages, height, length, weight, velocity, temperature, exam grades, IQ? How would we label our football players, serial numbers, IP addresses, phone numbers, tax forms? Clearly, numbers are important for almost everything we do. Beyond simply representing numbers, we calculate and make complex predictions with numbers. Here, we ask whether there are evolutionary precursors to human mathematical ability.

At the turn of the 20th century, a horse named Clever Hans was purported to be able to add, subtract, multiply, divide, work with fractions, tell time, and keep track of the calendar (Hothersall, 2004). The horse's owner, high school math teacher Mr. von Osten, would ask Hans a mathematical question and Clever Hans would answer by tapping his foot the correct number of times. Clever Hans had everyone fooled until one of von Osten's brighter graduate students determined that the horse was not performing any numerical calculations, but was instead merely watching the reactions and body language of von Osten or anyone else posing the question who was providing him with unintentional cues. Clever Hans produced the correct answer only when the questioner knew the answer and the horse could see the subtle, unconscious body cues indicating that the questioner expected Hans to cease tapping. The discrediting of Clever Hans' mathematical prowess created a healthy skepticism of any study purporting to show complex cognitive abilities in nonhuman animals. And not surprisingly, the effect of the Clever Hans story was most dramatic for research on animal numerical abilities. However, over the last 100 years, a vast number of experiments have now shown that many animal species are sensitive to number.

Beyond the Clever Hans problem, another issue for demonstrating that animals represent number is that many parameters typically covary with numerosity. Ten mangoes are more numerous than five mangoes but they also take up more space, take longer to eat, and have a higher hedonic value. Through careful stimulus control, research over the last century has compellingly demonstrated that many different nonhuman animal species can ignore nonnumerical stimulus dimensions and hone in on number (e.g., Brannon & Terrace, 1998; Dehaene, 2001; Emmerton et al., 1997; Jordan & Brannon, 2006a; Matsuzawa, 1985; Meck & Church, 1983; Nieder et al., 2002; Olthof & Roberts, 2000; Roberts, 2005).

For example, Jordan and Brannon (2006a) recently trained rhesus macaques to numerically match visual arrays in a delayed match-to-sample task on a touchscreen computer. In order to successfully match based on number, monkeys had to ignore continuous dimensions such as element size, cumulative surface area, and density. To assess whether monkeys attended to such continuous variables and whether these variables impacted numerical judgments, Jordan and Brannon analyzed accuracy as a function of whether continuous variables were congruent or incongruent with number. On trials in which number was considered congruent with cumulative surface area, the numerical match was more similar to the sample in cumulative surface area; in contrast, on trials in which number was considered incongruent with cumulative surface area, the distractor (or value that did not match the sample in

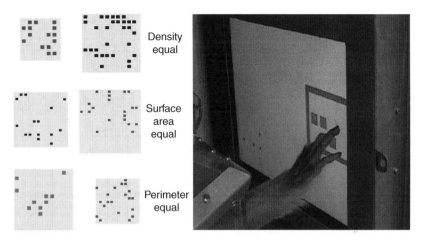

Fig. 3.1 Example stimuli used in a numerical ordering task. On some trials in this study, number covaried with cumulative surface area, density, or perimeter, whereas on other trials as shown in this figure, these variables were equated for larger and smaller numerosity. (Reproduced from Cantlon, J. F., & Brannon, E. M. (2006a). Shared system for ordering small and large numbers in monkeys and humans. *Psychological Science*, *17*, 402–407. With permission from Wiley-Blackwell.)

numerosity) was more similar to the sample in cumulative surface area. These analyses showed that the behavior of the monkeys was controlled by numerosity and not by continuous variables that often covary with numerosity.

Studies of numerical ordering in monkeys have used similar stringent stimulus controls and have demonstrated that monkeys can make purely numerical judgments (e.g., Brannon & Terrace, 1998, 2000; Brannon et al., 2006; Cantlon & Brannon, 2005, 2006a, 2006b; Judge et al., 2005; Smith et al., 2003; see Fig. 3.1 for example stimuli and for setup). There can be little doubt that nonhuman primates, and possibly many other animal species, have the capacity to discriminate stimuli based solely on number and to ignore nonnumerical dimensions that typically covary with number in nature.

3.3 **An analog magnitude system for representing number nonverbally**

The key finding throughout the literature on animal numerical competence is that discrimination depends on the ratio between numerical values (e.g., Beran, 2004; Beran et al., 2005; Cantlon & Brannon, 2006a; Gallistel & Gelman, 1992; Jordan & Brannon, 2006a; Judge et al., 2005; Olthof et al., 1997; Smith et al., 2003; Washburn & Rumbaugh, 1991). For example, Cantlon and Brannon (2006a) found that when rhesus monkeys were presented with pairs

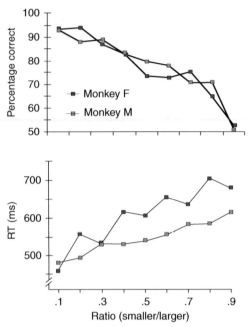

Fig. 3.2 Accuracy (top) and reaction time (RT; bottom) for two monkeys (Monkey F and Monkey M) as a function of the ratio between numerical values in a numerical ordering task. For both monkeys, accuracy decreased and reaction time increased as the ratio approached 1. (Reproduced from Cantlon, J. F., & Brannon, E. M. (2006a). Shared system for ordering small and large numbers in monkeys and humans. *Psychological Science, 17,* 402–407. With permission from Wiley-Blackwell.)

of the numerosities 2–30 and required to choose the numerically smaller, their accuracy and reaction time to respond was modulated by the ratio between the compared values (Fig. 3.2). Similarly, Jordan and Brannon (2006a) found that monkeys were more accurate and made faster responses in a numerical match-to-sample task when the ratio between the correct choice and incorrect choice was favorable (Fig. 3.3).

Ratio dependence has also been found in food choice tasks (e.g., Beran, 2001; Beran & Beran, 2004; Call, 2000; Lewis et al., 2005). Furthermore, when animals and humans are tested on numerical bisection tasks in which they are first trained to categorize small and large anchor values and then required to classify intermediate values as closer to the small or large anchor, their performance is best explained by models that assume they use a ratio comparison rule (Church & Deluty, 1977; Emmerton & Renner, 2006; Fetterman, 1993; Jordan & Brannon, 2006a, 2006b; Meck & Church, 1983; Meck et al., 1985; Platt & Davis, 1983; Roberts, 2005; Stubbs, 1976; Fig. 3.4).

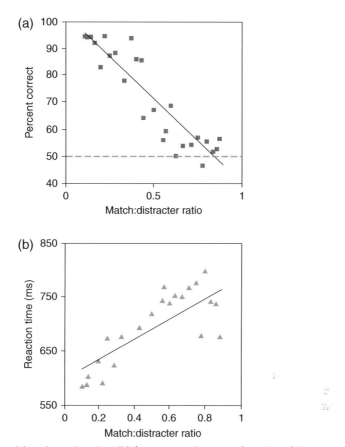

Fig. 3.3 Accuracy (a) and reaction time (b) for two monkeys as a function of the ratio between the correct numerical match and the numerically nonmatching stimulus (Jordan & Brannon, 2006a). Chance performance is 50%.

One explanation for ratio dependence is that the underlying representation for numerosities is in analog format (e.g., Gallistel & Gelman, 1992; Dehaene, 1992). In this format, numerosity is represented as a mental magnitude that is proportional to the quantity it represents. The signature property of this analog magnitude system is that it obeys Weber's Law: discrimination between two quantities depends on their ratio. Weber's Law states that $\Delta I/I = C$, where ΔI is the increase in stimulus intensity to a stimulus of intensity I that is required to produce a detectable change in intensity and C is a constant. Therefore, if a graduate student detects a change in a 20-pound backpack full of books when his advisor adds a 4-pound book, he would need an 8-pound book to detect a change in a 40-pound backpack. Previous research has revealed that under many circumstances, human infants also show ratio-dependent number

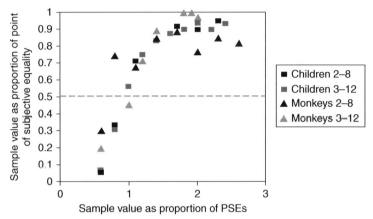

Fig. 3.4 The probability of classifying a numerical stimulus as more similar to the numerically large anchor value compared with the numerically small anchor value for 5-year-old children (squares) and monkeys (triangles). Anchor values were 2 and 8 (black) or 3 and 12 (gray). As predicted by Weber's Law, the psychometric functions that relate the probability of a 'choose large' response to the test numerosity superimpose different sets of anchor values with the same ratio in these two species (Jordan & Brannon, 2006a, 2006b).

judgments, suggesting that an analog magnitude system for representing number approximately may have both evolutionary and developmental origins (e.g., Jordan, Suanda, & Brannon, in press; Lipton & Spelke, 2003, 2004; Wood & Spelke, 2005; Xu & Spelke, 2000; Xu et al., 2005).

3.4 Parallels between numerical representations of adult humans and animals

Although adult humans from most parts of the world are highly adept at verbal counting and using symbolic number systems to perform complex mathematical operations, they simultaneously possess a nonverbal system for representing number. A strong possibility is that this nonverbal system is an analog magnitude system shared by nonhuman animals and in place early in human development. When adults are tested in nonverbal tasks that are designed to emulate animal tasks, their performance often looks virtually indistinguishable (e.g., Barth et al., 2006; Boisvert et al., 2003; Cantlon & Brannon, 2006a Cordes et al., 2001; Moyer & Landauer, 1967; Whalen et al., 1999).

For instance, Whalen and colleagues (1999) as well as Cordes and colleagues (2001) adapted a classic paradigm from the animal literature for use with humans. In the animal paradigm, rats were required to press a lever a target number of times to gain reward (Platt & Johnson, 1971). The mean number

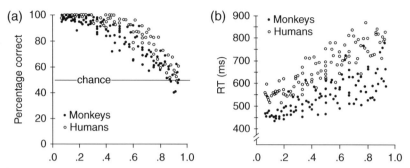

Fig. 3.5 Accuracy (a) and reaction time (b) for monkeys (filled circles) and college students (open circles) as a function of the ratio between the numerical values in a pair. (Reproduced from Cantlon, J. F., & Brannon, E. M. (2006a). Shared system for ordering small and large numbers in monkeys and humans. *Psychological Science*, *17*, 402–407. With permission from Wiley-Blackwell.)

of responses the rats made increased with the required number; importantly, the variability (standard deviation) in their response distributions was proportional to the required number of responses. In the human analog, subjects were either required to press at rates so fast they were prevented from verbally counting or were engaged in a verbal distracter task. Similar to rats, the mean number of key presses made by human subjects was proportional to the target number, and representations showed scalar variability in that the standard deviation of the response distributions increased with target magnitude (Cordes et al., 2001; Whalen et al., 1999).

Cantlon and Brannon (2006a) directly compared adult humans' and rhesus monkeys' abilities to order numerosities between 2 and 30. Qualitative and quantitative evidence suggest a shared system governed by Weber's Law for representing and comparing small and large numbers in these two species (Fig. 3.5). In a similar numerical ordering task, Beran (2006) uncovered an intriguing parallel between monkey and human numerical cognition. Beran found that monkeys, similar to humans, are sensitive to the regular–random numerosity illusion (RRNI). Under this illusion, we overestimate the number of items in sets of stimuli that are regularly (rather than randomly) arranged.

Another intriguing parallel between the numerical representations of adult humans and rhesus monkeys is the effect of semantic congruity on both species' numerical judgments (Cantlon & Brannon, 2005). An example of the semantic congruity effect is that people are faster at judging which of two small animals (i.e., a rat and a rabbit) is smaller than they are at judging which of these two small animals is larger. In contrast, we are faster at judging which of

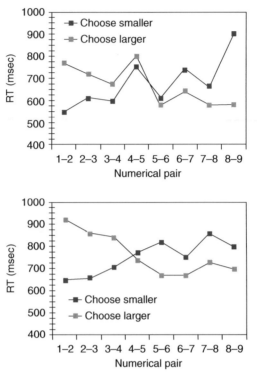

Fig. 3.6 Reaction time (RT) as a function of numerical pair for monkeys making an ordinal number judgment illustrates the semantic congruity effect. Monkeys were faster at choosing the smaller of two small numbers than they were at choosing the larger of two small numbers (black line). Conversely, when required to choose the larger of two large numbers, they were faster than when they were required to choose the smaller of two large numbers (grey line) (From Cantlon and Brannon, 2005).

two large animals (i.e., a zebra and an elephant) is larger than we are at judging which of two large animals is smaller (Banks et al., 1983; Shaki & Algom, 2002). This phenomenon had been shown to hold for various comparisons, including numerical contrasts (Moyer & Bayer, 1976; Banks et al., 1976). Intuitively, this effect seems driven by language. However, Cantlon and Brannon (2005) found that monkeys were faster at choosing the smaller of two small numerosities (i.e., 2 vs. 3) than they were at choosing the larger of two small numerosities (Fig. 3.6). Conversely, when required to choose the larger of two large numerosities, they were faster than when they were required to choose the smaller of two large numerosities. Thus, monkeys share with adult humans susceptibility to the semantic congruity effect in numerical comparisons.

Recent studies also demonstrate that nonhuman animals, similar to adult humans, can perform mathematical operations on their numerical representations. In one compelling study, a chimpanzee (Sheba) was first trained to map symbols to numerosities and subsequently tested on her ability to add symbols or sets of objects (Boysen & Berntson, 1989). The chimpanzee was led around a room to various hiding places where she saw Arabic numerals or sets of oranges. She was then required to choose the Arabic numeral that corresponded to the sum of the values she had seen. Amazingly, the chimpanzee performed well on the 14 test trials.

Taking a different approach, Hauser and colleagues adapted a paradigm, first developed by Wynn (1992) to study human infant numerical cognition, to test whether untrained monkeys spontaneously look longer at physical outcomes that violate their arithmetic expectations (Hauser et al., 1996). Monkeys watch as eggplants (or lemons) are placed on a stage. A screen is then raised to occlude the eggplants and more eggplants are then placed behind the screen. The screen is raised to reveal either the expected outcome or an arithmetically impossible outcome. In multiple studies, untrained monkeys have now been found to look longer when the outcome is mathematically impossible (e.g., Hauser et al., 1996; Flombaum et al., 2005). Beran and colleagues have also found that nonhuman primates reliably choose the larger of two food quantities, even when this requires tracking one-by-one additions to multiple caches over time (Beran, 2004; Beran & Beran, 2004).

In the most parametric study of addition in nonhuman animals to date, Cantlon and Brannon (2007b) directly compared monkeys and humans in an explicit addition task. Subjects viewed two addend arrays presented in succession on a touch sensitive screen and were required to choose the array (from two arrays) that was equal to the sum of the two addend arrays (Fig. 3.7a). The monkeys were trained on a few addition problems ($1 + 1 = 2$, 4, or 8; $2 + 2 = 2$, 4, or 8; $4 + 4 = 2$, 4, or 8) and then tested on novel problems. Monkeys performed at a level significantly greater than chance on each of these three problems within 500 trials. In the critical test, monkeys were presented with all possible addends of the novel sums 3, 7, 11, and 17. Monkeys were rewarded regardless of which of the two choice stimuli they selected as the sum to prevent learning during the experiment. Performance on the novel problems was significantly greater than that predicted by chance and performance was modulated by numerical ratio. Importantly, as shown in Fig. 3.7b, humans and monkeys tested on the same nonverbal addition task showed very similar performance (see also Barth et al., 2006).

Finally, recent studies of two Amazonian groups that lack a verbal counting system indicate that such people nevertheless possess nonverbal numerical

(a) Addition task

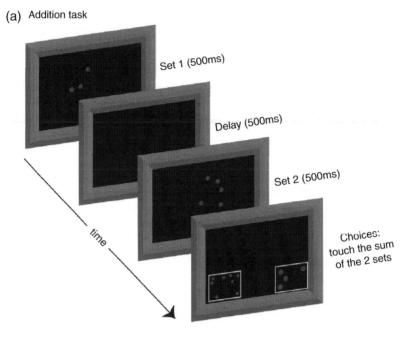

(b)

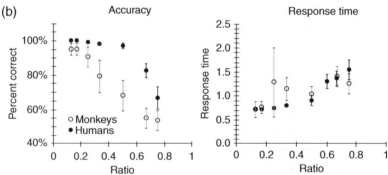

Fig. 3.7 (a) Stimuli and task design used to test nonverbal addition by monkeys and college students. Monkeys and humans were presented with one set of dots (Set 1), followed by a brief delay, after which a second set of dots was presented (Set 2). Then, two choices (the sum and the distractor) were presented, and monkeys were rewarded for touching the choice that represented the numerical sum of the two sets (Cantlon & Brannon, 2007). (b) Monkeys and humans exhibited ratio-dependent accuracy (left panel) and response time (right panel) when solving addition problems. Error bars reflect the standard error among subjects (Cantlon & Brannon, 2007b). See colour plates for (a).

representations and that their sensitivity to quantity is roughly similar to Europeans with verbal counting systems (Gordon, 2004; Pica et al., 2004). Such data indicate that the nonverbal system for representing number is likely universal among humans and not culturally specific.

Collectively, studies comparing nonverbal number representations and operations on numerical representations in animals and humans suggest that we share a system for representing numerosities as mental magnitudes that is governed by Weber's Law and supports arithmetic computations.

3.5 Is representing number a last-resort strategy?

Although animals can represent number in the laboratory when there is no other way to solve a task and gain rewards, do they represent number in their daily lives? One view has been that animals only represent number as a last resort after extensive laboratory training (Breukelaar & Dalrymple-Alford, 1998; Davis, 1993; Davis & Memmot, 1982; Davis & Perusse, 1988; Seron & Pesenti, 2001). In other words, their capacity to represent number is not apparent unless number is the *only* dimension through which they can make a response and obtain a reward. For example, Breukelaar and Dalrymple-Alford (1998) found that, even after rats were trained extensively in making numerical discriminations, when given a choice to discriminate stimuli based on time or number, rats overwhelmingly responded based on time.

Cantlon and Brannon (2007a), however, recently provided evidence that number may be more salient to monkeys than some other dimensions such as surface area. Monkeys were trained in a match-to-sample task in which the sample and correct match were the same in both numerosity *and* in an additional dimension (color, shape, or cumulative surface area of the elements). The incorrect choice differed from the sample and match both in numerosity and on the alternative dimension. After the monkeys reached a criterial level of performance, they were tested on nondifferentially reinforced probe trials in which one choice matched the sample in numerosity and the other choice matched the sample on an alternative dimension (color, shape, or cumulative surface area of the elements). They found that, for all dimensions contrasted with numerosity, the probability that monkeys made a numerosity match increased with the numerical distance between the numerosity match and the numerosity of the alternative stimulus. Furthermore, at all distances, monkeys were more likely to match stimuli based on numerosity than cumulative surface area; this was true both for the monkeys that had prior numerosity training *and* a single monkey who had never been trained on a numerical discrimination task. These data provide strong evidence that, for a monkey, number is more salient than other set summary statistics, such as cumulative surface area.

Thus, the alternative view to number as a last-resort strategy is that many or perhaps even all animals represent number spontaneously, and do so automatically in their everyday lives (e.g., Cantlon & Brannon, 2007a; Flombaum et al., 2005; Hauser et al., 2000; Hauser et al., 2003; Jordan & Brannon, 2005; Lyon, 2003; Wilson et al., 2001). But why might an animal need to represent number in the wild? One important selective pressure for representing number may be to maximize food intake. Not surprisingly, multiple studies have found that when animals are presented with a choice between two food quantities, they spontaneously choose the set with the largest number of food pieces (e.g., Beran, 2001; Beran et al., 2005; Boysen & Berntson, 1995; Call, 2000).

It is not only nonhuman primates, or even mammals, that have been found to represent number spontaneously in their everyday lives. In a remarkable example of defense against parasitism, American coots have been found to keep track of the number of their own eggs in a set of eggs that contains both their eggs and those of conspecific parasites (Lyon, 2003). Determining how many eggs in the female coot's nest actually belong to her provides the visual cue needed for the female to stop developing new egg follicles. Thus, counting a subset of eggs allows coots to make a valuable reproductive decision by avoiding a maladaptive reduction in clutch size.

A nonhuman animal may also find it useful to determine whether it has a numerical advantage in situations involving territorial defense. For example, an animal might benefit from knowing whether there are more members present in a defending group than there are members of any potential attacking party. Wilson et al. (2001) conducted a playback experiment in which the pant hoot of a single male (who was not a member of the chimpanzee group being tested) was presented to variable numbers of adult males in the test group. They found that groups of three or more males consistently chorused loudly in response to the playback and approached the speaker. In contrast, groups containing fewer than three males usually failed to make such responses. Chimpanzees may thus calculate whether they have 'strength in numbers' before deciding whether to defend their territory.

Hauser and colleagues (2002) tested whether untrained cotton-top tamarins could recognize the numerical equivalence between auditory stimuli presented in different formats. Using a habituation–discrimination procedure, they presented cotton-top tamarins with a mixture of either 2- or 3-syllable speech sequences varying in overall duration, intersyllable duration, and pitch. After the tamarins habituated to this repeated presentation of speech syllables of either numerosity, they presented the tamarins with novel 2- or 3-tone sequences in a test phase. They found that tamarins oriented to the speaker longer when the number of tones in the test phase differed from the number of speech syllables in the habituation phase. Because Hauser and colleagues controlled for various nonnumerical parameters such as duration and tempo that are often confounded with number in the real world, their study showed that without any reinforcement or training, tamarin monkeys could discriminate numerical values in the auditory modality—even when this required comparing sounds that were quite different (also see Hauser et al., 2003).

The ability to assess numerosity in the auditory modality might be useful in the wild when trying to determine how many friends or foe are nearby. But, are the numerical representations of nonhuman animals truly abstract enough to equate the number of voices they hear to the number of animals they expect to see? In other words, do the numerical representations of nonhuman animals extend across sensory modality?

3.6 **Cross-modal representations of number in animals**

Four flamingoes and four subway cars have little in common except for their numerosity. Yet clearly, adult humans have no trouble recognizing such numerical equivalence. Number can be extracted from sets of simultaneously visible individuals or from sequentially presented sets such as a sequence of tones. Furthermore, numerical representations are not specific to the sensory modalities in which they are established. Three telephone rings, three taps on your shoulder, and three political candidates are equally good examples of threeness; *hearing* someone's exclamation of 'Look, four deer!' causes us to visually search the space around us with the expectation we will *see* four animals. Is this type of abstract number representation unique to adult humans, or is there an evolutionary basis for our capacities? The ability to represent number without regard to stimulus modality is integral to any notion of a truly abstract concept of number. Here, we explore whether numerical representations without language are sufficiently abstract to be independent of stimulus modality. If so, is this a fundamental part of animals' and infants' numerical perception and cognition, or does it depend upon extensive training?

Barth and colleagues (2003) have shown that human adults show virtually no performance cost of comparing numerosities across versus within visual and auditory stimulus sets when using nonverbal numerical representations, suggesting that they possess number representations independent of stimulus modality. Thus, if nonverbal number representations are independent of stimulus modality, prelinguistic human infants and nonlinguistic animals should be able to detect the numerical correspondence between sets of entities presented in different sensory modalities. In other words, even without language, infants and monkeys should appreciate the correspondence between, for example, three notes of a flute and three sunsets. Yet, there have only been a few tests of cross-modal number representation in infants and animals, and data from such studies have proven controversial.

For example, Church and Meck (1984) found that rats trained to discriminate two from four sounds or light flashes later responded to compound cues of two lights and two sounds as if four events had occurred, suggesting that rats can transfer numerical representations across modalities. Yet, when Davis and Albert (1987) trained rats to discriminate three sequentially presented sounds from two or four sounds and then exposed rats to sequences of two, three, and four lights, they found no evidence that the rats transferred their auditory numerical discrimination to the visual modality. The Davis and Albert (1987) results raise the possibility that the rats in the Church and Meck study (1984) made a dichotomous discrimination that was purely intensity-based (i.e., they equated the less intense sound with the less intense light).

Field playback studies have yielded complementary evidence suggesting that animals predict the number of intruders they expect to see based on the number of vocalizing intruders they hear. In these studies, the probability that an animal from a focal group approached a speaker emitting vocalizations from foreign conspecifics depended on the relationship between the number of vocalizing foreign animals and the number of animals present in the focal group (Kitchen, 2004; McComb et al., 1994). For example, McComb and colleagues (1994) found that lions were more likely to approach a speaker emitting the roar of a single unfamiliar lion than a chorus of three unfamiliar lions, suggesting that lions decide whether to defend their territory based on the perceived number of intruders. However, such studies did not control for all possible nonnumerical auditory cues that covary with number (e.g., some aspects of duration), leaving open the question of whether the calculations made by the animals were in fact based on number.

Studies of cross-modal number representation in human infants has yielded similarly conflicting results. Starkey et al. (1983, 1990) tested whether infants detected numerical correspondences between visual and auditory stimuli by presenting side-by-side slides of two or three household objects, while a hidden experimenter hit a drum two or three times. Infants preferentially looked toward the visual display that numerically matched the number of drumbeats they heard. Unfortunately, other researchers had difficulty replicating these results, finding in some cases no preference for the matching visual array and in others a reverse preference for the nonmatching array (Mix et al., 1997; Moore et al., 1987).

A more recent study by Kobayashi and colleagues (2005) suggested that infants represented the numerical equivalence between objects and sounds when the visual and auditory stimuli were first given a natural, explicit relationship. However, similar to previous studies, this study used a within-subject design, allowing infants to experience multiple trials and thus conceivably learn to match stimuli on the basis of nonnumerical attributes such as intensity by comparing stimuli within the session over these multiple trials. Thus, the existence of evolutionarily and developmentally primitive, modality-independent, nonverbal numerical representations remained largely an open question.

To more definitively determine whether nonlinguistic organisms can match number across stimulus modalities, a recent experiment capitalized upon the social expertise of nonhuman primates by framing a numerical problem within a social context: specifically, researchers tested whether rhesus monkeys spontaneously matched the number of dynamic conspecific faces they saw with the number of vocalizations they simultaneously heard by employing the sort of preferential looking paradigm that had been used extensively with human infants (Jordan et al., 2005). Shortly thereafter, Jordan and Brannon (2006c) tested 7-month-old human infants on representing the equivalence between the number of human voices they heard and the number of faces they saw. Both laboratory studies employed strict stimulus controls for temporal attributes that often covary with number, used between-subject designs, and tested the numerical contrast of 2 vs. 3. The parallel between infants' and rhesus monkeys' performance on this task was striking. Both populations looked significantly longer at the matching display than the nonmatching display, and in both species, the effect held for individuals who heard two sounds or three sounds (Fig. 3.8a and 3.8b).

Thus, monkeys and infants recognize the numerical correspondence between two or three dynamic faces and two or three concurrent voices. Convergent results from Feron et al. (2006) also provide evidence of a developmental basis for language-independent numerical representations that extend across the visual and haptic sensory modalities.

Taken together, this matching of numerosities across various modalities supports the contention that human infants, human adults, and nonhuman primates share at least one common nonverbal numerical representational system. Although the neurobiological underpinnings of multisensory numerical perception remain unknown, these clear behavioral parallels argue for the possibility of a shared neurobiological substrate in disparate populations. Future studies should attempt to pinpoint the format of the numerical representations underlying behavior in this task. Because the numerical values

(a)   (b)

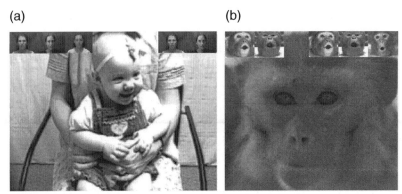

Fig. 3.8 Static images from video displays used to test whether human infants (a) and rhesus monkeys (b) spontaneously matched the number of dynamic conspecific faces they saw with the number of vocalizations they simultaneously heard in a preferential looking paradigm (Reproduced from Brannon, E. M. (2006). The representation of numerical magnitude. *Current Opinion in Neurobiology*, *16*, 222–229.) See colour plates.

tested in Jordan and Brannon (2005, 2006b) are within the capacity of either the analog magnitude system or the object file system, future studies are needed to determine whether monkeys and infants can spontaneously match larger numerical values across modality and whether spontaneous matching depends on the ratio between the two numerical values compared.

Regardless of representational system used, it is clear that monkeys and infants can spontaneously match nonarbitrarily related auditory and visual stimuli to detect numerical equivalence between modalities. However, these experiments left open the possibility that this ability was some context-specific capacity peculiar to social judgments. It was possible that these experiments succeeded because they tapped into a socioecologically relevant scenario; in their everyday lives, for example, territorial animals might be helped by being able to assess the number of individuals they will likely encounter by how many individuals they hear. Thus, another study used a direct, explicit measure of numerical knowledge (in contrast to relying on measuring looking time, a more indirect, implicit measure of knowledge) to show that monkeys can also learn to numerically match arbitrarily related stimuli across sensory modalities.

Jordan, MacLean, and Brannon (2008) specifically used a delayed match-to-sample paradigm to provide a more controlled environment in which rhesus monkeys made an active choice in numerically matching auditorily presented tones and visually presented squares. This study helped confirm that these cross-modal number-matching abilities in monkeys are parallel to our non-verbal numerical abilities as human adults, because these capacities in this study extended to a larger range of values and proved dependent on the ratio between the compared values. Such results showed that monkeys can learn to represent the numerical equivalence between arbitrarily related stimuli across modalities, but may require explicit reinforcement to attend to such equivalence. In sum, results gleaned from this combination of two distinct methods—one that relies on spontaneous cognition and the other that probes an animal's capacities under optimal circumstances—have helped shed light on the degree to which rhesus monkeys' numerical representations are independent of modality and the extent to which monkeys' cross-modal matching abilities are limited by ratio.

The use of dynamic displays and ecologically valid stimuli have thus revealed spontaneous capacities for cross-modal number representation in animals and importantly allowed a direct comparison with human infants. The use of convergent methods to investigate spontaneous and ecologically relevant abilities– but also more trained capacities with more carefully controlled stimuli–has provided clear evidence of cross-modal numerical matching, and can serve as a model for other domains.

3.7 How are analog magnitude representations of numerosity formed?

We know that animals can represent number, but how do they do it? There are multiple parts to this question. First, we can ask what cognitive algorithm allows an animal to convert a set of elements into an analog magnitude representation. Which properties of the set are preserved, and which are lost? Is the process serial (as in counting) or parallel (as in subitizing)? Which regions of the brain are involved in encoding number?

A host of models have been proposed to explain how number might be represented without language. Gelman and Gallistel (1978; Gallistel & Gelman, 1992) suggested that animals and young children use a nonverbal counting process that obeys three critical principles. The one-to-one principle states that there is a one-to-one correspondence between the number of labels applied and the number of to-be-counted elements in a set (labels can be nonverbal). The stable order principle states that the labels are applied in a stable order across counting episodes (one cannot count 1-2-3 today and 3-1-2 tomorrow). The cardinal principle states that the last label applied serves to represent the cardinal value of the set.

The mode-control model, developed to describe how rats enumerate serial arrays (sequences of sounds or light flashes), follows the counting principles as defined by Gelman and Gallistel (Meck & Church, 1983). Under this model, a pacemaker emits a regular stream of pulses at a constant frequency. When a stimulus begins, pulses are gated into an accumulator, which integrates the number of pulses over time. Depending upon the nature of the stimulus, a mode switch that closes after stimulus onset gates the pulses to the accumulator in one of three different modes: in the 'run' mode, the stimulus starts an accumulation process that continues until the end of the signal; in the 'stop' mode, the process occurs whenever the stimulus occurs; and in the 'event' mode, each onset of the stimulus produces a relatively fixed duration of the process regardless of stimulus duration. This mechanism can thus be used as a counter (the event mode) or a timer (the run and stop modes). In all modes, the value stored in the accumulator increases with duration or number. When the stimulus stops, the mode switch opens, stopping the gating of pulses to the accumulator. The final magnitude is placed into memory, while the accumulator is reset to zero and the organism is considered ready to time or count another stimulus. The representation of the magnitude in memory is noisy and obeys Weber's Law. Importantly, such a mode-control mechanism can represent and integrate sequentially processed numerical stimuli presented in any sensory modality, potentially accounting for highly abstract numerical representations.

It seems obvious that when elements within a set are presented serially (e.g., sequences of light flashes or tones, as used by Church & Meck, 1984), animals must process them serially. However, when stimuli are presented as simultaneous visual arrays, it is unclear whether the enumeration process is serial. It is possible that organisms serially allocate attention to each element in an array and thus convert a simultaneous array into a sequential array. However, the behavioral and neurobiological evidence to date suggests this is unlikely. Nieder and colleagues (2006) found that neurons in the prefrontal cortex (PFC) of the macaque brain that were selective for 1, 2, 3, 4, or 5 elements showed similar response latencies of approximately 120 ms (Nieder et al., 2002). Furthermore, if animals were serially allocating attention to elements in an array, we might expect to find that the number of visual saccades increases with the number of elements in an array. However, Nieder and Miller (2004b) found that the number of visual saccades made by monkeys did not increase with the number of display items in a numerical same–different task as set size increased from 1 to 7.

Similarly, analysis of reaction time for monkeys engaged in the numerical delayed match-to-sample task described earlier in this chapter provided no evidence that monkeys serially enumerate elements when forming numerical representations of simultaneously presented visual arrays (Jordan & Brannon, 2006a). Because subjects controlled the duration of the sample array and hence the processing time for the sample numerosity, a serial process should be reflected by increased reaction times to larger numerical samples. Reaction time, however, did not increase with sample numerosity. Barth and colleagues (2003) also found that it took adults no longer to compare large sets than to compare small sets, suggesting that adults may also use a parallel enumeration mechanism for nonverbally estimating and comparing large sets.

There are a few proposals for how numerosity might be computed as a parallel rather than a serial process. The notion of subitizing was invoked to explain the subjective feeling that when we see small collections of objects, we automatically apprehend the number of elements without the need for verbal counting (e.g., Kaufmann et al., 1949; Mandler & Shebo, 1982; Trick & Pylyshyn, 1994). The values in the tasks used by many of the animal studies described here exceed the values that are thought to be within the subitizing range. However, alternative parallel enumeration processes have been proposed that can theoretically handle larger values. Dehaene and Changeux's (1993) neural network model comprises four primary levels: the topographically organized input retina, an organized map of element positions from this retina, summation units that sum the input from the organized position map, and an array of numerosity detectors. These numerosity detectors respond selectively to certain numerosities (i.e., certain ranges of activity from the summation clusters). The numerosity detection system ultimately represents the numerosity of a set of simultaneously presented elements regardless of the size and position of the elements, and in this way, could account for the nonverbal parallel enumeration strategies observed in the studies by Nieder and Miller and Jordan and Brannon.

Another model put forth by Verguts and Fias (2004) attempts to explain how nonsymbolic numerical processing can arise from initially uncommitted neurons and how these same neurons under this summation coding system could be responsible for more precise *symbolic* numerical processing. This model posits an intermediate representational layer similar to that of Dehaene and Changeux (1993) that allows efficient mapping of sensory input in the form of spatially individuated elements to numerosity detectors. The total amount of activation from these number-sensitive 'summation units' reflects the numerosity presented in the input. Verguts and Fias (2004) presented different numbers of objects to an uncommitted neural network, which, equipped with an unsupervised competitive learning rule, developed numerosity detectors. The detectors were able to account for behavioral data such as modulation of numerical representations by numerical distance and size; furthermore, the detectors also conformed to neurophysiological data from the Nieder and Miller studies. Crucial to this model is that, after the numerosity detectors had developed, the same network nodes that were originally devoted to processing a given nonsymbolic numerosity also learned mappings to the value of the corresponding *symbolic* input. Key behavioral signature properties such as the distance effect transferred to symbolic processing; but interestingly, representational efficiency increased with symbolic input. Verguts and Fias (2004) argue that such an easily learned number detection system disputes the hypothesis that numerical representation systems are innate (although see Feigenson et al., 2004a, 2004b for arguments against this premise, e.g., that the Verguts and Fias model is structured in an inherently numerical fashion even before any learning occurs).

Although the notion of subitizing, the Dehaene and Changeux model, and the Verguts and Fias model are all proposals that achieve representations without serial enumeration, they are fundamentally different in that the idea of subitizing suggests that there are distinct cognitive processes at work for small and large sets whereas the other two models have no set-size limitations. In fact, there is growing evidence that ratio dependence in number discrimination does not always hold for human infants, and that instead in many situations their ability to represent multiple objects is limited by set size. For example, when presented with crackers sequentially placed into two different containers, human infants spontaneously chose the container with the larger number of crackers when acting upon small numerical sets, but were at chance with large numerical sets or with sets contrasting small and large numerical values (Feigenson et al., 2002; Fig. 3.9a). Similarly, when infants observe toys placed into an opaque box, their search time suggests that they represent only up to three objects in the box (Feigenson & Carey, 2003). To explain these results, the idea has been suggested that infants rely on an object file system that tracks and represents small numbers of individual objects precisely (Feigenson et al., 2002; Hauser & Carey, 1998; Hauser & Spelke, 2004; Zosh & Feigenson, Chapter 2).

Evidence also exists for set-size limitations indicative of an object file system in nonhuman primates. Hauser and colleagues (2000) found that when free-ranging untrained monkeys were tested in the food choice task described earlier, they chose the larger number of apple slices for sets of four or fewer but failed to represent sets larger than five (Fig. 3.9b). In one surprising condition, monkeys failed to choose a bucket with eight apple slices compared to a bucket with three apple slices. However, these results have yet to be reconciled with the fact that primates have not shown similar set-size effects in any other context or task in which they have been tested—even in similar food choice or food search tasks with limited numbers of trials (Beran, 2001; Beran & Beran, 2004; Call, 2000; Lewis et al., 2005). More research is needed to understand the conditions that may differentially invoke analog magnitude and object file representations and whether these conditions differ across species or over development.

3.8 **Neurobiological underpinnings**

The behavioral studies reviewed in the preceding sections show strong parallels between the numerical representations of adult humans and

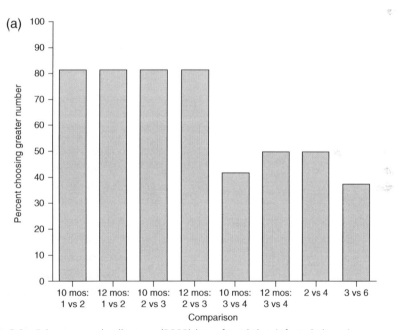

Fig. 3.9a Feigenson and colleagues (2002) have found that infants behave in some experiments as if they cannot represent sets larger than 3. As shown in this graph, when presented with crackers sequentially placed into two different containers, 10- and 12-month-old infants spontaneously chose the container with the larger number of crackers when acting upon small numerical sets, but were at chance with large numerical sets or with sets contrasting small and large numerical values. Infants, here, may thus be relying on an object file system that tracks and represents small numbers of individual objects precisely, rather than an analog magnitude system. (Reproduced from Feigenson, L., Carey, S., & Hauser, M. (2002). The representations underlying infants' choice of more: object files versus analog magnitudes. *Psychological Science*, *13*, 150–156. With permission from Wiley-Blackwell.)

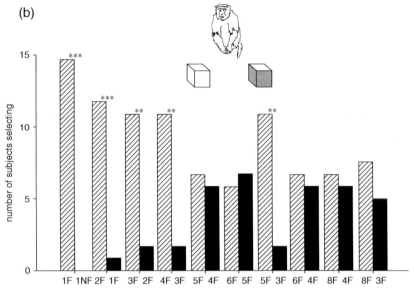

Fig. 3.9b Free-ranging rhesus monkeys watched as apple pieces were added, one at a time, to two containers. When required to keep track of a small total number of apple pieces, monkeys successfully chose the container with the larger number of pieces. F refers to food item and NF refers to nonfood item. (Reproduced from Hauser, M. D., Carey, S., & Hauser L. B. (2000). Spontaneous number representation in semi-free-ranging rhesus monkeys. *Proceedings of the Royal Society of London, Part B: Biological Sciences, 267*, 829–833. With permission from the Royal Society.)

nonhuman animals. Recent neurobiological work has also revealed striking similarities that support the possibility of a shared system for representing number nonverbally. The parietal cortex and especially the intraparietal sulcus (IPS) has been implicated in human number processing by neuroimaging and patient studies (e.g., Dehaene et al., 1999; Eger et al., 2003; Naccache & Dehaene, 2001; Piazza et al., 2004; Pinel et al., 2001). Importantly, activation in the IPS is modulated by the numerical distance between to-be-compared symbols (Pinel et al., 2001). Furthermore, recent studies indicate that the IPS, in adults and even children as young as 4 years of age, is also selectively responsive to changes in the numerosity of arrays and not to changes in shape (Cantlon et al., 2006b; Piazza et al., 2004)

In studies with nonhuman animals, neurons in a somatosensory-responsive area in the superior parietal lobe have been found to keep track of the number of hand taps by a trained monkey when the monkey was required to alternate between five arm movements of one type and five of another (Sawamura et al., 2002). In an extensive series of studies, Nieder and

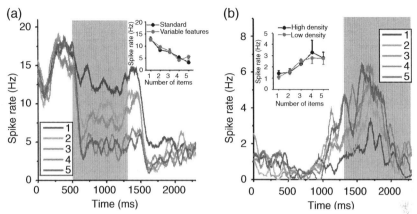

Fig. 3.10 Example numerosity-selective cells from the fundus of the intraparietal sulcus (IPS) in a macaque monkey. Neuron A was selective in the sample presentation and shows maximum firing to the numerosity 1. Neuron B was selective during the memory delay and fired maximally to numerosity 4. Distributions of preferred numerosities across the cells recorded from during the sample (a) and delay (b) periods (Reproduced with permission from Nieder & Miller, © 2004 National Academy of Science USA). See colour plates.

colleagues (Diester & Nieder, 2007; Nieder et al., 2002, 2006; Nieder & Merten, 2007; Nieder & Miller, 2003, 2004; Tudusciuc & Nieder, 2007) found cells in both the lateral PFC and ventral segment of the parietal cortex (VIP) of rhesus macaques that represent the quantity of visual items when monkeys are judging whether two visual arrays contain the same number of items (Fig. 3.10).

Interestingly, the tuning curves of these neurons overlapped, providing a possible physiological basis for the behavioral phenomenon that discrimination improves with increasing numerical distance—that is, the distance effect. Nieder and Miller (2004) also found that neurons in the IPS also responded to and differentiated numerosity earlier than the lateral PFC neurons, which suggests that information about numerosity flows from the IPS in posterior parietal cortex to lateral PFC. Nieder and Miller (2004) conclude that this network for processing numerosity in monkeys is similar to that in the adult human brain suggested by recent fMRI studies (e.g., Cantlon et al., 2006b; Dehaene et al., 1999; Naccache & Dehaene, 2001; Piazza et al., 2004; Pinel et al., 2002). It is not only simultaneously presented visual items that invoke number-sensitive neurons but also temporally distributed arrays (Nieder et al., 2006). Although this different format initially activates a separate population of neurons, yet another population represents the final quantity whether the initial input was spatial or temporal in form. Furthermore, when monkeys trained to associate symbols with numerosities in the form of visual arrays performed a numerical matching task, prefrontal but not parietal neurons responded selectively to both the numerosities and the associated visual shapes (Diester & Nieder, 2007)—suggesting that the PFC may prove part of a basis for higher-level, symbolic understanding of number.

Whether such neuronal populations specifically encode number or encode a host of quantitative dimensions is an important question. Recent research suggests that the posterior parietal cortex may indeed subserve a sort of generalized magnitude system encoding both continuous and discrete quantity. Tudusciuc and Nieder (2007) specifically showed that functionally overlapping sets of parietal neurons encode length and numerosity. Another crucial question is how exactly the quantitative output in this frontoparietal network comes about: What processes in the brain might precede the eventual output of the cardinal value of a set? In other words, what neuronal populations might act as the *input* for the populations of neurons identified by Nieder and colleagues as being tuned for specific cardinal values? A recent study by Roitman et al. (2007) may provide an answer. They identified two populations of neurons in the lateral intraparietal area (LIP) of the macaque brain that acted as quantitative 'accumulators', integrating or summing individual items by encoding the total number of elements in their response fields in a graded fashion (Fig. 3.11).

Specifically, about half the neurons they recorded from showed increasing firing rate as a function of the number of elements in the receptive field. For the other half of the neurons, firing rate decreased with the number of elements in the neuron's receptive fields. Thus, rather than being tuned for a preferred numerical position within a sequence, activity for these accumulator neurons either systematically increased or decreased with number for a large range of values. Roitman and colleagues (2007) suggest that the cardinal numerical representations studied by Nieder and colleagues may be based on computations upon input from these accumulator neurons, and that both number-selective neuronal populations may provide a physiological basis for components (such as the summation units and numerosity detectors) of the neural network models of Dehaene and Changeux (1993) and Verguts and Fias (2004).

Collectively, the bulk of research on the neural bases of number representations in humans and nonhuman animals implicates that homologous brain regions of parietal cortex are critical for representing number.

3.9 Conclusion

Although introspection may give the faulty impression that all of human cognition is supported by language, comparative research continues to uncover

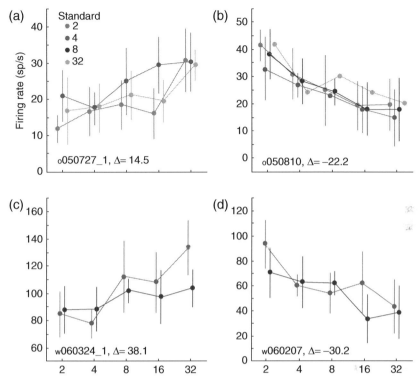

Fig. 3.11 Single lateral intraparietal (LIP) neurons respond in a graded fashion to the total number of elements in the response field (Roitman et al., 2007). Neurons shown in (a) and (c) increased firing rate with numerosity, whereas those shown in (b) and (d) had larger responses for smaller numerosities. See colour plates.

the links between the cognitive abilities of humans and other animal species that lack language. Representing and manipulating numbers are important for most aspects of human life, and much of this involves abstract symbolic representations that are culturally specific and may in fact intersect with language abilities. However, the work reviewed in this chapter should make it readily apparent that humans and many nonhuman animal species share a system for representing number nonverbally as mental magnitudes that enter into mathematical operations.

We have reviewed a host of behavioral parallels between human and animal numerical cognition such as ratio dependence, semantic congruity, cross-modal matching, and nonverbal arithmetic. Furthermore, homologous brain structures appear to support numerical representations in humans and macaque monkeys. Collectively, behavioral and neurobiological data strongly support an evolutionary basis to human numerical representations. The multitude of experiments showing that many animal species possess numerical abilities should now trump the skepticism created by the Clever Hans story. Although a nonhuman animal will never tally the votes on election night or calculate the likely return on your taxes, number representation is likely an integral cognitive component for the survival and sociopolitical success of many animals. The comparative approach has shown that, indeed, the actions of animals in the wild and the laboratory may be much more calculated than once thought.

References

Banks, W. P., Fujii, M, & Kayra-Stuart, F. (1976). Semantic congruity effects in comparative judgment effects in comparative judgments of magnitudes of digits. *Journal of Experimental Psychology: Human Perception and Performance, 2,* 435–447.

Banks, W. P., White, H., Sturgill, W., & Mermelstein, R. (1983). Semantic congruity and expectancy in symbolic judgments. *Journal of Experimental Psychology: Human Perception and Performance, 9,* 580–582.

Barth, H., Kanwisher, N., & Spelke, E. S. (2003). The construction of large number representations in adults. *Cognition, 86,* 201–221.

Barth, H., LaMont, K, Lipton, J., Dehaene, S., Kanwisher, N., & Spelke, E. S. (2006). Nonsymbolic arithmetic in adults and young children. *Cognition, 98,* 199–222.

Beck, B. B. (1980). *Animal Tool Use: The Use and Manufacture of Tools byAnimals.* New York: Garland.

Beran, M .J. (2001). Summation and numerousness judgments of sequentially presented sets of items by chimpanzees (*Pan troglodytes*). *Journal of Comparative Psychology, 115,* 181–191.

Beran, M. J. (2004). Chimpanzees (*Pan troglodytes*) respond to nonvisible sets after one-by-one addition and removal of items. *Journal of Comparative Psychology, 118,* 25–36.

Beran, M. J. (2006). Quantity perception by adult humans (*Homo sapiens*), chimpanzees (*Pan troglodytes*), and rhesus macaques (*Macaca mulatta*) as a function of stimulus organization. *International Journal of Comparative Psychology, 19,* 386–397.

Beran, M. J., & Beran, M. M. (2004). Chimpanzees remember the results of one-by-one addition of food items to sets over extended time periods. *Psychological Science, 15,* 94–99.

Beran, M. J., Beran, M. M., Harris, E. H, & Washburn, D. A. (2005). Ordinal judgments and summation of nonvisible sets of food items by two chimpanzees and a rhesus macaque. *Journal of Experimental Psychology: Animal Behavior Processes, 31,* 351–362.

Boesch, C. (1995). Innovation in wild chimpanzees (*Pan troglodytes*). *International Journal of Primatology, 16,* 1–16.

Boisvert, M. J., Abroms, B. D., & Roberts, W. A. (2003). Human nonverbal counting estimated by response production and verbal report. *Psychonomic Bulletin and Review, 10,* 683–690.

Boysen, S. T., & Berntson, G. G. (1989). Numerical competence in a chimpanzee (*Pan troglodytes*). *Journal of Comparative Psychology, 103,* 23–31.

Boysen, S. T., & Berntson, G. G. (1995). Responses to quantity: perceptual versus cognitive mechanisms in chimpanzees (*Pan troglodytes*). *Journal of Experimental Psychology: Animal Behavior Processes, 21,* 82–86.

Brannon, E. M. (2006). The representation of numerical magnitude. *Current Opinion in Neurobiology, 16*, 222–229.

Brannon, E. M., Cantlon, J. F., & Terrace, H. S. (2006). The role of reference points in ordinal numerical comparisons by rhesus macaques (*Macaca mulatta*). *Journal of Experimental Psychology: Animal Behavior Processes, 32*, 120–134.

Brannon, E. M., & Terrace, H. S. (1998). Ordering of the numerosities 1 to 9 by monkeys. *Science, 282*, 746–749.

Brannon, E. M., & Terrace, H. S. (2000). Representation of the numerosities 1–9 by rhesus macaques (*Macaca mulatta*). *Journal of Experimental Psychology: Animal Behavior Processes, 26*, 31–49.

Breukelaar, J. W. C., & Dalrymple-Alford, J. C. (1998). Timing ability and numerical competence in rats. *Journal of Experimental Psychology: Animal Behavior Processes, 24*, 84–97.

Call, J. (2000). Estimating and operating on discrete quantities in orangutans (*Pongo pygmaeus*). *Journal of Comparative Psychology, 114*, 136–147.

Cantlon, J. F., & Brannon, E. M. (2005). Semantic congruity affects numerical judgments similarly in monkeys and humans. *Proceedings of the National Academy of Sciences, 102*, 16507–16511.

Cantlon, J. F., & Brannon, E. M. (2006a). Shared system for ordering small and large numbers in monkeys and humans. *Psychological Science, 17*, 402–407.

Cantlon, J. F., & Brannon, E. M. (2006b). The effect of heterogeneity on numerical ordering in rhesus monkeys. *Infancy, 9*, 173–189.

Cantlon, J. F., & Brannon, E. M. (2007a). How much does number matter to a monkey (*Macaca mulatta*)? *Journal of Experimental Psychology: Animal Behavior Processes, 33*, 32–41.

Cantlon, J. F., & Brannon, E. M. (2007b). Basic math in monkeys and college students. *PLoS Biology, 5(12)*, e328.

Cantlon, J. F., Brannon, E. M., Carter, E. J., & Pelphrey, K. A. (2006). Functional imaging of numerical processing in adults and four-year-old children. *PLoS Biology, 4*, e125.

Church, R., & Meck, W. (1984). The numerical attribute of stimuli. In H. L. Roitblat, T. G. Bever, & H. S. Terrace (Eds.), *Animal Cognition* (pp. 445–464). Hillsdale, NJ: Erlbaum.

Church, R. M., & Deluty, M. Z. (1977). Bisection of temporal intervals. *Journal of Experimental Psychology: Animal Behavior Processes, 3*, 216–228.

Cordes, S., Gelman, R., & Gallistel, C. R. (2001). Variability signatures distinguish verbal from nonverbal counting for both large and small numbers. *Psychological Bulletin and Review, 8*, 698–707.

Davis, H. (1993). Numerical competence in animals: life beyond Clever Hans. In S. T. Boysen, & E. J. Capaldi (Eds.), *The Development of Numerical Competence: Animal and Human Models* (pp. 109–125). Hillsdale, NJ: Erlbaum.

Davis, H., & Albert, M. (1987). Failure to transfer or train a numerical discrimination using sequential visual stimuli in rats. *Bulletin of the Psychonomic Society, 25*, 472–474.

Davis, H., & Memmott, J. (1982). Counting behavior in animals: a critical evaluation. *Psychological Bulletin, 92*, 547–571.

Davis, H., & Perusse, R. (1988). Numerical competence in animals: definitional issues, current evidence, and a new research agenda. *Behavioral and Brain Sciences, 11*, 561–615.

Dehaene, S. (1992). Varieties of numerical abilities. *Cognition, 44,* 1–42.

Dehaene, S. (2001). Subtracting pigeons: logarithmic or linear? *Psychological Science, 12,* 244–246.

Dehaene, S., & Changeux, J. P. (1993). Development of elementary numerical abilities: a neuronal model. *Journal of Cognitive Neuroscience, 5,* 390–407.

Dehaene, S., Spelke, E. S., Pinel, P., Stanescu, R., & Tsivkin, S. (1999). Sources of mathematical thinking: behavioral and brain-imaging evidence. *Science, 284,* 970–974.

Diester, I., & Nieder, M. (2007). Semantic associations between signs and numerical categories in the prefrontal cortex. *PLoS Biology, 5,* e294.

Eger, E., Sterzer, P., Russ, M., Giraud, A., & Kleinschmidt, A. (2003). A supramodal number representation in human intraparietal cortex. *Neuron, 37,* 719–725.

Emmerton, J., Lohmann, A., & Niemann, J. (1997). Pigeons' serial ordering of numerosity with visual arrays. *Animal Learning and Behavior, 25,* 234–244.

Emmerton, J., & Renner, J. C. (2006). Scalar effects in the visual discrimination of numerosity by pigeons. *Learning and Behavior, 34,* 176–192.

Feigenson, L., & Carey, S. (2003). Tracking individuals via object-files: evidence from infants' manual search. *Developmental Science, 6,* 568–584.

Feigenson, L., Carey, S., & Hauser, M. (2002). The representations underlying infants' choice of more: object files versus analog magnitudes. *Psychological Science, 13,* 150–156.

Feigenson, L., Dehaene, S., & Spelke, E. S. (2004a). Core systems of number. *Trends in Cognitive Sciences, 8,* 307–314.

Feigenson, L., Dehaene, S., & Spelke, E. S. (2004b). Origins and endpoints of the core systems of number: reply to Fias and Verguts. *Trends in Cognitive Sciences, 8,* 448.

Feron, J., Gentaz, E., & Streri, A. (2006). Evidence for amodal representation of small numbers across visuo-tactile modalities in 5-month-old infants. *Cognitive Development, 21,* 81–92.

Fetterman, J. G. (1993). Numerosity discrimination: both time and number matter. *Journal of Experimental Psychology: Animal Behavior Processes, 19,* 149–164.

Flombaum, J. I., Junge, J. A., & Hauser, M. D. (2005). Rhesus monkeys (*Macaca mulatta*) spontaneously compute addition operations over large numbers. *Cognition, 97,* 315–325.

Gallistel, C. R., & Gelman, R. (1992). Preverbal and verbal counting and computation. *Cognition, 44,* 43–74.

Gelman, R., & Gallistel, C. R. (1978). *The Child's Understanding of Number.* Cambridge, MA: Harvard University Press.

Gordon, P. (2004). Numerical cognition without words: evidence from Amazonia. *Science, 306*(5695), 496–499.

Hare, B., Call, J., Agnetta, B., & Tomasello, M. (2000). Chimpanzees know what conspecifics do and do not see. *Animal Behaviour, 59,* 771–786.

Hauser, M. D. (1997). *The Evolution of Communication.* Boston: MIT Press.

Hauser, M. D. (2006). *Moral Minds: How Nature Designed Our Universal Sense of Right and Wrong.* New York: HarperCollins.

Hauser, M., & Carey, S. (1998). Building a cognitive creature from a set of primitives: evolutionary and developmental insights. In D. Cummins Dellarosa, & C. Allen (Eds.), *The Evolution of Mind* (pp. 51–106). New York: Oxford University Press.

Hauser, M. D., Carey, S., & Hauser L. B. (2000). Spontaneous number representation in semi-free-ranging rhesus monkeys. *Proceedings of the Royal Society of London, Part B: Biological Sciences,* 267, 829–833.

Hauser, M. D., Dehaene, S., Dehaene-Lambertz, G., & Patalano, A. (2002). Spontaneous number discrimination of multi-format auditory stimuli in cotton-top tamarins. *Cognition,* 86, B23–B32.

Hauser, M. D., MacNeilage, P., & Ware, M. (1996). Numerical representations in primates. *Proceedings of the National Academy of Science,* 93, 1514–1517.

Hauser, M. D., & Spelke, S. (2004). Evolutionary and developmental foundations of human knowledge: a case study of mathematics. In M. Gazzaniga (Ed.), *The Cognitive Neurosciences III* (pp. 853–864). Cambridge, MA: MIT Press.

Hauser, M. D., Tsao, F. T., Garcia, P., & Spelke, E. S. (2003). Evolutionary foundations of number: spontaneous representation of numerical magnitudes by cotton-top tamarins. *Proceedings of the Royal Society of London, Part B: Biological Sciences,* 270, 1441–1446.

Hothersall, D. (2004). *History of Psychology.* New York: McGraw-Hill.

Jordan, K. E., & Brannon, E. M. (2006a). Weber's Law influences the numerical representations in rhesus macaques (*Macaca mulatta*). *Animal Cognition,* 9, 159–172.

Jordan, K. E., & Brannon, E. M. (2006b). A common representational system governed by Weber's Law: nonverbal numerical similarity judgments in six-year-old children and rhesus macaques. *Journal of Experimental Child Psychology,* 95, 215–229.

Jordan, K. E., & Brannon, E. M. (2006c). The multisensory representation of number in infancy. *Proceedings of the National Academy of Sciences,* 103, 3486–3489.

Jordan, K. E., Brannon, E. M., Logothetis, N. K., & Ghazanfar, A. A. (2005). Monkeys match the number of voices they hear to the number of faces they see. *Current Biology,* 15, 1–5.

Jordan, K. E., MacLean, E., & Brannon, E. M. (2008). Monkeys match and tally quantities across senses. *Cognition,* 108, 617–625.

Jordan, K. E., Suanda, S., & Brannon, E. M. (2008). Intersensory redundancy accelerates preverbal numerical competence. *Cognition,* 108, 210–221.

Judge, P. G., Evans, T. A., & Vyas, D. K. (2005). Ordinal representation of numeric quantities by brown capuchin monkeys (*Cebus apella*). *Journal of Experimental Psychology: Animal Behavior Processes,* 31, 79–94.

Kaufman, E., Lord, M., Reese, T., & Volkmann, J. (1949). The discrimination of visual number. *American Journal of Psychology,* 62, 498–525.

Kitchen, D. M. (2004). Alpha male black howler monkey responses to loud calls: effect of numeric odds, male companion behaviour and reproductive investment. *Animal Behaviour,* 67, 125–139.

Kobayashi, T., Hiraki, K., & Hasegawa, T. (2005). Auditory-visual intermodal matching of small numerosities in 6-month-old infants. *Developmental Science,* 8, 409–419.

Kornell, N., Son, L. K., Terrace, H. S. (2007). Transfer of metacognitive skills and hint seeking in monkeys. *Psychological Science,* 18, 64–71.

Lewis, K. P., Jaffe, S., Brannon, E. M. (2005). Analog number representations in mongoose lemurs (*Eulemur mongoz*): evidence from a search task. *Animal Cognition,* 8, 247–252.

Lipton, J., & Spelke, E. (2003). Origins of number sense: large-number discrimination in human infants. *Psychological Science,* 14, 396–401.

Lipton, J. S., & Spelke, E. S. (2004). Discrimination of large and small numerosities by human infants. *Infancy*, *5*, 271–290.

Lyon, B. E. (2003). Egg recognition and counting reduce costs of avian conspecific brood parasitism. *Nature*, *422*, 495–499.

Mandler, G., & Shebo, B. J. (1982). Subitizing: an analysis of its component processes. *Journal of Experimental Psychology: General*, *111*, 1–22.

Matsuzawa, T. (1985). Use of numbers by a chimpanzee. *Nature*, *315*, 57–59.

McComb, K., Packer, C., & Pusey, A. (1994). Roaring and numerical assessment in contests between groups of female lions, *Panthera leo*. *Animal Behaviour*, *47*, 379–387.

Meck, W., & Church, R. (1983). A mode control model of counting and timing processes. *Journal of Experimental Psychology: Animal Behavior Processes*, *9*, 320–334.

Meck, W. H., Church, R. M., & Gibbon, J. (1985). Temporal integration in duration and number discrimination. *Journal of Experimental Psychology: Animal Behavior Processes*, *11*, 591–597.

Mix, K., Levine, S., & Huttenlocher, J. (1997). Numerical abstraction in infants: another look. *Developmental Psychology*, *33*, 423–428.

Moore, D., Benenson, J., Reznick, J. S., Peterson, M., & Kagan, J. (1987) Effect of auditory numerical information on infants' looking behavior: contradictory evidence, *Developmental Psychology*, *23*, 665–670.

Moyer, R. S., & Bayer, R. H. (1976). Mental comparison and the symbolic distance effect. *Cognitive Psychology*, *8*, 228–246.

Moyer, R., & Landauer, T. (1967). Time required for judgments of numerical inequality. *Nature*, *215*, 1519–1520.

Naccache, L., & Dehaene, S. (2001). The priming method: imaging unconscious repetition priming reveals an abstract representation of number in the parietal lobes. *Cerebral Cortex*, *11*, 966–974.

Nieder, A., Diester, I., & Tudusciuc, O. (2006). Temporal and spatial enumeration in the primate parietal cortex. *Science*, *313*, 1431–1435.

Nieder, A., Freedman, D. J., & Miller, E. K. (2002). Representation of the quantity of visual items in the primate prefrontal cortex. *Science*, *297*, 1708–1711.

Nieder, A., & Merten, K. (2007). A labeled-line code for small and large numerosities in the monkey prefrontal cortex. *Journal of Neuroscience*, *27*, 5986–5993.

Nieder, A., & Miller, E. K. (2003). Coding of cognitive magnitude: compressed scaling of numerical information in the primate prefrontal cortex. *Neuron*, *37*, 149–157.

Nieder, A., & Miller, E. K. (2004a). A parieto-frontal network for visual numerical information in the monkey. *Proceedings of the National Academy of Sciences*, *101*, 7457–7462.

Nieder, A., & Miller, E. K. (2004b). Analog numerical representations in rhesus monkeys: evidence for parallel processing. *Journal of Cognitive Neuroscience*, *16*, 889–901.

Olthof, A., Iden, C. M., & Roberts, W. A. (1997). Judgments of ordinality and summation of number symbols by squirrel monkeys (*Saimiri sciureus*). *Journal of Experimental Psychology: Animal Behavior Processes*, *23*, 325–339.

Otlhof, A., & Roberts, W. A. (2000). Summation of symbols by pigeons (*Columba livia*): the importance of number and mass of reward items. *Journal of Comparative Psychology*, *114*, 158–166.

Piazza, M., Izard, V., Pinel, P., LeBihan, D., & Dehaene, S. (2004). Tuning curves for approximate numerosity in the human intraparietal sulcus. *Neuron, 44*, 547–555.

Pica, P., Lemer, C., Izard, V., & Dehaene, S. (2004). Exact and approximate arithmetic in an Amazonian indigene group. *Science, 306*, 499–503.

Pinel, P., Dehaene, S., Riviere, D., & LeBihan, D. (2001). Modulation of parietal activation by semantic distance in a number comparison task. *NeuroImage, 14*, 1013–1026.

Platt, J. R., & Davis, E. R. (1983). Bisection of temporal intervals by pigeons. *Journal of Experimental Psychology: Animal Behavioral Processes, 9*, 160–170.

Platt, J. R., & Johnson, D. M. (1971). Localization of position within a homogeneous behavior chain: effects of error contingencies. *Learning and Motivation, 2*, 386–414.

Roberts, W. A. (2005). How do pigeons represent numbers? Studies of number scale bisection. *Behavioral Processes, 69*, 33–43.

Roitman, J. D., Brannon, E. M., & Platt, M. L. (2007). Monotonic coding of numerosity in macaque lateral intraparietal area. *PLoS Biology, 5*, e208.

Santos, L. R., Sulkowski, G. M., Spaepen, G. M., & Hauser, M. D. (2002). Object individuation using property/kind information in rhesus macaques (*Macaca mulatta*). *Cognition, 83*, 241–264.

Sawamura, H., Shirna, K., & Tanji, J. (2002). Numerical representation for action in the parietal cortex of the monkey. *Nature, 415*, 918.

Seron, X., & Pesenti, M. (2001). The number sense theory needs more empirical evidence. *Mind and Language, 16*, 76–89.

Shaki, S., & Algom, D. (2002). The locus and nature of semantic congruity in symbolic comparison: evidence from the Stroop effect. *Memory and Cognition, 30*, 3–17.

Smith, B. R., Piel, A. K., & Candland, D. K. (2003). Numerity of a socially housed hamadryas baboon (*Papio hamadryas*) and a socially housed squirrel monkey (*Saimiri sciureus*). *Journal of Comparative Psychology, 117*, 217–225.

Starkey, P., Spelke, E., & Gelman, R. (1983). Detection of intermodal numerical correspondences by human infants. *Science, 222*, 179–181.

Starkey, P., Spelke, E., & Gelman, R. (1990). Numerical abstraction by human infants. *Cognition, 36*, 97–127.

Stubbs, D. A. (1976). Scaling of stimulus duration by pigeons. *Journal of the Experimental Analysis of Behavior, 26*, 15–25.

Tomasello, M., Call, J., & Hare, B. (2003). Chimpanzees understand psychological states—the question is which ones and to what extent. *Trends in Cognitive Sciences, 7*, 153–156.

Trick, L. M., & Pylyshyn, Z. W. (1994). Why are small and large numbers enumerated ifferently? A limited capacity preattentive stage in vision. *Psychological Review, 101*, 80–102.

Tudusciuc, O., & Nieder, A. (2007). Neuronal population coding of continuous and discrete quantity in the primate posterior parietal cortex. *Proceedings of the National Academy of Sciences, 104*, 14513–14518.

Van Schaik, C. P., Ancrenaz, M., Borgen, G., et al. (2003). Orangutan cultures and the evolution of material culture. *Science, 299*, 102–105.

Verguts, T., & Fias, W. (2004). Representation of number in animals and humans: a neural model. *Journal of Cognitive Neuroscience, 16*, 1493–1504.

Washburn, D. A., & Rumbaugh, D. M. (1991). Ordinal judgments of numerical symbols by macaques (*Macaca mulatta*). *Psychological Science, 2,* 190–193.

Whalen, J., Gallistel, C. R., & Gelman, R. (1999). Nonverbal counting in humans: the psychophysics of number representation. *Psychological Science, 10,* 130–137.

Whiten, A., Goodall, J., McGrew, W. C., et al. (1999). Cultures in chimpanzees. *Nature, 6737,* 682–685.

Wilson, M., Hauser, M., & Wrangham, R. (2001). Does participation in intergroup conflict depend on numerical assessment, range location, or rank for wild chimpanzees? *Animal Behaviour, 61,* 1203–1216.

Wood, J. N., & Spelke, E. S. (2005). Infants' enumeration of actions: numerical discrimination and its signature limits. *Developmental Science, 8,* 173–181.

Wynn, K. (1992). Addition and subtraction by human infants. *Nature, 358,* 749–750.

Xu, F., & Spelke, E. (2000). Large number discrimination in 6-month-old infants. *Cognition, 74,* B1–B11.

Xu, F., Spelke, E. S., & Goddard, S. (2005). Number sense in human infants. *Developmental Science, 8,* 88–101.

Chapter 4

Multiple object tracking in infants: Four (or so) ways of being discrete

Marian L. Chen & Alan M. Leslie

4.1 Introduction

The traditional view of infancy held that babies could not track even one object if it passed out of view (Piaget, 1955). For babies, the world was considered to be literally 'out of sight, out of mind'. More recently, a revolution in our thinking occurred with the discovery that infants represent the continued existence of an object through occlusion (Baillargeon, 1986, 1987; Spelke, 1990) and can track even multiple objects (Wynn, 1992a). What kinds of information form the basis for infant object representations? Do infants represent objects on the basis of their continuous properties, such as total area and perimeter, or as discrete individuals? If infants represent discrete individuals, how do they do so? Is this ability numerical in nature or simply to do with the resolving power of attention and working memory?

The question of whether infants perceive objects based on their continuous or discrete properties intersects with and informs the debate over infants' numerical abilities. A substantial body of research has traced continuity between animal and human quantitative abilities, suggesting that number is an innate, evolutionarily specified endowment (e.g., Gallistel, 1990; Gallistel & Gelman, 2005; Gelman, 1990; Gelman & Gallistel, 1978; Jordan & Brannon, Chapter 3). At the heart of this proposal lies a brain mechanism that can represent both an individual object and its extended properties (e.g., size) as a continuous magnitude. Furthermore, this mechanism can accumulate such quantities across multiple objects, producing and storing in memory a summed quantity that represents the number of objects counted. This mechanism is known as the *accumulator* (Dehaene, 1997; Gallistel, 1990; Meck & Church, 1983). The possibility that infants may represent a discrete number of individuals by way of continuous brain magnitudes (Wynn, 1992b) adds to our questions.

The nature of the debate over whether infants represent small sets continuously or exactly is further clouded by the fact that continuous and discrete quantities are for the most part confounded in sets of everyday objects. If one has two apples and receives a third, one not only has more apples but also has more total apple stuff. When continuous quantity has been controlled, infants' ability to make judgments on the basis of discrete quantity has been called into question (Clearfield & Mix, 1999; Feigenson, Carey & Spelke, 2002; Zosh & Feigenson, Chapter 2). According to some accounts, infants must develop or extract discrete representations from continuous ones, whereas the latter are directly apprehended through sensory input (Mix et al., 2002). This issue is yet further clouded by the possibility that the total continuous stuff comprising a set is also derived by summing (e.g., accumulating) across the continuous extents of multiple objects. In this case, the accumulator mechanism could play a role in both discrete and continuous representations.

Clearly, the innocent question of whether infants represent objects based on their continuous or discrete properties is far more complicated than it appears at first glance. In this chapter, we lay out the several issues surrounding how infants represent multiple objects in order to evaluate the strengths and weaknesses of the theories proposed to explain infant object representations and to identify still open questions. First, we examine the question of whether infants utilize discrete or continuous object representations, or both. We then consider four possible mechanisms for forming discrete representations, some of which have been the focus of extensive research and some of which have not—object tracking, fixed-set representations, mental magnitudes, and integer representations. Throughout this discussion, we will need to recognize two distinct questions. The first is whether infants can represent the discrete number of objects in a set or only continuous properties of objects and sets, or whether they represent both. The second question is how infants represent these things: by continuous brain magnitudes or by discrete brain symbols for quantity. These questions, although easily confused, are in fact orthogonal.

4.2 **Continuous or discrete?**

Many studies have found that infants track the discrete numerosity of small sets of objects in multiple modalities, but the interpretation of these findings remains controversial. The bulk of these studies have looked at whether infants visually detect numerical equivalence of objects in small sets. Four-month-old infants who are habituated to sets of two or three dots dishabituate when shown a novel numerosity (Starkey & Cooper, 1980); even newborns make this discrimination (Antell & Keating, 1983). Five-month-old infants, when shown displays of simple addition and subtraction problems, looked longer at unexpected and impossible outcomes of $1 + 1 = 1$ and $2 - 1 = 2$ (Wynn, 1992a; Simon et al., 1995). Ten- to 12-month-old infants succeed at comparing two and three when presented with arrays of both homogeneous and heterogeneous objects (Strauss & Curtis, 1981). Converging evidence from a reaching task shows that 12-month-old infants correctly select a larger number of crackers when presented with comparisons of 1 vs. 2, 1 vs. 3, and 2 vs. 3 crackers (Feigenson, Carey & Hauser, 2002). Adult primates exhibit similar limitations in their numerical comparisons, although they are able to discriminate smaller ratios than human infants, succeeding on comparisons of 1 vs. 2, 1 vs. 3, 1 vs. 4, 2 vs. 3, and 3 vs. 4, but failing on comparisons involving quantities larger than 5 (Hauser et al., 2000).

The ability to discriminate between small numerosities extends beyond objects to groups, events, and sounds, and across sensory modalities. Five-month-olds, when habituated to either two groups of three objects or four groups of two objects, look longer when shown a novel number of groups (either four groups of two objects or two groups of four objects), even though the total number of items remains constant across test trials (Wynn et al., 2002). Six-month-olds dishabituate to novel numbers of visual events, such as jumps (Wynn, 1996). Seven-month-old infants cross-modally match equivalent sets of two and three, preferring to look at a display that shows the same number of objects as sounds heard (Starkey et al., 1983). Infants also seem to enumerate auditory stimuli, such as syllables, at 4 days (Bijeljac-Babic et al., 1993), and tones, at 7 months (vanMarle & Wynn, 2006). Intriguingly, infants even appear to add across sensory modalities. Kobayashi et al. (2004) trained 5-month-old infants to associate a tone with the introduction of an object. In test trials, infants saw a display of one object, which was then occluded, and then heard either one or two tones, indicating that one or two objects had been introduced to the display. The occluder was then dropped to reveal a display of two or three objects. Infants looked longer when the total number of objects viewed and tones heard did not match the expected outcomes.

This ability to discriminate between small sets seems to be limited to numbers smaller than four, leading some researchers to describe a 'set-size limitation' for comparisons involving four. Somewhat surprisingly, 12-month-old infants choose randomly when given the option of one cracker hidden in a pot or four crackers hidden in another pot, even though they correctly choose three crackers over two. Both comparisons involve a total of five crackers, and the one versus four comparison presents a far more favorable ratio, but infants still fail (Feigenson, Carey & Hauser, 2002). Fourteen-month-old infants also fail to search longer for a total of four objects hidden inside a box (Feigenson & Carey, 2003). However, there is evidence that infants have some limited ability to reason about sets of four. Infants do correctly choose four crackers over one cracker when both sets are in plain view, and reliably choose four crackers over no crackers in occlusion (Feigenson & Carey, 2003). Infants will also search longer for a total of four hidden objects if the objects are introduced into the box in two groups of two (Feigenson & Halberda, 2004). Twelve-month-old infants who are familiarized to two distinct sets of objects (two circles and two triangles) appearing from behind a screen look longer at an unexpected outcome of only two objects (one circle and one triangle), whereas infants who are familiarized to two identical sets of objects (one circle and one triangle) show the opposite result, looking longer only at an unexpected outcome of four objects (two circles and two triangles; Leslie & Chen, 2007).

4.3 Confounds in the evidence

A fair number of studies indicate that infants can discriminate the numerosity of small sets of objects; what, exactly, is driving infants' behavior on these tasks? Although it is tempting to conclude from these many results that infants are sensitive to discrete quantity and perhaps possess concepts of number, such studies have not always sufficiently unconfounded continuous variables and discrete quantity. If infants simply track a continuous amount of stuff, they do not even need to individuate objects (much as one can assess the length of a paragraph without counting the words), let alone possess any numerical competency. And indeed, when tested on displays controlling for continuous variables, infants typically fail to respond on the basis of discrete quantity.

Clearfield and Mix (1999) attempted to replicate Starkey et al. (1990) while controlling for continuous quantity—specifically, total perimeter. They found that infants failed to detect a change in number when perimeter was held constant, but looked longer at changes in perimeter when number was held constant. Infants show the same pattern of results for changes in area (Clearfield & Mix, 2001). Feigenson, Carey and Spelke (2002) replicated Wynn's arithmetic task using controlled stimuli, showing 7-month-old infants one small doll + one small doll = one large doll (with the same total area as the two small dolls together). They failed to find longer looking times for the numerically unexpected outcome with an expected continuous extent. In light of these results, the claims that infants have sophisticated and complex number concepts must be reexamined. Instead, Mix et al. (2002) argue that infants may be equipped only with the ability to monitor continuous quantities, such as area or perimeter, and through experience, such as applying counting routines, eventually derive or extract ever more precise concepts of number. So, is there any evidence that infants represent discrete number?

4.4 **Controlling for stuff**

Few studies to date have shown unambiguously that infants represent small sets of objects as discrete entities: that is, infants respond based on discrete number when continuous variables are controlled. To further complicate the issue, it is very difficult to control for changes in number, area, and perimeter simultaneously, particularly for smaller sets. Only a handful studies looking at the small number range have found compelling evidence for discrete number, rather than continuous quantity. One study eliminated continuous variables as a possible dimension of interest altogether by always varying the total area and perimeter of the habituation and test arrays (Feigenson, 2005). Seven-month-old infants were habituated to either one or two objects that differed in both color and texture both within and between displays. In the one-object habituation condition, the object had a total of two colors and two textures, to provide an equivalent control to the two-object condition. Infants in this study detected a change in numerosity when shown a novel numerical outcome. These results contrasted with those from an earlier study, which found that infants did not notice changes in number when objects differed only in color (Feigenson, Carey & Spelke, 2002).

In addition, at least three studies have shown that infants can respond on the basis of discrete representations even when they could have responded on the basis of continuous ones. Brannon et al. (2004) found that 6-month-old infants could detect a twofold change in number when area was held constant, but not a twofold change in area when number was held constant. Another set of studies used a reaching paradigm to investigate discrete number representations (Feigenson & Carey, 2003). Infants aged 12–14 months were shown items being introduced sequentially into a box and then encouraged to search for the objects. Infants represented up to three hidden objects, even when objects retrieved were larger than the objects concealed (Feigenson & Carey, 2003). However, they failed when four objects were hidden. For numbers up to three, infants tracked how many objects came out of the box, not a total amount of stuff.

In our laboratory, we have found that 12-month-olds detect a change from two to three and a change from two to one when area is held constant. Nine-month-olds, however, detect only the change from two to three, failing to look longer at a change from two to one (Chen & Leslie, in preparation). We used a two-screen methodology developed by Káldy and Leslie (2003), and tested infants on their ability to track the locations of a group of one and a group of two by number.

The design of our study is shown in Fig. 4.1. The groups were shown on alternating sides during familiarization events to prevent infants from associating one group with a particular location; during test trials, both groups were hidden

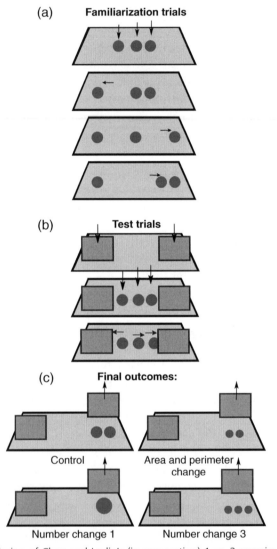

Fig. 4.1 The design of Chen and Leslie's (in preparation) 1 vs. 2 experiment

behind screens on either side of the stage and the screen occluding the group of two was lifted to show one of four outcomes. As illustrated in the bottom panel of Fig. 4.1, the possible outcomes were: Control: a final outcome showing the two original disks; Area and Perimeter Change: a final outcome showing the expected number of disks with an unexpected total area and perimeter (area 66% of original disks); Number Change 1: an outcome showing an unexpected number of disks (one) with the same area as the original two disks;

Number Change 3: an outcome showing an unexpected number of disks (three) with the same area as the original two disks. (a) a control outcome of the two original discs; number change outcomes with the same total area as the original two discs showing either (b) one large disc or (c) three smaller discs, or (d) an area and/or perimeter change outcome of two smaller discs, which constituted 66% of the area of the original two discs. Consistent with Brannon et al. (2004), we found that both the 9- and 12-month-old infants did not look significantly longer at the change in area and perimeter when number was held constant, and both age groups looked significantly longer at the number change to three. However, only 12-month-olds detected the number change from two to one. Data are still being collected but current results indicate that 9-month-olds do not look reliably longer when the two discs change to one large disc; these results are consistent with the findings of Feigenson, Carey and Spelke (2002) that 7-month-olds do not look longer at the outcome of one small doll + one small doll = one large doll

4.5 **But what about stuff?**

Infants' ability to represent the continuous extents of objects and sets of objects may be severely limited by a large Weber fraction. Brannon et al. (2004) compared 6-month-old infants' ability to discriminate between outcomes differing in discrete or continuous quantity. They found, as expected, that 6-month-old babies, when familiarized to displays of constant number but with large variations in area (up to a fivefold change), were able to differentiate 8 elements from 16 elements, but failed to notice an equivalent twofold change in total area when familiarized to displays of constant area with large variations in number (again, up to a fivefold change). Brannon et al. (2006) found that 6-month-old infants could discriminate between successive presentations of Elmo faces varying in size for ratios of 1:2, 1:3, and 1:4, but failed for ratios of 2:3. For comparison, adults have a Weber fraction for area judgment of 10–20% when comparing two ellipses or rectangles (Morgan, 2005); the adult Weber fraction for number in rapid non-verbal counting is somewhat larger, in the 15–25% range (Whalen et al., 1999).

Furthermore, when asked to track substances that can be measured only by continuous properties, such as sand or liquid, infants' performance is highly variable. Gao et al. (2000) familiarized infants to half a cup of pink liquid being poured into another container containing a quarter of a cup of pink liquid, and found that infants looked longer when shown a result of a quarter cup of liquid than the correct outcome of three-quarters of a cup, a 1:3 ratio. However, infants do not look longer at an incorrect outcome when the substances are piles of sand. In fact, even when a cup of sand is poured behind a screen next to and distinct from another pile of sand, infants do not look longer when only the original pile is shown, suggesting that their ability to reason about continuous substances is very different from their ability to reason about discrete entities (Huntley-Fenner et al., 2002). Ten- to 12-month-old infants also appear not to represent amount of food very precisely, choosing the larger quantity of Cheerios only when the two amounts differ by a ratio of at least 1:4 (vanMarle, under review). At this age, infants' ability to quantify food substances also seems to rely largely on perimeter and density cues, as their ability to distinguish between amounts of food diminishes with changes to these variables. When these cues are removed, infants perform only at chance. (For a review of primate discrimination of continuous quantities, see Jordan & Brannon, Chapter 3.)

Infants show no greater precision in their representations of continuous extent than in their representations of discrete number. In fact, Brannon et al. (2006) found that infants' ability to discriminate between two different continuous extents seems to be governed by exactly the same Weber fractions as their ability to discriminate between discrete numbers and their ability to discriminate durations (1:2, compared with the 1:4 ratio found by vanMarle in her Cheerios task). It appears that even for very young infants, representations of continuous amount and number seem to develop in parallel. Infants clearly do not have to learn to ignore continuous amount as a property of a set of objects in favor of discrete number. Perhaps, under certain circumstances, they may not even encode continuous amount as a relevant dimension of a set of objects (Brannon et al., 2006; Feigenson & Halberda, 2004).

In addition, studies looking at whether infants can track continuous properties of sets of objects through occlusion events indicate that these representations are fragile. Although Brannon and her colleagues found that infants could succeed in discriminating between the continuous extents of visual elements in large ratios, none of their studies involved occlusion (Brannon et al., 2004, 2006). VanMarle's (under review) results suggest that even at 12 months of age, representations of continuous quantity, sensitive as they are to visual cues such as density, may be subject to more variability than representations of discrete quantity. Feigenson and her colleagues found that infants tested in different reaching paradigms sometimes failed to respond on the basis of continuous quantity, for example, when choosing between a quantity of one and four crackers (Feigenson, Carey & Hauser, 2002) or when searching for a number of toys hidden in a box (Feigenson & Halberda, 2004). It is therefore an open question whether infants' relatively noisy representations of continuous amount are robust enough to survive occlusion events. Baillargeon (2004) reviewed a series of studies that detail a developmental pathway stretching throughout the first year in which infants gradually learn to attend to and reason about extensive properties of physical objects under different types of occlusion events.

4.6 **Having it both ways**

The pattern of failures and successes exhibited by infants when reasoning quantitatively about objects and about the stuff they are made of raises the question of how to reconcile the many apparently contradictory results. Infants do seem to represent the discrete properties of objects when continuous variables are controlled, both for studies looking at equivalence of sets and for studies of arithmetic. However, they fail to respond to discrete number under certain circumstances, instead using continuous quantity information as the basis for their representations. But these representations of continuous quantity may be very approximate and noisy. How can we best account for their behavior?

It seems to us that the answer to whether infants represent objects based on their continuous or discrete properties falls somewhere in the middle. Infants clearly can track the continuous properties of sets, although this ability may not be as robust as originally believed. It also seems to us most unlikely that the tracking of continuous properties provides the basis for developing discrete and/or exact quantity representations. At the same time, infants appear able to track discrete quantities as well. The nature of the underlying competence in this case is likely to remain controversial for some time. Do infants actually have number concepts that enable them, for example, to nonverbally count (Brannon, 1992; Gallistel & Gelman, 1992; Gelman & Gallistel, 1978; Leslie et al., 2007; Leslie et al., 2008; Simon et al., 1995; Wynn, 1992a; Xu & Spelke, 2000)? Or is their ability nonnumerical in nature, and simply subserved by a limited-capacity attentional mechanism (Leslie et al., 1998; Scholl & Leslie, 1999; Uller et al., 1999)? Or do infants represent sets as such, rather than simply multiple individuals (LeCorre & Carey, 2007)?

4.7 **Four (or so) ways to be discrete**

In this section, we evaluate the available evidence for four theories that have been proposed to explain how infants track discrete quantity.

4.7.1 **Object indexing**

Even if infants do use discrete number to discriminate between sets of objects, infants may not necessarily possess truly numerical concepts. Failures with comparisons involving four (Feigenson & Carey, 2003; Feigenson, Carey & Hauser, 2002) instead point to the possibility that infants track small sets of objects using a limited-capacity object-tracking system such as one demonstrated in adults (Pylyshyn & Storm, 1988; Trick & Pylyshyn, 1994; Flombaum et al., Chapter 6). In an adult multiple-tracking paradigm, for example, subjects view a set of 8 featurally identical dots that move with random trajectories. Four of these dots are identified momentarily by appearing on screen slightly later than the other dots, which act as distractors. The subject's task is to mentally track the late-onset dots and pick them out from the others after several seconds of movement. Subjects can perform this task surprisingly well even though it requires that attention be split across multiple randomly varying locations that overlap with the locations traversed by the distractors.

To account for this and related abilities, Pylyshyn proposed a visual system for object tracking. This system tracks visual objects by assigning a mental finger, also known as an *object file* or *object index* (henceforth, OI), that points at each object (or to a collection of objects such as a flock of birds).[1] The OI 'sticks' to the object as it changes location over time and continues to point at the object even if the object passes behind or inside an occluder. This simple mechanism will track the continued existence of an individual object through 3-dimensional space, thus implementing Spelke's spatiotemporal continuity principle (Spelke, 1994). Adults can track the Brownian motion of up to four objects at a time, even through occlusion (Scholl & Pylyshyn, 1999); in infants, this system may be limited to three objects (Leslie et al., 1998; Scholl & Leslie, 1999). The indexing limit may be the source of the 'set-size limitation' exhibited by infants when making comparisons involving sets of four.

By nature, the pointing finger is agnostic about the objects it points out (Leslie et al., 1998; Pylyshyn, 2003; Scholl & Leslie, 1999). Specific featural information is stored in a separate object representation (OR), which is bound to the OI. Exactly what property information goes into these ORs and when it is used remains largely undefined, although infants use shape information to distinguish objects by about 6 months (Káldy & Leslie, 2005) and color information at about 12 months (Tremoulet et al., 2000).

Object indexes are only implicitly numerical because they do not in themselves directly support arithmetic inference (Leslie et al., 2007). In other words, without counting or an equivalent process to map OI's onto numbers, one cannot know the number of objects one is currently indexing. Because of this, the object indexing account is equally compatible with both discrete and continuous accounts of infants' quantity representations. If infants represent

---

[1] We prefer the term *object index* to *object file* in this context for reasons explained at some length in Leslie and Káldy (2007). Briefly, an object file contains two parts: an index to the location of an object and a description of the object's features. Many phenomena indicate that the latter part may be empty (no description available) although subjects are still able to track the object's location and/or trajectory. It is this indexing function, rather than the descriptive function, that is most relevant to multiple object tracking and therefore to number tracking.

objects only by their continuous quantities, object indexing could account for how they also seem to sometimes respond based on discrete variables. If infants do represent objects discretely, indexing may complement nonverbal counting by keeping track of what is being counted, what has been counted, and what is yet to be counted. Alternatively, indexing may be the sole mechanism used by infants to track sets of objects in the small number range. The latter possibility seems unlikely, given that infants appear to enumerate nonobjects, such as events (Wood & Spelke, 2005; Wynn, 1996) and sounds (Bijeljac-Babic et al., 1993; vanMarle & Wynn, 2006), although these may be discriminated on the basis of continuous variables such as duration, tempo, and so on. Wood and Spelke (2005) suggest that infants may form 'event files', parallel representations similar to object files, but which pick out transitory events in the world rather than enduring objects.

Although object indexing is compatible with a model in which infants rely mostly on continuous quantity representations, it cannot fulfill one function—providing the basis for learning to count discrete objects. Neither OIs nor ORs can provide the basis for small number concepts because both are only implicitly numerical. In order to enumerate the number of assigned indexes, one must already be able to count. If infants can only represent small numbers by using object indexes, how do they compare sets of objects without resorting to counting or concepts of number?

4.7.2 Sets

An alternative account proposes that infants represent the small number range by in some way representing sets of (small) specific sizes (Carey, 2001, 2004; Feigenson & Carey, 2005; Feigenson et al., 2004; Feigenson & Halberda, 2004; LeCorre & Carey, 2007). Some of these set theories have been advanced to explain how infants can come to derive small number concepts using only object tracking plus general inductive reasoning. One version, recalling the Piagetian tradition, suggests that infants make one-to-one mappings between individuals in different sets (LeCorre & Carey, 2007). These set comparisons require that infants represent individuals at a highly abstract level of individual$_x$, individual$_y$, individual$_z$ and as belonging to sets represented by the concept {}: thus, {individual$_x$}, {individual$_x$, individual$_y$,}, and {individual$_x$, individual$_y$, individual$_z$}. Infants are supposed, furthermore, to be limited to just these set sizes until the preschool period during which children begin to learn words for numbers. Word learning then leads the child to bootstrap into arithmetic (for critiques of the bootstrapping account, see Leslie et al. [2007] and Rips et al. [2006, 2008]).

Theories of set representations often posit a core numerical representation system, 'parallel individuation', which is sometimes related to object files

(Carey, 2004) and sometimes not (LeCorre & Carey, 2007). Parallel individuation gives infants the ability to store representations of at least two sets of objects in working or long-term memory (Feigenson & Carey, 2003, 2005; LeCorre & Carey, 2007). In such systems, memory, not attention, determines the limits of infants' representations. Exactly how infants represent elements within the set has not been established (essentially, how specific the ORs for each element are), but 'each individual is represented by a unique mental symbol' (LeCorre & Carey, 2007). In essence, sets appear to be a list structure containing one or more of these mental tokens. Set-size limitations indicate that items are represented discretely—each represented set can hold only up to three (or perhaps four) individuals (Feigenson & Carey, 2003; Feigenson, Carey & Hauser, 2002). In addition, these sets cannot be added to without destroying the existing representation (Feigenson, 2005). Similar to object indexing, parallel individuation is only implicitly numerical. The system contains no symbols for number, such as those represented by the analog magnitudes, and the set representations cannot enter into arithmetic inferences directly.

However, infants are able to evaluate objects on the basis of *numerical identity*: that is, whether the object they saw is the same as one they saw earlier (Xu & Carey, 1996), and can compare the sizes of represented sets by one-to-one correspondence (Feigenson & Carey, 2005). This system attempts to explain how infants can simultaneously represent at least two sets with a total of more than three objects without resorting to counting, for example, in the cracker comparisons of 2 vs. 3 (Feigenson, Carey & Hauser, 2002). In such cases, five objects in total exceeds the limit of items that can be concurrently individuated by the indexing system. By placing the set representations of these items into memory, 'chunking' them, infants can use tracking to individuate objects and memory to compare them without having to count.

How do infants make the transition from these one-to-one comparisons to judgments on the basis of numerical concepts? How do infants go from representing only these small sets to larger number representations? Carey and her colleagues propose that three core endowments do the work. The first is the ability to represent large numbers as mental magnitudes, the accumulator mechanism, discussed in the next section (Gallistel & Gelman, 1992; Meck & Church, 1983). Secondly, infants represent the existence of small discrete sets using parallel individuation; these sets are represented on the level of the individual or unordered lists thereof. They also have access to yet another core system of numerical knowledge, 'set-based quantification', which allows infants to form summary representations of the sets picked out by parallel individuation and which provides the meanings of natural language quantifiers, the morphemes denoting sets (such as 'a' and plural '-s'), and in languages that feature such terms, markers for concepts such as 'dual' and 'trial' (Corbett, 2000).

Infants who grow up speaking languages with these morphemes first map between these terms and the small sets, which they can individuate in parallel, and from there induce concepts of small integers (up to the limit of three). Infants further come to understand that sets of two are one item larger than sets of one, and sets of three are one larger than sets of two, and from this realization induce the successor function, which allows them to map into even larger integers, assuming the count terms for such concepts are available in one's language—if not, these larger numbers are never learned. LeCorre and Carey (2007) call this integration process *enriched parallel individuation*.

This process of 'bootstrapping' into specific small number concepts and from there into larger number concepts via quantifiers and the count list (Carey, 2004; Feigenson & Carey, 2005) suggests a relationship between language and numerical competence, a relationship supported by data from Carey and her colleagues. Infants will search for one, two, and three objects hidden in a box, but when four objects are hidden, they fail to search longer than for one object (Feigenson & Carey, 2003). Infants begin to pass this task at around 24 months of age; this ability is highly correlated with acquisition of the plural marker -*s* (Barner et al., in press) and varies cross-linguistically. Infants learning languages with redundant linguistic cues for plurality pass this task earlier than English learners (Kouider et al., 2006).

However, the fact that nonhuman primates also make the singular–plural distinction suggests that this ability may not be completely linguistically driven (Barner et al., 2007). In addition, studies from adult speakers of languages with impoverished count list inventories have found that adults in these cultures show less precision in their mathematical abilities than do individuals speaking languages with terms for large numbers (Dehaene, 1999; Gordon, 2004), although these conclusions have been challenged (Gelman & Butterworth, 2005). Once infants have established the correspondence between the count list items 'one', 'two', 'three', and 'four', and the relationship between those concepts, they are then able to induce the underlying successor function, which allows them to learn terms for ever larger integers and map them correctly to the appropriate number representation.

However, Rips et al. (2006) argue that using language to 'bootstrap' into an infinite system of number concepts does not work without specifying a more restricted definition of the concept 'next number word'. Simply learning a count list could not itself impart the means to induce the successor function because the count list, comprising meaningless sounds, cannot specify whether the next-to-be-encountered item in the list will in fact be the next larger number (for instance, FIVE following FOUR) or simply the restarting of a cyclical system (as SUNDAY follows SATURDAY), or a modulo *n* system for numbers. Children learning a finite set of words for numbers can only distinguish between these options if he or she understands that the 'next' word maps to the output of the successor function—namely, the well-defined next number. Such a restricted definition of the 'next number word', however, implies an innate or at least prior understanding of the successor function, rendering bootstrapping unnecessary.

LeCorre and Carey (2007) can still argue that they describe only how young children learn the count terms for the limited and finite set of small numbers that they have mapped to their set representations. However, this restriction postpones but does not answer the question of how children ultimately break out of these small number representations into larger numbers. Infants may start with a limited number of (small) number concepts, but they still at some point must deduce the larger integers on the number line, and Rips et al.'s (2006) criticism still holds for that process.

Indeed, why are infants on this account limited to the small number range for their set representations? The answer appears to have something to do with the capacity of working memory: one might think of attention as a funnel allowing only a certain number of items to fit into a slot. If the funnel overloads, then nothing gets placed into the slot, resulting in the failure to represent larger sets of four and greater (Feigenson, Carey & Hauser, 2002; Feigenson & Halberda, 2004). However, long-term memory should not be subject to such limitations. In addition, the capacity of working memory increases over the first year from one item at 6 months to three (or four) by 12 months (Káldy & Leslie, 2003, 2005; Leslie & Káldy, 2007; Ross-Sheehy et al., 2003), although nothing suggests that the set limitation must change along with it. Indeed the data from numerous studies reviewed earlier suggest this limit is already at three by the age of 6 months. If working memory dictates what can be placed into these set representations, then the set limitation must start at one for 6-month-old infants and increase over time to three only by about 10 months of age. LeCorre and Carey do not offer this restriction and it is unclear whether any data support this claim. But if working memory constrains long-term memory, then the issue of how 6-month-old infants can form representations of sets up to three must be clarified while restricting older infants from representing still larger sets in long-term memory.

Another possible approach to set representation is that infants represent specific sets using summary representations limited to SINGLE, PAIR, and TRIPLE (Leslie & Chen, 2007; Leslie & Káldy, 2007). Such representations provide only a limited basis for comparing sets on number: namely, whether they are the same or different. This follows from these particular representations having no internal structure, in contrast to the sets hypothesized by LeCorre and Carey, which have the internal structure of an unordered list. Central to the Leslie and Chen proposal is that SINGLE, PAIR, and TRIPLE neither come preordered by magnitude nor are analyzable by projective set operations such as mapping onto a magnitude order. They are simply labels for different set types, based on indexing or other types of subitizing, and so remain merely implicitly numerical. Yet, within the limit, they will allow infants to distinguish sets of different magnitudes. If infants represent sets along the lines of SINGLE, PAIR, and TRIPLE, exactly how these representations eventually match up with integer concepts will remain to be determined. Perhaps, they play little or no role in integer development yet underlie the acquisition of morphosyntactic 'number' distinctions in language, such as singular or plural, and dual, and trial, much as Carey and colleagues have suggested for their list representations.

4.7.3 **Mental magnitudes/accumulator**

Another possibility is that infants represent small quantities using mental magnitudes, or an accumulator mechanism. There is compelling evidence that the accumulator mechanism subserves various numerical abilities in primates, rats and pigeons, as well as human adults (e.g., Cordes et al., 2001; Gallistel & Gelman, 1992; Meck & Church, 1983). The accumulator is amodal and represents quantity (both discrete and continuous) using continuous mental magnitudes, which by nature are imprecise and noisy. In other words, representations of numbers such as two and three are approximate, not exact. As the magnitude represented grows larger, the variability around the magnitude increases as a constant ratio. As a result of this increase in variability, human ability to discriminate between two numbers exhibits both size and distance effects consistent with Weber's law. In other words, the discrimination of two magnitudes depends on their ratio, rather than the absolute difference between them.

  Although the idea that infants represent at least the large number range (numbers greater than four) using the accumulator is relatively uncontroversial (Lipton & Spelke, 2003; Xu, 2003; Xu & Spelke, 2000), infants' discriminations of the small number range are exact and not noisy. In addition, the same ratios governing their large number discriminations do not appear to hold for numbers less than four (Feigenson & Carey, 2003; Feigenson, Carey & Hauser, 2002). These findings suggest that infants represent small and large numbers using different numerical systems: the accumulator for the large number range, and perhaps, an object-based or set mechanism for the small number range. A disconnect between the small and large number range is also seen in children's understanding of count terms, suggesting that the discontinuity in number representations exhibited by infants may extend into later development. Children learning English seem to laboriously learn the referents for one, two, and three, but after acquiring *four*, they appear to grasp the idea of all numbers larger than four as well (Bloom & Wynn, 1997; Wynn, 1992b).

The data do appear to favor the hypothesis that there is some difference in the systems infants use to operate over the small and large number ranges. However, an apparent discontinuity does not necessarily entail two distinct systems of representation of number. The fact that infants can make comparisons across the small and number ranges (from two to eight) suggests that these two systems are not incommensurable after all (Cordes et al., 2007).

The main failure of the accumulator as a system of representation for infant number is that it offers no explanation for why infants show set-size limitations for small sets and for why small number judgments do not exhibit a Weber fraction. If infants do in fact represent the small number range using the accumulator, an explanation must be found for their various failures in small number discrimination. One possibility is that object indexing—specifically, the limit on how many objects can be tracked concurrently—rather than being the source of these representations, may interfere with small number representations.

4.7.4 **Integers**

Yet another possibility, which has only recently been advanced in the literature, is that infants have a capacity to represent integers (Leslie & Chen, 2007; Leslie et al., 2007; Leslie et al., 2008). The proposal is not of course that infants have all the integers handy, as it were, and already stored in memory. This would be impossible, if for no other reason than that there are infinitely many integers, exceeding the capacity of any person's memory, whether young or old. Instead, the proposal is that infants are equipped with a rule for generating this infinite set. The rule, called the successor function S, recursively defines the integers by way of a minimal piece of algebra: $S(x) = x + ONE$. Formulating the successor function this way requires that infants have 'innate knowledge' of at least one number and only one number—namely, the number ONE (1). To represent all the other numbers will require work, principally, computing the next value of 'x' and storing it in memory in an ordered list of symbols.

For this approach, numbers are fundamentally related to a formal system of a particular sort—namely, to arithmetic. This contrasts with the Piagetian approach of thinking about numbers as fundamentally properties of sets (of physical objects or events) and derived developmentally from understanding operations on sets (of physical objects or events). Instead, number representation may better be thought of as falling out of arithmetic and developmentally derived from arithmetic inference (Gelman & Gallistel, 1978; Gelman & Meck, 1992; Leslie et al., 2008). Of course, the formal system of arithmetic can be brought to bear on the physical and other domains, but that may be something the infant, the child, and the adult have to discover and learn about. At any rate, an emphasis on the formal origins of number representation, even in infants, may lead to fresh insights and new lines of investigation.

Early and/or nonverbal integer representation has been largely overlooked in the psychological literature in favor of real-valued continuous magnitudes representations. Continuous magnitude representations are inherently noisy and variable. Yet the natural numbers, including the first few natural numbers, have exact values and indeed have exactly integer values. This underlies our intuition that one instance of the second integer is perfectly substitutable for another instance of the second integer (they are necessarily exactly equal). This intuition is hard to explain on the basis of noisy continuous representations. In general, two instances of a continuous magnitude representation will never be exactly equal.

Integer concepts, recursively generated, would provide not only a way for infants to represent small numbers exactly, but also, via the successor function, provide the concept of 'next number'. That is to say, infants may begin with limited and exact cardinal values that can then be added to by realizing the next number in the integer series defined by the successor function. Leslie and colleagues argue that integer representations must be calibrated against the system of continuous mental magnitudes (the example given is of numbers on a speedometer corresponding to the analog representation of speed). Integer values have no special status in a continuous representation, which represents (infinitely many) values between any two integer values; in fact, integer positions cannot be represented exactly in a noisy continuous system. Yet eventually, we are able to align the two systems so that, for example, the ratio of an integer value to a continuous magnitude can be calculated (as in estimates of rates of occurrence). This requires the two systems to be computationally compatible and thus calibrated. This defines a further type of quantitative learning: calibration learning, which is necessary to ensure the computational compatibility of the two kinds of number representation. Finally, an important role is allotted to learning the 'compact' number notation provided by languages such as English. For further discussion of these ideas, see Leslie et al. (2007) and Leslie et al. (2008).

Investigators have yet to seriously study the possibility of an infant integer representation. Key features to look for include exact numerical representations (e.g., lack of Weber fraction) combined with ordinality in the small number range.

4.8 Summary

Of the four possible systems by which infants might represent the discrete quantity of small sets of objects, only the accumulator and the generative integer views posit an irreducibly numerical basis to infants' number representations. The object indexing and set accounts provide a mechanism by which infants might be able to track small numbers of discrete objects and compare them on the basis of their numerical identity without actually being able to count. In addition, many of the accounts are to some extent compatible with each other, and indeed, often may complement each other (e.g., infants may represent large numbers using the accumulator but small numbers using sets or object tracking). No one theory on its own fully accounts for the experimental results on studies of infants' quantity representations provided to date; so, exploring how the interaction of different systems may account for different pieces of evidence becomes an even more critical task. Ultimately, a theory of infant number representations should provide a satisfactory and comprehensive explanation for the many disparate results arrived at in the field, as well as be consistent with evidence for number representation from the animal kingdom.

Understanding what kind of information forms the basis of the representations infants use to track sets of objects in the world sheds light on what humans start out knowing about objects and number, and helps to specify the learning tasks that lie ahead. Is number learning a culturally determined process of drawing connections between the physical environment and linguistic terms? If so, then the behavior of children before and after learning this mapping should be discontinuous, and qualitatively different. Or does knowing about numbers reflect evolutionarily advantageous systems that allow us to exploit numerical properties of the environment? If that is the case, then the behavior of infants, young children, older children, and adults should exhibit strong continuity. Or do we have to untangle a complex weave of both kinds of threads? Establishing the nature of infants' numerical competence will provide basic guiding principles regarding these questions, and will have far-reaching implications for the fields of cognitive science, developmental psychology, mathematics, and education.

References

Antell, S. R., & Keating, D. (1983). Perception of numerical invariance by neonates. *Child Development, 54,* 695–701.

Baillargeon, R. (1986). Representing the existence and the location of hidden objects: object permanence in 6- and 8-month-old infants. *Cognition, 23,* 21–41.

Baillargeon, R. (1987). Object permanence in 3.5 and 4.5 month old infants. *Developmental Psychology, 23*, 655–664.

Baillargeon, R. (2004). Infants' reasoning about hidden objects: evidence for event-general and event-specific expectations. *Developmental Science, 7*, 391–424.

Barner, D., Thalwitz, D., Wood, J., & Carey, S. (2007). On the relation between the acquisition of singular-plural morpho-syntax and the conceptual distinction between one and more than one. *Developmental Science, 10(3)*, 365–373.

Bijeljac-Babic, R., Bertoncini, J., & Mehler, J. (1993). How do 4-day-old infants categorize multisyllabic utterances? *Developmental Psychology, 29*, 711–721.

Bloom, P., & Wynn, K. (1997). Linguistic cues in the acquisition of number words. *Journal of Child Language, 24*, 511–533.

Brannon, E. M. (2002). The development of ordinal numerical knowledge in infancy. *Cognition, 83*, 223–240.

Brannon, E. M., Abbott, S., & Lutz, D. J. (2004). Number bias for the discrimination of large visual sets in infancy. *Cognition, 93*, B59–B68.

Brannon, E. M., Lutz, D., & Cordes, S. (2006). The development of area discrimination and its implications for number representation in infancy. *Developmental Science, 9*, F59–F64.

Carey, S. (2001). Cognitive foundations of arithmetic: evolution and ontogenesis. *Mind and Language, 16*, 37–55.

Carey, S. (2004). Bootstrapping and the origin of concepts. *Daedalus, Winter*, 59–68.

Clearfield, M. W., & Mix, K. S. (1999). Number versus contour length in infants' discrimination of small visual sets. *Psychological Science, 10*, 408–411.

Clearfield, M. W., & Mix, K. S. (2001). Amount versus number: infants' use of area and contour length to discriminate small sets. *Journal of Cognition and Development, 2*, 243–260.

Corbett, G. C. (2000). *Number*. Cambridge, UK: Cambridge University Press.

Cordes, S., Gelman, R., Gallistel, C. R., & Whalen, J. (2001). Variability signatures distinguish verbal from nonverbal counting for both large and small numbers. *Psychonomic Bulletin and Review, 8(4)*, 698–707.

Cordes, S., Lutz, D., & Brannon, E.M. (2007). Discriminations of small from large sets in human infants. Poster presented at the 2007 Biennial Society For Research in Child Development Meeting, Boston, MA. March 31.

Dehaene, S. (1997). *The Number Sense*. Oxford, UK: Oxford University Press.

Feigenson, L., & Carey, S. (2003). Tracking individuals via object-files: evidence from infants' manual search. *Developmental Science, 6*, 568–584.

Feigenson, L., Carey, S., & Hauser, M. (2002). The representations underlying infants' choice of more: object files versus analog magnitudes. *Psychological Science, 13*, 150–156.

Feigenson, L., Carey, S., & Spelke, E. (2002). Infants' discrimination of number vs. continuous extent. *Cognitive Psychology, 44*, 33–66.

Feigenson, L., Dehaene, S., & Spelke, E. (2004). Core systems of number. *Trends in Cognitive Sciences, 8*, 307–314.

Feigenson, L., & Halberda, J. (2004). Infants chunk object arrays into sets of individuals. *Cognition, 91*, 173–190.

Feigenson, L. (2005). *A double dissociation in infants' representation of object arrays. Cognition, 95*, B37–B48.

Gao, F., Levine, S. C., & Huttenlocher, J. (2000). What do infants know about continuous quantity? *Journal of Experimental Child Psychology, 77,* 20–29.

Gallistel, C. R. (1990). *The Organization of Learning.* Cambridge, MA.: MIT Press.

Gallistel, C. R., & Gelman, R. (1992). Preverbal and verbal counting and computation. *Cognition, 44,* 43–74.

Gallistel, C. R., & Gelman, R. (2005). Mathematical cognition. In K. Holyoak, & R. Morrison (Eds.), *Cambridge Handbook of Thinking and Reasoning* (pp. 559–588). New York: Cambridge University Press.

Gelman, R. (1990). First principles organize attention to and learning about relevant data: number and the animate-inanimate distinction. *Cognitive Science, 14,* 79–106.

Gelman, R., & Butterworth, B. (2005). Language and number: How are they related? *Trends in Cognitive Sciences, 9,* 6–10.

Gelman, R., & Gallistel, C. R. (1978). *The Child's Understanding of Number.* Cambridge, MA.: Harvard University Press.

Gelman, R., & Meck, B. (1992). Early principles aid initial but not later conceptions of number. In J. Bideaud, & C. Meljac (Eds.), *Pathways to Number: Children's Developing Numerical Abilities* (pp. 171–189). Hillsdale, NJ: Lawrence Erlbaum.

Gordon, P. (2004). Numerical cognition without words: evidence from Amazonia. *Nature, 306,* 496–499.

Hauser, M. D., Carey, S., & Hauser, L. B. (2000). Spontaneous number representation in semi-free-ranging rhesus monkeys. *Proceedings of the Royal Society of London, Part B: Biological Sciences, 267,* 829–833.

Huntley-Fenner, G., Carey, S., & Solimando, A. (2002). Objects are individuals but stuff doesn't count: perceived rigidity and cohesiveness influence infants' representations of small numbers of discrete entities. *Cognition, 85,* 203–221.

Káldy, Z., & Leslie, A. M. (2003). The identification of objects by 9-month-old infants: integrating 'what' and 'where' information. *Developmental Science, 6,* 360–373.

Káldy, Z., & Leslie, A. M. (2005). A memory span of one? Object identification in 6.5-month-old infants. *Cognition, 97,* 153–177.

Kobayashi, T., Hiraki, K., Mugitani, R., & Hasegawa, T. (2004). Baby arithmetic: one object plus one tone. *Cognition, 91,* B23–B34.

Kouider, S., Halberda, J., Wood, J., & Carey, S. (2006). Acquisition of English number marking: the singular-plural distinction. *Language Learning and Development, 2,* 1–25.

LeCorre, M., & Carey, S. (2007). One, two, three, four, nothing more: an investigation of the conceptual sources of the verbal counting principles. *Cognition, 105,* 395–438.

Leslie, A. M., & Chen, M. L. (2007). Individuation of pairs of objects in infancy. *Developmental Science, 10,* 423–430.

Leslie, A. M., Gallistel, C. R., & Gelman, R. (2007). Where integers come from. In P. Carruthers, S. Laurence, & S. Stich (Eds.), *The Innate Mind: Foundations and the Future* (pp. 103–138). Oxford, UK: Oxford University Press.

Leslie, A. M., Gelman, R., & Gallistel, C. R. (2008). The generative basis of natural number concepts. *Trends in Cognitive Sciences, 12,* 213–218.

Leslie, A. M., & Káldy, Z. (2007). Things to remember: limits, codes, and the development of object working memory in the first year. In L.M. Oakes, & P.J. Bauer (Eds.), *Short- and Long-Term Memory in Infancy and Early Childhood* (pp. 103–125). Oxford, UK: Oxford University Press.

Leslie, A. M., Xu, F., Tremoulet, P. D., & Scholl, B .J. (1998). Indexing and the object concept: developing 'what' and 'where' systems. *Trends in Cognitive Sciences, 2*, 10–18.

Lipton, J. S., & Spelke, E. S. (2003). Origins of number sense: large-number discrimination in human infants. *Psychological Science, 14*, 397–401.

Meck, W. H., & Church, R. M. (1983). A mode control model of counting and timing processes. *Journal of Experimental Psychology: Animal Behavior Processes, 9*, 320–334.

Mix, K. S., Huttenlocher, J., & Levine, S. C. (2002). Multiple cues for quantification in infancy: Is number one of them? *Psychological Bulletin, 128*, 278–294.

Morgan, M. J. (2005). The visual computation of 2-D area by human observers. *Vision Research, 45*, 2564–2570.

Piaget, J. (1955). *The Child's Construction of Reality*. London: Routledge & Kegan Paul.

Pylyshyn, Z. (2003). *Seeing and Visualizing: It's Not What You Think*. Cambridge, MA: MIT Press.

Pylyshyn, Z., & Storm, R. (1988). Tracking multiple independent targets: evidence for both serial and parallel stages. *Spatial Vision, 3*, 179–197.

Rips, L .J., Asmuth, J., & Bloomfield, A. (2006). Giving the boot to the bootstrap: how not to learn the natural numbers. *Cognition, 101*, B51–B60.

Rips, L. J., Asmuth, J., & Bloomfield, A. (2008). Do children learn the integers by induction? *Cognition, 106*, 940–951.

Ross-Sheehy, S., Oakes, L. M., & Luck, S. J. (2003). The development of visual short-term memory capacity in infants. *Child Development, 74*, 1807–1822.

Scholl, B. J., & Leslie, A. M. (1999). Explaining the infant's object concept: beyond the perception/cognition dichotomy. In E. Lepore, & Z. Pylyshyn (Eds.), *What is Cognitive Science?* (pp. 26–73). Oxford, UK: Blackwell.

Scholl, B. J., & Pylyshyn, Z. W. (1999). Tracking multiple objects through occlusion: clues to visual objecthood. *Cognitive Psychology, 38*, 259–290.

Simon, T. J., Hespos, S .J., & Rochat, P. (1995). Do infants understand simple arithmetic? A replication of Wynn (1992). *Cognitive Development, 10*, 253–269.

Spelke, E. S. (1990). Principles of object perception. *Cognitive Science, 14*, 29–56.

Spelke, E. S. (1994). Initial knowledge: six suggestions. *Cognition, 50*, 431–445.

Starkey, P., & Cooper, R. G. Jr. (1980). Perception of numbers by human infants. *Science, 210*, 1033–1035.

Starkey, P. D., Spelke, E. S., & Gelman, R. (1983). Detection of numerical correspondences by human infants. *Science, 222*, 179–181.

Strauss, M. S., & Curtis, L .E. (1981). Infant perception of numerosity. *Child Development, 52*, 1146–1152.

Tremoulet, P. D., Leslie, A. M., & Hall, D. G. (2000). Infant individuation and identification of objects. *Cognitive Development, 15*, 499–522.

Trick, L. M., & Pylyshyn, Z. (1994). Why are small and large numbers enumerated differently? A limited-capacity preattentive stage in vision. *Psychological Review, 101*, 80–102.

Uller, C., Carey, S., Huntley-Fenner, G., & Klatt, L. (1999). What representations might underlie infant numerical knowledge? *Cognitive Development, 14*, 1–36.

VanMarle, K. (under review). Infants' sensitivity to continuous quantity: the relationship between discrete and continuous quantification.

VanMarle, K., & Wynn, K. (2006). 6-month-old infants use analog magnitudes to represent duration. *Developmental Science, 9*, F41–F49.

Whalen, J., Gallistel, C. R., & Gelman, R. (1999). Non-verbal counting in humans: the psychophysics of number representation. *Psychological Science, 10*, 130–137.

Wood, J. N., & Spelke, E. S. (2005). Infants' enumeration of actions: numerical discrimination and its signature limits. *Developmental Science, 8*, 173–181.

Wynn, K. (1992a). Addition and subtraction by human infants. *Nature, 358*, 749–750.

Wynn, K. (1992b). Evidence against empiricist accounts of the origins of numerical knowledge. *Mind and Language, 7*, 315–332.

Wynn, K. (1996). Infants' individuation and enumeration of actions. *Psychological Science, 7*, 164–169.

Wynn, K., Bloom, P., & Chiang, W. (2002). Enumeration of collective entities by 5-month-old infants. *Cognition, 83*, B55–B62.

Xu, F. (2003). Numerosity discrimination in infants: evidence for two systems of representations. *Cognition, 89*, B15–B25.

Xu, F., & Carey, S. (1996). Infants' metaphysics: the case of numerical identity. *Cognitive Psychology, 30*, 111–153.

Xu, F., & Spelke, E. S. (2000). Large number discrimination in 6-month-old infants. *Cognition, 74*, B1–B11.

Chapter 5

Do the same principles constrain persisting object representations in infant cognition and adult perception?: The cases of continuity and cohesion

Erik W. Cheries, Stephen R. Mitroff,
Karen Wynn, & Brian J. Scholl

5.1 Introduction

In recent years, the study of object persistence—how the mind identifies objects as the same individuals over time—has been undergoing a renaissance in (at least) two different fields of cognitive science. First, vision scientists have come to understand some of the principles that control the construction, maintenance, and destruction of object representations in mid-level vision. Second, developmental researchers have identified several principles of 'core knowledge' that constrain object permanence in infants. These two fields have traditionally operated largely independently, but some researchers have suggested that they may in fact be studying the same underlying mental processes.

This interesting idea has been used in the past to interpret various empirical results in each field, but the real promise of this approach lies in its ability to drive further progress by generating novel predictions that can then be tested in both fields. The hope is that this approach could spark a useful feedback loop of sorts: for example, infancy research may give rise to specific predictions for adult perception experiments, whose subsequent results may in turn give rise to additional specific predictions for infant cognition experiments. To the extent that this strategy succeeds—confirming ever more specific predictions as hypotheses are carried back and forth across these fields—we may obtain support for the idea that these two fields are studying the same thing.

In this chapter we describe two examples of attempts to implement this strategy in practice, while studying two of the most salient principles of core knowledge: *continuity* and *cohesion*. In each case, earlier infant research was used to motivate adult perception experiments, which were in turn used to generate and test more specific predictions in further infant studies. These case studies illustrate the utility of bridging the gaps between these two fields, as our knowledge of each is deepened as a result of exploring the connections. In particular, this process has revealed in new ways how violations of these principles of core knowledge in turn have deleterious effects on the underlying object representations themselves. In addition, the results in each case are consistent with the possibility that representations of persisting objects in each domain are controlled by the same principles, and perhaps even the same underlying processes.

5.1.1 **Object persistence**

Many of the mind's most extraordinary accomplishments are achieved with deceptively little conscious effort. A striking example of this is the apparent ease with which we perceive the many objects that populate our everyday visual experience. By merely opening our eyes, it seems that the undifferentiated wash of light captured on the surface of our retinas is instantly transformed into representations of discrete objects. However, the principal lesson from research in cognitive science (underscored by the amount of attention given to the topic in this book!) is that even a seemingly effortless ability such as object perception is in fact the result of complicated cognitive processing beneath the surface.

This is true not only for the perception of objects but also for the perception of *persisting objects*—our ability to perceive objects as the very same individuals over time, motion, featural changes, and despite interruptions such as occlusion (for a summary, see Scholl & Flombaum, in press). Without such processing, visual experience would be incoherent: we would be able to perceive objects, but it would be as if the world was created from scratch at every instant. In addition, recent empirical work has shown that computations of object persistence are critical for understanding many other processes such as visual memory (e.g., Cheries et al., 2006; Flombaum & Scholl, 2006), implicit learning (e.g., Fiser et al., 2007), numerical cognition (e.g., Feigenson et al., 2004), motion perception (e.g., Dawson, 1991), search and foraging (e.g., Flombaum et al., 2004; Santos, 2004), and even visual awareness in the first place (e.g., Mitroff & Scholl, 2005; Moore & Lleras, 2005).

In recent years, researchers in several areas of psychology have made great strides in elucidating the principles that guide the computation of object persistence. Here, we focus on two such domains: infant cognitive development and adult vision science.[1] Collectively, the results of these studies suggest that there are mental mechanisms for computing object persistence that are *primitive* in at least two senses: (1) they occur relatively early in perceptual processing, such that they are largely 'hardwired' parts of perception that then constrain later cognition; and (2) they arise early in human development.

5.1.2 Object persistence in infant cognition

Research in infant cognition across the last two decades has generated a wealth of evidence that even young infants (a) experience the world in terms of discrete persisting objects and (b) have relatively sophisticated expectations about how objects in their physical environment should behave (for a review, see Santos & Hood, Chapter 1). For instance, infants expect that objects hidden from view continue to exist (Baillargeon, 1987; Baillargeon & DeVos, 1991; Shinskey & Munakata, 2003), move in spatially continuous paths over time (Spelke et al., 1995; Xu & Carey, 1996), occupy physically distinct locations from other objects (Baillargeon et al., 1985; Spelke et al., 1992), and maintain cohesive boundaries over time (Needham, 1999; Spelke & van de Walle, 1993). These findings are collectively thought to reflect a set of 'core knowledge' principles involving (among others) continuity, solidity, and cohesion; these principles guide infants' expectations about how objects will behave and serve as the foundation of our physical understanding of the world throughout adulthood (Carey & Spelke, 1996; Spelke, 2000; Spelke & Kinzler, 2007).

A growing number of studies have also demonstrated that infants possess sophisticated numerical abilities, and these studies provide a particularly strong demonstration of infants' ability to represent objects as persisting individuals. After all, establishing a correct numerical representation of any array requires that each of the individual objects in that array be represented as the same individual over time. As a simple demonstration of this fact, imagine a ball rolling behind a screen and emerging from the other side. How many objects were there? Adult observers, of course, would say (and see) 'one' (Burke, 1952; Michotte et al., 1964/1991). However, if we were unable to represent the pre- and post-occlusion encounters as the same individual, we might instead say and see 'two' objects. As this illustrates, the mind must somehow collate the multiple 'snapshots' of the occluding object before successfully representing the number involved.

---

[1] Although we limit ourselves to these two areas of psychology in this chapter, note that the nature of object persistence has also been the focus of a great deal of recent research in other areas of cognitive science, such as computer science (for a review, see Yilmaz et al., 2006) and philosophy (for a review that highlights connections with psychological research, see Scholl, 2007).

Even at an early age, infants show precocious numerical abilities. For instance, infants can represent both small and large numbers of objects (Antell & Keating, 1983; Feigenson, 2005; Starkey & Cooper, 1980; Strauss & Curtis, 1981; van Loosbroek & Smitsman, 1990; Wynn et al., 2002; Xu, 2003; Xu & Spelke, 2000), actions (Sharon & Wynn, 1998; Wood & Spelke, 2005; Wynn, 1996), and sounds (Lipton & Spelke, 2004). Moreover, they not only represent the number of individuals under occlusion but also successfully update this representation in their minds as individuals are either added to or subtracted from the set, in a form of primitive arithmetic (Cheries & Wynn, 2007; Koechlin et al., 1997; McCrink & Wynn, 2004; Simon et al., 1995; Wynn, 1992).

5.1.3 Object persistence in adult visual cognition

We interpret the world in terms of persisting objects in part because that matches the inferences that we make during reasoning and other forms of higher-level cognition (e.g., Rips et al., 2006; Scholl, 2007). However, we also *perceive* the world in terms of persisting objects in the first place, driven by more hardwired principles of persistence that appear to be a part of visual processing. These visual processes may even cause us to perceive persisting objects even when we simultaneously *judge* that in fact there is no persistence—as occurs, for example, in some cases of apparent motion (Anstis, 1980; Wertheimer, 1912/1961) or the tunnel effect (Flombaum & Scholl, 2006; Michotte et al., 1964/1991).

Much of the work on object persistence in adult visual cognition occurs at the level of what is often called *mid-level vision* (Nakayama et al., 1995). At this level, objects may be represented as the same individuals over time despite changes to both their lower-level visual features (e.g., red, round) and their higher-level category descriptions (e.g., 'apple'). These mid-level object representations—often referred to as *object files* (Kahneman & Treisman, 1984; Kahneman et al., 1992)—may store information about objects' visual features, but their construction, maintenance, and destruction appears to be controlled by purely spatiotemporal aspects of how the objects move across space (Gao & Scholl, in press; Kahneman et al., 1992; Mitroff & Alvarez, 2007; for a review, see Flombaum et al., Chapter 6).

Some of the evidence for this system of representation comes from the *object-reviewing* paradigm (Kahneman et al., 1992; see Fig. 5.1).

In a typical task, adult subjects are shown a video screen with two small outlined boxes, and distinct single letters (or other distinguishable features) are briefly presented in each box. After the letters disappear, the (now empty) boxes move to different locations on the screen, after which a single probe letter appears on just one of the boxes. The subject's task, in one variant of this paradigm (see Noles et al., 2005) is to use a key 'press' to indicate whether

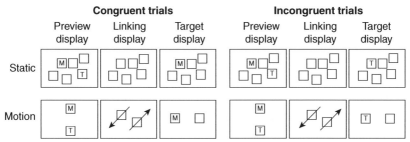

Fig. 5.1 Sample displays used in the object-reviewing paradigm (Kahneman et al., 1992). Subjects see two preview letters in an initial display and a single probe letter in a final display, and must simply indicate whether the final probe was present in the initial preview display. Responses are faster when the probe letter had initially appeared in that same object during the preview display, compared with when it had appeared in the other object. In the static displays, the target is seen as the same object as one of the previews, because it appears on the same object, in the same location. Objecthood and location are unconfounded in the moving displays.

the final probe letter was the same as *either* of the initially presented letters. The basic finding is that subjects are quicker to name the probe letter when it had been a preview letter than when it is novel (a type of display-wide priming), but that they are faster still to name the letter if it reappears in the *same* box in which it had been previewed, regardless of the new location that box now occupies. This latter response time advantage (for 'congruent' over 'incongruent' trials; see Fig. 5.1) has been termed the *object-specific preview benefit* (OSPB), and is thought to reveal the computation of persisting objects in mid-level vision.

Other research has explored object persistence in perception by directly evaluating the ability to keep a set of target objects distinct over time and motion from a featurally identical set of distractor objects, using attentional tracking. For instance, in multiple-object tracking (MOT) tasks (Pylyshyn & Storm, 1988), subjects initially see a number of qualitatively identical objects. A subset of these are then flashed to indicate their status as targets, after which all of the (again identical) objects begin moving independently and unpredictably about the display. When they stop moving, subjects must indicate which of the objects are the original targets. Subjects are able to succeed at MOT when tracking up to 3 or 4 objects, but tracking more is nearly impossible for most adult subjects because of the limits on parallel attention (Pylyshyn & Storm, 1988). This task has been used to reveal several mechanisms of object persistence that operate beneath the surface of conscious awareness (see Scholl, in press, for a review) such as the automatic allocation of attention to objects' centers of gravity (Alvarez & Scholl, 2005), the automatic inhibition of distractors during tracking (Pylyshyn, 2006; Pylyshyn et al., 2008), and the engagement of extra pools of resources in situations such as occlusion that pose severe challenges for maintaining persisting representations (Flombaum et al., 2008).

5.1.4 Do the same principles constrain object persistence in infant cognition and adult perception?

Despite the wealth of recent research on object persistence in infant cognition and adult perception, these two fields have traditionally operated largely independently. Nevertheless, some researchers have suggested that they may be related—reflecting the same underlying principles of persistence, and perhaps even some of the same underlying processes (e.g., Carey & Xu, 2001; Chiang & Wynn, 2000; Feigenson, Carey & Hauser, 2002; Scholl & Leslie, 1999). These suggestions have been based in part on various analogies between the results that have been obtained in the two fields. Three examples (drawn from Scholl & Leslie, 1999):

Spatiotemporal priority: Both fields have converged on a core principle that guides the creation and maintenance of persisting object representations—the principle of 'spatiotemporal priority'. When identifying objects as the same individuals over time, the visual system appears to rely on their spatiotemporal histories—that is, where, when, and how they were encountered—to a greater degree than their visual surface features (for a review, see Flombaum et al., Chapter 6).

Numerical limits: The ability to maintain persisting objects in both fields appears to be numerically constrained to only a small number (3–4) of simultaneously active representations (e.g., Feigenson et al., 2002; Pylyshyn & Storm, 1988).

Surviving occlusion: Persisting representations as studied in both fields appear to support online visual experience of the world, but they are not entirely fleeting; rather, such representations can survive periods of complete occlusion (e.g. Scholl & Pylyshyn, 1999; Spelke et al., 1995).

Exploring such analogies is valuable, insofar as it may help to theoretically bridge these two otherwise-disparate disciplines. If nothing else, doing so can reveal a wealth of new ideas for experiments in each area, as researchers discover how strikingly similar questions have been explored in various ways in each domain. However, the real promise of this (or any such) project lies in its ability to drive further concrete progress in each field. And so we might ask: can attending to the connections between these fields actually lead to a greater understanding of how object persistence is achieved in infant cognition and/or adult perception?

We think the answer to this question is 'yes', and in the remainder of this chapter, we discuss two case studies of such progress in practice. In each case, the initial spark for our research was drawn from studies of object persistence in infant cognition. These studies prompted us to ask similar questions about how such manipulations might or might not operate in adult perception. In turn, though, the results we obtained in the adult perception experiments revealed new nuances to such processing that then deserved and received further testing in infant cognition—implementing a type of feedback as we moved back and forth between these domains. The results we obtained along each step of this process deepened our understanding of some of the core principles of persistence in a way that would have been difficult to discover without bridging these disciplines. And the strikingly similar patterns of results that we observed across these areas is consistent with the possibility that we have in fact been studying the same underlying principles and/or processes.

5.2 Case study 1: Continuity through occlusion

A basic fact about the world is that objects cannot simply go in and out of existence over time: for two objects encountered at different locations to be subsequent stages of the same individual, there must be a spatiotemporally continuous path between them. If an object disappears at one location, and an object immediately appears at a different spatially separated location, then those two instances cannot be the same object, because physical laws do not allow for that sort of thing (at least at the spatial and temporal scales that characterize our everyday interaction with objects). As such, tracking an object's continuous movement across space could serve as a reliable guide for perceiving it as the same persisting individual over time. One problem with this constraint in practice, however, is that our eyes frequently lose perceptual contact with many of the objects we may be tracking. Along with the effects of blinking, perhaps the most severe form of this type of interruption is occlusion, where one object may disappear entirely behind another object before reappearing. In order to perceive objects as they really are—individuals that continue to persist over time—rather than how they literally appear to our eyes, our mind must account for ecologically valid disappearances such as occlusion.

5.2.1 Initial infant research

There is now ample evidence that the ability to maintain object representations throughout visual interruptions such as occlusion develops quite early in ontogeny (for reviews, see Baillargeon, 1999; Santos & Hood, Chapter 1). For instance, even newborn infants are able to perceive partly occluded objects

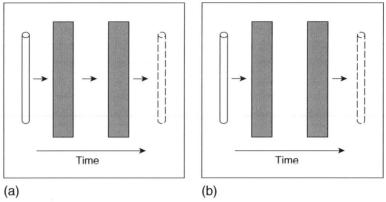

Fig. 5.2 A schematic of events used to study spatiotemporal continuity in infancy studies (Spelke et al., 1995). (a) An object moves behind a first screen, then an object moves between the two screens, then an object emerges from the second screen and continues moving (after which it may change direction and these events occur again in reverse order). It is natural to experience this event (as infants seem to do) as a single object that moves behind two screens. (b) When the same event proceeds but without an object ever appearing between the two screens, it is natural to experience it (as infants seem to do) as involving two distinct objects, one moving behind each screen.

as complete wholes rather than as the fragmented parts that are immediately perceivable (Valenza et al., 2006; cf., Amso & Johnson, Chapter 9), and by at least 3.5 months, infants expect objects that have completely disappeared to persist and move continuously during momentary disappearances (Aguiar & Baillargeon, 1999, 2002; Baillargeon & DeVos, 1991; Spelke et al., 1995). In one study, for example, the looking-time behavior of 5-month-old infants who observed a rod that moved sequentially behind two screens (see Fig. 5.2a) indicates that they perceive the event in terms of a single persisting object. In contrast, however, they instead seem to perceive two distinct objects if the rod does not traverse the space between the two screens (Fig. 5.2b; Spelke et al., 1995). This simultaneously illustrates (a) the operation of a constraint on persistence based on spatiotemporal continuity and (b) the ability of infants to keep track of objects through periods of occlusion.

5.2.2 Step 1: Testing for persistence through occlusion in adult perception

Directly inspired by such demonstrations in the infant cognition literature (and especially by Spelke et al., 1995), one of our early experiments (Scholl & Pylyshyn, 1999) sought to determine whether object tracking in adult perception is also able to survive periods of occlusion—or whether

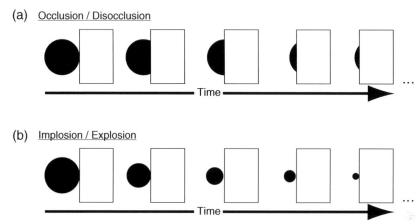

Fig. 5.3 Depictions of how an object might interact with an occluder in two conditions in studies of object tracking through occlusion in adults (Scholl & Pylyshyn, 1999) and infants (Cheries, Feigenson et al., 2008, in preparation). (a) The object is momentarily occluded—deleting from its trailing edge as it disappears and then accreting from its leading edge upon its reappearance. Tracking in this condition is unimpaired. (b) The object moves through the same trajectory, disappearing at the same time and the same rate as in (a), but now it gradually 'implodes' to a point and then later 'explodes' from a point. This violates spatiotemporal continuity, greatly impairing tracking.

constant perceptual contact must be maintained with objects in order to track them over time as the same individuals. In an MOT task, adult subjects had to track 4 out of 8 moving objects as they moved about a display that also contained two occluders. Each time a moving object intersected an occluder, it disappeared, and later reappeared from the opposite side of the occluder. Across trial types, the specific manner of these disappearances and reappearances was varied (see Fig. 5.3). On *Occlusion/Disocclusion* trials, whenever an object intersected the edge of an occluder, it would disappear gradually at its leading edge (as if it were moving behind the occluder) and then later gradually reappear along its trailing edge (see Fig. 5.3a). Tracking performance on such trials was excellent, and not significantly different from the performance obtained when the objects simply moved atop the 'occluder' contours, so that they were always visible. Thus, it seems as if persisting representations in adult perception, similar to those in infant cognition, can readily survive occlusion.[2]

---

[2] Later experiments (e.g., Flombaum et al., 2008; Scholl & Feigenson, 2004) have sometimes found a slight impairment for tracking through occlusion compared with tracking without any occluders—but in all cases, the magnitude of this impairment has been small, and tracking performance in both conditions has been excellent.

The ability to track well in Occlusion/Disocclusion trials does not itself provide evidence for any principles that control object representations; rather, such success could simply reflect a general tolerance of tracking through any form of brief interruption. These adult perception experiments also tested other types of manipulations, however, beyond the familiar types of occlusion. On *Implosion/Explosion* trials, whenever an object intersected the edge of an occluder, it would shrink to a central point at the entering edge of the occluder, and then later expand out of a central point at the exiting edge (see Fig. 5.3b).

These trials were constructed so that the objects were always visible and invisible for the same amounts of time as in the Occlusion/Disocclusion trials, and the disappearances always occurred at the same times and at the same rates. Nevertheless, performance on Implosion/Explosion trials was radically impaired relative to Occlusion/Disocclusion trials, and was often near chance. (Moreover, similar results occur with Implosion vs. Occlusion in experiments involving the tunnel effect that do not require attentive tracking or explicit responses involving persistence over time; Flombaum & Scholl, 2006.)

In sum, when subtle visual cues indicated that the momentary disappearances reflected the objects going out of sight, the disappearances did not affect tracking—but when these cues indicated that the objects were going out of existence, subjects were no longer able to track them as persisting individuals, despite their brute visual similarity to the 'trackable' displays (Scholl & Feigenson, 2004; Scholl & Pylyshyn, 1999). Critically, notice that this inability did not reflect subjects' beliefs or strategies: they knew perfectly well what was going on during the Implosion/Explosion trials, and would have preferred to ignore those cues. But they could not—indicating that this particular type of principle of spatiotemporal continuity is encapsulated from our beliefs and preferences, and is part of the basic processes that help to generate visual experience.

5.2.3 Step 2: Testing occlusion versus implosion in infant cognition

The pattern of results obtained in the studies described in the previous section succeeded in taking a prediction from the infant cognition literature and testing (and confirming) it in the adult perception literature. In our attempt to unconfound the specific principle of continuity through occlusion from a more general tolerance for interruptions, however, we also uncovered a new effect of the *manner* of disappearance at occluding boundaries. This effect (operationalized as occlusion vs. implosion) may also reflect a type of principle governing the maintenance of persisting object representations: only objects that disappear in specific and ecologically valid ways can be maintained through interruptions. If this type of principle is truly primitive in the mind, however—and if the adult perception and infant cognition literatures are exploring related processes—then we should similarly find that infants' representational abilities are constrained in this fashion.

In fact, two recent studies have demonstrated that such cues can influence infants' representations of hidden objects. First, infants' ability to predict whether a ball will reappear after disappearing behind an opaque screen depends upon such cues (Bertenthal et al., 2007): infants who observe a ball that disappears via 'occlusion' (as in Fig. 5.3a) make significantly more saccades to the opposite side of the screen than infants who see the ball 'implode' behind the screen (as in Fig. 5.3b). In this way, the cue that signals an object's spatiotemporal continuity controls whether infants anticipate that the object will reemerge from the other side of a screen. Similarly, an electroencephalography (EEG) study with 7-month-old infants has shown that such cues control activity levels in brain regions that correlate with the maintenance of object representations (Kaufman et al., 2005). Significantly more gamma-band activity was detected over these brain areas when infant subjects viewed an object being covered by a screen in a way that was consistent with occlusion, compared with trials when the object gradually dissolved as it was covered.

Both of these studies underscore how object persistence in infancy is constrained by the same visual cues that support object tracking in adult perception. However, we might still wonder whether this manipulation disrupts infants' representations of persisting objects per se. In particular, note that adults' failure to track multiple imploding and exploding objects in the MOT task may reflect the disruption of two separate computations. First, the implosion cue at the entering edge of the occluder may have disrupted the visual system's ability to infer the continued existence of the object behind the barrier (as demonstrated in the aforementioned infant studies). Additionally, however, this cue was also sufficient to destroy adults' ability to track the emerging object as the same individual once it reappeared. This second result is not a necessary consequence of the first, because the continuity of speed, trajectory, and featural similarity could in principle be sufficient for the numerical identity of the object to be maintained once it reappears. ('I thought it was gone, but wait—it's back now!')

Does this second type of disruption—the inability to 'reacquire' an object as the same individual once it does reappear, after an Implosion/Explosion event—also occur in infant cognition? To test this, we adapted the adult

MOT task for infant subjects (Cheries et al., in preparation; see also Cheries, Feigenson et al., 2008). Ten-month-old infants were habituated to dynamic displays of either 2 or 3 randomly moving identical items, which disappeared and reappeared from behind two long and narrow occluders. What varied across experimental conditions (and subjects) was precisely how these objects disappeared behind the opaque barriers: they either occluded and disoccluded (Fig. 5.3a) or imploded and exploded (Fig. 5.3b) as in the previous adult perception studies. The critical question was whether infants would be able to establish representations of a stable number of individuals across these habituation trials. To assess this, infants in both types of disappearance conditions were shown the identical displays of 2 or 3 moving objects at test but without any barriers or disappearances. If infants maintained the number of individuals across habituations trials, then infants who were habituated to 2 objects should respond by looking longer at test displays of 3 objects and vice versa.

As predicted, infants who were habituated to objects that disappeared behind the barriers via 'occlusion' and 'disocclusion' successfully dishabituated to the test displays containing a novel number of objects (see Fig. 5.4a). In contrast, infants who were habituated to object arrays that disappeared and reappeared from behind the screens via 'implosion' and 'explosion' failed to differentiate the number of objects present in the proceeding test trials (see Fig. 5.4b). Apparently, infants were unable to perceive a stable number of individuals across habituation in this condition, even though the objects moved and disappeared equally gradually and at the same rates as the objects in the occlusion condition.

These results are consistent with the interpretation that occlusion is a cue that an object has gone out of sight, whereas implosion is a cue that an object has gone *out of existence*. However, an additional possibility is that the imploding motion pattern is so anomalous and distracting that infants were unable to successfully represent anything at all about the display over the course of habituation, due to a general distraction. After all, infants have no experience observing objects behaving in this manner.

We tested these two possibilities by determining whether infants are able to represent a *nonnumerical* property of the objects in the 'implosion/explosion' condition. Infants were again habituated to displays of moving objects that imploded and exploded from behind the barriers. Some infants were shown 2 or 3 disc-shaped objects as before, whereas another group of infants were habituated to 2 or 3 square-shaped objects. After this habituation phase, infants saw test trials that always contained the same number of objects they were habituated to, but the shapes of the object were alternated across test trials.

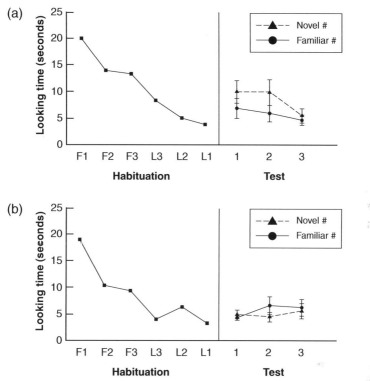

Fig. 5.4 Results from Cheries, Feigenson et al. (2008, in preparation). Habituation and test-trial looking times are presented for infants in the (a) 'occlusion' condition and (b) 'implosion/explosion' condition, collapsed across habituation group. Error bars represent standard errors.

This design allowed for a simple test of whether infants were able to encode and represent the shape of the objects during habituation, despite the potentially distracting implosion and explosion cues. Indeed, infants who were habituated to imploding/exploding discs were found to successfully dishabituate to test displays containing the same number of squares and vice versa. This rules out the possibility that infants are just generally distracted by the implosion/explosion motion, such that they fail to represent any feature of the objects from the habituation trials at all. Rather, the disruptive effect of the anomalous disappearance cue is specific to maintaining representations of the objects' numerical identity over time.

The experiments reviewed in this section illustrate the utility of bridging the adult perception and infant cognition literatures in the context of object persistence in general, and spatiotemporal continuity in particular. As a result, we have learned about the role of spatiotemporal continuity in adult perception, and we have learned about the importance of the *manner* of disappearances and reappearances in infant cognition. In particular, the most recent step in this feedback loop has revealed that violations of spatiotemporal continuity via implosion and explosion cues serve not only to guide orienting (Bertenthal et al., 2007) but also to actively disrupt the underlying numerical representations of infants during passive viewing (Cheries, Feigenson et al., 2008, in preparation).

5.3 Case study 2: Cohesion violations

One of the most powerful principles determining whether something can be tracked as the same persisting individual over time may be that of cohesion: objects must maintain rigid boundaries and internal connectedness as they move over time. This may also be the most intuitive defining characteristic of what it means to be an object in the first place. For instance, to determine whether something is an object, you might just 'grab some portion of stuff and pull: all the stuff that comes with you belongs to the same object; the stuff that remains behind does not' (Bloom, 2000, p. 94; Pinker, 1997). In this way, a cohesion violation differs from other core principles (e.g., continuity) in that an entity's noncohesive motion may both (a) violate how an object is expected to move and, in some conditions, (b) call into question whether the entity was correctly categorized as an object in the first place.

5.3.1 Initial infant research

One way that the principle of cohesion may disrupt our persisting representations is by causing some entity to be categorized as a nonsolid *substance* rather than an object. The 'core knowledge' framework (Spelke, 2000; Spelke & Kinzler, 2007) stipulates that principles such as solidity, continuity, and cohesion selectively apply only to the domain of physical objects per se—and as such, this framework predicts that infants will have few (if any) expectations about events involving entities that are categorized as noncohesive substances. Indeed, infants demonstrate a surprising lack of expectation about physical events involving substances, compared to their apparent savviness when it comes to objects. Even at the same age when infants can successfully remember the precise number of objects that have disappeared behind an occluder (e.g., Wynn, 1992), they fail to demonstrate any expectation about whether a poured substance, such as sand, should continue to exist (Huntley-Fenner et al., 2002; for reviews, see Rosenberg & Carey, Chapter 7; vanMarle, 2004). In this way, the work on noncohesive substances provides some of the strongest evidence to date of the domain-specific nature of our early physical reasoning abilities.

Another way that the principle of cohesion might constrain our representations is by guiding our expectations about how objects ought to behave. Nearly all of our visual experience supports the notion that objects maintain their boundaries and move as connected wholes over time. In fact, even young infants expect that objects will remain cohesive over time. For example, in a display wherein a hand grabs an object from above, infants look longer at events where an object appears split apart due to the grabbing, compared with similar grabbing events involving two objects that already appear separated (Needham, 1999; Spelke & van de Walle, 1993; Xu et al., 1999). This demonstrates one way in which infants' expectations about objects are constrained by cohesion: this principle requires that a solid-looking object will maintain a single cohesive boundary over time.

Previous work from our laboratories has also demonstrated how certain complex types of cohesion violations impair infants' expectations about object persistence. For example, infants' fail to detect the magical disappearance of a pyramid object that has been disassembled into 5 separate blocks, reassembled into its pyramid shape, and then pushed behind a screen (Chiang & Wynn, 2000). This, and a series of control studies, showed how infants' persisting object representations are perturbed by the process of reconstruing a single object as a collection of multiple objects. This could be due to the type of categorization effects discussed earlier, where an object breaking into five smaller pieces is recategorized as a substance that is then no longer bound by the principle of continuity. Alternatively, this disruption may have been due to the fact that a single object file was attempted to be reassigned to multiple objects that exceed the capacity limits of attention in infants (for a review, see Zosh & Feigenson, Chapter 2).

5.3.2 Step 1: Testing for cohesion violations in adult perception

In adult perception research, objects are often contrasted with spatial regions or visual surface features (for a review, see Scholl, 2001), but they had never to our knowledge been contrasted with nonsolid substances—as was so prominent in the infant cognition research noted in the previous section. This observation by itself illustrates the usefulness of exploring object persistence across subfields of cognitive science—because in this case an entire class of entities had been ignored in one field but was prominent in another.

Directly inspired by demonstrations of the importance of cohesion in the infant cognition literature, we sought to determine whether this principle also constrains persisting object representations in adult perception. In an initial study, we used the MOT paradigm (described in Section 5.1.3) to test adults' ability to track objects that move from location to location in a non-cohesive manner (vanMarle & Scholl, 2003). As in the standard MOT task (e.g., Pylyshyn & Storm, 1988; Scholl & Pylyshyn, 1999), adults were presented with a homogeneous array of 8 rectangular objects and were asked to track a particular subset of 4. On *Object* trials, the shapes moved as in typical MOT experiments, maintaining their boundaries over time while their locations shifted. On *Substance* trials, however, the objects moved by disintegrating into streams of pixels, as if being *poured* from one location to the next. Although this 'pouring' motion traced exactly the same trajectories and shifted at the same rates as various other control conditions, subjects' tracking performance was significantly impaired.

This MOT research suggested that tracking (nonsolid) substances was markedly more difficult than tracking discrete bounded objects, but the underlying reason for this difference was unclear. Rather than being due to some sort of categorization *as* a substance, the 'substance tracking' impairment may have been due to a characteristic dynamic *property* of nonsolid substances (vs. objects), which is that they do not have a consistent center of mass over time, to which attention might be locked during tracking (vanMarle & Scholl, 2003; for evidence that tracking does prioritize such a location, see Alvarez & Scholl, 2005). As a result, however, it was an open question whether cohesion violations directly impaired persisting object representations per se.

To study this more specific question, we employed the object-reviewing paradigm as discussed earlier (see Section 5.1.3), and did so with an extremely simplified and 'pure' form of cohesion violation: a single object splitting smoothly into two. This seems like a rather pedestrian type of event, but note that it introduces a critical type of ambiguity. Suppose that you witnessed such an event and were then asked where the initial object was. None of the obvious possible answers (it's just one of the resulting 'twins'; it's neither of them; it's both of them) seems especially satisfying.

To explore the visual system's answer to such questions, adult subjects viewed two circular objects that moved from left to right across a display. During the motion, one of the objects 'split': as it continued to move, it gradually separated into two identical resulting objects (Mitroff et al., 2004; see Fig. 5.5). Critically, this splitting was smooth and symmetrical, so that there was nothing to bias one of the resulting objects over the other. (A second nonsplitting object is also present in each display as a control.) The theoretical question then concerned what would happen to the underlying object representation of the initial object—its 'object file'—as a result of the fission. There are several possibilities that correspond to the intuitive possibilities noted in the preceding: (1) the cohesion violation might obliterate the object file's contents entirely;

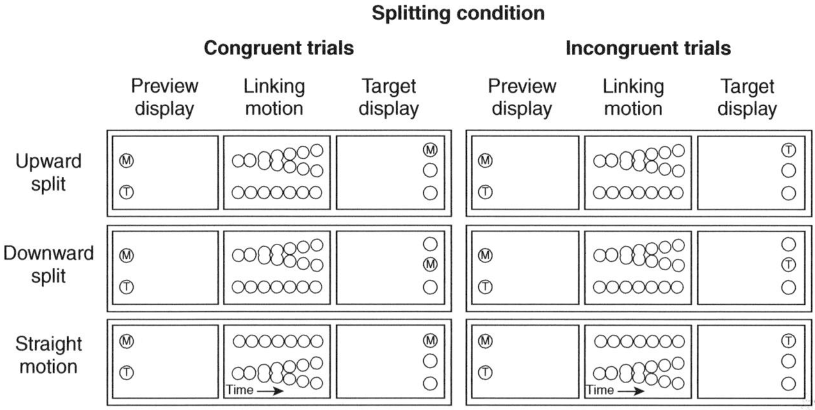

Splitting condition

	Congruent trials			Incongruent trials		
	Preview display	Linking motion	Target display	Preview display	Linking motion	Target display
Upward split	Ⓜ Ⓣ		Ⓜ O	Ⓜ Ⓣ		Ⓣ O
Downward split	Ⓜ Ⓣ		O Ⓜ O	Ⓜ Ⓣ		O Ⓣ O
Straight motion	Ⓜ Ⓣ	Time →	Ⓜ O O	Ⓜ Ⓣ	Time →	Ⓣ O O

Fig. 5.5 A subset of the trial types from a study of cohesion violations using the object-reviewing paradigm (Mitroff et al., 2004). In each case, subjects simply responded as quickly as possible whether the final letter appeared anywhere in the initial preview display on that trial. Objects either traveled a straight trajectory, a curved trajectory, or smoothly split into two separate objects. (The actual experiment also included No-Match trials for each condition, in which the final probe letter was neither of the initially presented letters, and factors such as the relative orientations were always counterbalanced and randomized, such that the final probe letter could appear on any final object.) As described in the text, these cohesion violations produced considerable costs in visual processing, relative to controls that are not depicted here.

(2) the information about the preview letter might survive the 'splitting' intact, but stay bound to only one of the two resulting objects, indicating that object files cannot themselves split into two; or (3) the object file's contents might essentially be 'copied' to both of the two resulting objects.

In fact, this cohesion violation detrimentally affected the subjects' ability to maintain a persisting representation over time and motion in two ways. First, the magnitude of the OSPB for a 'split' object was significantly smaller than that obtained during control trials where there were similar types of motions but no splitting. Second, the OSPB for an additional third object in the display that simply moved across the screen unperturbed was completely eliminated by the existence of splitting elsewhere in the display. These costs suggest that the visual system ends up effectively splitting the actual object representations that underlie the object(s) in this event, such that one object file is eventually replaced with two object files, into which the initial contents of the first file are copied. (There is no indication in these studies of bimodal response patterns, which would suggest that the object file 'went with' only one of the post-split objects.) The fact that this process resulted in substantial costs to visual processing, however, indicates that this event is seen as exceptional, and requires more resources to handle than is the norm in the perception of simple events.

This result demonstrated for the first time how the active maintenance of adults' object representations can be constrained by the principle of cohesion. We may be able to readily *see* objects that split in half (as we commonly do for various types of food, pieces of paper, etc.), but this work suggests that the cohesion violations that accompany such events nevertheless impair forms of underlying visual processing.

5.3.3 Step 2: Testing for impairments due to simple splitting events in infant cognition

The adult perception work described in the previous section was motivated by earlier infant research, but the manipulation that we employed in the object-reviewing study—a single object smoothly splitting into two—was markedly different (and simpler) than the manipulations used in the previous infancy experiments (e.g., pouring sand or disassembled blocks). If cohesion truly operates in infancy as a principle, however, then such a simple violation should nevertheless also impair infants' object representations. (Indeed, although such an event is so simple, that simplicity also serves to make the violation itself that much more 'flagrant'.)

So, directly motivated by our object-reviewing experiments, we tested this prediction using a forced-choice crawling procedure that has been previously used as a direct behavioral measure of infants' quantification abilities (Feigenson et al., 2002). In our version of this task (Cheries, Mitroff et al., 2008), 11-month-old infants witnessed a single trial of an experimenter placing a different number of graham crackers into two spatially separated containers. All infants observed the experimenter placing one graham cracker into one bucket and two graham crackers sequentially placed into the other (a 1 vs. 2 cracker choice). What we varied across subjects was whether the two crackers were initially presented (a) as already-separated entities or (b) created from the experimenter splitting a larger cracker in two (see Fig. 5.6). After observing one of these events, infants were allowed to crawl toward and choose either of the containers.

We replicated previous results demonstrating that a significant majority of infants will reliably crawl to the bucket containing two crackers (Feigenson et al., 2002). However, despite controlling for the overall presentation time and hand motions across conditions, we found that infants in the 'Split Cracker' condition chose randomly between the two buckets (see Fig. 5.7). This result was surprising, seeing as how the crackers entered the buckets in exactly the

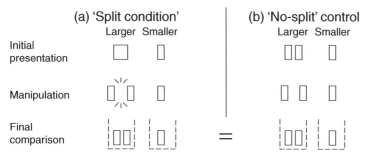

Fig. 5.6 A schematic comparing the key events in the (a) Split condition and (b) No-Split condition of Cheries, Mitroff et al. (2008).

same manner across both conditions; what varied was only how the crackers first appeared to the infant. Also, by this age, infants have had many experiences seeing crackers and other food objects split in half. Although it is possible that some infants, over time, have developed a preference for 'whole' crackers over broken ones, this preference was shown to have no effect in other control conditions.

Even a cohesion violation as simple as a single object splitting in half was sufficient to disrupt infants' ability to choose the container with the greater cracker quantity. However, there are at least two different ways to characterize the nature of this disruption. Attending to a cohesion violation may impair infants' ability to maintain representations of an object's persisting numerical identity, or it may interfere with their ability to represent and use a

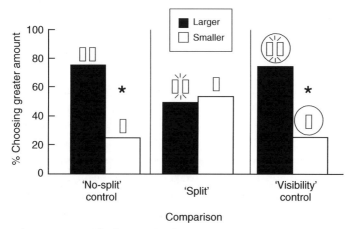

Fig. 5.7 The percentage of subjects who chose the container with the larger amount of crackers in each condition of Cheries, Mitroff et al. (2008).

particular feature of those objects, such as their overall volumes. The distinction between these two interpretations remains ambiguous in the current study because previous research has demonstrated how infants' choosing in this paradigm is based on the relative amount of cracker material (i.e., collapsed across individual crackers) in either of the buckets. The manual-search paradigm (Feigenson & Carey, 2003, 2005; van de Walle et al., 2000; for a review, see Zosh & Feigenson, Chapter 2), on the other hand, has been shown to bias infants' judgments away from their expectations about surface area. Instead, this paradigm elicits infant responses based on the number of individuals that are retrieved from the box (regardless of their size) that are matched to infants' representations of those objects on the basis of one-to-one correspondence (Feigenson & Carey, 2003).

In order to provide convergent evidence for our crawling study and better characterize the nature of the observed disruption, we have recently run an analogous study in slightly older infants using a manual-search paradigm. This allowed us to test, within subjects, whether infants' specific numerical expectations about objects placed into a box were affected by a simple cohesion violation. In this version of the task (Cheries & Carey, in preparation), 12.5-month-old infants witnessed an experimenter place 1 or 2 Lego pieces (4 trials each) into a box that they could reach but could not see into (see Fig. 5.8). In both trial types, infants were allowed to retrieve a single Lego piece by reaching through the fabric on the front of the box. The experimenter would then code the number and duration of reaches during a 10-second coding window. If infants successfully remembered how many Lego pieces entered the box, they should reach relatively less on 1-object trials, when the box should be empty, than on 2-object trials, when there should still be one Lego piece remaining. What varied across the two blocks of trials (in a within-subjects manipulation) was whether the Lego pieces in 2-object trials were initially presented as one larger Lego piece (Fig. 5.8b) or were already separated into two (Fig. 5.8a). As in the previous study, the timing and hand motions were completely controlled across 'Split' and 'No-Split' conditions.

Replicating previous studies using this method, infants successfully reached more on 2-object trials than on 1-object trials when the two Lego pieces were initially presented as two separate objects. However, infants failed to reach significantly more on 2-object trials when the two Lego pieces were created from a larger one splitting in half, even though every other aspect of the presentation was identical. Thus, even the simple and extremely familiar act of a Lego block splitting into two was sufficient to disrupt infants' representations of how many objects were involved in the event. These data demonstrate how

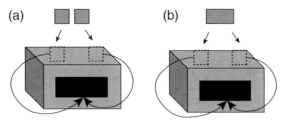

Fig. 5.8 A schematic of the manual search procedure used in Cheries and Carey (in preparation).(a) 'No-Split' trials began with the experimenter placing the box on the table in front of the infant, reaching in, and retrieving two Lego objects with one hand. The experimenter briefly waved the two objects above the box and then sequentially placed each one on opposite corners of the box while saying 'Look!' for each one. After 3 seconds, the experimenter picked up each block one at a time with a single hand and placed the objects in the box. (b) 'Split' trials began with the experimenter placing the box on the table in front of the infant, reaching in, and retrieving a single larger Lego object with one hand. The experimenter briefly waved the single object above the box, split it into two identically sized objects, and sequentially placed each one on opposite corners of the box while saying 'Look!' for each one. After 3 seconds, the experimenter picked up each block one at a time with a single hand and placed the objects in the box.

infants' persisting object representations appear to be powerfully constrained by the principle of cohesion.

The experiments reviewed in this section illustrate the utility of bridging the adult perception and infant cognition literatures in the context of object persistence in general, and cohesion violations in particular. As a result, we have demonstrated for the first time that cohesion plays a role in driving object persistence in adult perception, and that at least some similar types of cohesion violations produce impairments in the contexts of both adult perception and infant cognition. In particular, the most recent step in this feedback loop has revealed that even the simplest possible cohesion violation—of a single familiar object splitting into two—dramatically impairs the ability of infants to maintain persisting representations.

5.4 **Concluding discussion**

Explaining the mind's ability to represent objects as persisting individuals has been a major preoccupation of several fields within the cognitive sciences. The promise of the approach presented here is that empirical results from disparate subject populations and research methodologies can be compared with one another to generate novel and testable hypotheses that are unlikely to have arisen otherwise. The goal of the current chapter was to describe a successful implementation of this approach across the historically independent fields of infant cognition and adult vision science.

In particular, this chapter has focused on how our understanding of two core principles of persistence—continuity and cohesion—has been significantly enhanced by the seesaw relationship between studies in these two fields. The initial explorations of both of these principles in infant cognition directly inspired research in adult vision science, which in turn sparked further and more specific explorations of the operation of these principles back in studies with infant subjects. This feedback loop has advanced our understanding of how these principles influence our persisting object representations in several ways.

First, without noticing the emphasis placed on such cues in the infant literature, vision scientists might not have ever thought to test for the effects that cues to occlusion or cohesion have on adults' persisting object representations. (Indeed, as noted earlier, entire distinctions—such as objects vs. substances—have been prominent in one field but entirely absent in the other.) As a result, we have learned how these principles continue to govern the online maintenance of adults' object representations in mid-level vision in a way that appears to be automatic and remarkably encapsulated from the observer's high-order beliefs. Observing the operation of these principles at this level in adults may also help direct the characterization of infants' performance along the implicit/explicit divide. Before a certain age, infants may only 'know' that objects should remain cohesive in the same way that adults' mid-level visual representations 'know' about cohesion.

In turn, without the corresponding adult vision studies, the infant literature might not have predicted the relatively subtle cues that articulate these constraints. For example, success and failure on the adult tasks was determined by subtle differences (a) between an object gradually disappearing along a fixed contour versus disappearing just as gradually but along all contours at once or (b) between a single object splitting in half versus remaining whole. These manipulations might have first appeared as unlikely candidates to affect infants' representations in the typical free-viewing tasks. (Indeed, one author of this chapter thought it not worth running our initial infant 'graham cracker splitting' study, because he found it so intuitively unlikely that it would succeed!) However, emboldened by the findings with adults, we have discovered how even the relatively subtle object behaviors that define these principles hinder object processing.

Observing the relative strength of these cues across both subject populations has also demonstrated the relative severity of the cost for violating these principles. Each of the subtle manipulations employed in these studies was found to significantly impair or destroy subjects' ability to represent the objects involved in the event. It seems that objects that violate these principles frustrate the computations that support our ability to represent them as the same individuals over time. The representational costs observed in infant subjects were directly predicted by adults' performance using analogous manipulations. Moreover, these deleterious effects constitute a somewhat new amendment to the traditional characterization of the operation of object constraints in infancy. Infants' performance across a large number of physical reasoning tasks is consistent with the idea that the principles of cohesion and continuity constrain their expectations and interpretations of physical events.

For instance, infants often look reliably longer at physical events that violate these principles (e.g., Baillargeon et al., 1985), and tend to favor event interpretations that avoid such violations altogether, inferring the presence of additional objects if necessary (e.g., Spelke et al., 1995; Xu & Carey, 1996). However, these studies did not indicate whether these core principles similarly constrain the maintenance of infants' persisting object representations per se. It is well established that infants will react by looking longer to various types of object violations, but most studies stop short of asking whether the object representations themselves incur any type of penalty. However, the studies discussed in this chapter, motivated by the adult vision results, show how violating these principles imposes additional processing demands that severely disrupt infants' representations of the objects involved in the event. A failure to represent objects through such violations is suggestive that the computations involved in object persistence are constrained by these principles.

Finally, the studies reviewed in this chapter have also demonstrated how violating the principles of cohesion and spatiotemporal continuity produce deleterious effects that are remarkably continuous across development. It is unlikely that the subtle processing costs for such violations in adult perception are due to a lifetime of experience viewing objects as they normally behave in the world, because these effects seem to operate even more powerfully in infants who lack as much experience. This pattern suggests how these constraints may constitute the foundation of our object understanding from very early on or possibly even from birth. The effects may become less severe across development as we gradually develop auxiliary resources that can compensate for these representational limitations, but these results reinforce the 'core' nature of these principles of core knowledge. In summary, the two case studies presented in this chapter—focusing on the principles of spatiotemporal continuity and cohesion, respectively—highlight the benefits of explicitly and directly exploring how infant cognition research can inform adult perception research, and vice versa.

References

Aguiar, A., & Baillargeon, R. (1999). 2.5-month-old infants reasoning about when objects should and should not be occluded. *Cognitive Psychology, 39,* 116–157.

Aguiar, A., & Baillargeon, R. (2002). Developments in young infants' reasoning about occluded objects. *Cognitive Psychology, 45,* 267–336.

Alvarez, G. A., & Scholl, B. J. (2005). How does attention select and track spatially extended objects? New effects of attentional concentration and amplification. *Journal of Experimental Psychology: General, 134,* 461–476.

Anstis, S. M. (1980). The perception of apparent movement. *Philosophical Transactions of the Royal Society of London B, 290,* 153–168.

Antell, S., & Keating, D. (1983). Perception of numerical invariance in neonates. *Child Development, 54,* 695–701.

Baillargeon, R. (1987). Object permanence in 3.5- and 4.5-month-old infants. *Developmental Psychology, 23,* 655–664.

Baillargeon, R. (1999). Young infants' expectations about hidden objects: a reply to three challenges. *Developmental Science, 2,* 115–132.

Baillargeon, R., & DeVos, J. (1991). Object permanence in young infants: further evidence. *Child Development, 62,* 1227–1246.

Baillargeon, R., Spelke, E. S., & Wasserman, S. (1985). Object permanence in five-month-old infants. *Cognition, 20,* 191–208.

Bertenthal, B. I., Longo, M. R., & Kenny, S. (2007). Phenomenal permanence and the development of predictive tracking in infancy. *Child Development, 78,* 350–363.

Bloom, P. (2000). *How Children Learn the Meanings of Words.* Cambridge, MA: MIT Press.

Burke, L. (1952). On the tunnel effect. *Quarterly Journal of Experimental Psychology, 4,* 121–138.

Carey, S., & Spelke, E. S. (1996). Science and core knowledge. *Philosophy of Science, 63,* 515–533.

Carey, S., & Xu, F. (2001). Infants knowledge of objects: beyond object-files and object tracking. *Cognition, 80,* 179–213.

Cheries, E. W., & Carey, S. (in preparation). Cohesion disrupts infants' representations of numerical identity.

Cheries, E. W., Feigenson, L., Scholl, B. J., & Carey, S. (2008). Cues to object persistence in infancy: tracking objects through occlusion vs. implosion. Poster presented at the International Conference on Infant Studies, 29 March 2008, Vancouver, BC, Canada.

Cheries, E. W., Feigenson, L., Scholl, B. J., & Carey, S. (in preparation). Cues to object persistence in infancy: tracking objects through occlusion vs. implosion.

Cheries, E. W., Mitroff, S. R., Wynn, K., & Scholl, B. J. (2008). Cohesion as a constraint on object persistence in infancy. *Developmental Science, 11,* 427–432.

Cheries, E. W., & Wynn, K. (2007). Individual-tracking in infants' arithmetic. Symposium talk presented at the Harvard NSRCD Mini-Conference, 28 March 2007, Cambridge, MA.

Cheries, E. W., Wynn, K., & Scholl, B. J. (2006). Interrupting infants' persisting object representations: an object-based limit? *Developmental Science, 9,* F50–F58.

Chiang, W. C., & Wynn, K. (2000). Infants' tracking of objects and collections. *Cognition*, *77*, 169–195.

Dawson, M. (1991). The how and why of what went where in apparent motion: modeling solutions to the motion correspondence problem. *Psychological Review*, *98*, 569–603.

Feigenson, L. (2005). A double dissociation in infants' representation of object arrays. *Cognition*, *95*, B37–B48.

Feigenson, L., & Carey, S. (2003). Tracking individuals via object-files: evidence from infants' manual search. *Developmental Science*, *6*, 568–584.

Feigenson, L., & Carey, S. (2005). On the limits of infants' quantification of small object arrays. *Cognition*, *97*, 295–313.

Feigenson, L., Carey, S., & Hauser, M. (2002). The representations underlying infants' choice of more: object files versus analog magnitudes. *Psychological Science*, *13*, 150–156.

Feigenson, L., Dehaene, S., & Spelke, E. S. (2004). Core systems of number. *Trends in Cognitive Sciences*, *7*, 307–314.

Fiser, J., Scholl, D. J., & Aslin, R. N. (2007). Perceived object trajectories during occlusion constrain visual statistical learning. *Psychological Bulletin and Review*, *14*, 173–178.

Flombaum, J. I., Kundey, S. M., Santos, L. R., & Scholl, B. J. (2004). Dynamic object individuation in rhesus macaques: a study of the tunnel effect. *Psychological Science*, *15*, 795–800.

Flombaum, J. I., & Scholl, B. J. (2006). A temporal same-object advantage in the tunnel effect: facilitated change detection for persisting objects. *Journal of Experimental Psychology: Human Perception and Performance*, *32*(4), 840–853.

Flombaum, J. I., Scholl, B. J., & Pylyshyn, Z. W. (2008). Attentional resources in visual tracking through occlusion: the high-beams effect. *Cognition*, *107*, 904–931.

Gao, T., & Scholl, B. J. (in press). Are objects required for object-files? Roles of segmentation and spatiotemporal continuity in computing object persistence. *Visual Cognition*.

Huntley-Fenner, G., Carey, S., & Solimando, A. (2002). Objects are individuals but stuff doesn't count: perceived rigidity and cohesiveness influence infants' representations of small numbers of discrete entities. *Cognition*, *85*, 203–221.

Kahneman, D., & Treisman, A. (1984). Changing views of attention and automaticity. In R. Parasuraman, & D. R. Davies (Eds.), *Varieties of Attention* (pp. 29–61). New York: Academic Press.

Kahneman, D., Treisman, A., & Gibbs, B. (1992). The reviewing of object files: object-specific integration of information. *Cognitive Psychology*, *24*, 175–219.

Kaufman, J., Csibra, G., & Johnson, M. (2005). Oscillatory activity in the infant brain reflects object maintenance. *Proceedings of the National Academy of Sciences*, *102*, 15271–15274.

Koechlin, E., Dehaene, S., & Mehler, J. (1997). Numerical transformations in five-month-old human infants. *Mathematical Cognition*, *3*, 89–104.

Lipton, J. S., & Spelke, E. S. (2004). Discrimination of large and small numerosities by human infants. *Infancy*, *5*, 271–290.

McCrink, K., & Wynn, K. (2004). Large number addition and subtraction by 9-month-old infants. *Psychological Science*, *15*, 776–781.

Michotte, A., Thinès, G., & Crabbé, G. (1964/1991). Les complements amodaux des structures perceptives. In *Studia Psychologica*. Louvain: Publications Universitaires. Reprinted and translated as Michotte, A., Thinès, G., & Crabbé, G. (1991). Amodal completion of perceptual structures. In G. Thines, A. Costall, & G. Butterworth (Eds.), *Michotte's Experimental Phenomenology of Perception* (pp. 140–167). Hillsdale, NJ: Erlbaum.

Mitroff, S. R., & Alvarez, G. A. (2007). Space and time, not surface features, underlie object persistence. *Psychonomic Bulletin and Review, 14*, 1199–1204.

Mitroff, S. R., & Scholl, B. J. (2005). Forming and updating object representations without awareness: evidence from motion-induced blindness. *Vision Research, 45*, 961–967.

Mitroff, S. R., Scholl, B. J., & Wynn, K. (2004). Divide and conquer: how object files adapt when a persisting object splits into two. *Psychological Science, 15*, 420–425.

Moore, C. M., & Lleras, A. (2005). On the role of object representations in substitution masking. *Journal of Experimental Psychology: Human Perception and Performance, 31*, 1171–1180.

Nakayama, K., He, Z. J., & Shimojo, S. (1995). Visual surface representation: a critical link between lower-level and higher-level vision. In S. Kosslyn (Ed.), *An Invitation to Cognitive Science, Vol. 2: Visual Cognition*, 2nd edn. (pp. 1–70). Cambridge, MA: MIT Press.

Needham, A. (1999). The role of shape in 4-month-old infants' segregation of adjacent objects. *Infant Behavior and Development, 22*, 161–178.

Noles, N. S., Scholl, B. J., & Mitroff, S. R. (2005). The persistence of object file representations. *Perception and Psychophysics, 67*, 324–334.

Pinker, S. (1997). *How the Mind Works*. New York: Norton; London: Penguin.

Pylyshyn, Z. (2006). Some puzzling findings in multiple object tracking (MOT): II. Inhibition of moving nontargets. *Visual Cognition, 14*, 175–198.

Pylyshyn, Z., Haladjian, H., King, C., & Reilly, J. (2008). Selective nontarget inhibition in multiple object tracking (MOT). *Visual Cognition, 16*, 1011–1021.

Pylyshyn, Z., & Storm, R. (1988). Tracking multiple independent targets: evidence for a parallel tracking mechanism. *Spatial Vision, 2*, 179–197.

Rips, L., Blok, S., & Newman, G. (2006). Tracing the identity of objects. *Psychological Review, 113*, 1–30.

Santos, L. R. (2004). 'Core knowledges': a dissociation between spatiotemporal knowledge and contact-mechanics in a non-human primate? *Developmental Science, 7*, 164–174.

Scholl, B. J. (2001). Objects and attention: the state of the art. *Cognition, 80*, 1–46.

Scholl, B. J. (2007). Object persistence in philosophy and psychology. *Mind and Language, 22*, 563–591.

Scholl, B. J. (in press). What have we learned about attention from multiple object tracking (and vice versa)? In D. Dedrick, & L. Trick (Eds.), *Computation, Cognition, and Pylyshyn*. Cambridge, MA: MIT Press.

Scholl, B. J., & Feigenson, L. (2004). When out of sight is out of mind: perceiving object persistence through occlusion vs. implosion [Abstract]. *Journal of Vision, 4*, 26a. Available at: http://journalofvision.org/4/8/26/ [Last accessed: 10 December 2008].

Scholl, B. J., & Flombaum, J. I. (in press). Object persistence. In B. Goldstein (Ed.), *Sage Encyclopedia of Perception*. Thousand Oaks, CA: Sage Publications.

Scholl, B. J., & Leslie, A. M. (1999). Explaining the infant's object concept: beyond the perception/cognition dichotomy. In E. Lepore, & Z. Pylyshyn (Eds.), *What Is Cognitive Science?* (pp. 26–73). Oxford, UK: Blackwell.

Scholl, B. J., & Pylyshyn, Z. W. (1999). Tracking multiple items through occlusion: clues to visual objecthood. *Cognitive Psychology, 38,* 259–290.

Sharon, T., & Wynn, K. (1998). Infants' individuation of actions from continuous motion. *Psychological Science, 9,* 357–362.

Shinskey, J. L., & Munakata, Y. (2003). Are infants in the dark about hidden objects? *Developmental Science, 6,* 273–282.

Simon, T. J., Hespos, S. J., & Rochat, P. (1995). Do infants understand simple arithmetic? A replication of Wynn (1992). *Cognitive Development, 10,* 253–269.

Spelke, E. S. (2000). Core knowledge. *American Psychologist, 55,* 1233–1243.

Spelke, E. S., Breinlinger, K., Macomber, J., & Jacobson, K. (1992). Origins of knowledge. *Psychological Review, 99,* 605–632.

Spelke, E. S., Kestenbaum, R., Simons, D. & Wein, D. (1995). Spatiotemporal continuity, smoothness of motion and object identity in infancy. *The British Journal of Developmental Psychology, 13,* 113–142.

Spelke, E. S., & Kinzler, K. D. (2007). Core knowledge. *Developmental Science, 10,* 89–96.

Spelke, E. S., & van de Walle, G. (1993). Perceiving and reasoning about objects: insights from infants. In N. Eilan, R. McCarthy, & W. Brewer (Eds.), *Spatial Representation* (pp. 132–161). Oxford, UK: Basil Blackwell.

Starkey, P., & Cooper, R. (1980). Perception of numbers by human infants. *Science, 210,* 1033–1035.

Strauss, M. S., & Curtis, L. E. (1981). Infant perception of numerosity. *Child Development, 52,* 1146–52.

Valenza, E., Leo, I., Gava, L., & Simion, F. (2006). Perceptual completion in newborn infants. *Child Development, 77,* 1810–1821.

van de Walle, G., Carey, S., & Prevor, M. (2000). Bases for object individuation in infancy: evidence from manual search. *Journal of Cognition and Development, 1,* 249–280.

van Loosbroek, E., & Smitsman, A. (1990). Visual perception of numerosity in infancy. *Developmental Psychology, 26,* 911–922.

vanMarle, K. L. (2004). Infants' understanding of number: the relationship between discrete and continuous quantity. *Dissertation Abstracts International, 65*(3), 1582B.

vanMarle, K., & Scholl, B. J. (2003). Attentive tracking of objects versus substances. *Psychological Science, 14,* 498–504.

Wertheimer, M. (1912/1961). Experimentelle Studien über das Sehen von Bewegung. Zeitschrift für Psychologie, *61,* 161–265. Reprinted and translated as Wertheimer, M. (1961). Experimental studies on the seeing of motion. In T. Shipley (Ed. and Trans.), *Classics in Psychology* (pp. 1032–1089). New York: Philosophical Library.

Wood, J. N., & Spelke, E. S. (2005). Infants' enumeration of actions: numerical discrimination and its signature limits. *Developmental Science, 8,* 173–181.

Wynn, K. (1992). Addition and subtraction by human infants. *Nature, 358,* 749–750.

Wynn, K. (1996). Infants' individuation and enumeration of actions. *Psychological Science, 7,* 165–169.

Wynn, K., Bloom, P., & Chiang, W-C. (2002). Enumeration of collective entities by 5-month-old infants. *Cognition*, *83*, B55–B62.

Xu, F. (2003). Numerosity discrimination in infants: evidence for two systems of representations. *Cognition*, *89*, B15–B25.

Xu, F., & Carey, S. (1996). Infants' metaphysics: the case of numerical identity. *Cognitive Psychology*, *30*, 111–153.

Xu, F., Carey, S., & Welch, J. (1999). Infants' ability to use object kind information for object individuation. *Cognition*, *70*, 137–166.

Xu, F., & Spelke, E. S. (2000). Large number discrimination in 6-month-old infants. *Cognition*, *74*, B1–B11.

Yilmaz, A., Javed, O., & Shah, M. (2006). Object tracking: a survey. *ACM Computing Surveys*, *38*, 13.

Chapter 6

Spatiotemporal priority as a fundamental principle of object persistence

Jonathan I. Flombaum, Brian J. Scholl, & Laurie R. Santos

6.1 Introduction

The impoverished and rapidly changing stimulation on the retina looks very different from the stable world of discrete persisting objects that populate our visual experience. To get from the features on the retina to the objects that we experience, the visual system must solve several correspondence problems. One of these problems has to do with *sameness*: the visual system must decide whether each bit of stimulation reflects an object that has already been encountered (which might occasion the *updating* of an existing object representation) or a new one (which might occasion the *creation* of a new object representation). This problem of object persistence has been studied with a wide array of visual phenomena and paradigms, and in several disciplines in cognitive science—including vision science, developmental psychology, and comparative cognition.

The study of object persistence in these different fields has progressed largely independently. Yet strikingly, they have converged on a core principle that guides the creation and maintenance of persisting object representations: the principle of *spatiotemporal priority*. When identifying objects as the same individuals over the time, the visual system appears to rely on their spatiotemporal histories—that is, where, when, and how they were encountered—to a greater degree than their visual surface features. In this chapter, we review the many contexts in which spatiotemporal priority drives computations of object persistence, and we propose explanations at several levels for why spatiotemporal priority plays this dominant role.

6.1.1 **The problem of persistence**

Suppose that you have just spent several hours at a large suburban shopping mall, and you must now retrieve your Prius from the parking lot. When you exit the mall, a sea of cars overwhelms you. How will you decide which is yours? This is a type of correspondence problem: you must find the car that corresponds to the one in which you arrived. These kinds of problems are extremely prevalent in moment-to-moment visual experience, but because they are solved so efficiently, we may not always realize it. Indeed, the problem of object persistence is fundamentally a problem of correspondence: our visual system must constantly decide whether current stimulation reflects a novel object, or whether it corresponds to an object that was already encountered a moment ago (Scholl & Flombaum, in press). If we couldn't solve this type of problem, visual experience would be incoherent. This is a problem in part due to the sheer information load involved, and in part because a previously experienced object may be reencountered—even a moment later—in a different location (perhaps after a visual interruption such as occlusion), and/or with different visual surface features. How are these challenges overcome? How do we readily see objects as the *same* enduring individuals from moment to moment?

In the case of finding your Prius in the mall's crowded parking lot, there are at least two ways to solve the problem: you might scan the lot for a car that *looks* like yours or you might try to remember where exactly you parked it. These same two solutions are available to meet the challenges of persistence in online perception. First, the visual system can rely on what objects look like to reidentify them: 'this red square must be the same red square that I just saw a moment ago.' Second, the visual system can rely on where and when various objects appear: 'this object *here* must be same object that was previously over *there* but was moving fast in exactly this direction.' Research across a wide array of disciplines and phenomena converges on a simple pattern of results: the second kind of solution trumps the first. That is, the correspondences favored by spatiotemporal considerations will almost always trump those favored by featural similarity. We will term this the *principle of spatiotemporal priority* (see also Scholl, 2001b).

This bias may seem intuitively surprising. If in the mall parking lot you arrived at the location where you left your Prius but found an Escalade in that location, you would not naturally assume that your car had somehow changed its appearance while you were busy shopping. Yet, the visual system seems comfortable making analogous assumptions. In fact, because of spatiotemporal priority, we readily see impossible featural transformations in a variety of visual phenomena, and infants and nonhuman primates often make rather large errors when keeping track of objects because they discount objects' surface properties. In the next two sections, we review this evidence.

6.2 **Spatiotemporal priority in adult visual cognition**
6.2.1 **Amodal completion**

Among the most extensively studied correspondence problems in visual perception is the phenomenon of amodal completion—our ability to perceive objects as completing behind occluders (Kanizsa, 1979; Michotte et al., 1964/1991; Wertheimer, 1912/1961). For example, we naturally see two of the line segments in Fig. 6.1a as two ends of the same line, occluded by the box. And, despite the 'ink spills', we can naturally bind together the many segments in Fig. 6.1b in order to recognize the necker cube. This is a spatial effect, of course, rather than a spatiotemporal effect, but it illustrates the character of the problem and its solutions. In particular, note that the completion in Fig. 6.1a cannot be based only on the surface similarity of the line segments, because there are many other identical segments that are not bound to one another. Instead, visual completion in such spatial contexts is driven by subtle factors of how the line segments are aligned relative to each other (e.g., Kellman & Shipley, 1991; Singh & Fulvio, 2005). One way to explain such effects is in terms of the visual system's tendency to avoid coincidences: in these cases, the occluded fragments are aligned in a way that would be highly coincidental if they were in fact unrelated. This is a conclusion that the visual system is unwilling to accept, and so it settles on an interpretation of occluded objects, which 'explains away' the coincidence.

This emphasis on spatial alignment rather than featural similarity is notable in two ways. First, it means that segments may be bound into the same (occluded) object representations even when those segments look different (as in Fig. 6.1c; e.g., Walker & Davies, 2003); inconsistencies in surface appearances, in other words, do not preclude completion. Second, an emphasis on spatial alignment means that we almost always perceive the most direct link between unoccluded segments, as in Fig. 6.1d and 6.1e (adapted from examples in Kanizsa, 1982). These cases also highlight the nature of such processing as fundamentally perceptual rather than cognitive—because it might be more natural to *think* that regular patterns in these images simply continue behind the occluders, although this clearly not what you see.

6.2.2 **Amodal integration and the tunnel effect**

The previous section lingered on a type of *spatial* correspondence problem largely because the nature of the problem—and its solution—is entirely

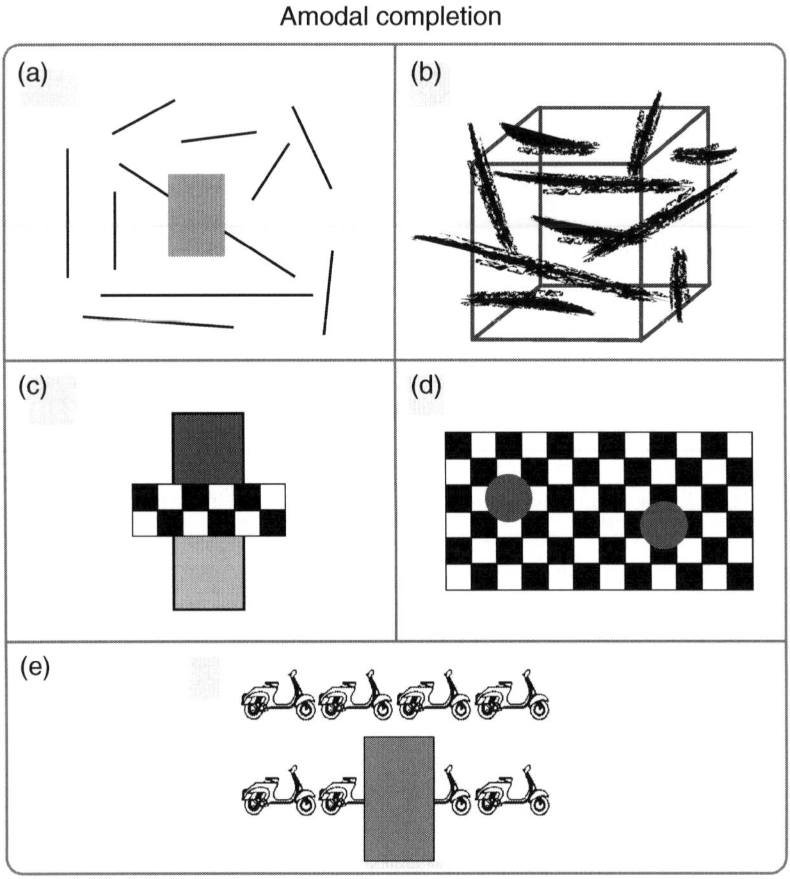

Amodal completion

Fig. 6.1 Examples of amodal completion. (a) We readily bind segments together to perceive whole objects despite occlusion. (b) This phenomenon is robust, and we can even recognize large objects that are occluded in multiple places. (c) Completion can occur on the basis of spatial alignment, despite differences in surface features. (d) The binding process often ignores featural regularities, for example, leading us to see the circles as occluding black and white crosses, even though it makes more 'sense', cognitively, to interpret the entire background as a checkerboard (adapted from Kanizsa, 1982). (e) Similarly, we see a single 'anomalous' extended scooter behind the occluder, even though it makes more 'sense', cognitively, to interpret all the scooters as identical (adapted from Kanizsa, 1982).

analogous in spatio*temporal* contexts that require correspondences among objects encountered at different times and places. Inspired by the phenomenon of amodal completion, Luke Burke and Albert Michotte realized in the 1950s that we do not only see *parts* of a static object that are currently occluded but we also readily see *entire* objects as persisting through periods of occlusion. Here is their elegant description of the problem:

> Let us suppose a cyclist has to pass behind some stationary object in the centre of the street in which we are standing. He moves towards the object, disappears from view, and a moment later reappears at the other side. In this every day fact we have ... an intriguing problem in the psychology of perception. Every observer is convinced that cyclist has been continuously in motion. Is this merely a matter of belief or of knowledge based on past experience or is the continuity of the movement actually 'seen' by the observer?

(Burke, 1959, p. 122)

To answer these questions, they constructed demonstrations of various objects passing at different speeds behind occluders of various lengths, and they simply asked observers to report their percepts. The responses they collected (and indeed, their own visual experiences) confirmed that we really do see such events in terms of the (occluded) motion of a single persisting object. This type of dynamic 'amodal integration' is the spatiotemporal analogue of spatial amodal completion. And similar to amodal completion, the phenomenon is exquisitely sensitive to the details: when the conditions are not quite right for amodal integration, observers will instead see two distinct objects—one which disappears behind an occluder and another that later emerges. Thus, the computations that underlie amodal integration influence the contents of our mental experience—determining whether we perceive one object or two (Burke, 1952; Michotte et al., 1964/1991).

Burke and Michotte also made two other key observations about amodal integration. First, they observed that we may often see a single occluded moving object even if the object that enters an occluder looks very different from the one that later emerges. For example, the occluding object might be light and the disoccluding object might be dark—but we would (often irresistibly) perceive this in terms of a single object that *changed* from light to dark, rather than as two separate objects (Fig. 6.2a). They termed this phenomenon of amodal integration despite featural heterogeneity the *tunnel effect*. Conversely, they noted that we *fail* to perceive an amodally integrated object—even if its features do *not* change—if the disoccluding object emerges at the wrong time (Fig. 6.2b) or place (Fig. 6.2c) given its initial trajectory. To summarize both observations, spatiotemporal factors such as continuity trump objects' surface features during computations of object persistence.

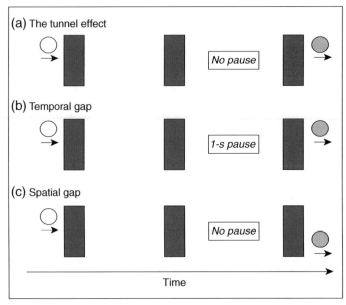

Fig. 6.2 The tunnel effect. (a) We readily perceive a persisting object through occlusion, even if the pre- and post-occlusion views have distinct features (e.g., color), provided that the disoccluding object appears at the right time and place. The percept does not obtain, however, when the trajectories are discontinuous as a result of either a temporal gap (b) or spatial gap (c).

This spatiotemporal bias is more than just a quirk in perception. Instead, it appears to be a central feature of our underlying representations of persisting objects—and as a result, spatiotemporal priority can impact the downstream processes and behaviors that rely on these representations. For example, in a study of the influence of object persistence on visual memory, we recently discovered that an amodally integrated percept facilitates change detection of objects' colors (Flombaum & Scholl, 2006). Our displays included several independent dynamic events in which an object disappeared behind an occluder, and then an object emerged from the other side of the occluder, as depicted in Fig. 6.3. (These effects are inherently dynamic, and readers can view example displays at http://www.yale.edu/perception/tunnel/.)

Observers' task was simply to press a key when they detected a color change (i.e., when a disoccluding object was a different color from an occluding object) in any of the simultaneously moving events. Subjects were more accurate in these judgments under conditions when the tunnel effect obtained— that is, when the two objects were bound into the same underlying object representation—compared with when two objects were perceived (such as

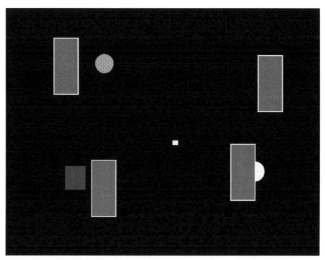

Fig. 6.3 The tunnel effect and visual memory. A static snapshot (not to scale) of a sample display in Experiment 1 from Flombaum and Scholl (2006). Readers can view dynamic animations of the conditions from each experiment online at http://www.yale.edu/perception/tunnel/.

cases involving spatial and temporal gaps, as in Fig. 6.2b and 6.2c). In other words, visual memory was better when the color change involved *updating* a single representation, rather than comparing two distinct representations. These studies indicate that spatiotemporal priority determines not just what we see, but also how well we remember it. Spatiotemporal priority is evidently not just a heuristic for perceiving persisting objects, but it underlies the way that we represent objects from moment to moment.

6.2.3 **Apparent motion**

Perhaps the most extensively studied example of spatiotemporal priority in visual cognition is apparent motion. In apparent motion, we readily see a continuous motion trajectory when an object appears in one location, disappears, and then an object quickly appears in another nearby location (Anstis, 1980; Wertheimer, 1912/1961; see Fig. 6.4a). This is another example of a type of coincidence avoidance in perception: the two spatiotemporally proximate flashes are judged unlikely to be independent, and the result is a percept that binds them together.

As in the tunnel effect and amodal completion, spatiotemporal factors primarily determine whether and when this percept obtains. We can readily see apparent motion when the two discrete flashes involve objects that

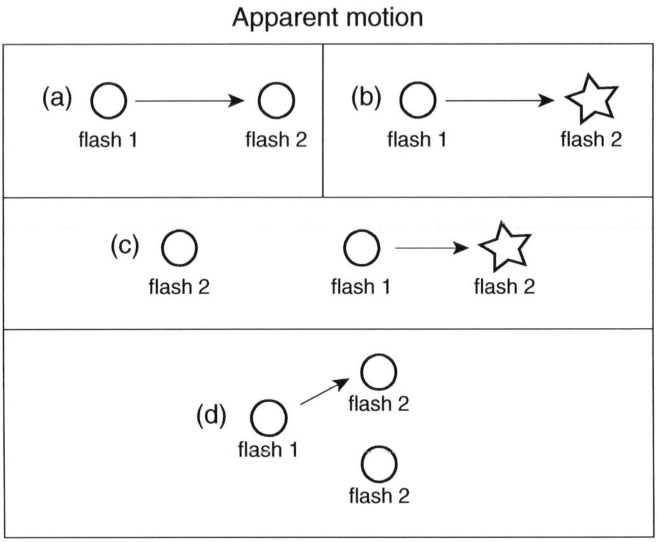

Fig. 6.4 Apparent motion. (a) In apparent motion, we are presented with two discrete stationary flashes, but we see a single object move between the flashed locations. (b) This percept obtains even if the two flashes look dissimilar, and (c) distance trumps featural similarity when matches favoring these factors are both available. (d) Apparent motion also obeys the spatiotemporal rule of solidity, or object integrity: when two equidistant correspondences are available, we see only a single motion trajectory.

look very different from each other, so long as the flashes are close enough in time and space (Kolers, 1972; Fig. 6.4b). Conversely, we will fail to see apparent motion when the flashes are not sufficiently spatiotemporally proximate, even if they look identical (e.g., Dawson, 1991). Moreover, distance trumps surface appearance. When an object disappears and then two objects appear simultaneously, another correspondence problem arises: which of the two new objects (if either) is the same individual as the one that disappeared? The visual system's solution to this correspondence problem depends on distance: we will see apparent motion linking the disappeared object with the one that appears closer to the disappearance, even if the more distant one would avoid a large featural transformation, as in Fig. 6.4c (Kolers & Pomerantz, 1971). In some experiments, there appears to be no preference at all for featurally consistent versus inconsistent percepts, even with all other spatiotemporal factors held equal (Burt & Sperling, 1981). Thus, at best, surface features play a weak, secondary, and indirect role in generating apparent motion percepts. Changes in surface features are not sufficient to produce motion on their own; they must be accompanied by spatiotemporal changes (Navon, 1976). When they do have an impact, they do so merely by modulating sensitivity to distance (Shechter et al., 1988), and models of apparent motion have estimated the impact of surface features on motion correspondence is as much as 80 times weaker than the impact of spatiotemporal factors (Dawson, 1991).

In fact, successful models of apparent motion are best characterized in terms of a handful of simple spatiotemporal rules that also seem to apply in related phenomena such as amodal completion and integration (Dawson, 1991). In particular, because of the *nearest neighbor principle*, we tend to perceive apparent motion trajectories that minimize the distance traveled (Fig. 6.4c). Similarly, in displays where several correspondence problems need to be solved simultaneously, the *relative velocity principle* leads to a minimization of the amount of relative motion between corresponding pairs. In other words, global spatiotemporal properties in a display, not just local ones, also drive apparent motion—but once again, these computations function irrespective of surface features (e.g., Dawson, 1991; Ramachandran & Anstis, 1986). Finally, according to the *element integrity principle*, perception avoids generating correspondences whereby an element is split into parts (i.e., one element moves to two new locations simultaneously; see Fig. 6.4d), or whereby two elements fuse together (e.g., Dawson, 1991; Ullman, 1979). As we discuss later, a similar spatiotemporal principle, often called *cohesion*, seems to drive infants' reasoning about persisting objects.

As in amodal integration and the tunnel effect, the principle of spatiotemporal priority in apparent motion affects more than just what we see. In one relevant study, for example, observers had to detect repeated letters that appeared in two rapid serial visual presentation (RSVP) streams (Chun & Cavanagh, 1997). These two RSVP streams were not spatially stationary, however; instead, they constituted locations in two different apparent motion streams that passed by one another. Thus, as depicted in Fig. 6.5, letter repetitions could occur in a single apparent motion stream (making those letters the changing features of a single object over time)—or in two different apparent motion streams (making each cross-stream appearance of a repeated letter a feature of a different object). A common phenomenon in RSVP displays is that closely spaced repetitions are difficult to detect and perceive—a phenomenon known as *repetition blindness* (Kanwisher, 1987). In this experiment, however, observers experienced more repetition blindness for repeated letters that appeared in a single apparent motion stream, compared with those that appeared in distinct motion streams—even though the timing and spacing of these repetitions were identical in all conditions (Chun & Cavanagh, 1997). Thus, the spatiotemporal rules that guide the experience of apparent motion can also impact how we attend to the world

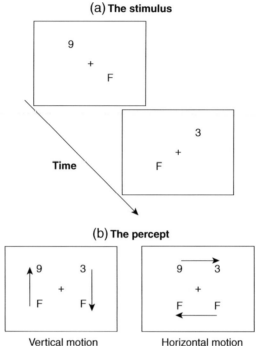

Fig. 6.5 Apparent motion and repetition blindness. (a) Chun and Cavanagh (1997) presented observers with motion quartets that could be biased toward a percept of either vertical or horizontal motion by the preceding apparent motion streams. (b) These observers detected fewer letter repetitions (i.e., they exhibited more repetition blindness) when repeated letters appeared in the same apparent motion stream (e.g., as in the 'Horizontal motion' panel), compared with when they appeared in different apparent motion streams (e.g., as in the 'Vertical motion' panel). (Adapted from Chun & Cavanagh, 1997)

and can ultimately even influence whether we will be visually aware of an object in the first place.

6.2.4 Illusory conjunctions

Similar to many of the challenges faced by the visual system, the challenge of object persistence is at root a type of inverse problem. Discrete and persisting objects exist in the real world, but this information is lost during optical transmission and must be reconstructed. One idiosyncratic aspect of this challenge is known as the *binding problem*. Objects in the real world possess a variety of features such as color, shape, size, and position. During the earliest phases of visual processing, these features are processed by distinct neural circuitry, and so this information must be later rebound in order to produce the impression

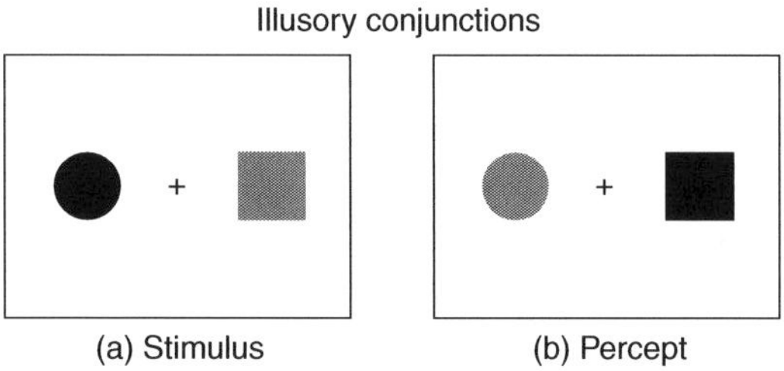

Illusory conjunctions

(a) Stimulus   (b) Percept

Fig. 6.6 Illusory conjunctions. Treisman and Schmidt (1982) demonstrated that under high attentional loads, observers sometimes misbind objects' surface features, such as lightness or color.

of coherent persisting individuals, with the right features attached to the right objects. In everyday life, it is difficult to recognize this challenge, because it is almost always met so successfully. Sometimes the binding operation does not work as accurately as it should, however, and we perceive *illusory conjunctions* between features and objects (Treisman & Schmidt, 1982; see Fig. 6.6).

An interesting aspect of such illusory conjunctions is that they appear to preserve spatiotemporal features at the expense of surface features. That is, the surface features, not the spatiotemporal features, seem capable of being bound to the wrong object. For example, if you are quickly presented with a red triangle on the left and a blue circle on the right, you might see a red circle on the left (misbinding shape to the wrong object), but you will not see a red triangle on the right (misbinding location to the wrong object). If all features were created equal—shape, color, and location, in this example—then these two illusory conjunctions would be equally likely. But all features are not created equal, and in the case of such illusory conjunctions, location seems privileged.

This same pattern occurs in more extreme cases of illusory conjunctions that arise in certain neuropsychological syndromes. For example, patients with Balint syndrome are frequently able to perceive only a single object at a time (for a review, see Rafal, 1997). Despite seeing only one object in a display filled with multiple objects, however, the single perceived object will occasionally serially adopt the surface properties of the other objects in the display—so that, for example, they might see a red circle that shifts to blue, then green, and so on (Humphreys et al., 2000; Robertson et al., 1997). Again, this is a case of a surface feature (color) floating free of an object. In contrast, spatial location does not seem to do this: these patients never report seeing a red circle in one place, and then having it shift to another location. It has even been suggested that Balint syndrome actually reflects an inability to represent more than a single spatial location at a time, which in turn results in the inability to perceive more than one object at a time (Rafal, 1997).

A more recent example of illusory conjunctions makes this type of spatiotemporal priority especially salient, extending the priority to direction of motion (Wu et al., 2004). In this demonstration, observers fixate the center of a large display with an array of many moving dots. Some of the dots move upward, whereas some of the dots move downward; likewise, some of the dots are red and some are green. In the center of the display, all the green dots move up and all the red move down. But at the peripheries, these motion directions are reversed: red dots move up and green dots move down. Nonetheless, observers perceive the peripheral dots as obeying the regularity set by the dots near fixation: they perceive *all* of the green dots in the display as moving up, and *all* the red dots as moving down.

This is a striking example of illusory conjunctions persisting over time and on a large scale, and it occurs because of a type of spatiotemporal priority: global motion coherence appears to be more important to the visual system than correctly locating green things and red things. Illusory conjunctions thus suggest that position appears privileged relative to color and other surface properties, and that it seems to form the scaffolding over which object representations are built. In other words, at least some surface features merely ride on the backs of object representations that are set up on the basis of spatiotemporal considerations. (This is a conclusion that we will return to in a discussion of 'object files'.)

6.3 Ontogenetic and phylogenetic origins of spatiotemporal priority

In the previous section, we reviewed evidence for spatiotemporal priority in adult visual cognition. In this section, we turn to the origins of this phenomenon. Does spatiotemporal priority develop only after extended experience with the behavior of visual objects, or does this bias emerge early in development? Similarly, is this phenomenon uniquely human, or is it shared more widely in the animal kingdom? Put differently, do infants and nonhuman animals experience objects as persisting individuals over time—and if so, do they prioritize spatiotemporal features when determining persistence?

6.3.1 Spatiotemporal priority in infant object cognition

The question of whether infants recognize that objects persist over time (even when they are not always in view) has played a prominent role in research on infant object cognition, ever since Piaget's time. Piaget famously claimed on the basis of observing infants' overt behaviors that they do not see objects as persisting through interruptions such as occlusion—that they lack what he called *object permanence* (Piaget, 1954). It took nearly 30 years for clever researchers armed with new tools such as the measurement of looking times to prove him wrong (e.g., Baillargeon, 1986). Since then, a growing body of work suggests that infants recognize that objects continue to persist over time, and that their persisting object representations survive periods of occlusion and several sorts of manipulations during periods of occlusion (e.g., Cheries et al., 2006; Spelke et al., 1992; Wynn, 1992; Xu & Carey, 1996; for reviews, see Baillargeon, 2008; Carey & Xu, 2001; Spelke, 2000). Moreover, infants maintain their persisting object representations according to several spatiotemporal principles—for example, involving spatiotemporal continuity (e.g., Aguiar & Baillargeon, 1999, 2002; Spelke et al., 1995) and cohesion (Cheries et al., 2008; Chiang & Wynn, 2000; Huntley-Fenner et al., 2002; Wynn et al., 2000).

In the process of exploring the principles that control object persistence in infancy, researchers have also discovered striking examples of spatiotemporal priority. In a now-classic set of studies, Xu and colleagues explored the features that 10- and 12-month-old infants use to determine the number of objects hidden behind an occluder (Xu, 2002; Xu & Carey, 1996; Xu et al., 2004). This work revealed that 10-month-old infants reliably use spatiotemporal information to track the number of objects behind a screen. For example, they will reliably infer that two objects exist behind a screen on the basis of seeing them both at the same time, as in Fig. 6.7a. At the same time, however, infants of the same age will not reliably use contrasting surface features to draw this same inference. For example, they will not reliably infer that there are two objects behind the screen on the basis of seeing a truck and a duck sequentially emerge, as in Fig. 6.7b. Twelve-month-olds, in contrast, will use both sorts of information, similar to adults.

In a similar vein, 4-month-old infants have been shown to infer that two parts are in fact a single unitary occluded object (as shown in Fig. 6.1a) on the basis of spatiotemporal information (e.g., the fact that two parts separated by an occluder undergo common motion) but not featural information (e.g., the fact that two stationary parts separated by an occluder have similar colors and/or shapes; e.g., Kellman & Spelke, 1983; Kestenbaum et al., 1987). (Again, adults and older children will use both sorts of information.) Furthermore, some studies suggest that infants at these ages appear to use *only* spatiotemporal information to assess an object's unity: in the situation described earlier, for example, infants are perfectly happy to conceive of the two parts in common motion as a single object, despite the fact that their colors and shapes suggest strongly (to older children and adults) that they are distinct objects (but cf. Needham, 1997). Although the overall question of whether young infants *can* use surface features to fuel inferences about object persistence

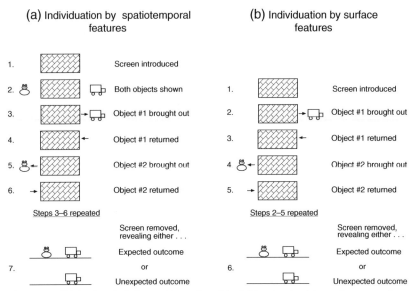

Fig. 6.7 Individuation in infancy. Examples of individuation by (a) spatiotemporal factors and (b) surface features in the seminal infancy studies of Xu and Carey (1996). (Adapted from Xu & Carey, 1996)

remains controversial (e.g., Leslie et al., 1998; Needham, 1998, 1999; Needham & Baillargeon, 1997, 1998; Needham et al., 2005; Wilcox, 1999; Wilcox & Baillargeon, 1998), this debate does not tar the overall conclusion of spatio-temporal priority. Overall, object persistence and the spatiotemporal rules that guide it appear to come online early in development, and these abilities may even reflect parts of 'core knowledge' that are a part of our genetic endowment (Spelke, 1988, 2000; Spelke & Kinzler, 2007).

6.3.2 **The evolution of spatiotemporal priority**

The developmental priority of spatiotemporal information raises the possibility that it may be evolutionarily prior as well. Over the past several years, comparative studies of other animals (typically, nonhuman primates) have demonstrated—perhaps unsurprisingly—that object persistence is a relatively ancient cognitive achievement. Using tasks similar to those used with human infants, researchers have discovered that several species of nonhuman primates represent objects as the same individuals over time and through occlusion. Similar to infants, they understand that objects continue to exist when occluded (e.g., chimpanzees: Beran, 2004; Beran & Beran, 2004; rhesus macaques: Hauser & Carey, 2003; Hauser et al., 1996, 2000; Santos et al., 2002; tamarins: Uller et al., 2001), retain their boundaries across motion (e.g., rhesus macaques: Munakata et al., 2001), and trace continuous paths in space and time (e.g., rhesus monkeys: Santos, 2004; Santos & Hauser, 2002; tamarins: Santos et al., 2006).

Do nonhuman primates also prioritize spatiotemporal information when tracking persisting objects? We recently demonstrated that they do—and moreover that spatiotemporal priority can have powerful consequences for real-world behaviors such as foraging for food (Flombaum et al., 2004). In these experiments, rhesus macaques watched as a lemon rolled down a ramp and came to rest behind a tunnel (Occluder 1), and then as a kiwi emerged and became occluded at the end of its path behind a screen (Occluder 2; see Fig. 6.8).

When the kiwi emerged at about the time that the lemon should have (had it continued its motion), subjects searched for food only behind Occluder 2—apparently perceiving the lemon transform into a kiwi on the basis of spatiotemporally continuous motion. (Other control conditions verified that the monkeys did in fact recognize the featural difference.) In contrast, when a brief pause interrupted the occlusion of the lemon and the emergence of the kiwi, monkeys searched for food behind both occluders—apparently perceiving two distinct objects, and assuming (on the basis of the featural difference) that the lemon must have remained in the tunnel. In this way, the tunnel effect directly influenced not only the monkeys' percepts but also their subsequent spontaneous behaviors.

Fig. 6.8 The tunnel effect in rhesus macaques. Sample stills from a study of the tunnel effect in rhesus macaques (Flombaum et al., 2004). A monkey watches as a lemon rolls down a ramp (Frames A–B) and becomes concealed by Occluder 1 (Frame C), and then as kiwi rolls down the remainder of the ramp (Frames D–E) and becomes concealed by Occluder 2 (Frame F). Finally, the experimenter walks away, and the subject is given the opportunity to search (Frame F). (Adapted from Flombaum et al., 2004)

6.4 **A neural signature of spatiotemporal cues to object persistence**

The demonstrations of spatiotemporal priority discussed in the previous sections were drawn from many different kinds of behavioral studies. In contrast, the nature of spatiotemporal cues to object persistence has received much less study in cognitive neuroscience. Of course, the distinction between featural and spatiotemporal processing has been well characterized in neural terms. Perhaps most famously, these sorts of processes seem to be partially localized in anatomically distinct cortical streams (e.g., Livingstone & Hubel, 1988), with the ventral pathway corresponding to identification (i.e., the processing of *what* an object is, on the basis of surface features) and the dorsal pathway corresponding to individuation (i.e., how and *where* objects move, on the basis of spatiotemporal information). And a wealth of research in cognitive neuroscience has explored the neural bases of object identification on the basis of surface features. There have been few cognitive neuroscience studies of persistence as driven by spatiotemporal factors, however—and fewer still have studied both spatiotemporal properties and surface features at the same time. Several neuroscientific studies have demonstrated that neural processing of objects persists even when the objects are invisible, such as while momentarily occluded (e.g., Assad & Maunsell, 1995; Baker et al., 2001; Hulme & Zeki, 2007; Kaufman et al., 2005; Olson et al., 2003; Shuwairi et al., 2007). But few studies have examined the role of spatiotemporal principles such as continuity directly.

One recent exception is a functional magnetic resonance imaging (fMRI) study that compared spatiotemporal and featural processing (Yi et al., 2008). This study did not attempt to directly pit these types of processing against each other in general, as would be required in a comprehensive study of the neural bases of spatiotemporal priority. Instead, this study sought to explore how spatiotemporal factors might play a role even in some of the most staunchly 'featural' areas of visual cortex. We relied in this study on the phenomenon of neural *repetition attenuation* (e.g., Grill-Spector & Malach, 2001): a weaker neural response is typically observed to a repeated stimulus compared with a novel stimulus. For example, presenting two identical faces results in an attenuated fMRI response to the second face in the fusiform face area (FFA; an area of the visual cortex that responds selectively to faces), compared with the response to a second novel face. Thus, similar to the looking-time methods that are commonly employed in developmental and comparative studies (see Turk-Browne et al., 2008), repetition attenuation can help to reveal whether particular brain regions treat two

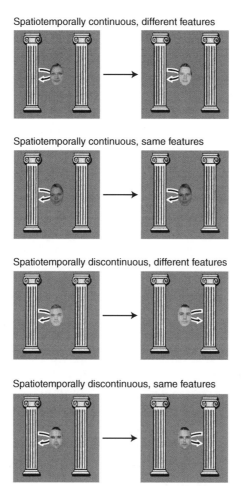

Fig. 6.9 Spatiotemporal continuity and surface features in an fMRI study. In an fMRI study of object persistence (Yi et al., 2008), faces could appear sequentially in a spatiotemporally continuous or discontinuous manner, and could look the same or different. Repetition attenuation in ventral cortical regions was weaker (or sometimes nonexistent) for repeated visual features in the spatiotemporally discontinuous condition, compared with the spatiotemporally continuous condition. (Dynamic animations are available online at http://www.yale.edu/perception/tunnel/.)

stimuli as two different objects or as instances of the same object—the key question in studies of persistence.

In our fMRI study (Yi et al., 2008), we presented two faces sequentially in a variety of situations. One situation—depicted in Fig. 6.9—involved dynamic occlusion: the faces could appear sequentially from behind the same occluder (and thus could be the same individual) or could appear sequentially from behind two different occluders (and thus could not be the same individual, given the lack of a spatiotemporally continuous path between them). In addition, the two faces on each trial could *look* identical or different, in terms of their surface features. By measuring repetition attenuation in the FFA (and in other regions of the ventral cortex), we were thus able to ask about whether even these 'featural' areas of visual processing would take spatiotemporal factors into account.

In particular, we were able to ask whether spatiotemporal object discontinuity would affect the representation of objects as 'the same' (as revealed by repetition attenuation), even when those objects' visual surface features were (and appeared to be) identical. This was in fact the case: repetition attenuation for faces that looked identical was always weaker (and was sometimes nonexistent) in ventral cortical regions when the faces appeared in spatiotemporally discontinuous ways (from behind different occluders), compared with when they appeared in spatiotemporally continuous ways (from behind the same occluder). These results were also replicated in another very different type of display, based on persistence in apparent-motion streams (as in Fig. 6.5; Chun & Cavanagh, 1997).

These results indicate for the first time that spatiotemporal continuity modulates neural representations of object identity, influencing judgments of object persistence even in the most staunchly featural areas of the ventral visual cortex. This is not a demonstration of spatiotemporal priority per se, because we were not pitting spatiotemporal factors directly against featural factors. But, it is nevertheless a surprising demonstration of the power of spatiotemporal cues to object persistence in neural terms, as it shows the influence of spatiotemporal processing even on the 'home cortical turf' of featural processing. Indeed, the brain regions that exhibited these effects—the fusiform gyrus and lateral occipital cortex—are perhaps among the least likely places to find effects of spatiotemporal continuity, given their long association with the processing of what an object is on the basis of its surface features (e.g., Ungerleider & Mishkin, 1982). Thus, these results suggest that spatiotemporal object continuity is an important constraint on neural processing of identity in some of the best characterized regions of the visual cortex. This paves the way for future neuroscientific research to explore the existence of spatiotemporal priority per se.

6.5 Explaining spatiotemporal priority

The evidence reviewed in the preceding sections converges on spatiotemporal priority as a key principle of object persistence. Having now reviewed such a broad range of demonstrations of spatiotemporal priority, it is perhaps worth stepping back to again note how intuitively surprising it is. After all, when you reason using higher-level cognition through your own correspondence problems—such as finding your Prius in the crowded mall parking lot or determining which beverage belongs to whom on your dinner table—you do not exercise spatiotemporal priority! You might wonder just how your glass of milk got over *there* (where your friend's beer was a moment ago), but you wouldn't wonder just how your milk turned into beer.

Why, then, is spatiotemporal priority so powerful in more automatic processes of visual cognition? There are two ways to answer this question. In Section 6.5.2, we will approach it from a functional perspective by considering the computational advantages that might emerge from spatiotemporal priority. But first we consider the question from a mechanistic perspective: how are persisting object representations implemented in the mind so that spatiotemporal properties play such a dominant role?

6.5.1 A mechanistic explanation (and some thoughts on object files)

How are persisting objects mentally represented in the visual system? The most influential answer to this question appeals to a kind of representation called an *object file* (Kahneman & Treisman, 1984; Kahneman et al., 1992). An object file is a mid-level visual representation that 'sticks' to a moving object over time on the basis of spatiotemporal properties, and stores (and updates) information about that object's surface features. In this way, object files help to construct our conscious perception of objects and how they behave—for example, telling us 'which went where' or underlying the perception of object persistence despite featural change or momentary periods of occlusion. Critically, note that spatiotemporal and surface features are treated very differently in this framework. Object files can be thought of as analogous to 'file folders'—with one folder per salient object in the visual field, up to some limit of roughly 4 available folders—with addresses written on their covers that identify the object's current location and with various papers inside describing the object's features (perhaps including its past features). Spatiotemporal features can update a folder's label, perhaps even occasioning the creation of a new folder or the destruction of a current folder. Surface features, in contrast, are just along for the ride: when they change, the only result may be that the description stored inside the folder is modified.

Object files are thought to underlie object persistence via three steps (Kahneman et al., 1992): (a) a *correspondence* operation, which uses spatiotemporal information for each visual object to determine whether it is novel or whether it moved from a previous location; (b) a *reviewing* operation, which retrieves previously stored object properties (e.g., color, shape) of those objects; and (c) an *impletion* operation, which uses both current and reviewed information to construct an evolving conscious percept, perhaps of object motion. Spatiotemporal priority arises in this model due to the assumption that only spatiotemporal information drives the correspondence operation, combined with the assumption that conflicting features are simply overwritten during the reviewing operation (although the previous features may also still be stored).

These three steps can account for a variety of the empirical demonstrations of spatiotemporal priority that were introduced in Sections 6.2 and 6.3. For example, the spatiotemporal rules that characterize amodal integration and apparent motion—such as the *nearest neighbor principle*, the *relative velocity principle*, and more generally, the attempt to minimize the distance and time interpolated—are presumably the very rules underlying the correspondence operation. Additionally, by the time that a change in surface features is processed in this framework (during the reviewing operation), decisions about object persistence have already been made (during the correspondence operation). As a result, property changes on their own cannot induce apparent motion (Navon, 1976), they have little or no impact on motion correspondences in apparent motion (Burt & Sperling, 1981), and they do not preclude amodal integration as in the tunnel effect (Burke, 1952; Flombaum & Scholl, 2006). Finally, illusory conjunctions seem less mysterious in this context: when the impletion operation makes an error while building a percept, it can only make the error by misbinding ('misfiling') one of the surface properties collected during the reviewing procedure; the object's locations, in contrast, have already been determined by the correspondence operation. In many ways, the object representation *is* the object's location—such that the file can only be addressed via its spatiotemporal label—which is perhaps why surface features can be illusorily bound to the wrong locations, but not vice versa.

What evidence is there that object files exist and work in these ways? Object files are typically studied with a paradigm known as object reviewing, depicted in Fig. 6.10a. In the initial preview display, a number of distinct objects are presented and then letters (or other symbols) briefly appear on some or all of them. After the letters disappear, the objects begin moving about the display. Once they come to rest, a single target letter appears on one of the objects, and the observer's task is simply to name that letter as quickly as possible. This response is typically slightly faster when the letter matches one of the initially presented letters (a type of display-wide priming). However, observers are faster still to name the target letter when it is the same letter that initially appeared on that same object (in a congruent trial), compared with when the

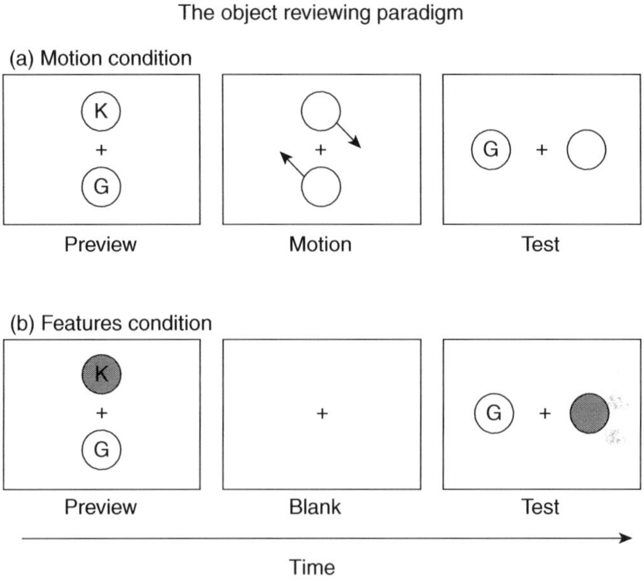

The object reviewing paradigm

Fig. 6.10 Object reviewing. (a) In the standard 'object reviewing paradigm' (Kahneman et al., 1992), observers first see two objects with a letter presented in each one (the preview screen). Next, the letters disappear and the two objects move to new positions. Finally, the objects stop moving, a letter appears in one of the objects (the test screen), and observers must indicate whether the letter had appeared in the preview screen. A response-time advantage (called an 'object-specific preview benefit', or OSPB) is obtained when the test letter appears in the same object as it had in the preview screen, compared with when it appears in a different object. (b) As demonstrated by Mitroff and Alvarez (2007), however, no OSPB occurs when shared surface features (e.g., color) link the objects in the preview and test screens, without continuous motion.

final letter initially appeared on a different object (in an incongruent trial). This is termed an *object-specific preview benefit* (OSPB). This relative response-time advantage for congruent trials over incongruent trials is necessarily object-based because the objects' spatial locations change from the preview to the target displays.

Several more recent object reviewing studies have employed a different method wherein the task is to answer as quickly as possible whether the target letter matches *either* of the initial previews. This forces subjects to attend to the preview information (which otherwise can be completely ignored), and perhaps for that reason it tends to produce more robust OSPBs (Kruschke & Fragassi, 1996; Noles et al., 2005). Object reviewing studies of this sort have recently been used to explore the rules that govern the creation and maintenance of object files, focusing on spatiotemporal principles such as continuity (Gao & Scholl, in press) and cohesion (Mitroff et al., 2004).

One recent object reviewing study even demonstrated directly that surface features do not drive object file correspondence in the absence of spatiotemporal continuity (Mitroff & Alvarez, 2007; see Fig. 6.10b). Even if the two objects in the preview and test displays can be easily disambiguated on the basis of their surface features (e.g., if one is blue and one is red), an OSPB is not obtained unless spatiotemporally continuous motions link the objects. Conversely, even when the object that moves looks entirely featurally distinct from the initial features that established the object file, OSPBs are still reliably obtained (Gao & Scholl, in press). Thus, spatiotemporal priority is salient not only in various phenomena of visual cognition but also in direct tests of the object file framework.

6.5.2 A functional explanation (and some thoughts on the computational advantages of spatiotemporal priority)

Object file theory provides an elegant explanation for how spatiotemporal priority is implemented, but it does not explain *why* the visual system would be constructed in this way. We suggest, however, that there are at least two reasons for why spatiotemporal priority is an adaptive solution for the kinds of correspondence problems typically faced by the visual system.

6.5.2.1 Avoiding coincidences

The first reason why spatiotemporal priority might be adaptive is that, statistically speaking, spatiotemporal priority means that the visual system rejects coincidences—and coincidences, by definition, are statistically improbable, and thus *should* be avoided.

On the face of it, ignoring surface features altogether can seem shortsighted. In our experiments on the tunnel effect with monkeys, for example, a kiwi enters an occluder and then a lemon exits on the other side, and because of spatiotemporal continuity monkeys perceive a single enduring object (Flombaum et al., 2004). Why does their visual system ignore the fact that the two objects look so different, leading them to search for only a single piece of food? (After all, this means that they get less food!)

Although it is true that featural evidence is being ignored in the tunnel effect, it is also true that the spatiotemporal evidence is statistically more reliable. The particular spatiotemporal evidence that drives the tunnel effect is the continuous motion that links the occluding and disoccluding objects. If the events on either side of the occluder reflected two distinct objects, then this continuity would be unexplained: in other words, it would just be a coincidence that the second object happened to appear when (and moving at the speed) it did. The visual system, however, is in the business of trying to infer the structure of the world from utterly insufficient data, and as a general rule it would be unwise for it to settle on interpretations that are by definition judged to be unlikely. As such, the visual system avoids coincidences when settling on interpretations of visual input (e.g., Rock, 1983).

This reasoning is general, and so it also applies to other phenomena such as amodal completion and apparent motion. Perfect alignment drives amodal completion because it would be improbable to find two perfectly aligned segments that were not parts of the same extended object. (If you were to toss two physical segments up in the air, what is the likelihood that they would land perfectly aligned?) Similarly, in apparent motion, it would be an unexplained coincidence for the second flash to reflect an entirely new object that just happened to appear so close to an object that had just disappeared a moment before—and thus, we instead see motion.

In fact, evidence that the logic of spatiotemporal priority has something to do with coincidences can be adduced from one study where surface features have actually been shown to affect object persistence. In the *flash-lag illusion*, observers misperceive the spatial relationship between a moving object and a briefly flashed object (MacKay, 1958; Nijhawan, 2002). The illusion is not obtained, however, if the moving object stops at exactly the moment that the flash takes place. In other words, the object's trajectory must persist following the flash to induce the misperception. The illusion also is not obtained if the moving object changes its size or shape—but still continues to move—at the very moment that the second object is flashed (Moore & Enns, 2004; see also Moore et al., 2007).

Putting these facts together suggests that the sudden featural change induces the individuation of a new object, thus fracturing the motion trajectories before and after the flash. This is atypical: here a featural change seems to cause the creation of a new object, rather than just updating the features of an existing object representation. This special case can be reconciled with spatiotemporal priority, however, in terms of coincidences: here the change in surface features is occurring at a particular time—at the exact moment of the sudden, unexpected flash—and this coincidence is 'explained' by the visual system in terms of the flash and the feature change both reflecting the appearance of a new object[1].

---

[1] There is at least one other way that this type of study (see also Moore et al., 2007) may be reconciled with spatiotemporal priority. The particular 'surface features' used here (size and shape) may in fact be better characterized as spatial features of a sort—part of the

6.5.2.2 Surface features are unreliable, but spatiotemporal rules can be implemented without exceptions

The second reason why spatiotemporal priority might be adaptive is simply that surface features are often more unreliable guides to persistence than are spatiotemporal cues. The former must be indirectly inferred, and an instance of a changing surface feature may or may not reliably signal a new object. In contrast, some spatiotemporal rules for persistence can be computationally implemented without exception, as extremely reliable guides to persistence.

In the first place, it is obvious that surface features alone could never be a sole guide to object persistence. If they were, then we could never keep track of multiple individuals that looked the same. This would render certain types of real-world hunting and predation impossible, because when chasing a herd of animals it may often be impossible in practice to discriminate individual prey on the basis of their surface features. We can obviously still keep track of individuals in such contexts, though, and this is also possible in the laboratory. In multiple object tracking (MOT) experiments, for example, observers must track a group of haphazardly and independently moving targets among a group of moving distractors, and this is possible (for up to 4 targets) even when all of the objects look identical (Pylyshyn & Storm, 1988; for a review, see Scholl, in press). Indeed, recent experiments have demonstrated that MOT seems to rely solely on spatiotemporal cues in some ways: for example, additional moving objects in the display will be treated as distractors even if they have completely different surface properties, but additional static objects will not be treated as distractors even if they are identical to the targets (Pylyshyn et al., in press).

Even when distinctive surface features are present in a display, however, they still may not be reliable guides to identity over time. In part, this is because many objects can change their surface properties over time, although not becoming new individuals: chameleons and octopuses can change their colors from moment to moment, for example, and even humans can radically change their postures and facial expressions, and so on.

In addition, however, many surface features cannot be directly recovered from retinal input, but must be inferred indirectly. We think of lightness, for example, as a surface feature of objects, but what we actually need to perceive

---

global spatial signature of *where* an object is. It is seductive to think of locations as single points, but in fact the spatiotemporally encoded locations of objects may have spatial extent and even a rough type of overall boundary shape (cf. Alvarez & Cavanagh, 2008). We are exploring this possibility in current research.

in order for lightness to be useful is the *reflectance* of the object. Recovering reflectance is technically impossible to reliably infer, however, because the actual number of photons reaching the eyes after reflecting off a surface will always be the product of the illumination from the light source(s) (which we want to discount) and the reflectance of the surface (the 'paint', which we want to know about). Separating these sources is not strictly possible, as it would essentially require the visual system to 'unmultiply', for example, solving for R in the equation $R \times I = 12$ (see Adelson, 2000). Instead, the visual system must infer reflectance indirectly using a set of heuristic assumptions. These indirect inferences typically succeed in everyday life, of course, but in general the visual system has no way of checking the reliability of such inference in individual cases.

In contrast, some spatiotemporal properties such as relative position can be much more reliably recovered from retinal input, because relative separation on the retina directly entails relative separation in the world. And, when computations of such features are recovered, they are much more reliable cues to persistence. If two objects are encountered in distinct locations without a possible spatiotemporally continuous path between them, for example, then they cannot be the same individual—no matter how similar they might appear. (And as we saw in Section 6.4, even those areas of the visual cortex that are most involved in the processing of surface features appear to be sensitive to this fact.) Indeed, this can be a direct reflection of physical laws, whereas surface features can at best be merely strongly suggestive of persistence or the lack thereof. As a result, the reliability of such spatiotemporal cues to persistence may also give them a computational advantage: they can be implemented in the mind *without exception*.

6.6 Conclusion

The principle of spatiotemporal priority, as we have seen, has considerable scope in accounting for phenomena of object persistence. It describes a general solution to types of correspondence problems as they are grappled with in many guises in visual cognition research—including the tunnel effect, apparent motion, illusory conjunctions, and object reviewing. It captures some of the primary features of the dominant 'object file' model of object persistence. It accounts for the perception of persisting objects not only in adult humans but also in infants and nonhuman primates. And it may have a firm foundation in both mechanistic and functional terms. We suggest, as captured in the title of this chapter, that it constitutes a fundamental principle of object persistence.

References

Adelson, E. H. (2000). Lightness perception and lightness illusions. In M. Gazzaniga (Ed.), *The New Cognitive Neurosciences*, 2nd edn. (pp. 339–351). Cambridge, MA: MIT Press.

Aguiar, A., & Baillargeon, R. (1999). 2.5-month-old infants' reasoning about when objects should and should not be occluded. *Cognitive Psychology*, *39*, 116–157.

Aguiar, A., & Baillargeon, R. (2002). Developments in young infants' reasoning about occluded objects. *Cognitive Psychology*, *45*, 267–336.

Alvarez, G. A., & Cavanagh, P. (2008). Visual short-term memory operates more efficiently on boundary features than on surface features. *Perception and Psychophysics*, *70*, 346–364.

Anstis, S. M. (1980). The perception of apparent movement. *Philosophical Transactions of the Royal Society of London B*, *290*, 153–168.

Assad, J., & Maunsell, J. (1995) Neuronal correlates of inferred motion in primate posterior parietal cortex. *Nature*, *373*, 518–521.

Baillargeon, R. (1986). Representing the existence and the location of hidden objects: object permanence in 6- and 8-month old infants. *Cognition*, *23*, 21–41.

Baillargeon, R. (2008). Innate ideas revisited: for a principle of persistence in infants' physical reasoning. *Perspectives on Psychological Science*, *3*, 2–13.

Baker, C. I., Keysers, C., Jellema, T., Wicker, B., & Perrett, D. I. (2001). Neuronal representation of disappearing and hidden objects in temporal cortex of the macaque. *Experimental Brain Research*, *140*, 375–381.

Beran, M. J. (2004). Chimpanzees (*Pan troglodytes*) respond to nonvisible sets after one-by-one addition and removal of items. *Journal of Comparative Psychology*, *118*, 25–36.

Beran, M. J., & Beran, M. M. (2004) Chimpanzees remember the results of one-by-one addition of food items to sets over extended time periods. *Psychological Science*, *15*, 94–99.

Burke, L. (1952). On the tunnel effect. *Quarterly Journal of Experimental Psychology*, *4*, 121–138.

Burt, P., & Sperling, G. (1981). Time, distance, and feature trade-offs in visual apparent motion. *Psychological Review*, *88*, 171–195.

Carey, S., & Xu, F. (2001). Infant knowledge of objects: Beyond object files and object tracking. *Cognition*, *80*, 179–213.

Cheries, E. W., Mitroff, S. R., Wynn, K., & Scholl, B. J. (2008). Cohesion as a principle of object persistence in infancy. *Developmental Science*, *11*, 427–432.

Cheries, E. W., Wynn, K., & Scholl, B. J. (2006). Interrupting infants' persisting object representations: An object-based limit? *Developmental Science*, *9*, F50–F58.

Chiang, W-C., & Wynn, K. (2000). Infants' representation and tracking of multiple objects. *Cognition*, *77*, 169–195.

Chun, M. M., & Cavanagh, P. (1997). Seeing two as one: linking apparent motion and repetition blindness. *Psychological Science*, *8*, 74–79.

Dawson, M. (1991). The how and why of what went where in apparent motion: modeling solutions to the motion correspondence problem. *Psychological Review*, *98*, 569–603.

Flombaum, J. I., Kundey, S., Santos, L. R., & Scholl, B. J. (2004). Dynamic object individuation in rhesus macaques: a study of the tunnel effect. *Psychological Science*, *15*, 795–800.

Flombaum, J. I., & Scholl, B. J. (2006). A temporal same-object advantage in the tunnel effect: facilitated change detection for persisting objects. *Journal of Experimental Psychology: Human Perception and Performance*, *32*, 840–853.

Gao, T., & Scholl, B. J. (in press). Are objects required for object-files? Roles of segmentation and spatiotemporal continuity in computing object persistence. *Visual Cognition*.

Grill-Spector, K., & Malach, R. (2001). fMR-adaptation: a tool for studying the functional properties of human cortical neurons. *Acta Psychologica*, *107*, 293–321.

Hauser, M. D., & Carey, S. (2003). Spontaneous representations of small numbers of objects by rhesus macaques: examinations of content and format. *Cognitive Psychology*, *47*, 367–401.

Hauser, M. D., Carey, S., & Hauser, L. B. (2000). Spontaneous number representation in semi-free-ranging rhesus monkeys. *Proceedings of the Royal Society of London: Biological Science*, *267*, 829–833.

Hauser, M. D., MacNeilage, P., & Ware, M. (1996). Numerical representations in primates. *Proceedings of the National Academy of Science*, *93*, 1514–1517.

Hulme, O. J., & Zeki, S. (2007). The sightless view: neural correlates of occluded objects *Cerebral Cortex*, *17*, 1197–1205.

Humphreys, G. W., Cinel, C., Wolfe, J., Olson, A., & Klempen, N. (2000). Fractionating the binding process: Neuropsychological evidence distinguishing binding of form from binding of features. *Vision Research*, *40*, 1569–1596.

Huntley-Fenner, G., Carey, S., & Solimando, A. (2002). Objects are individuals but stuff doesn't count: perceived rigidity and cohesiveness influence infants' representations of small groups of discrete entities. *Cognition*, *85*, 203–221.

Kahneman, D., & Treisman, A. (1984). Changing views of attention and automaticity. In R. Parasuraman, & D. R. Davies (Eds.), *Varieties of Attention*. New York: Academic Press.

Kahneman, D., Treisman, A., & Gibbs, B. J. (1992). The reviewing of object files: object-specific integration of information. *Cognitive Psychology*, *24*, 175–219.

Kanizsa, G. (1979). *Organization in Vision*. New York: Praeger.

Kanizsa, G. (1982). Amodal completion: Seeing or thinking? In J. Beck (Ed.), *Organisation and Representation in Perception* (pp. 167–190). New Jersey: Erlbaum.

Kanwisher, N. G. (1987). Repetition blindness: type recognition without token individuation. *Cognition*, *27*, 117–143.

Kaufman, J., Csibra, G., & Johnson, M. H. (2005). Oscillatory activity in the infant brain reflects object maintenance. *Proceedings of the National Academy of Sciences*, *102*, 15271–15274.

Kellman, P. J., & Shipley, T. F. (1991). A theory of visual interpolation in object perception. *Cognitive Psychology*, *23*, 141–221.

Kellman, P. J., & Spelke, E. S. (1983). Perception of partly occluded objects in infancy. *Cognitive Psychology*, *15*, 483–524.

Kestenbaum, R., Termine, N., & Spelke, E. S. (1987). Perception of objects and object boundaries by three-month-old infants. *British Journal of Developmental Psychology*, *5*, 367–383.

Kolers, E. (1972). *Aspects of Motion Perception*. New York: Pergamon Press.

Kolers, P., & Pomerantz, J. (1971). Figural change in apparent motion. *Journal of Experimental Psychology*, *87*, 99–108.

Kruschke, J. K., & Fragassi, M. M. (1996). The perception of causality: feature binding in interacting objects. In *Proceedings of the Eighteenth Annual Conference of the Cognitive Science Society* (pp. 441–446). Hillsdale, NJ: Erlbaum.

Leslie, A. M., Xu, F., Tremoulet, P., & Scholl, B. J. (1998). Indexing and the object concept: developing 'what' and 'where' systems. *Trends in Cognitive Sciences, 2,* 10–18.

Livingstone, M. S., & Hubel, D. H. (1988). Segregation of form, color, movement, and depth: anatomy, physiology, and perception. *Science, 240,* 740–749.

MacKay, D. M. (1958). Perceptual stability of a stroboscopically lit visual field containing self-luminous objects. *Nature, 181,* 507–508.

Michotte, A., Thinès, G., & Crabbé, G. (1964/1991). Les complements amodaux des structures perceptives. In *Studia Psychologica.* Louvain: Publications Universitaires. Reprinted and translated as Michotte, A., Thinès, G., & Crabbé, G. (1991). Amodal completion of perceptual structures. In G. Thines, A. Costall, & G. Butterworth (Eds.) *Michotte's Experimental Phenomenology of Perception* (pp. 140–167). Hillsdale, NJ: Erlbaum.

Mitroff, S. R., & Alvarez, G. A. (2007). Space and time, not surface features, underlie object persistence. *Psychonomic Bulletin and Review, 14,* 1199–1204.

Mitroff, S. R., Scholl, B. J., & Wynn, K. (2004). Divide and conquer: how object files adapt when a persisting object splits into two. *Psychological Science, 15,* 420–425.

Moore, C. N., & Enns, J. T. (2004). Object updating and the flash-lag effect. *Psychological Science, 15,* 866–871.

Moore, C. M., Mordkoff, J. T, & Enns, J. T. (2007). The path of least persistence: evidence of object-mediated visual updating. *Vision Research, 47,* 1624–1630.

Navon, D. (1976). Irrelevance of figural identity for resolving ambiguities in apparent motion. *Journal of Experimental Psychology: Human Perception and Performance, 2,* 130–138.

Needham, A. (1997). Factors affecting infants' use of featural information in object segregation. *Current Directions in Psychological Science, 6,* 26–33.

Needham, A. (1998). Infants' use of featural information in the segregation of stationary objects. *Infant Behavior and Development, 21,* 47–76.

Needham, A. (1999). How infants grasp two adjacent objects: effects of perceived display composition on infants' actions. *Developmental Science, 2,* 219–233.

Needham, A., & Baillargeon, R. (1997). Object segregation in 8-month-old infants. *Cognition, 62,* 121–149.

Needham, A., & Baillargeon, R. (1998). Effects of prior experience in 4.5-month-old infants' object segregation. *Infant Behavior and Development, 21,* 1–24.

Needham, A., Dueker, G. L., & Lockhead, G. (2005). Infants' formation and use of categories to segregate objects. *Cognition, 94,* 215–240.

Nijhawan, R. (2002). Neural delays, visual motion and the flash-lag effect. *Trends in Cognitive Sciences, 6,* 387–393.

Noles, N. S., Scholl, B. J., & Mitroff, S. R. (2005). The persistence of object file representations. *Perception and Psychophysics, 67,* 324–334.

Olson, I. R., Gatenby, J. C., Leung, H. C., Skudlarski, P., & Gore, J. C. (2003). Neuronal representation of occluded objects in the human brain. *Neuropsychologia, 42,* 95–104.

Piaget, J. (1954). *The construction of reality in the child.* New York: Basic Books.

Pylyshyn, Z. W., Haladjian, H., King, C., & Reilly, J. (in press). Selective nontarget inhibition in multiple object tracking (MOT). *Visual Cognition.*

Pylyshyn, Z. W., & Storm, R. W. (1988). Tracking multiple independent targets: evidence for a parallel tracking mechanism. *Spatial Vision, 3,* 179–197.

Rafal, R. D. (1997). Balint syndrome. In T. Feinberg, & M. Farah (Eds.), *Behavioral Neurology and Neuropsychology* (pp. 337–356). New York: McGraw-Hill.

Ramachandran, V. S., & Anstis, S. M. (1986). The perception of apparent motion. *Scientific American, 245,* 102–109.

Robertson, L., Treisman, A., Freidman-Hill, S., & Grabowecky, M. (1997). The interaction of spatial and object pathways: evidence from Balint's syndrome. *Journal of Cognitive Neuroscience, 9,* 254–276.

Rock, I. (1983). *The Logic of Perception.* Cambridge, MA: MIT Press.

Santos, L. R. (2004). 'Core knowledges': a dissociation between spatiotemporal knowledge and contact-mechanics in a non-human primate? *Developmental Science, 7,* 167–174.

Santos, L. R., & Hauser, M. D. (2002). Dissociations between implicit knowledge and search behavior in cotton-top tamarins. *Developmental Science, 5,* F1–F7.

Santos, L. R., Seelig, D., & Hauser, M. D. (2006). Cotton-top tamarins' (*Saguinus oedipus*) expectations about occluded objects: a dissociation between looking and reaching tasks. *Infancy, 9,* 147–171.

Santos, L. R., Sulkowski, G., Spaepen, G. M., & Hauser, M. D. (2002). Object individuation using property/kind information in rhesus macaques (*Macaca mulatta*). *Cognition, 83,* 241–264.

Scholl, B. J. (2001b). Spatiotemporal priority and object identity. *Cahiers de Psychologie Cognitive, 20,* 359–371.

Scholl, B. J. (in press). What have we learned about attention from multiple object tracking (and vice versa)? In D. Dedrick, & L. Trick (Eds.), *Computation, Cognition, and Pylyshyn.* Cambridge, MA: MIT Press.

Scholl, B. J., & Flombaum, J. I. (in press). Object persistence. In B. Goldstein (Ed.), Encyclopedia of Perception. Thousand Oaks, CA: Sage Publications.

Shechter, S., Hochstein, S., & Hillman, P. (1988). Shape similarity and distance disparity as apparent motion correspondence cues. *Vision Research, 28,* 1013–1021.

Shuwairi, S. M., Curtis, C. E., & Johnson, S. P. (2007). Neural substrates of dynamic object occlusion. *Journal of Cognitive Neuroscience, 19,* 1275–1285.

Singh, M., & Fulvio, J. (2005). Visual extrapolation of contour geometry. *Proceedings of the National Academy of Sciences, 102,* 939–944.

Spelke, E. (1988). The origins of physical knowledge. In L. Weiskrantz (Ed.), *Thought without language* (pp. 168–184). Oxford: Oxford Science Publications.

Spelke, E.S. (2000). Core knowledge. *American Psychologist, 55,* 1233–1243.

Spelke, E. S., Breinlinger, K., Macomber, J., & Jacobson, K. (1992). Origins of knowledge. *Psychological Review, 99,* 605–632.

Spelke, E. S., Kestenbaum, R., Simons, D., & Wein, D. (1995). Spatiotemporal continuity, smoothness of motion and object identity in infancy. *The British Journal of Developmental Psychology, 13,* 113–142.

Spelke, E. S., & Kinzler, K. D. (2007). Core knowledge. *Developmental Science, 10,* 89–96.

Treisman, A., & Schmidt, H. (1982). Illusory conjunctions in the perception of objects. *Cognitive Psychology, 14,* 107–141.

Turk-Browne, N. B., Scholl, B. J., & Chun, M. M. (2008). Babies and brains: habituation in infant cognition and functional neuroimaging. *Frontiers in Human Neuroscience, 2,* 16. doi: 10.3389/neuro.09.016.2008.

Uller, C., Hauser, M., & Carey, S. (2001). The spontaneous representation of number in a New World primate species, cotton-top tamarins. *Journal of Comparative Psychology, 115,* 1–10.

Ullman, S. (1979). *The Interpretation of Visual Motion.* Cambridge, MA: MIT Press.

Ungerleider, L. G., & Mishkin, M. (1982). Two cortical visual systems. In D. J. Ingle, M. A. Goodale, & R. Mansfield (Eds.), *Analysis of Visual Behaviour* (pp. 549–586). Cambridge, MA: MIT Press.

Walker, P., & Davies, S. J. (2003). Perceptual completion and object-based representations in short-term visual memory. *Memory and Cognition, 31,* 746–760.

Wertheimer, M. (1912/1961). Experimentelle Studien über das Sehen von Bewegung. *Zeitschrift für Psychologie, 61,*161–265. Reprinted and translated as Wertheimer, M. (1961). Experimental studies on the seeing of motion. In T. Shipley (Ed. and Trans.) *Classics in Psychology* (pp. 1032–1089). New York: Philosophical Library.

Wilcox, T. (1999). Object individuation: infants use of shape, size, pattern, and color. *Cognition, 72,* 125–166.

Wilcox, T., & Baillargeon, R. (1998). Object individuation in infancy: the use of featural information in reasoning about occlusion events. *Cognitive Psychology, 37,* 97–155.

Wu, D. A., Kanai, R., & Shimojo, S. (2004). Steady-state misbinding of colour and motion. *Nature, 429,* 262.

Wynn, K. (1992). Addition and subtraction by human infants. *Nature, 358,* 749–750.

Wynn, K., Bloom, P., & Chiang, W. C. (2002). Enumeration of collective entities by 5-month-old infants. *Cognition, 83,* B55–B62.

Xu, F. (2002). The role of language in acquiring object kind concepts in infancy. *Cognition, 85,* 223–250.

Xu, F., & Carey, S. (1996). Infants' metaphysics: the case of numerical identity. *Cognitive Psychology, 30,* 111–153.

Xu, F., Carey, S., & Quint, N. (2004). The emergence of kind-based object individuation in infancy. *Cognitive Psychology, 49,* 155–190.

Yi, D-J., Turk-Browne, N. B., Flombaum, J. I., Kim, M-S., Scholl, B. J., & Chun, M. M. (2008). Spatiotemporal object continuity in human ventral visual cortex. *Proceedings of the National Academy of Sciences, 105,* 8840–8845.

Chapter 7

Infants' representations of material entities

Rebecca D. Rosenberg & Susan Carey

7.1 Infants' representations of material entities

Although the core cognition hypothesis is controversial, many researchers endorse the existence of systems of core cognition. Hypothesized domains of core cognition include objects and physical causality, agents, and number (e.g., Baillargeon, 2001; Carey, in press; Carey & Spelke, 1994, 1996; Leslie, 1994; Spelke & Kinzler, 2007). By hypothesis, systems of core cognition exhibit several properties that distinguish the representations within them from other types of mental representations. These distinctive properties include (1) conceptual content, (2) innate input analyzers that pick out entities in core domains and constrain representations of the events these entities participate in, (3) continuity through the lifespan, (4) domain-specific learning mechanisms, and (5) modularity.

The first of these properties differentiate the representations in core cognition from perceptual representations; the content of the symbols in core cognition go beyond the vocabulary of sensory and perceptual primitives and the outputs of core cognition participate in central inferential processes. The remaining properties differentiate core cognition from most human conceptual representations. There are no innate input analyzers that identify most of the entities in the world we think about (from electrons to ghosts and Gods to hammers), most concepts are vulnerable to change, even abandonment, and although intuitive theories provide constraints on the information relevant to confirmation of hypotheses within them, these processes are neither modular nor encapsulated (Fodor, 1983).

Cognition about objects was the first system of core cognition to be studied (e.g., Baillargeon, 1986; Spelke et al., 1992) and it remains a parade case. Object representations go beyond the vocabulary of sensorimotor primitives and in this sense are conceptual. Bounded, coherent, independently movable entities are represented as spatiotemporally continuous and as continuing to exist when out of sight, and representations of their motion are subject to the constraints of solidity and contact causality. Representations with these properties are evident by 2 months of age.

Two lines of argument convince us of the innateness of object representations. First, the learnability challenge to those who deny innateness has not been met—nobody has provided an alternative analysis of developmental primitives that does not include object representations and a learning mechanism through which such representations might come into being (see Berkeley, 1732/1919; Locke, 1690/1975; Piaget, 1954; Quine, 1953/1980, 1960 for valiant attempts to do so). Second, the representations within systems of core cognition emerge as an integrated whole. For example, as soon as young infants provide evidence of using spatiotemporal information to create representations of individual objects that continue to exist behind barriers (e.g., 3-month-olds; Baillargeon & DeVos, 1991), they also display evidence that they expect such individuals to obey the solidity constraint (e.g., 2-month-olds; Hespos & Baillargeon, 2001; Spelke et al., 1992). Such integrated emergence would not be expected on a picture in which specific generalizations about the behavior of entities are abstracted by statistical analysis of the perceptual input (although see Amso & Johnson, Chapter 9; Mareschal & Bremner, Chapter 10, for discussions of statistical learning).

The hypothesis that there are systems of core cognition, systems of representations with the earlier-mentioned properties, is an empirical one, and it is beyond the scope of this chapter to review the evidence for it (see Carey, in press, for an extensive review). Rather, our goal in this chapter is to explore some consequences of the core cognition hypothesis. We assume that evolutionary processes created systems of core cognition for a limited set of domains, and the rest of our conceptual apparatus is built from the resources of perception and core cognition, drawing on domain-general learning mechanisms. Representations within core cognition will be privileged in various ways. Infants will be poised to learn about the entities identified by innate perceptual input analyzers, and their learning will be efficient due to the constraints imposed by domain-specific learning mechanisms. In this chapter, we explore whether we can distinguish representations of entities that fall within core domains and those that do not, with respect to these putative privileges. We then pose a challenge to the field of cognitive development: How do infants come to represent entities that are not part of core cognition?

7.2 Case study: Cohesive versus noncohesive material entities

It is trivially easy to come up with entities that are not directly represented within some system of core cognition: money, movies, universities, genes.

More interesting cases are entities in the child's environment, entities for which one could imagine an adaptationist just-so story that might lead us to expect that evolution may have built some specialized representational and learning machinery. Which domains of core cognition exist, if any, is an empirical question. Some expect intuitive biology might be a domain of core cognition, that we are built to form representations not only of agents but also of living things (Medin & Atran, 2004; Wellman & Gelman, 1992; but see Carey, 1985, 1988, for counter arguments).

Another possible domain of core cognition might be substances, both solid and noncohesive substances. Any material individual (my computer, my table) is potentially a member of an object kind and also made of some substance (metal, wood, respectively), and the child's world is full of important noncohesive substances whose substance kind has consequences for the child (the water they bathe in, the pureed food they eat, the juice and milk they drink). The ontological distinction between objects and substances interacts with the quantificational distinction between individuated and nonindividuated entities, and that quantificational distinction is central to the syntax and semantics of natural language (Samuelson & Smith, 1999, 2000, 2005; Soja et al., 1991).

These considerations might lead us to expect core cognition of substances. Nonetheless, there is considerable evidence against this hypothesis. Infants seem robustly impaired in representing and reasoning about certain material entities that are ubiquitous in their experience, namely, noncohesive substances, in the face of success at reasoning about cohesive objects in the same circumstances. This failure is predicted by the characterization of core object cognition, but only on the assumption that there is not also core cognition of substances. One of the spatiotemporal cues used by the input analyzer that picks out objects in the world is cohesiveness or boundedness. Objects maintain their boundaries over time, and spatiotemporal continuity (both spatial—cohesiveness—and temporal) is the fundamental condition on object individuation and numerical identity (e.g., Scholl, 2001; Scholl & Pylyshyn, 1999; Spelke et al., 1992; Xu & Carey, 1996).

Evidence for noncohesiveness signals that an entity is not a single object (as when an object breaks in two) or not an object at all (as with water or sand). If there is indeed core cognition of objects, with dedicated input analyzers poised to analyze perceptual input for boundedness and spatiotemporal continuity in order to pick out the objects in the world, and if the further computations that create models of the world in terms of spatial and causal relations among objects operate only on the outputs of these dedicated input analyzers, then the infant would be expected to be unable to create comparable models of portions of nonsolid substances or broken objects. And so it seems to be.

Several studies have compared infants' representations of entities that do not maintain boundaries as they move through space with those of bounded, cohesive objects that appear identical to the noncohesive ones at rest. Wen-Chi Chiang and Karen Wynn (2000) were the first to report success at reasoning about objects in the face of failure at reasoning about perceptually identical (when at rest) noncohesive entities. They compared 8-month-old infants' representations of little piles of Lego blocks, either glued together to create solid objects or merely stacked so that they could be disassembled and restacked as the child watched. Stimulus condition (object vs. collection) was a between-subject variable. The task was a variant of Wynn's (1992) 1 + 1 = 2 or 1 violation of expectancy paradigm. As the trial began, the curtain opened to reveal an entity on one side of the stage, ambiguously the glued object or a stack of blocks, for the two looked identical. This entity was then occluded by a large screen.

In the object condition, another identical glued object was slid onto the stage and moved back and forth while the infants watched. It was then slid behind a second screen. This is a 1 object + 1 object trial. The collection condition began in the same manner. After the screen had occluded the original entity, a second pile of blocks was introduced onto the stage and was taken apart in front of the child, the blocks placed in a straight line, clearly separated from one another. Then, the blocks were reassembled into a small pile that was then slid, as a pile, behind a second occluder. In both conditions, the occluders were then removed, revealing either a single pile/object (unexpected outcome) or two piles/objects (expected outcome). Infants in the collection condition failed to differentiate the outcome: their attention was not drawn to the impossible outcome in which one of the piles placed behind the screen was not present. Infants in the object condition succeeded at the task: they looked reliably longer at the unexpected outcome of a single object. Apparently, seeing the pile taken apart and reassembled disrupted the infants' subsequent capacity to track it through time and occlusion. Infants in this study failed to exhibit 'pile permanence', in the face of robust object permanence.

Chiang and Wynn (2000) replicated this pattern of results in several different versions of the study, but they suggested that the failure is not absolute, for infants succeeded if given approximately 10 seconds of exposure to the already separated Lego blocks in the waiting room before the experiment. Of course, we do not know whether this experience helped infants represent the pile as a single collection that they tracked through time, as opposed to transforming the study into a 5 + 5 = 10 or 5 experiment, which McCrink and Wynn (2004) have shown is within infant's competence. The success could also reflect the infants' focusing on a single small block within the pile.

Gavin Huntley-Fenner and his colleagues (Huntley-Fenner et al., 2002) studied a different noncohesive entity and found results entirely comparable to those of Chiang and Wynn's, except that preexposure to sand did not lead to success in the sand condition. We describe here only one of the versions of the experiment; Huntley-Fenner et al. obtained the result in two different versions. Eight-month-old infants were assigned either to the sand condition or the object condition. The object was a pile-shaped sand-coated object that looked like a pile of sand when at rest on the stage. It had a black thread embedded in it so that it could be picked up and moved as a solid, coherent whole, dangling from the thread. Infants in each condition were familiarized to the entity they would see in the experiment before they were shown the stage. Those in the sand condition were placed in a high chair, where they witnessed sand being poured back and forth between two beakers and then poured into a pile on the high-chair tray. They were encouraged to touch the sand for a period of 30 seconds, and they witnessed their mother and the experimenter picking up small portions of the sand, putting their fingers in the pile, and moving the sand around. Those in the object condition witnessed the object being dangled in mid air before them, jiggled in position, and then lowered onto the high-chair tray. They too were encouraged to touch the object over a period of 30 seconds, and witnessed their mother and the experimenter slide the object around on the tray.

After this familiarization, the high chair was turned to face the stage and the experiment proper began. Infants watched as either a pile of sand was poured onto the stage or the pile-shaped object was lowered onto the stage. The entity was then occluded by a small screen, and a second screen, clearly distinct from the first one, was placed on the stage 16 cm from the first. Sand was then poured behind that second screen. The two screens were then removed revealing either the expected outcome of two piles of sand or the unexpected outcome of the single pile behind the first occluder. The object condition was identical, except that the entities involved were the solid sand-covered pile-shaped objects. Infants distinguished the expected and unexpected outcomes in the object condition but failed to do so in the sand condition.

Eric Cheries and colleagues (2008; see also Chapter 5) have recently provided evidence for a particularly striking failure to track entities through time and occlusion. Cheries began with a conceptual replication of Feigenson, Carey and Hauser's (2002) finding that 12-month-old infants choose a container into which two crackers have been put over one into which only a single cracker has been put. In Cheries' version, the single cracker was one half of a full-sized graham cracker. The two crackers were each the same size as one half of a full-sized graham cracker and were introduced at once, held in front of the child, moved sideways away from each other and then back toward each other, and then put one at a time into the bucket. Replicating Feigenson, Carey and Hauser (2002), infants chose the bucket with two crackers when allowed to approach the buckets. The noncohesive condition was identical, except that the two-cracker choice was initially introduced as a single double-sized cracker, then broken in half in front of the child, after which the trial unfolded exactly the same. Infants were at chance in this latter condition: they did not systematically choose the bucket with two crackers over the bucket with a single cracker.

Infants' failure to track noncohesive entities through time and occlusion is one source of evidence for the identification of infant object representations with those that articulate mid-level object-based attention. Object tracking in the multiple object tracking paradigm is also impaired by the noncohesion of the entities being tracked (vanMarle & Scholl, 2003), and computations of object identity are impaired by splitting (Mitroff et al., 2004).

These failures to represent nonohesive entities, in the face of success at representing perceptually identical cohesive objects, is consistent with the core cognition hypothesis: object representations appear privileged in infants' representations of the physical world. However, the earlier-mentioned experiments leave a very important question about the nature of this privilege open: Where in processing do representations of the sand entities, collections, and broken crackers get lost? Do infants fail to attend to them at all, failing to create working models that contain these entities? Getting a purchase on this question would serve a dual purpose. First, it will bear on the nature of core cognition. Second, it will bear on the severity and nature of the problems a learner faces in gaining knowledge of material entities that are not in the domain of core cognition of objects.

7.3 Where in processing does the disruption of representations of noncohesive entities occur?

In Zenon Pylyshyn's terminology (1989), in order to attend to some aspect of the world, a perceiver must index it, or assign a mental pointer to it. Pylyshyn assumes that many aspects of the world can be indexed: colors, objects, sounds, anything we can attend to. But in the tradition of object-based attention, perhaps indices can only be assigned to individuated entities such as objects, such that attention to a color or a sound must be attention to a color of or sound emitted by some object. Perhaps young infants cannot even attend to portions of nonsolid substances, and therefore form no representations of them whatsoever.

This seems unlikely. Although the matter has not been systematically studied, infants in the earlier-mentioned studies were clearly looking at the noncohesive entities, watching intently as the events unfold. It is highly likely that they attend to (and hence index) the collections of blocks, the sand, and the cracker pieces after they have been broken. If infants could not even index nonobjects, it would seem impossible for infants to learn about noncohesive entities—one cannot form generalizations about entities one cannot represent. Clearly, humans *eventually* have robust representations of substances including noncohesive ones, although the studies reviewed in the preceding section suggest that 8-month-olds have not yet done so!

A second hypothesis is that these failures reflect difficulties in entity tracking alone, difficulties in computations of numerical identity (maintaining a representation of a given entity as the same one as an entity viewed earlier). It stands to reason that representations of numerical identity would be impaired by noncohesion. When an entity breaks apart, it truly is ambiguous whether one of the resulting parts is to be thought of as the same entity as the original one, or whether new 'entity files' (akin to object files) should be established for each of the parts. Perhaps attempting to resolve that ambiguity might cause a young infant to lose the representation altogether. This hypothesis nicely covers the sand findings of Huntley-Fenner et al. (2002), but both Cheries' (2008; Chapter 5) and Chiang and Wynn's (2000) paradigms provide the child with quite a bit of experience of the entities after the cohesion violation. If this hypothesis is correct, it requires that the costs of reassigning indices after a cohesion violation are high. This hypothesis would be supported by evidence that representations of noncohesive entities are not impaired if the child is not required to track them through trajectories in which they fall apart.

A third hypothesis is a special case of the second. The collection, sand, and cracker permanence studies described earlier require not only that the child establish representations of individuated entities and track these through time but also that they create working memory models of these entities when they are occluded behind screens or in buckets. Perhaps, infants are unable to form working-memory entity files for portions of nonsolid substances.

We carried out three studies designed to adjudicate among these three hypotheses concerning exactly how representations of noncohesive entities are vulnerable, relative to those of objects (Rosenberg & Carey, under review). In these studies, we eliminated the requirement that the infant track particular entities through occlusion. As in Huntley-Fenner's studies, entity type (sand vs. object that was a sand-pile look-alike) was a between-participants variable, and infants were tactually familiarized with the relevant entity before the study began. If the second hypothesis is correct, infants should succeed at representing the piles of sand in these studies, for they do not require the child to create working memory models of particular individuals they have tracked through time and occlusion.

The experiments were based on the simple 1 vs. 2 habituation design of Feigenson, Carey and Spelke (2002). In each habituation trial of the sand condition, 8-month-old infants watched as one or two piles of red sand were poured onto a stage from hidden beakers above the stage. Infants' looking to the display was recorded once the entities were at rest. The stage curtain was then closed while the display was cleared. The experimenter reopened the curtain and again poured one or two new piles of sand onto the stage. After infants were habituated or familiarized to these arrays, test trials that alternated between the same number and different number of piles were presented (see Fig. 7.1a and 7.1b). In the object condition, habituation and test trials were identical to those in the sand condition, except they involved one or two objects being lowered onto the stage rather than sand being poured onto it (see Fig. 7.1c and 7.1d).

If infants can index visible piles of sand, and can create entity files for them, then they should succeed at this task, looking longer at the novel number of sand piles during test trials. Failure would be consistent with the possibility that 8-month-old infants cannot index portions of sand at all, or cannot create entity files for them. To abstract what is common among the habituation trials (e.g., always a single pile of sand), the child must have some memory of what was seen on a previous trial to compare to what is currently presented, even if he or she needn't represent it as the same individual. Thus, entity files for each pile are required. We of course expect infants to succeed in the object condition, for this is merely a conceptual replication of Feigenson, Carey and Spelke (2002), with different objects. It is important to note that infants' looking time is measured as they gaze at the piles of sand or the sand-pile objects resting on the stage floor, entities that are as perceptually identical as we could make them.

As shown in Fig. 7.2a infants looked equally long at the novel and familiar number of sand piles during test trials. This is a remarkable failure; there were several possible bases for infant success on this task. They could have responded to the number of individuals on the stage from trial to trial (1 vs. 2), to the amount of 'stuff' on the stage (twice as much on the two-pile trials than on the one-pile trials), to the locations filled or empty on the stage, or even to perceptual properties such as the amount of 'redness' on the stage; yet infants looked equally long at the two outcomes! In contrast, as expected, infants showed a significant preference for the novel versus familiar number of objects.

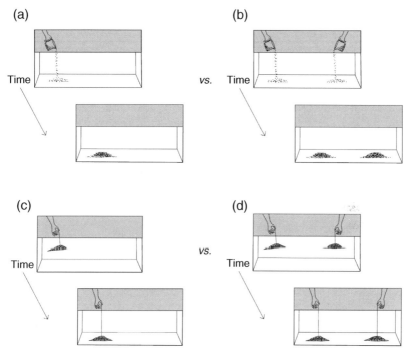

Fig. 7.1 Stimuli from Experiment 1 of Rosenberg and Carey (under review). In the sand condition, a hidden experimenter pours one (a) or two (b) portions of sand onto the stage. In the object condition, a hidden experimenter lowers one (c) or two (d) solid objects onto the stage.

Although Experiment 1 was based on the procedure by Feigenson, Carey and Spelke (2002), it actually provided one less cue to novelty. In Feigenson, Carey and Spelke (2002), the location of the objects in two-entity trials varied such that there was never an object in the same location from trial to trial. Thus, infants would never assign attentional indices to the same spatiotemporal location for two trials in a row. Furthermore, the single-object trials involved an object in the middle of the stage, again not in a position ever occupied in the two-object trials. In Experiment 1, however, the single entity was always in the same location for every trial (the left or the right of the stage, counterbalanced across infants). For single-entity trials, the rest of the stage was empty, whereas for two-entity trials, there was a second entity on the opposite side of the stage. The positions of the entities were constant across trials.

Thus, assuming that attentional indices specify location in the world, the novel trials differed more from the familiar trials in the Feigenson, Carey and Spelke (2002) design than in this one. These extra cues were not needed in

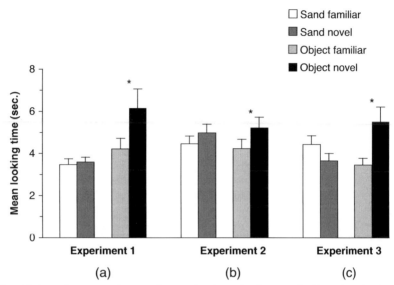

Fig. 7.2 Data from Rosenberg and Carey (under review). Mean looking time (and single standard error) during test trials to sand and object piles in (a) Experiment 1, (b) Experiment 2, and (c) Experiment 3. Note that for each sand condition *N* = 22, and for each object condition *N* = 16.

the object condition (infants succeeded with the sand-pile look-alike objects). Perhaps the cost for representing sand is small, and infants would succeed in indexing the piles, abstracting what is common across habituation trials, and differentiating these from the novel test trials if given these extra cues that the familiarization and test arrays are distinct.

To test this possibility, we instituted one change from Experiment 1 to Experiment 2: the single entity was poured or lowered onto the center of the stage whereas the two entities were poured or lowered onto each side of the stage. Thus, infants familiarized to single-entity trials saw two entities in two new locations during novel test trials, whereas the previously filled location (the center of the stage) was empty. If infants were able to index the location of a poured portion of sand, we would have expected them to respond to the novelty of a previously poured pile versus an empty location and vice versa. Yet, despite this added cue to novelty on the novel test trials, infants' performance in Experiment 2 mimicked that of Experiment 1 (see Fig. 7.2b). When familiarized to a single entity or a pair of entities, infants looked longer at test trials involving a novel number of entities in the object condition whereas they did not look significantly longer than the novel and familiar test outcomes in the sand condition.

These data suggest that the disruptions of entity tracking in the studies by Chiang and Wynn (2000), Huntley-Fenner et al. (2002), and Cheries et al. (2008) are not limited to cases in which representations of particular individuals must be tracked through time and occlusion. Rather, the disruption of encoding caused by noncohesion must occur in the process of indexing or in the process of forming an entity file

A third study assessed whether difficulty tracking noncohesive entities through time might after all have interfered with infants' encoding of the sand piles. Infants of this age might have difficulty tracking the narrow, dynamic stream of sand during pouring as the same entity as the static, pile-shaped mound on the stage. That is, the state change and/or change in center of gravity of the entity might disrupt infants' ability to track the portion of substance as an individual. Indeed, the streaming motion of the entities in vanMarle & Scholl's (2003) MOT study disrupted entity tracking in adults. Even though infants' looking time in Experiments 1 and 2 was recorded once the entities were at rest on the stage, perhaps infants in the sand conditions could not recover from the confusion caused by the pouring motion of the sand. If so, then indexing piles of sand and creating entity files should be possible if the sand is never poured in view of the infants.

Experiment 3 tested this hypothesis. As before, infants were given 30 seconds of tactile exploration with the sand or object prior to the study. But in each habituation or test trial, the curtains opened on the stage revealing the entities already at rest on the stage floor. Except for infants never seeing the entity poured or lowered onto the stage, the experiment was almost identical to Experiment 2.

A color change was introduced to help increase attention to repeated presentations of static piles. During habituation, infants saw alternating presentations of red and green piles from one habituation trial to the next (e.g., in the one-entity habituation condition, single red pile trials alternated with single green pile trials). The entities in all test trials were yellow. This study allowed us to explore another issue—namely, what cues to noncohesion infants are using in these studies. In the studies described in the preceding, there were multiple cues to the noncohesiveness of sand: the tactual prefamiliarization, the pouring during habituation and test trials, and the appearance of the entity resting on the stage.

Although we attempted to make the sand-pile objects perceptually indistinguishable from the piles of sand, they were not actually indistinguishable. Necessarily, the sand scattered a bit at the edges upon pouring and the object had clear-cut edges. In this study, we eliminated the cues from pouring, and we also used the sand-pile objects in *both* conditions: that is, when the curtains opened during a habituation or test trial, it was a sand-pile object that was resting on the stage. The only evidence infants had that this was a sand pile rather than an object was that gained during the tactual prefamiliarization period in which they saw sand poured onto their high chair and were encouraged to touch it

The results of Experiment 3 echoed those of Experiments 1 and 2 (see Fig. 7.2c). Again, during test, infants looked longer at the novel number of objects but looked equally long at the familiar and novel number of what they construed to be sand piles. The failures observed in the two preceding studies persisted even when infants did not observe sand being poured during familiarization and test trials; they did not witness noncohesion during these trials, so their representations of the sand piles resting on the stage floor could not have been disrupted by difficulty maintaining representations of these entities in the face of changes of shape and cohesiveness. Please dwell on the fact that infants viewed *identical* static entities on the stage in the object and sand conditions. Their previous 30 seconds of tactile experience with the sand or object apparently led them to construe those same entities differently. And when these entities were construed as sand, infants failed to distinguish trials with two piles of sand (also, twice as much sand) as different from trials with one pile of sand (also, one half as much sand).

Experiments 1–3 provide remarkably convergent data. In each experiment, infants in the object condition looked longer at the novel than familiar test outcomes whereas infants in the sand condition looked equally at the novel and familiar outcomes. These data are the first to demonstrate that even when infants are not required to maintain a working memory representation of the specific individual portions of occluded noncohesive entities in order to choose which bucket contains more cracker (Cheries et al., 2008) or to predict how many entities will be observed when the occluder is removed (Chiang & Wynn, 2000; Huntley-Fenner et al., 2002), they nonetheless fail to distinguish the novel from the familiar number of sand piles.

So, where in processing are representations of noncohesive substances going wrong? These data are consistent with the possibility that infants fail to index portions of sand at all, or fail to create working memory entity files for piles of sand. As mentioned earlier, we find it highly unlikely that infants cannot index (attend to) sand. If noncohesion led infants to fail to attend to such entities, they could never learn about them. Furthermore, during the experiments, infants look intently at the sand, both during the tactual familiarization and the experiment itself, and they became habituated at comparable rates in each condition. If infants had not attended to the sand in the tactual familiarization condition, they would not have failed in the Experiment 3, for there would have been no representations that could have influenced their construal of the ambiguous entities they observed resting on the stage. Finally, there is other positive evidence infants attend to nonsolid substances. Two independent studies (Baillargeon, 1995, with 5.5-month-olds; Huntley-Fenner, 1995, with 8-month-olds) found that infants' attention was drawn when sand or salt apparently passed through a solid barrier. Infants cannot react to a violation of expectancy involving sand without attending to it (indexing it).

The data at hand are consistent with two possibilities concerning the locus of difficulty infants face in representing portions of sand. Perhaps, as we have discussed,they are impaired at creating working memory entity files for sand piles; these are needed to abstract what is common across successive habituation trials, as well as to solve the entity permanence tasks of previous studies. Alternatively the difficulty may be of an entirely different nature altogether: perhaps infants index portions of sand just fine, and even create entity files for them, but quantify over these representations differently than they do over representations of objects. The distinction between objects and substances has quantificational consequences; objects are lexicalized as count nouns and substances as mass nouns. Perhaps infants are representing the sand as 'some sand' and are simply not sensitive to whether it comes in scattered or continuous portions. Current studies in our laboratory seek to adjudicate between these two hypotheses.

7.4 Implications for the core cognition hypothesis

The findings we have described thus far are consistent with the claim that there is no core knowledge of noncohesive substance, as well as with the core cognition hypothesis as it applies to solid, cohesive objects. Infants are able to index and track entities within a putative domain of core cognition (e.g., solid objects) in the face of failure with perceptually similar objects outside of core cognition (e.g., noncohesive entities). Noncohesive entities are material ones, and thus are subject to some of the same physical constraints as material objects have. As previously stated, 5- and 8-month-old infants recognize that sand and salt should not pass through a solid barrier. We drew on this fact to argue that they must attend to these entities, but here we comment on the fact that they have come to apply one of the key constraints on the motion of objects to nonobjects. Is it possible that there really is core knowledge for substances that is just later appearing? If so, such knowledge should emerge in coherent way.

Preliminary evidence suggests that this is not the case. As mentioned earlier, the capacity to represent *objects* as spatiotemporally continuous (object permanence) and as uniquely occupying space (the solidity constraint) emerge together at approximately 2 months of age. But we have just seen that infants represent sand and salt as subject to the solidity constraint by 5–8 months of age, whereas 8- and 12-month-olds fail at tasks that tap their recognition that noncohesive entities are permanent at least until 12 months of age (Cheries et al., 2008; Chiang & Wynn, 2000; Huntley-Fenner et al., 2002). This is just exactly the piecemeal learning we might expect to find about entities whose representations are not supported by a system of core cognition.

Of course, at some point, we eventually come to understand the properties of nonobjects. How, then, might we come to this understanding? Infants might form statistical generalizations of the behavior of noncohesive entities, although to do so requires that infants attend to and create representations of them based on their understanding of the behavior of material entities in general. As previously reported, infants do appear to understand that noncohesive substances should not pass through solid barriers (5-month-olds: Baillargeon, 1995; 8- and 12-month-olds: Huntley-Fenner et al., 2002). Then again, this knowledge might have more to do with a generalization about solid barriers than about the types of entities that could or could not pass through them.

Here, we turn to a stronger test of the hypothesis that learning about noncohesive entities is piecemeal, and that there is no core knowledge of noncohesive entities. We explore infants' representations of cohesion and noncohesion per se. Cohesion is a basis of categorizing objects as objects, and it is also a constraint on object motion (objects do not fall apart as they move through space). Even 3-month-olds represent cohesion as such (Spelke et al., 1993). In Spelke's study, infants viewed a hand picking up a simple, regularly shaped static solid object that either lifted as a whole (the expected outcome) or came apart as it was lifted (the unexpected outcome). Infants looked longer when the object fell apart, suggesting that they expect solid objects to maintain their boundaries when moved. If knowledge about noncohesive entities must be acquired in a piecemeal way, perhaps the comparable fact about noncohesive entities (that they *are* noncohesive) must be painstakingly learned.

7.5 Do infants understand noncohesion as a projectable property?

Based on the Spelke et al. (1993) study of cohesion with 3-month-olds, Huntley-Fenner (1995) tested 8- and 12-month-old infants in a similar violation of expectancy paradigm. Now, however, infants were not only asked to reason about the future behavior of solid, cohesive objects but also about the future behavior of noncohesive entities. The stimuli (sand and a perceptually similar solid pile) were the same as in the sand studies previously described

(Huntley-Fenner et al., 2002; Rosenberg & Carey, under review). Unlike all of the studies discussed earlier, infants were given tactile exposure to *both* entities (sand and the sand-pile look-alike object). They were then randomly assigned to either the sand or the object condition.

For test trials in the object condition, an occluder that covered half of the previously empty stage was raised and the solid object was lowered behind the occluder. The occluder was then removed to reveal a hand reaching for the entity (on half the trials, the object had been surreptitiously switched with a pile of sand). Two test outcomes were alternated: the object was either lifted as a coherent whole and moved to a new location on the stage (the expected outcome) or the entity fell apart upon being lifted (the unexpected outcome). Test trials for the sand condition involved sand being poured behind the occluder, upon which the occluder was removed and the hand was shown reaching for the revealed entity.

On half of the trials, the sand had been surreptitiously switched with a sand-pile look-alike object. For sand trials, the expected outcome (for adults) was the entity falling apart upon being lifted and the unexpected outcome was the entity being lifted as a coherent whole. Replicating Spelke et al. (1993) with older children, infants in the object condition looked longer at the unexpected outcome, providing further evidence of their understanding of cohesion as an enduring property of solid objects. Infants in the sand condition, however, showed no expectation as to how the sand should behave: that is, they did not seem surprised when sand that they had seen poured behind an occluder magically lifted as a whole!

These data provide further evidence against core knowledge for noncohesive entities. Noncohesion is, as the name would suggest, a defining property of noncohesive entities. Yet, even 12-month-olds fail to understand that a pile of sand should remain noncohesive over time, occlusion, and movement. Thus, infants do not seem prepared to represent noncohesive entities, as they not only fail to distinguish one from two portions of them but also fail to recognize them as noncohesive. To further explore the protracted process through which infants learn about noncohesive entities, the last studies we report here attempt to find the earliest evidence for infants' reasoning about noncohesion per se (Rosenberg et al., in preparation). Just how delayed are infants in representing noncohesion as a projectable, stable property of some material entities, in the face of success at representing cohesiveness as an enduring property at least by 3 months of age? Finding the age of success will enable us to explore the relation between representing noncohesive entities as such and creating generalizations about the behavior of noncohesive substances that would allow them to be indexed and tracked through time.

7.6 **Differential reaching and grasping**

Because it is difficult to test infants over 12- to 14-months of age in looking time paradigms, we needed to develop a new method for assessing infants' understanding of non-cohesion. Based on extensive work showing that infants can perform anticipatory reaching and grasping movements based on the physical attributes of the objects for which they are reaching (e.g. Clifton et al., 1991; Hood & Willatts, 1986; Lockman et al., 1984; McCarty et al., 2001), we developed a reaching method that could be used on 13- to 18-month-old infants. Infants in our Experiment 1 were divided into a 'young' group (mean age = 15 months) and an 'old' group (mean age = 17 months). The stimuli were the actual sand and the sand-covered, sand-pile-shaped objects described earlier.

The experimenter performed four imitation-eliciting trials alternating sand and objects. For object trials, she introduced the object dangling from a string and lowered it, jiggling, onto a tray, tucking the string under the bottom of the pile. She then demonstrated an exaggerated patting motion on the pile using two flat hands to tap the pile three times. The infant was encouraged to copy the action, and the experimenter and/or parent continued to model the action and encourage the infant until the infant either imitated the action or 60 seconds passed. For sand trials, the experimenter poured the sand between two visible beakers and then onto the tray. Calling attention to her fingers, she made a clear pincer grasp and then reached down, picked up a bit of sand, and placed it to the side of the pile. Again, the infant was encouraged to imitate the action.

For test trials, the experimenter introduced the stimuli as in the imitation trials (lowering the object dangling from a string or pouring the sand between two beakers and onto the tray). Without performing any action on the entities herself, the experimenter asked the infant, 'What do you do with that?' and pushed the tray toward the infant. If infants had encoded the cohesive or noncohesive nature of the entity based on whether it was lowered as a whole or poured from a stream into a pile, we would expect them to perform the desired action. If, however, infants fail to represent the noncohesiveness of sand, they should not differentially try to pick up a bit of it.

Only infants who had correctly performed the desired action for each entity type at least once during familiarization were included in analysis of test trials. For test trials, infants' first contact with the entity was coded as +1 point for performing the object action (patting the object) and −1 point for performing the sand action (trying to grasp at the object as though to try and pick up a bit). Thus, a score of −1 on a sand trial would constitute performing the

Addition task

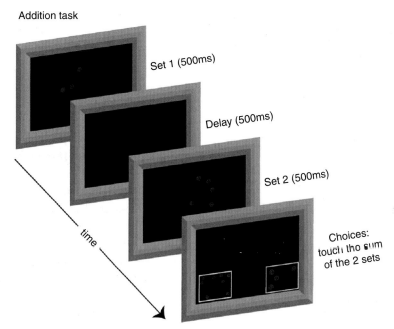

Set 1 (500ms)

Delay (500ms)

Set 2 (500ms)

time

Choices:
touch the sum
of the 2 sets

Fig. 3.7 (a) Stimuli and task design used to test nonverbal addition by monkeys and college students. Monkeys and humans were presented with one set of dots (Set 1), followed by a brief delay, after which a second set of dots was presented (Set 2). Then, two choices (the sum and the distractor) were presented, and monkeys were rewarded for touching the choice that represented the numerical sum of the two sets (Cantlon & Brannon, 2007). See p. 62.

(a)   (b)

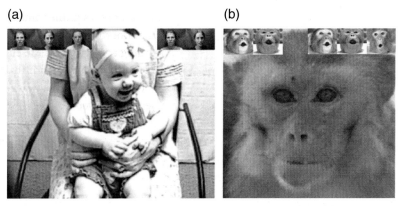

Fig. 3.8 Static images from video displays used to test whether human infants (a) and rhesus monkeys (b) spontaneously matched the number of dynamic conspecific faces they saw with the number of vocalizations they simultaneously heard in a preferential looking paradigm (Reproduced from Brannon, E. M. (2006). The representation of numerical magnitude. *Current Opinion in Neurobiology, 16,* 222–229.). See p. 68.

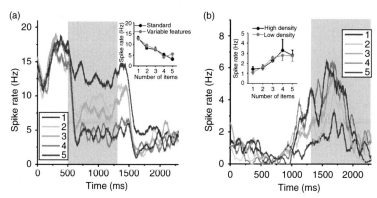

Fig. 3.10 Example numerosity-selective cells from the fundus of the intraparietal sulcus (IPS) in a macaque monkey. Neuron A was selective in the sample presentation and shows maximum firing to the numerosity 1. Neuron B was selective during the memory delay and fired maximally to numerosity 4. Distributions of preferred numerosities across the cells recorded from during the sample (a) and delay (b) periods (Nieder & Miller, 2004). See p. 75.

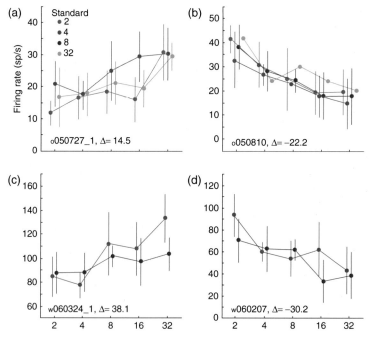

Fig. 3.11 Single lateral intraparietal (LIP) neurons respond in a graded fashion to the total number of elements in the response field (Roitman et al., 2007). Neurons shown in (a) and (c) increased firing rate with numerosity, whereas those shown in (b) and (d) had larger responses for smaller numerosities. See p. 77.

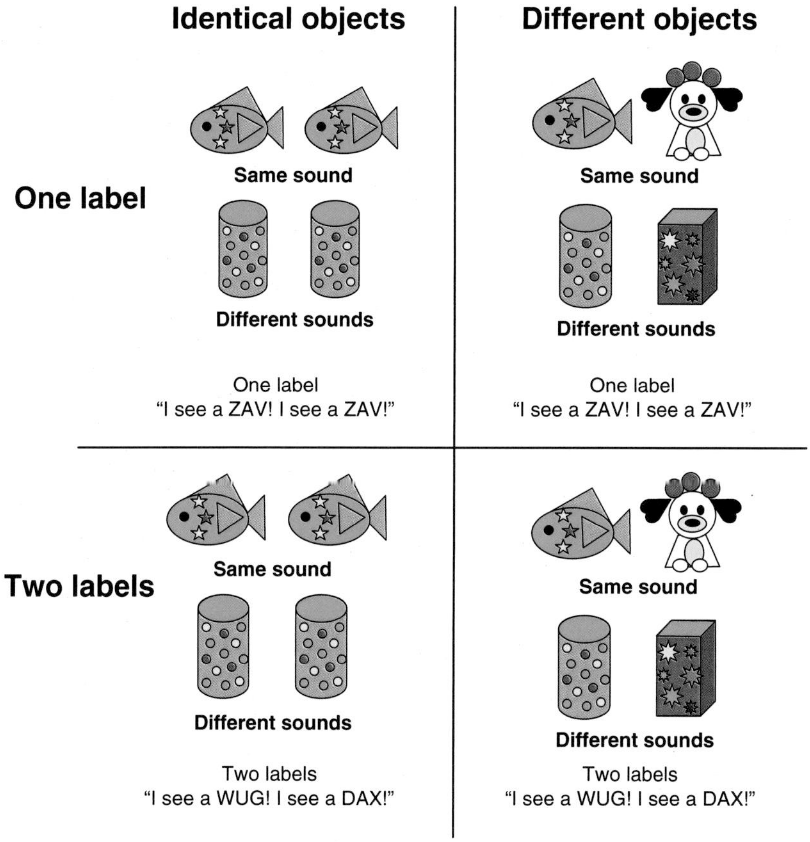

Fig. 11.2 Test trials for all four conditions (identical vs. different objects; one vs. two labels) from Dewar and Xu (in press). See p. 273.

Fig. 11.3 A schematic of the thought experiment on overhypothesis formation by Goodman (1955). See p. 275.

Fig. 13.2 The four-door solidity apparatus. This image illustrates the four-door apparatus showing the four doors, the partially visible wall, and an object rolling down the ramp. See p. 356.

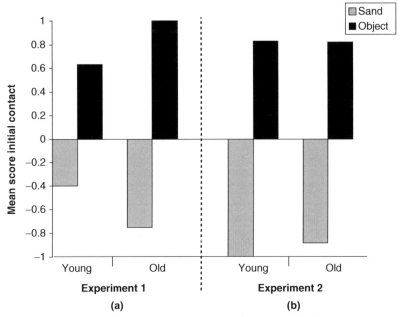

Fig. 7.3 Data from Rosenberg et al. (in preparation). Mean score of initial contacts in test trials in (a) Experiment 1 and (b) Experiment 2. A score of +1 represents performing the object action (patting in Experiment 1 and pushing in Experiment 2) and a score of −1 represents performing the sand action (grasping).

desired action whereas a score of +1 on a sand trial would represent performing the opposite action (patting the sand pile). Mean scores for each entity type were calculated using zero as chance performance. As shown in Fig. 7.3a, the younger group performed the correct action on almost all of the object trials but not on all the sand trials.

Not surprisingly, infants at both ages seem to represent the solid object as such, for they performed the modeled patting action once the object was lowered. In contrast, the younger group failed, as a group, to perform the modeled action on the sand. Thus, as a group, even 15-month-old infants failed to keep track of the history of the entity (poured in a stream from a beaker into a pile on a stage) so they knew to pick up a portion of it with a pincer grasp. These data confirm the conclusion of Huntley-Fenner's looking-time study that infants as old as 12–14 months of age have not yet formed the generalization that a noncohesive entity is likely to remain noncohesive in the immediate future.

The older group of infants, however, performed the correct action for both types of entities on almost every trial. Having just seen the object lowered as a whole, they immediately performed a patting action, and having just seen the sand poured, they performed a pincer-like action. These results suggest that by 17 months of age infants are sensitive to noncohesion as an enduring property of some material entities. That is, for the sand trials, they seem to have tracked the noncohesion of the pouring sand such that they expected it to be able to come apart if they attempted to grasp at it. These findings are some of the first to demonstrate a positive representation of noncohesion in infancy see also, Hespos et al., (in press).

These data confirm both predictions from the hypothesis that there is core cognition of objects but not of noncohesive entities. First, infants are sensitive to cohesion very early in infancy, and they appear to represent cohesion as a projectable property of objects over a year earlier than they represent non-cohesion as a projectable property of sand. This is what would be expected if there are innate constraints on representations of object motion, but not on representations of the motion of noncohesive entities. Second, learning about noncohesion apparently proceeds in a piecemeal manner: infants have learned that sand and salt should not pass through a barrier by 5–8 months of age, but there is no evidence that they can create entity files for particular portions of sand even at 12 months of age, nor is there evidence that they have even repre-sented sand as noncohesive until 17 months of age.

Still, 17 months is a relatively late age to demonstrate knowledge of non-cohesion as an enduring property of material entities, given that very young infants are *sensitive* to noncohesion in the sense that they must be able to represent sand as different from the sand-pile object look-alikes to respond to them differentially. It is possible that these tasks have underestimated infants' knowledge. One plausible explanation for the young groups' lesser perform-ance on our reaching task is that the actions we used were not particularly motivating for the infants. Patting the sand-pile object did not lead to some other interesting outcome. And although the grasping and picking up action modeled for the sand could not be (successfully) performed on the object, the patting action could certainly be performed on either entity. That is, whereas the grasping motion was intrinsically tied to the noncohesive nature of the sand, the patting motion was not tied to the object's cohesion or solidity. Perhaps using more relevant, motivating, and function-based actions would improve infants' performance.

7.7 The entity detector

The stimuli for Experiment 2 were the same as in the previous reaching study. Additionally, an 'entity detector' (a box that lit up and made noise every time the desired action was performed) was introduced. Infants, who again ranged in age from 13 to 18 months, were divided into younger and older groups (mean ages of 15 and 17 months, respectively). The experimenter first presented infants with one imitation trial for each entity without using the entity detector. The action for the sand was the same as in the previous study. The experimenter poured the sand between two beakers and then into a pile on a tray in front of the infant. She then modeled an exaggerated pincer grasp, picked up a bit of sand, and placed it to the side of the pile. The experimenter encouraged the infant to copy her action.

For the object trial, the experimenter dangled the object from a string, lowering it onto the tray. Rather than patting it, she modeled pushing the pile across the tray with a flat semi-upright hand and then encouraged the infant to do so. This action could only be successfully carried out on the object. Next, the entity detector was introduced and infants were given four imitation trials, alternating sand and objects. For sand trials, once the sand was at rest on the stage, the experimenter demonstrated making a pincer grasp, then picked up a bit of sand and placed it in a small funnel on top of the entity detector. As the sand entered the funnel, the experimenter surreptitiously activated the lights and sounds of the entity detector, creating a convincing cause and effect relationship between the desired action and the auditory and visual stimuli. For object trials, once the object was static on the tray, the experimenter demonstrated how she could push the object (with a flat, semi-upright hand) into a pile-shaped hole at the bottom of the entity detector. As the object entered the hole, the experimenter activated the lights and sounds. For the four test trials (two sand and two object, with order counterbalanced), stimuli were presented as described in the preceding, but the experimenter did not model any action. Once the stimuli were at rest on the tray, she asked, 'Can you make my machine work?' and waited for the infant to proceed.

Test trials were coded for initial contact using the same scoring system as in the previous experiment. Infants in *both* groups performed the desired actions in both their initial contact (see Fig. 7.3b) and their subsequent actions for *both* types of entities. These data suggest they had represented the cohesive state (cohesive or noncohesive) of each entity and created a working memory model that allowed them to plan and execute their reach and grasp according to the attributes of the entity for which they were reaching. Note that for the younger groups, the performance on the initial contacts to the stimuli was better in this experiment than in the previous one, suggesting that both functional demands of the task aided infants' representations of the cohesive state of each entity.

The entity detector study (Experiment 2) confirms that infants in their second year of life are able to represent noncohesion as a projectable property of material entities. In both experiments, the older infants demonstrated that they expected that sand will come apart upon being lifted, as evidenced by their pincer grasp and attempts to pick up a *portion* of the entity. What is new in the entity detector study is that given enough motivation, even 15-month-olds succeed. We do not yet know the youngest age at which functional relevance might lead infants to succeed. A looking-time version of the entity detector study could be brought to bear on the question. Nonetheless, consistent with the hypothesis that infants are still working out generalizations about noncohesive entities in their second year of life, whereas they have already worked out the comparable generalizations about cohesive entities early in their first year, the functional information was necessary for robust success on the sand trials but not on the object trials.

7.8 **Conclusions**

The core cognition hypothesis requires that the representations within core cognition be distinguishable from other representations. Most of human knowledge is *not* embedded within systems of core cognition. Almost certainly, there are no innate perceptual analyzers, nor innate learning mechanisms, that pick out the electrons, the tables, the stars, or the wombats in our environment. There is no a priori way of establishing which systems of core knowledge exist. As illustrated here, arguments from cross-cultural universality, centrality in thought, and ubiquity in the environment are not sufficient. Such considerations might lead us to expect core cognition of substances, including noncohesive ones.

On the contrary, coming to explicitly distinguish material from immaterial physical entities, representing the former as made of substances, is a protracted developmental process, extending over years in child development (see Carey, in press, for a review) and over centuries in historical development (Jammer, 1961; Toulmin & Goodfield, 1962). The present studies bring this point home; infants well into their first year of life have great difficulty creating representations of particular portions of nonsolid substances and tracking these through time, and apparently fail to recognize noncohesion as a stable property of entities until their second year of life.

One goal of the present chapter was to provide support for the core cognition hypothesis by demonstrating that the representations within core cognition have very different properties from representations not part of any core cognition system. Representations within core cognition are evident very early in development, and emerge coherently. Object representations display both of these signatures of core cognition. Finding that representations of nonsolid substances most emphatically do not do so bolsters our confidence that the representations of objects truly are privileged in development. This is especially important because the generalizations about nonsolid substances we explored here (substance permanence, the capacity to form entity files for individual portions of substance, and the recognition of noncohesion as a projectable property of some material entities) are closely related to central features of core cognition of objects.

In addition to providing evidence for the existence of core cognition in general, the present studies bear on the proper characterization of core object cognition. Several of the constraints on object motion infants represent in their models of the world actually follow from objects' status as material entities. It is true of all material entities that no two portions can be in the same place at the same time, it is true of all inanimate material entities that once at rest they remain at rest unless subject to some external force, and it is true of all material entities that they cannot blip in and out of existence. The present studies demonstrate that infants' generalizations about objects are not couched at this more abstract level. They are truly generalizations about *objects*—bounded, coherent wholes that maintain their boundaries as they move through space and time.

These studies leave many open questions. First, we have presented our arguments in terms of infants' knowledge of noncohesive entities, but we have primarily discussed one particular entity—sand. Sand, salt, and similar entities are certainly not ubiquitous in most infants' environment. Thus, it remains an open question whether infants might learn properties of other noncohesive entities, such as liquids or pureed food, earlier.[1] Again, such findings would be consistent with piecemeal learning about particular noncohesive substances, rather than constrained learning about substances in general. Perhaps the most important remaining question, then, is *how* infants learn about nonsolid substances?

Human beings, similar to all animals, are equipped with powerful, domain-general, learning mechanisms. These include the associative learning mechanisms captured, for example, in connectionist algorithms (e.g., Rogers & McClelland, 2004) and Bayesian learning mechanisms (e.g., Gopnick & Tenenbaum, 2007) that can abstract statistical regularities in the child's experience (see also Amso & Johnson, Chapter 9; Mareschal & Bremner, Chapter 10). To learn about the relevant properties of noncohesive entities, infants

---

[1] See Hespos et al. (in press) for evidence that 5-month-old infants distinguish liquids from perceptually similar solids based on movement cues. But see Shutts et al. (under review) for demonstrations of 9-month-old infants' limited understanding of the properties of food substances.

may draw on generalizations about objects by analogy. This might underlie infants' relatively early knowledge that sand or salt cannot pass through a solid barrier. Coming to see that sand and salt are subject to the same constraint on entity motion as are objects could be part of a protracted process through which certain properties of objects are generalized to become represented as properties of noncohesive entities. Such a process of forming representations of nonobjects is in stark contrast to infants' core representations of solid, cohesive objects.

Acknowledgements

This research was supported in part by an NSF GRF to the first author and NIH grant R01 HD 038338 to the second author. We are grateful to the following researchers for their assistance: Alene Anello, Leah Casner, Rebecca Doggett, Caryn Harris, Eileen Matias, and Paul Muentener. We also thank Gavin Huntley-Fenner for the wonderful set of studies on which we based our work. Finally, we are indebted to all of the families who have participated in our research.

References

Baillargeon, R. (1986). Representing the existence and the location of hidden objects: object permanence in 6- and 8-month-old infants. *Cognition*, *23*, 21–41.

Baillargeon, R. (1995). A model of physical reasoning in infancy. In C. Rovee-Collier, & L. Lipsett (Eds.), *Advances in Infancy Research* (p. 9). Norwood, NJ: Ablex.

Baillargeon, R. (2001). Infants' physical knowledge: of acquired expectations and core knowledge. In E. Dupoux (Ed.), *Language, Brain, and Cognitive Development: Essays in Honor of Jacques Mehler* (pp. 341–361). Cambridge, MA: MIT Press.

Baillargeon, R., & DeVos, J. (1991). Object permanence in young infants: further evidence. *Child Development*, *62*, 1227–1246.

Berkeley, G. (1732/1919). *A New Theory of Vision and Other Select Philosophical Writings*. New York: E.P. Dutton & Co.

Carey, S. (1985). *Conceptual Change in Childhood*. Cambridge, MA: MIT Press.

Carey, S. (1988). Conceptual differences between children and adults. *Mind and Language*, *3*, 167–181.

Carey, S. (in press). *The Origins of Concepts*. New York: Oxford University Press.

Carey, S., & Spelke, E. (1994). Domain-specific knowledge and conceptual change. In L. Hirshfeld, & S. Gelman (Eds.), *Mapping the Mind: Domain Specificity in Cognition and Culture* (pp. 169–200). New York: Cambridge University Press.

Carey, S., & Spelke, E. (1996). Science and Core Knowledge. *Journal of Philosophy of Science*, *63*, 515–533.

Cheries, E. W., Mitroff, S., Wynn, K., & Scholl, B. (2008). Cohesion as a constraint on object persistence in infancy. *Cognition*, *80*, 179–213.

Chiang, W., & Wynn, K. (2000). Infants' tracking of objects and collections. *Cognition, 77,* 169–195.

Clifton, R. K., Rochat, P., Litovsky, R. Y., & Perris, E. E. (1991). Object representation guides infants' reaching in the dark. *Journal of Experimental Psychology: Human Perception and Performance, 17,* 323–329.

Feigenson, L., Carey, S., & Hauser, M. (2002). The representations underlying infants' choice of more: object files versus analog magnitudes. *Psychological Science, 13,* 150–156.

Feigenson, L., Carey, S., & Spelke, E. (2002). Infants' discrimination of number vs. continuous extent. *Cognitive Psychology, 44,* 33–66.

Fodor, J. A. (1983). *Modularity of Mind.* Cambridge, MA. MIT Press.

Gopnick, A., & Tenenbaum, J. B. (2007). Bayesian networks, Bayesian learning and cognitive development. *Developmental Science, 10,* 281–287.

Hespos, S., & Baillargeon, R. (2001). Reasoning about containment events in very young infants. *Cognition, 78,* 207–245.

Hespos, S. J., Ferry, A., & Rips, L .J. (in press). Five month old infants have different expectations for solids and substances. *Psychological Science.*

Hood, B., & Willatts, P. (1986). Reaching in the dark to an objects' remembered position: evidence for object permanence in 5-month-old infants. *British Journal of Developmental Psychology, 4,* 57–65.

Huntley-Fenner, G. (1995). The representations of objects, non-solid substances, and collections in infancy and early childhood (Doctoral Dissertation: MIT, 1995). *Dissertation Abstracts International: Section B: The Sciences and Engineering, 56,* 2352.

Huntley-Fenner, G., Carey, S., & Solimondo, A. (2002). Objects are individuals but stuff doesn't count: perceived rigidity and cohesiveness influence infants' representations of small groups of entities. *Cognition, 85,* 203–221.

Jammer, M. (1961). *Concepts of Mass in Classical and Modern Physics.* Cambridge, MA: Harvard University Press.

Leslie, A. M. (1994). ToMM, ToBy, and Agency: core architecture and domain specificity. In L. Hirschfeld, & S. Gelman (Eds.), *Mapping the Mind: Domain Specificity in Cognition and Culture* (pp. 119–148). Cambridge: Cambridge University Press.

Locke, J. (1690/1975). *An Essay Concerning Human Understanding.* Oxford: Oxford University Press.

Lockman, J. J., Ashmead, D. H., & Bushnell, E. W. (1984). The development of anticipatory hand orientation during infancy. *Journal of Experimental Child Psychology, 37,* 176–186.

McCarty, M., Clifton R., Ashmead, D., Lee, P., & Goubet, N. (2001). How infants use vision for grasping objects. *Child Development, 72,* 973–987.

McCrink, K., & Wynn, K. (2004). Large-number addition and subtraction by 9-month-old infants. *Psychological Science, 15,* 776–781.

Medin, D. L., & Atran, S. (2004). The native mind: biological categorization and reasoning in development and across cultures. *Psychological Review, 111,* 960–983.

Mitroff, S. R., Scholl, B. J., & Wynn, K. (2004). Divide and conquer: how object files adapt when a persisting object splits into two. *Psychological Science, 15,* 420–425.

Piaget, J. (1954). *The Construction of Reality in the Child.* New York: Basic Books.

Pylyshyn, Z. W. (1989). The role of location indexes in spatial perception: a sketch of the FINST spatial-index model. *Cognition, 32*, 65–97.

Quine, W. V. O. (1953/1980). Two dogmas of empiricism. In *From a Logical Point of View: Nine Logico-Philisophical Essays* (pp. 20–46). Cambridge, MA: MIT Press.

Quine, W. V. O. (1960). *Word and Object.* Cambridge, MA: MIT Press.

Rogers, T., & McClelland, J. (2004). Semantic cognition: a parallel distributed approach. Cambridge, MA: MIT Press.

Rosenberg, R. D., & Carey, S. (under review). The effects of non-cohesion on entity indexing, entity tracking, and working-memory files.

Rosenberg, R. D., Huntley-Fenner, G., & Carey, S. (in preparation). Infants' perception of cohesion and non-cohesion as enduring properties of material entities.

Samuelson, L. K., & Smith, L. B. (1999). Early noun vocabularies: Do ontology, category structure and syntax correspond? *Cognition, 73*, 1–33.

Samuelson, L. K., & Smith, L. B. (2000). Children's attention to rigid and deformable shape in naming and non-naming tasks. *Child Development, 71*, 1555–1570.

Samuelson, L. K., & Smith, L. B. (2005). They call it like they see it: spontaneous naming and attention to shape. *Developmental Science, 8*, 182–198.

Scholl, B. J. (2001). Objects and attention: the state of the art. *Cognition, 80*, 1–46.

Scholl, B. J., & Pylyshyn, Z. W. (1999). Tracking multiple items through occlusion: clues to visual objecthood. *Cognitive Psychology, 38*, 259–290.

Shutts, K., Condry, K. F., Santos, L. R., & Spelke, E .S. (under review). Core knowledge and its limitations: the domain of food.

Soja, N., Carey, S., & Spelke, E.S. (1991). Ontological categories guide young children's inductions of word meaning: object terms and substance terms. *Cognition, 38*, 179–211.

Spelke, E. S., Brelinger, K., & Jacobson, K. (1993). Gestalt relations and object perception: a developmental study. *Perception, 22*, 1483–1501.

Spelke, E. S., Brelinger, K., Macomber, J., & Jacobsen, K. (1992). Origins of knowledge. *Psychological Review, 99*, 605–632.

Spelke, E., & Kinzler, K. (2007). Core knowledge. *Developmental Science, 10*, 89–96.

Toulmin, S., & Goodfield, J. (1962). *The Architecture of Matter.* NY: Harper & Row.

VanMarle, K., & Scholl, B. J. (2003). Attentive tracking of objects vs. substances. *Psychological Science, 14*, 498–504.

Wellman, H. M., & Gelman, S. (1992). Cognitive development: foundational theories of core domains. *Annual Review of Psychology, 43*, 337–375.

Wynn, K. (1992). Addition and subtraction by human infants. *Nature, 358*, 749–750.

Xu, F., & Carey, S. (1996). Infants' metaphysics: the case of numerical identity. *Cognitive Psychology, 30*, 111–153.

Chapter 8

The developmental origins of animal and artifact concepts

Kristin Shutts, Lori Markson, &
Elizabeth S. Spelke

As much of this book attests, a wealth of research provides evidence that human infants have a core capacity for representing objects and their motions. The environment contains a diversity of objects, however, with varied properties and behaviors. Objects such as pebbles and blocks are inert; they move or change only in response to an external force. Objects such as butterflies and cars have internal mechanisms generating forces that can propel them. Self-propelled objects can be further differentiated, according to the nature and characteristic pattern of their motions and the circumstances that evoke them. To navigate successfully in this diverse and changing environment, perceivers and actors must categorize the objects around them appropriately, determining what kind of thing each object is and how it is likely to behave.

Here we consider three general accounts of the development of this ability in humans. First, all human learning about objects may be supported by a single core domain that identifies and tracks objects through space and time (e.g., Flombaum et al., Chapter 6; but see Amso and Johnson, Chapter 9). As infants track pebbles and parrots, balls and cars, they may gradually learn that objects fall into general kinds with distinctive properties and behavior (e.g., Spelke, 1990). Second, humans may possess a wealth of distinct core systems for representing objects of different kinds. Early in development, infants may distinguish natural from artifact objects, and they may further distinguish animals, plants, and nonliving natural kinds, as well as people from different social groups and with various properties (Cosmides & Tooby, 1994; Cosmides et al., 2003). Finally, human learning may stem from a very limited set of core domains, such as one for reasoning about social or sentient objects and another for reasoning about all other kinds of objects (e.g., Bloom, 2004; Johnson et al., 1998), or one for reasoning about objects with the capacity for autonomous motion and another for reasoning about objects that lack this capacity (e.g., Baillargeon et al., Chapter 12; R. Gelman, 1990).

Behind these contrasting proposals is a longstanding question, still unresolved, concerning the origins and nature of concepts in human infancy. Are humans' most fundamental concepts, including *person*, *object*, *animal*, and *artifact*, inherent in the human mind and manifest throughout human development, or are they products of learning and experience? Studies of human infants are needed to address this question, using methods that can reveal the signatures of mature conceptual distinctions. In the present chapter, we discuss a new line of experiments on infants that follow this strategy, probing infants' concepts of autonomously moving objects that are natural (i.e., animals) or artifacts (i.e., vehicles). We consider these concepts in relation to two more general ones: the concept *self-propelled object*, which includes both animals and vehicles, and the concept *object*, which includes both self-propelled objects and inert objects such as plants, cups, and rocks.

8.1 **The concept** *animal*

Extensive research on the origins of human concepts has focused on the concept *animal* in adults and children. This concept is universal across humans (Atran et al., 2002) and is well established in children by the time they enter school (Carey, 1985; Keil, 1989; S. Gelman, 2003). At the center of this concept are two principles. First, animals belong to *kinds*, whose members share not only perceptible properties but also common internal properties and predispositions (R. Gelman, 1990; S. Gelman & Wellman, 1991; Simons & Keil, 1995). Second, animals move on their own, and their motion is internally generated, directed to goals, and takes efficient paths to those goals (R. Gelman & Spelke, 1981; Massey & R. Gelman, 1988; Viviani & Stucchi, 1992).

Nevertheless, research on children and adults does not clarify the origins of these principles. It is possible that the concept *animal* extends back to infancy. Alternatively, infants may be attuned only to object motions and visual attributes, and they may construct the concept *animal* by learning about correlations of these features with one another and with deeper properties of animals (see Quinn, 2002; Rakison, 2003). Intermediate positions also are possible: Infants may be predisposed to focus on objects and their sources of motion and to form concepts that account for regularities in object structures and functions, fostering rapid learning of concepts of animals and vehicles during infancy (Mandler, 2004).

In recent years, research probing the origins of the concepts *animal* and *vehicle* has centered on methods that probe infants' categorization of objects (for reviews, see Mandler, 2004; Rakison & Poulin-Dubois, 2001; Rakison & Oakes, 2003). Behind this research is the assumption that infants' concepts will be revealed through the categories they form: If infants have a concept *animal*, then they will categorize together perceptually dissimilar objects with the critical attributes of animals (e.g., Mandler & McDonough, 1993, 1998). If infants lack such a concept, then their categorization of objects will depend more directly on the objects' perceptual characteristics, such as possession of particular parts (e.g., Rakison & Butterworth, 1998).

8.2 **Methods for studying infants' concepts**

Infants' categorization of objects has been tested by means of a suite of methods for eliciting object categorization, focusing on visual preference, object manipulation, and deferred imitation. Studies using these methods reveal that infants have an impressive capacity for categorizing animals as distinct from other objects such as vehicles and furniture, on the basis of object appearance (e.g., Behl-Chada, 1996; Mandler & McDonough, 1993, 1996, 1998; McDonough & Mandler, 1998; Pauen, 2002). Because animals and artifacts are highly complex, however, it is not clear what aspects of their appearance are critical to infants' categorization (Pauen, 2002; Rakison & Butterworth, 1998). Moreover, the findings of this research have produced no consensus concerning either the status of infants' categories or the course of conceptual development (see Rakison & Poulin-Dubois, 2001, for a review).

The problem, we believe, lies in the strategy of inferring concepts from the perceptual features used in categorization (Shutts & Spelke, 2004). All categorization of perceptible objects must depend on some perceived properties of those objects, whether or not that categorization is guided by abstract conceptual distinctions. Moreover, there is no systematic metric of shape perception or catalog of object features that would dictate how objects should be categorized in the absence of abstract concepts. For these reasons, studies of feature-based categorization do not reveal whether infants share adults' conceptual categories of *animal* and *vehicle* or form meaningless groupings of objects that are similar in appearance. A consideration of adults' and young children's concepts suggests both the limitations of this strategy and a different approach to the study of concepts in infancy.

Research with adults and preschool children suggests two signature properties of mature *animal* and *vehicle* concepts. First, adults and children expect different kinds of motion from animals versus other artifacts (e.g., R. Gelman & Spelke, 1981; Massey & R. Gelman, 1988). In one study (Massey & Gelman,

1988), for example, 3- and 4-year-old children were shown photographs of animals, vehicles, and rigid objects, and they were asked whether each thing could go up and down a hill on its own. Children judged that only the animals could move in both directions, and reported that even the vehicles could move only downhill by themselves. These findings suggest that children distinguish animals from artifacts of all kinds by three years of age.

Second, adults and children expect animals of the same kind to have similar substance properties (colors and textures) as well as similar shapes, whereas they expect artifacts to vary along substance dimensions. Thus, adults and children attend to information about color and texture when reasoning about animals, but not about artifacts (e.g., Booth & Waxman, 2002; Brown, 1990; Jones & Smith, 1998; Jones et al., 1991; Keil et al., 1998; Lavin & Hall, 2002; Massey & R. Gelman, 1988; McManus & Keil, 2001; Santos et al., 2002). Preschool children tested by Massey and Gelman (1988), for example, used texture information to distinguish photographs of real animals from photographs of animal statues (both of which had animal shapes), and correctly judged that only the former was capable of autonomous motion.

In summary, the mature concept *animal* captures a more abstract set of processes and properties: processes that reveal themselves in the object's behavior, and properties that are specific to an object's substance. These observations suggest an approach to the study of the origins of the concepts in infants. If the mature concepts *animal* and *vehicle* originate in infancy, then infants should show the two same signature patterns of inference. Presented with an object in motion, they should expect the object to move independently only if it possesses animal features and moves like an animal. Moreover, when presented with an object that looks like an animal, infants should generalize learning about that animal's motion to other objects that share its underlying form and substance.

Testing for these signatures requires a method for determining when infants consider an object to be an animal. In the natural world in which human conceptual capacities evolved, the primary perceptual signature of animals is autonomous motion: only animals moved in the absence of an external force. In the modern world, autonomous motion is less clearly a cue to animacy, because vehicles, fans, blenders, and other machines also move through internal forces. These objects appeared only recently in human history, however, and most of them are both started and guided by human agents. If the concept *animal* depends on a cognitive system that emerges early in infancy under the shaping effects of natural selection, then it may be revealed through a method that taps infants' predisposition to attend to and learn about self-propelled motion.

8.3 **Infants' learning about self-propelled objects**

Our first line of research focuses on infants' reasoning about the movement behaviors of different classes of objects, using a procedure developed by Markson and Spelke (2006) for testing young infants' rapid learning about self-propelled objects. In their experiments, 7-month-old infants were familiarized to events in which one windup toy object engaged in self-propelled motion, whereas a different windup toy object was moved across a stage by hand. Infants were then presented with stationary test trials in which both objects were shown side-by-side alone on the stage. Markson and Spelke (2006) predicted that infants would look longer in stationary test trials at the object that had been previously self-propelled than at the object that had been previously hand-moved, because only the former would be capable of future autonomous motion. The predicted results were obtained in experiments with objects that had animal features and engaged in articulated motion. However, in experiments with toy vehicles or nonsense objects that displayed rigid translatory motion, infants did not demonstrate learning about the differential movement capacities of the objects: they looked equally long at the two objects in stationary test trials.

The pattern of results observed by Markson and Spelke (2006) could be explained in two ways. First, 7-month-old infants' learning about self-propelled motion may be restricted to the domain of animals: Infants may attribute self-propelled motion only to objects with animate features (e.g., eyes, limbs, articulated movement). An experiment by Pauen and Träuble (submitted) supports the idea that infants' attributions of self-propelled motion are specific to objects with animal features. Seven-month-old infants were familiarized to scenes in which two objects—a plastic ball and a hairy worm-like stuffed animal with a face—moved around a stage together. An invisible thread conjoined the two objects so that the source of their joint motion was ambiguous. Following familiarization, infants viewed test trials in which the objects were separated and presented motionless next to one another on a stage. Infants looked longer at the stuffed animal than at the ball, suggesting that they attributed the source of the motion to the object with animal features.

An alternative explanation of the findings of Markson and Spelke (2006) is that infants learn about self-propelled motion for all kinds of objects, but only when the autonomous motion is more complex than rigid translation. Rigid translation may be a poor indicator of self-propelled motion for several reasons. First, in Newtonian mechanics, rigid uniform translatory motion is a default state of all objects, animate or inanimate. As a consequence, children often observe inanimate objects undergoing rigid translation (e.g., a ball that is thrown or struck, an apple that falls from a tree). Consistent with this possibility, research provides evidence that infants who view an object moving after contact with another object do not endow the pushed object with self-propelled motion (e.g., Leslie & Keeble, 1987). Thus, Markson and Spelke's findings are consistent with two quite different views of the origins of infants' learning about objects.

To test the breadth of infants' learning about self-propelled objects in the first year of life, we manipulated category and motion information across three experiments. If young infants' conceptions of animate and inanimate objects are rooted in knowledge of different patterns of movement (e.g., Mandler, 2004), then infants might fail to learn about objects engaging in motions that are not characteristic of animals. Additionally, infants may not be able to learn about self-propelled motion for objects that lack animal features such as a face and limbs. If, however, young infants' learning about objects and their movements is supported by a domain-general system, then infants may learn readily about all kinds of objects, provided their motion is more complex than uniform rigid translation.

The second line of research focuses on infants' generalization of learning about animals. A substantive body of previous research has shown that infants, children, and adults attend to and generalize learning about artifacts by shape over changes in color and texture (e.g., Baldwin et al., 1993; Brown, 1990; Graham et al., 2004; Santos et al., 2002; Welder & Graham, 2001; Wilcox, 1999). In contrast, children and adults generalize learning about animals both by shape and by substance information (color and texture; Booth & Waxman, 2002; Jones & Smith, 1998; Jones et al., 1991; Keil et al., 1998; McManus & Keil, 2001). No research to our knowledge, however, has investigated whether young infants learn and generalize information about animals in accord with their substance properties. To address this question, we investigated younger infants' selective use of shape and color for learning about toy animals. Using Markson and Spelke's (2006) method, 7-month-old infants were given the opportunity to learn, during the experiment, that a toy animal was capable of autonomous, biological motion. Then, we tested whether, and on what basis, infants generalized the capacity for autonomous motion to other toy animals on the basis of shape and color.

8.3.1 Selective learning about autonomously moving animals

Our first study used a variation of the method of Markson and Spelke (2006) to investigate whether infants are capable of learning about the self-propelled motion of an object that has animal features, but undergoes rigid, rather than deforming, animate motion. In familiarization trials, 7-month-old infants saw two windup toy animals in alternation on a stage: a pink mouse and a black monkey (Fig. 8.1a). As in Markson and Spelke's (2006) studies, one of the animals was moved passively by a hand that grasped and moved it on the stage. In contrast to their research, however, the other animal moved actively in a motion that is not characteristic of animals: it flipped over backwards in a rigid rotation. After familiarization, infants were presented with the two objects side-by-side and their looking time to each object was recorded.[1] If infants' learning about self-propelled motion is restricted to the domain of objects that engage in the deforming motions characteristic of animals, we reasoned that they would fail to learn about these motion patterns, and their looking preferences at test would be unrelated to the objects' prior patterns of motion. In contrast, if infants learn more broadly about self-propelled motion, we reasoned that they would look longer at the previously self-propelled object during the stationary test trials.

During the familiarization phase, infants looked longer at self-propelled trials than hand-moved trials (M_{SP} = 42.30 s, SD = 4.95; M_{HM} = 40.05 s, SD = 5.56; $t(15)$ = 2.22, $p < 0.05$). During the test trials, infants looked longer at the object that was previously self-propelled than at the object that was previously hand-moved ($t(15)$ = 2.33, $p < 0.05$). Fig. 8.2 presents infants' average looking toward each of the objects during the test phase of this experiment.

Infants therefore looked longer, both during familiarization and during the stationary test trials, at the windup animal toy that was previously self-propelled. The present results provide evidence against the hypothesis that infants' capacity for learning about self-propulsion for animates is limited to cases of deforming motions characteristic of animals, as the objects displayed rigid, flipping movements. Infants showed reliable learning about a self-propelled object with animal features, even though the object underwent a rigid rotary motion.

These findings raise the question of whether infants' learning is specific to objects with animal features (e.g., faces, bodies) or whether it also occurs for familiar artifact objects. Although the infants in Markson and Spelke's (2006) experiments failed to learn about the self-propelled motion of a vehicle that underwent a rigid motion, the motion used in their experiment—uniform translation—may have appeared to be the passive response of an inanimate object rather than actively generated, self-propelled motion.

---

[1] Additional details about methods for all the studies presented in this chapter can be found online at http://www.wjh.harvard.edu/~lds

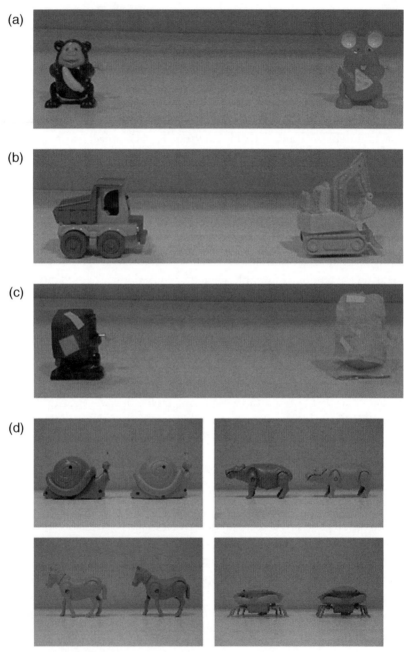

Fig. 8.1 (a) Animal windup toys, (b) vehicle windup toys, (c) nonsense windup toys, (d) painted animal windup toys used in the studies of learning and generalization.

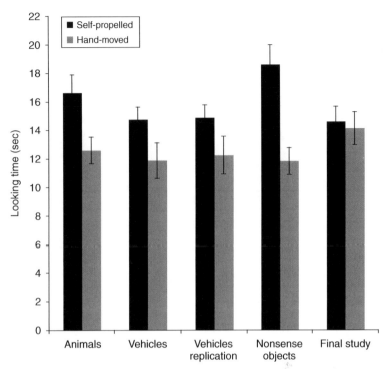

Fig. 8.2 Mean looking times of infants in stationary test trials toward the object that previously exhibited self-propelled versus hand-moved motion. Bars represent the standard error of the mean.

8.3.2 Selective learning about autonomously moving vehicles

Accordingly, we next investigated whether infants learn about the self-propelled motion of complex vehicles. During familiarization, 7-month-old infants saw trials in which one windup toy vehicle (e.g., a dump truck) engaged in nonuniform and nonrigid self-propelled motion, whereas another windup toy vehicle (e.g., a backhoe) was moved around the stage by hand. Following familiarization, infants viewed stationary test trials in which both objects appeared side by side on the stage (Fig. 8.1b). If infants are able to learn about the movement behaviors of vehicles displaying complex motion, they would be expected to look longer at the previously self-propelled object during the test phase.

Once again, infants looked longer during familiarization trials in which the vehicle exhibited self-propelled motion compared with hand-moved motion (M_{SP} = 45.29 s, SD = 1.58; M_{HM} = 41.67 s, SD = 3.23; $t(15)$ = 4.36, $p < 0.001$). During the test phase, infants looked longer at the object that was previously self-propelled than at the object that was previously hand-moved ($t(15)$ = 2.00, $p < 0.05$, one-tailed; Fig. 8.2). Infants therefore proved capable of learning about the self-propelled motion of vehicles. Because the test trial effects were relatively weak, however, we replicated the experiment with a new group of infants using the same procedure. Infants in the replication study also looked longer during the familiarization phase at trials with self-propelled motion (M_{SP} = 42.63 s, SD = 5.20; M_{HM} = 38.36 s, SD = 6.89; $t(15)$ = 3.91, $p < 0.001$) and looked longer during test trials at the previously self-propelled object ($t(15)$ = 2.01, $p < 0.05$, one-tailed; Fig. 8.2). A repeated-measures ANOVA with study (vehicles vs. vehicles replication) as a between-subject factor and test object (self-propelled vs. hand-moved) as a within-subject factor revealed only a main effect of test object ($F(1,30)$ = 8.03, $p < 0.01$).

These findings contrast with those of Markson and Spelke (2006), who did not observe rapid learning about vehicles. Interestingly, the rigid translatory motion displayed by Markson and Spelke's (2006) vehicles was more category-typical than the motions of the vehicles in the present experiments, yet learning occurred in the latter but not the former case. The vehicles we used displayed articulated movements of individual parts and spontaneous changes in path. One or both of these attributes may have contributed to infants' successful learning, perhaps by highlighting or confirming the self-propelled object's capacity for autonomous motion.

8.3.3 Selective learning about autonomously moving nonsense objects

Animals and vehicles are both familiar kinds of objects whose real-world counterparts possess internal sources of motion. Both types of objects possess salient features, such as faces and wheels, which infants may use to identify and categorize them. Do infants learn about self-propelled objects only when they are confronted with objects in these familiar categories? We next addressed this question by investigating whether infants are capable of learning about self-propelled 'nonsense' objects that are unfamiliar and that lack the identifying features of either animals or vehicles.

During familiarization trials with self-propelled motion, 7-month-old infants watched one windup toy object (e.g., a pink 'blob') flip over backward as in our first study: a rigid nontranslatory motion. During familiarization trials with passive motion, infants saw a different windup toy object (e.g., a black blob) being tipped forward and back by the experimenter. As in the previous experiments, infants then viewed test trials in which both objects were present but neither moved (Fig. 8.1c).

Yet again, infants' looking was significantly longer for the self-propelled object, both during the familiarization sequence ($M_{SP} = 42.89$ s, SD = 4.26; $M_{HM} = 37.96$ s, SD = 5.54; $t(15) = 4.21$, $p < 0.001$) and at test ($t(15) = 3.81$, $p < 0.01$; Fig. 8.2). Infants therefore learned about the self-propelled motion of unfamiliar objects without animal features or biological motion.

Taken together, these findings provide evidence that infants are broadly capable of learning about self-propelled objects and their movements. A comparison of the present findings to those of Markson and Spelke (2006) suggests that in order to learn about self-propulsion, infants require motion that is more complex than rigid translation of an object from one point to another. Infants may fail to learn from rigid translation because it fails to command their interest, or because it fails to convey that the object's motion is self-generated.

8.3.4 Probing the mechanisms that yield attention to self-propelled objects

These findings raise questions about the causes of infants' preferences for self-propelled objects. On average, infants looked significantly longer during familiarization trials with self-propelled motion than during familiarization trials with hand-moved motion. Infants' preference for active over passive motion is not altogether surprising, given that autonomous motion is a marker of agency and therefore might be intrinsically attractive to infants (Premack, 1990). Additionally, previous research has shown that young infants are more engaged by self-propelled than by induced motion (e.g., Crichton & Lange-Küttner, 1999). One concern, however, is that infants' test-trial preference for the object that previously moved autonomously might have been driven by a simple familiarity preference or by a simple preference for an object that previously engaged in complex motion, rather than by an expectation of future self-generated movement.

There are two reasons to doubt the former hypothesis: first, infants tested by Markson and Spelke (2006) did not show a significant preference for the self-propelled over the hand-moved animal during familiarization, but they nevertheless looked longer at that animal during the test trials. Second, infants tested with nonsense objects by Markson and Spelke (2006) *did* show a preference for the self-propelled object during familiarization, but did not look longer at the object during test. These findings suggest that a preference for self-propelled motion is neither necessary nor sufficient for demonstrating this preference when the object is stationary.

To explore further the relationship between familiarization and test preferences in the three studies, a self-propelled familiarization preference score was calculated for each infant by subtracting total looking during hand-moved familiarization trials from total looking during self-propelled familiarization trials. We then used this self-propelled familiarization preference score as a covariate in an analysis of variance. ANCOVA revealed that after controlling for preference during familiarization, preference at test (for the previously self-propelled object) was significant: ($F(1,62) = 4.98, p < 0.05$). This analysis also revealed a significant interaction of familiarization preference score and test object ($F(1,62) = 6.39, p < 0.05$), suggesting that even though familiarization preferences cannot fully account for test preferences, such preferences do play a role in test effects.

The final experiment in this series was designed to explore further the relationship between familiarization and test preferences by manipulating the relative attractiveness of the two types of familiarization events. As in previous experiments, infants were familiarized with two objects that underwent either autonomous or passive motion, and then they were shown the two stationary objects on test trials. We altered the familiarization events with passive motion, however, to make them more engaging to infants than the familiarization events with autonomous motion.[2] If looking patterns at test are a simple function of interest during familiarization, then infants should look longer, during stationary test trials, at the object whose previous motion was passive.

During the familiarization phase, infants looked significantly longer during the trials with passive motion than during the trials with self-propelled motion ($M_{SP} = 40.31$ s, SD = 4.27; $M_{HM} = 42.37$ s, SD = 3.12; $t(15) = 2.71, p < 0.05$). In stationary test trials, however, infants looked equally at both objects ($t < 1$; Fig. 8.2).

Because both the first study (8.3.1) and this last study used objects with animal features, but manipulated the complexity and salience of the motion, their findings were compared directly. To compare looking preferences across studies, we subtracted total looking to the hand-moved from total looking to the self-propelled object both during familiarization and during test, and we conducted a repeated-measures ANOVA with experiment (first study vs. last study) as a between-subject factor and phase (familiarization vs. test) as a within-subject factor. Critically, ANOVA revealed no interaction between experiment and phase ($F < 1$): the increase in infants' preference for the self-propelled object from familiarization to test was equal in both experiments.

---

[2] See online supporting materials for specific details about the motion.

Thus, presentation of self-propelled motion increased infants' test trial looking in this last study, as it did in the previous experiments, for reasons beyond a simple preference for more interesting motion. Importantly, reversing infants' preference for familiarization events (from a preference for autonomous motion to a preference for passive motion) did not result in a reversal in infants' test preferences, nor did it interfere with the attention-enhancing effects of self-propelled motion. These findings provide evidence that infants are sensitive to the pattern of autonomous motion and use that pattern to learn about self-propelled objects.

In sum, babies distinguish self-propelled objects from objects that cannot move on their own. Beyond the general concept *object*, infants possess and use a narrower concept *self-propelled object*. Nevertheless, the research discussed thus far provides no evidence that babies distinguish self-propelled objects that are *animals* from those that are *artifacts*. It is possible, however, that babies distinguish animals from artifacts such as vehicles, even though they expect both to move on their own. We turn, therefore, to a different series of experiments that probes for the *animal–artifact* distinction by focusing on the second signature of this distinction shown by older children and adults.

8.4 Learning and generalizing information about self-propelled objects

Adults and preschool children view animals, but not artifacts, as members of kinds with a common structure and material composition. As a consequence, adults and children generalize learning about animals both by their shape properties and their substance properties (Booth & Waxman, 2002; Jones & Smith, 1998; Jones et al., 1991; Keil et al., 1998; McManus & Keil, 2001). If asked to imagine that they observe a novel animal with a particular set of properties, children and adults report that other animals of the same kind will be similar to the target animal in shape, texture, and color. In contrast, if asked to imagine that they observe a new artifact, children and adults report that other artifacts of the same kind will be similar in shape but not in texture or color (Keil et al., 1998).

To probe whether infants also distinguish animals from artifacts in this manner, we investigated infants' generalization of learning about animals. In different experiments, we probed generalization based either on the shapes of the animals or on their colors. If infants learn about animals as do older children, then they should generalize learning across animals on the basis of both shape and color.

8.4.1 **Generalizing across animals on the basis of shape**

In our first study in this series, we tested whether infants generalize learning about the autonomous motion of an animal on the basis of the information that adults and children use in generalizing about both animals and artifacts: shape. Seven-month-old infants participated in two experimental blocks, each comprising six alternating familiarization trials followed by two test trials, as in our previous studies. The stimuli were eight windup toy animals: a blue horse, a tan horse, a blue crab, a tan crab, a pink snail, a green snail, a pink hippo, and a green hippo (Fig. 8.1d). During the familiarization phase of each block, infants viewed windup toy animals differing in shape only (e.g., a blue crab and a blue horse), one of which moved on its own and one of which was moved passively by a hand. For the test, infants viewed new objects with the same shapes but a different color, presented without motion. If infants generalize learning by shape, we expected them to look longer during the test at the object with the same shape as the previously seen object that had moved autonomously.

Results were analyzed with a repeated-measures ANOVA with block (1 vs. 2) and movement (autonomous vs. passive) as within-subject factors. As in the previous experiments, infants looked reliably longer during the familiarization period at the event with autonomous motion, $F(1,15) = 8.03$, $p < 0.05$ ($M_{SP} = 43.27$ s, SD $= 2.56$; $M_{HM} = 39.26$ s, SD $= 5.17$). During the stationary test, infants looked longer at the object that shared the same shape as the toy animal that was self-propelled during familiarization ($F(1,15) = 14.84$, $p < 0.01$; Fig. 8.3, left).

Self-propelled familiarization preferences scores were calculated as in previous experiments, and used as a covariate in an analysis of variance. After controlling for preference during familiarization, infants showed a significant preference at test for the object that shared the same shape as the one that had previously moved autonomously ($F(1,14) = 5.13$, $p < 0.05$). Thus, similar to preschool children and adults, infants generalize learning about animals on the basis of shape.

8.4.2 **Generalizing across animals on the basis of color**

Accordingly, we next investigated whether infants also generalize their learning by color, over a change in shape. During familiarization, infants viewed windup animals differing in color only (e.g., a blue crab and a tan crab), one of which moved autonomously. For the test, infants viewed toy animals of the same colors but a different shape (e.g., a blue horse and a tan horse). If infants have a concept *animal* according to which animals divide into kinds with a common material composition as well as a common structure, then they may show successful generalization by color, just as they generalized by shape in the previous study.

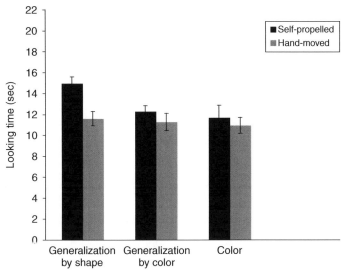

Fig. 8.3 Mean looking times of infants in stationary test trials toward the object that shared the same property (shape or color) as the one that was previously self-propelled versus hand-moved. The graph presents average looking time across two blocks of trials. Bars represent the standard error of the mean.

Infants in this second study looked longer during familiarization trials with autonomous motion compared with passive motion (M_{SP} = 43.57 s, SD = 2.79; M_{HM} = 37.43 s, SD = 4.09, $F(1,15)$ = 43.69, $p < 0.001$). There was no significant effect of block and no significant interaction between movement and block. In contrast, infants showed no looking preference, on the stationary test trials, for the object with the same color and texture as the animal that moved autonomously during familiarization ($F(1,15)$ = 1.13, NS; Fig. 8.3).

Infants therefore showed no evidence of generalizing on the basis of color what they learned about the objects they viewed during familiarization. These findings suggest that only shape serves as a basis for infants' learning about animals. Because preschool children and adults show this learning pattern for artifacts but not for animals, the experiment provides no evidence for differentiated animal and artifact concepts in infancy. Nevertheless, it is possible that children take account of substance properties in learning about animals, but do so only when the animals have the same shape (e.g., Jones et al., 1991).

Accordingly, we next investigated whether infants take account of color in learning about animals that are similar in shape. In this third study, infants were familiarized with two toy animals of the same shape but different colors (e.g., a blue crab and a tan crab), one of which engaged in autonomous motion. For test trials, infants viewed the same objects (e.g., the blue crab and the tan crab) without motion. This study therefore required no generalization of learning over a change in shape. Rather, it investigated whether infants can learn about the motion properties of individual toy animals based on color differences alone, when shape is held constant.

Infants again looked longer, during the familiarization period, at the animal that moved autonomously ($M_{SP} = 40.35$ s, SD = 4.06; $M_{HM} = 35.97$ s, SD = 5.16; $F(1,15) = 19.64$, $p < 0.001$). For the stationary test, however, infants looked equally long at the two animals ($F < 1$; Fig. 8.3). To compare the test results from the first study (shape) to the test results of the second and third studies (color), we subtracted each infant's total looking toward the (previously) hand-moved object from their looking toward the (previously) self-propelled object. We then compared the test preference scores of infants in these experiments. Infants showed reliably more generalization by shape than by color ($t(46) = 2.30$, $p < 0.05$).

8.4.3 The mechanisms subserving infants' privileging of shape over color

Infants showed no evidence of learning about the movement properties of toy animals on the basis of color, when shape was held constant. In this respect, infants' performance contrasts with that of adults and older children, who use both color and shape in learning about kinds of animals. There are at least two possible interpretations of this negative finding. First, infants may not consider color information when learning about animals. Learning that a given animal engages in self-generated motion may generalize to other animals with the same shape, even if infants only see the movement exhibited by one object of a particular color. Alternatively, infants may not have been able to discriminate between, or remember, the two colors presented during familiarization. The latter alternative is unlikely, because infants have been shown to detect, discriminate, and remember colors in other experiments (e.g., Bornstein et al., 1976). It is possible, however, that this ability would not be shown with the present experiment and displays. A final study was conducted to distinguish between these two interpretations.

We created a test of visual discrimination between the pairs of objects used in the second and third studies. During familiarization, infants saw two motionless toy animals of the same shape and color (e.g., two blue horses) side by side on the stage. For the test, they saw one of the familiarization objects alongside another toy animal that differed from it only in color (e.g., the blue horse and the tan horse). If infants discriminate two animals differing only in color, and they remember the familiar color, they should look longer at the animal with the novel color in the test trials.

During the test trials, infants looked longer at the toy animal with the novel color (M_{NOV} = 3.40 s, SD = 1.37; M_{FAM} = 2.60 s, SD = 1.04; $F(1,15)$ = 9.42, $p < 0.01$). This finding provides evidence that infants can perceive, discriminate, and remember the color properties of each of the objects, and it therefore constrains our interpretation of the generalization studies. Although infants can perceive and remember both the shapes and colors of these objects, they learned and generalized learning about self-propelled motion on the basis of shape alone.

8.5 **The development of object concepts**

The present findings provide evidence that infants make a conceptual distinction between objects that are capable of autonomous motion and those that are not. In the studies described in Section 8.1, infants learned rapidly about the self-propelled motion of a broad class of objects, including animals that displayed rigid rotary motion, vehicles that displayed nonrigid and nontranslatory motion, and unfamiliar objects that engaged in rigid rotary motion. These findings accord with and extend those of previous research on infants' sensitivity to the sources of object motion (e.g., Luo & Baillargeon, 2005; Luo et al., in press; Markson & Spelke, 2006; Pauen & Träuble, submitted).

Nevertheless, the experiments in Sections 8.1 and 8.2 provide no evidence that infants possess the more specific conceptual distinction between self-propelled *animals* and *artifacts*. Infants showed neither of the two signatures of this distinction found in older children and adults. Unlike children and adults, infants' attributions of autonomous motion do not appear to be dependent on category information, or on motions typically associated with particular categories of objects. Infants learned no more readily about self-propelled objects with the features and characteristic motions of animals, than about self-propelled objects with the features and motions of vehicles, or about nonsense objects.

Additionally, unlike children and adults, infants did not learn about animals in accord with both shape and substance properties. Rather, they learned about animals according to the same property they employ when reasoning about novel artifacts: shape. Seven-month-olds infants' reliance on shape accords with findings from research on older infants' attention to shape when learning about artifact objects (e.g., Baldwin et al., 1993; Graham et al., 2004; Wilcox, 1999), as well as with research on children's reliance on shape for word learning (e.g., Graham & Poulin-Dubois, 1999; Jones & Smith, 1998; Jones et al., 1991; see Xu et al., Chapter 11). Their failure to use substance information learning about animals contrasts with the performance of older children and adults (Booth & Waxman, 2002; Jones & Smith, 1998; Jones et al., 1991; Keil et al., 1998; McManus & Keil, 2001), and suggests that infants lack a key signature of the distinction between artifact and natural kinds.

This conclusion is negative, and so it must be offered with caution. It is possible that future work, using different displays, methods, or signatures of the *animal–vehicle* distinction, will find evidence in young infants for some of the principles that guide young children and adults' reasoning about animals and artifacts. Nevertheless, several features of our findings render this possibility unlikely. First, the displays used in the present studies were the same sorts of toy animals and vehicles that have demonstrated successful categorization of animals and artifacts in older infants and children (e.g., Mandler & McDonough, 1998; Rakison & Butterworth, 1998). Second, the signatures for which we tested reflect what may be the deepest properties of animals in relation to artifacts: the role of substance properties in determining and constraining animals' behavior, and the role of autonomous motion in exhibiting that behavior.

Nevertheless, it is possible that other aspects of the *animal–artifact* distinction have earlier roots in human development. In particular, shape information may support generalizations differently over animals versus artifacts. Although infants in the present studies generalized learning about objects in both categories on the basis of object shape, it is possible that the shape descriptions given to animals and to artifacts differ for infants, as they do for older children and adults (e.g., Becker & Ward, 1991; Landau & Leyton, 1999). Despite this possibility, it is clear that some of the most striking markers of the *animal–vehicle* distinction found in children were not observed in the present studies.

Our findings present an interesting contrast with those obtained in studies of adult nonhuman primates using a related looking-time method (Hauser, 1998). Adult cotton-top tamarin monkeys were presented with objects that moved either autonomously or passively in response to external forces, and that either possessed or lacked animal features. Perception of the animacy of the objects was tested by presenting an object, occluding it, and then revealing the object at either the same or a new location. If monkeys represented an object as capable of self-generated motion, they were expected not to be surprised by its change in location, and therefore were expected to show equal looking whether the object was revealed in the same or a different location. By this measure, monkeys distinguished self-propelled animals from passively moved objects, as did the infants in our studies. In contrast to human infants, however, they also distinguished self-propelled animals from self-propelled objects of all other kinds, providing evidence for further distinctions between self-propelled objects that are animate versus inanimate. Because the monkeys were adults, it would be most interesting to repeat these studies with infant monkeys to chart the development of the latter distinction in this species.

Why might human infants have a general concept of *self-propelled object* but not the specific concepts *animal* and *vehicle*? One possible explanation, inspired by evolutionary psychology, is that artifacts such as vehicles are relatively recent inventions. In the environment in which humans evolved, the only objects with the capacity for autonomous motion were animals, and thus a system dedicated to perceiving and reasoning about self-propelled objects would have been sufficient for making inferences about animal kinds.

Researchers interested in the development of the animate–inanimate distinction have proposed a variety of accounts for how infants might construct concepts of animals and artifacts by attention to and analysis of motion information. Both R. Gelman (1990) and Mandler (2004) have suggested that infants' categories are inductively rich and structured around a causal analysis of object motion. Infants are predisposed to analyze the sources of motion of all perceived objects. When they view an object whose motion has no evident external cause, they posit an internal cause to the motion and take that cause to specify its kind. Mandler (2004) has posited that image schemas such as *self-motion* versus *caused motion* and *animate motion* (hypothesized to be 'rhythmic, up and down, and irregular', p. 96) versus *inanimate motion* distinguish animate from inanimate objects and form the basis of infants' earliest categories. On these views, infants' causal analysis gives rise to a primitive concept, *self-propelled object*, from which more specific concepts such as *animal* will arise.

A leaner view has been proposed by others (e.g., Rakison, 2003). Infants may be biased to attend both to object motion and to object parts of any kind. In the environments in which our species evolved, this bias would direct attention toward animals. Attention to global motion and motion of parts may be supported, in turn, by an evolved mechanism for predator and prey detection. Domain-general associative learning mechanisms therefore may allow infants to associate different kinds of static and dynamic object attributes and form categories such as *animals* and *artifacts*. Experiments with younger infants are needed to distinguish these views.

However these questions are resolved, the present research exemplifies a strategy for investigating the origins and early development of category-specific knowledge, modeled on strategies that have been used in recent years to investigate the development of many other aspects of object cognition that are treated in this volume and elsewhere (Carey & Xu, 2001; Scholl, 2001; Shutts & Spelke, 2004). In these studies, we investigated whether young infants show critical signatures of the conceptual distinctions made by older children and adults. Children and adults distinguish animals from artifacts on the basis of both their part structures and their characteristic motions. Moreover, children and adults selectively learn and generalize information about objects along different dimensions, depending on the domain to which the objects belong. With the present methods, investigators can ask when in development humans begin to display these signature patterns. In light of our findings that infants fail to show the central signatures of concepts such as *animal*, future studies can probe the circumstances under which these signatures begin to appear, thereby tracing how maturation and specific experiences shape children's emerging concepts.

Acknowledgements

This research was supported by NIH Grant H23103 to E.S.S. We thank Lysett Babocsai, Ariel Grace, and Liesje Spaepen for assistance with testing.

References

Atran, S., Medin, D. L., & Ross, N. (2002). Thinking about biology: modular constraints on categorization and reasoning in the every day life of Americans, Maya, and Scientists. *Mind and Society*, 6, 31–64.

Baldwin, D., Markman, E. M., & Melartin, R. L. (1993). Infants' ability to draw inferences about nonobvious object properties: evidence from exploratory play. *Child Development*, 64, 711–728.

Becker, A. H., & Ward, T. B. (1991). Children's use of shape in extending novel labels to animate objects: identity versus postural change. *Cognitive Development*, 6, 3–16.

Behl-Chada, G. (1996). Basic-level and superordinate-like categorical representations in infancy. *Cognition*, 60, 105–141.

Bloom, P. (2004). *Descartes' Baby: How Child Development Explains What Makes Us Human*. New York: Basic Books.

Booth, A. E., & Waxman, S. R. (2002). Word learning is 'smart': evidence that conceptual information affects preschoolers' extension of novel words. *Cognition*, 84, B11–B22.

Bornstein, M. H., Kessen, W., & Weiskopf, S. (1976). The categories of hue in infancy. *Science*, 191, 201–202.

Brown, A. L. (1990). Domain-specific principles affect learning and transfer in children. *Cognitive Science*, 14, 107–133.

Carey, S. (1985). *Conceptual Change in Childhood*. Cambridge, MA: MIT Press.

Carey, S., & Xu, F. (2001). Infant's knowledge of objects: beyond object files and object tracking. *Cognition*, 80, 179–213.

Cosmides, L., & Tooby, J. (1994). Origins of domain specificity: the evolution of functional organization. In L. A. Hirschfeld, & S. A. Gelman (Eds.), *Mapping the Mind: Domain Specificity in Cognition and Culture* (pp. 85–116). Cambridge University Press.

Cosmides, L., Tooby, J., & Kurzban, R. (2003). Perceptions of race. *Trends in Cognitive Sciences*, 7, 173–178.

Crichton, M. T., & Lange-Küttner, C. (1999). Animacy and propulsion in infancy: tracking, waving, and reaching to self-propelled and induced moving objects. *Developmental Science, 2*, 318–324.

Gelman, R. (1990). First principles organize attention to and learning about relevant data: number and the animate-inanimate distinction as examples. *Cognitive Science, 14*, 79–106.

Gelman, R., & Spelke, E. S. (1981). The development of thoughts about animate and inanimate objects: implications for research on social cognition. In J. H. Flavell, & L. Ross (Eds.), *Social Cognition* (pp. 43–66). New York: Academic Press.

Gelman, S. A. (2003). *The Essential Child: Origins of Essentialism in Everyday Thought.* Oxford: Oxford University Press.

Gelman, S., & Wellman, H. (1991). Insides and essences. *Cognition, 38*, 214–244.

Graham, S. A., Kilbreath, C. S., & Welder, A. N. (2004). 13-month-olds rely on shared labels and shape similarity for inductive inferences. *Child Development, 75*, 409–427.

Graham, S. A., & Poulin-Dubois, D. (1999). Infants' use of shape to extend novel labels to animate and inanimate objects. *Journal of Child Language, 26*, 295–320.

Hauser, M.D. (1998). A nonhuman primate's expectations about object motion and destination: The importance of self-propelled movement and animacy. *Developmental Science, 1*, 31–37.

Johnson, S., Slaughter, V., & Carey, S. (1998). Whose gaze will infants follow? The elicitation of gaze-following in 12-month-olds. *Developmental Science, 1*, 233–238.

Jones, S. S., & Smith, L. B. (1998). How children name objects with shoes. *Cognitive Development, 13*, 323–334.

Jones, S. S., Smith, L. B., & Landau, B. (1991). Object properties and knowledge in early lexical learning. *Child Development, 62*, 499–516.

Keil, F. C. (1989). *Concepts, Kinds, and Cognitive Development.* Cambridge, MA: MIT Press.

Keil, F. C., Smith, W. C., Simons, D. J., & Levin, D. T. (1998). Two dogmas of conceptual empiricism: implications for hybrid models of the structure of knowledge. *Cognition, 65*, 103–135.

Landau, B., & Leyton, M. (1999). Perception, object kind, and object naming. *Spatial Cognition and Computation, 1*, 1–29.

Lavin, T. A., & Hall, D. G. (2002). Domain effects in lexical development: learning words for foods and toys. *Cognitive Development, 16*, 929–950.

Leslie, A. M., & Keeble, S. (1987). Do six-month-olds perceive causality? *Cognition, 25*, 265–288.

Luo, Y., & Baillargeon, R. (2005). Can a self-propelled box have a goal? Psychological reasoning in 5-month-old infants. *Psychological Science, 16*, 601–608.

Luo, Y., Kaufman, L., & Baillargeon, R. (in press). Young infants' reasoning about physical events involving inert and self-propelled objects. *Cognitive Psychology.*

Mandler, J. M. (2004). *The Foundations of Mind.* New York: Oxford University Press.

Mandler, J. M., & McDonough, L. (1993). Concept formation in infancy. *Cognitive Development, 8*, 291–318.

Mandler, J. M., & McDonough, L. (1996). Drinking and driving don't mix: inductive generalizations in infancy. *Cognition, 59*, 307–335.

Mandler, J. M., & McDonough, L. (1998). On developing a knowledge base in infancy. *Developmental Psychology, 34*, 1274–1288.

Markson, L., & Spelke, E. S. (2006). Infants' rapid learning about self-propelled objects. *Infancy, 9*, 45–71.

Massey, C. M., & Gelman, R. (1988). Preschoolers' ability to decide whether a photographed unfamiliar object can move by itself. *Developmental Psychology, 24*, 307–317.

McDonough, L., & Mandler, J. M. (1998). Inductive generalization in 9- and 11-month-olds. *Developmental Science, 1*, 227–232.

McManus, C., & Keil, F. C. (2001, Oct). Framework knowledge about causal centrality. Paper presented at the 2nd Biennial Meeting of the Cognitive Development Society, Virginia Beach, VA.

Pauen, S. (2002). Evidence for knowledge-based category discrimination in infancy. *Child Development, 73*, 1016–1033.

Pauen, S., & Träuble, B. (submitted). How 7-month-olds interpret ambiguous motion events: Category-specific reasoning in infancy.

Premack, D. (1990). The infants' theory of self-propelled objects. *Cognition, 36*, 1–16.

Quinn, P. C. (2002). Category representation in young infants. *Current Directions in Psychological Science, 11*, 66–70.

Rakison, D. H. (2003). Parts, motion, and the development of the animate-inanimate distinction in infancy. In D. H. Rakison, & L. M. Oakes (Eds.), *Early Category and Concept Development: Making Sense of the Blooming, Buzzing Confusion* (pp. 159– 192). Oxford: Oxford University Press.

Rakison, D. H., & Butterworth, G. (1998). Infants' use of parts in early categorization. *Developmental Psychology, 34*, 49–62.

Rakison, D. H., & Oakes, L. M. (Eds.) (2003). *Early Category and Concept Development: Making Sense of the Blooming, Buzzing Confusion*. Oxford: Oxford University Press.

Rakison, D. H., & Poulin-Dubois, D. (2001). Developmental origin of the animate-inanimate distinction. *Psychological Bulletin, 127*, 209–228.

Santos, L. R., Hauser, M. D., & Spelke, E. S. (2002). Domain-specific knowledge in human children and non-human primates: artifact and food kinds. In M. Bekoff, C. Allen, & G. Burghardt (Eds.), *The Cognitive Animal* (pp. 205–216). Cambridge, MA: MIT Press.

Scholl, B. J. (2001). Objects and attention: the state of the art. *Cognition, 80*, 1–46.

Shutts, K., & Spelke, E. S. (2004). Straddling the perception-conception boundary. *Developmental Science, 7*, 507–511.

Simons, D. J., & Keil, F. (1995). An abstract to concrete shift in the development of biological thought: the insides story. *Cognition, 56*, 129–163.

Spelke, E. S. (1990). Principles of object perception. *Cognitive Science, 14*, 29–56.

Viviani, P., & Stucchi, N. (1992). Biological movements look uniform: evidence of motor-perceptual interactions. *Journal of Experimental Psychology: Human Perception and Performance, 18*, 603–623.

Welder, A. N., & Graham, A. (2001). The influence of shape similarity and shared labels on infants' inductive inferences about nonobvious object properties. *Child Development, 72*, 1653–1673.

Wilcox, T. (1999). Object individuation: infants' use of shape, size, pattern, and color. *Cognition, 72*, 125–166.

Chapter 9

Building object knowledge from perceptual input

Dima Amso & Scott P. Johnson

9.1 Building object knowledge from perceptual input

The development of object perception has received considerable scientific attention. Discoveries in this domain hold substantial promise to inform one of the most important questions in developmental cognitive and brain sciences: How do infants construct and act on an enduring representation of the external environment? Addressing this question involves examining the development, and effective use, of both perceptual and conceptual properties of objects. These include object unity, persistence or continuity, kinds, and so on. Experimentation in each of these domains adds an important piece to our understanding of the emergence of object knowledge.

Theoretical divisions in the research community arise not from the process of experimentation but from experimental interpretation. Rosenberg and Carey (Chapter 7), for example, elegantly lay out one theoretical perspective that argues that knowledge of objects, defined as spatiotemporally continuous bounded cohesive entities, is derived from a system of 'core cognition' (e.g., Carey & Spelke, 1994, 1996). That is to say that this object knowledge is innately endowed or present at birth independent of visual experience. Support for this perspective comes from well-conducted studies that provide evidence for the emergence of object knowledge substantially earlier than other types of knowledge—that is, that of noncohesive substances such as sand or salt. The interpretation is that knowledge of substances that do not satisfy the criteria for 'objecthood' are not core to the system and must be slowly learned, whereas those that do satisfy these criteria emerge earlier and are part of core cognition.

However, early competence for objects may also be a result of learning and experience with the environment, however brief it may seem. Certainly, a brief exposure to almost any visual scene in the real world will result in a higher frequency of encounters with 'objects' relative to nonobject substances. Hence, data can never directly show which knowledge is within the domain of core cognition once infants have had visual experience, but can only provide indirect support for core cognition by showing slower emergence of knowledge not within this realm (e.g., understanding of salt or sand substances). Comparative approaches vying to provide evidence for core cognition suffer the same fate. For example, primate work involves a similarly structured visual system to that of the human infant that interacts with an identical environment. Cross-species similarity with respect to the timing of emergence of knowledge would be expected.

The obvious alternative to core cognition is that the relatively high occurrence of objects (bounded, coherent, independently movable) in the external environment, in combination with a variety of developing information acquisition and/or learning mechanisms, results in an earlier emergence of object, relative to nonobject, knowledge. The empirical responsibility for developmental and cognitive scientists is to provide direct positive evidence for the existence of these short-term learning mechanisms and their function. We argue, in this chapter, that a variety of mechanisms come together to support short-term learning about objects and their properties (see also Mareschal & Bremner, Chapter 10). We focus on changes intrinsic to infants, including the development of neural circuits that afford effective *active* exploration of visual scenes. We also consider external conditions that optimize acquisition of the relevant information in otherwise complex environments.

9.2 Object unity and visual exploration

A substantial body of evidence suggests that there is progress over the first several postnatal months from a disorganized and fragmented perception of objects to a more mature perception of objects as continuing across space and time in the absence of visual input (Johnson & Aslin, 1995, 1996; Slater et al., 1990). *Perception of object unity* refers to the ability to perceive disjoint object parts as complete, as in situations involving partial object occlusion, supporting effective visually guided navigation and interaction with the environment. Traditional habituation methodology is often used to study object unity perception in young infants (Kellman & Spelke, 1983).

In the rod-and-box paradigm, infants are habituated to a partly occluded rod display followed by two test displays (Fig. 9.1). One test display is designed to match a percept of unity (a complete unoccluded rod) and the other to match a percept of disjoint surfaces. Longer looking to either test display provides information about how the rod parts were perceived

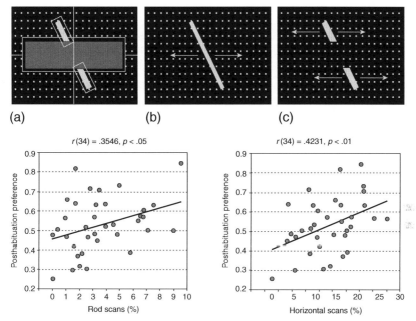

Fig. 9.1 Top panel: Schematic of displays presented to infants in experiments designed to tap perceptual completion. (a) Habituation display, consisting of a partly hidden rod and an occluding box. The grey outlines represent the areas of interest (AOIs) defined for eye movement data analyses and were not visible to infants. The AOIs containing the visible rod parts 'moved' with the rod for purposes of analysis. (b) Complete rod test stimulus. (c) Broken rod test stimulus. Lower panel: Average proportion of rod scans and vertical scans by each group as a function of posthabituation preference (Amso & Johnson, 2006; Johnson et al., 2004). Posthabituation preferences on the y-axis greater than 0.50 indicate unity perception when the infant viewed the occlusion stimulus during habituation; preferences less than 0.50 indicate perception of disjoint surfaces.

during habituation. Longer looking to the complete rod test display indicates that the rod parts were perceived as disjoint, whereas longer looking to the disjoint surfaces indicates that the rod parts were perceived as unified during habituation. A number of experiments that use this paradigm have shown that unity perception develops over the first postnatal months. Data from neonates suggest that they respond based on what is directly visible, rather than perceptually bridging the gap imposed by occlusion (Slater et al., 1990; Slater et al., 1996). In contrast, 2-month-old infants perceive unity under limited conditions and 4-month-olds exhibit more robust perceptual completion (Johnson, 2004). In this section, we consider the possibility that developments in visual exploration skills are a potential agent of this change.

9.3 **Active vision**

> Perceiving is active, a process of obtaining information about the world. We don't
> simply see, we look. The visual system is a motor system as well as a sensory one. As
> new actions become possible, new affordances are brought about; both the informa-
> tion available and the mechanisms for detecting it increase.
>
> (E. Gibson, 1988)

Active vision refers to a perceptual-motor skill comprising controlled exploration of a visual scene for optimal information gathering (Gibson, 1966).
This notion has important developmental implications. Developments in the
ability to control eye movements should bootstrap information gathering in
general, and object perception specifically.

Johnson et al. (2004) and Amso and Johnson (2006) combined looking time
methodology with corneal reflection eye tracking to examine the relations
between active exploration (infants' oculomotor scans and fixations) during
habituation and object unity perception. As noted previously, Johnson (2004)
showed that 2-month-olds provided evidence of unity perception under limited conditions, and it is not until 4 months that unity perception becomes
reliably robust. Therefore, in the Johnson et al. (2004) experiment, a group of
3-month-old infants was selected to study potential influences on differences
in unity perception during this transition. We reasoned that if development
of visual exploration skills is an important mechanism of change in veridical
object perception, infants whose novelty preference indicates unity perception should target scans and fixations to the relevant informative features of
the habituation display for optimal online information gathering.

The habituation display was divided into a series of *areas of interest* (AOIs)
for off-line coding (Fig. 9.1a). These included the top and bottom of the rod
parts, the four background quadrants, and the occluder. Scans and fixations
within and between these regions were examined as a function of each infant's
posthabituation preference. We found that infants who looked longer at the
broken rod display at test, indicating unity perception, provided evidence of
more effective visual exploration strategies during habituation. As a group,
they fixated the rod during habituation more frequently than infants whose
test display preference did not imply unity perception (Fig. 9.1). This group
also scanned more often across the rod parts as they translated back and forth.
These data suggest an association between object perception and infants'
visual experience, behavior, and interactions with the environment, and provide evidence for real-time visual information gathering occurring during
habituation.

The outstanding question is: What mechanisms drive the differences in looking behavior, and in turn unity perception, in this group? An important agent of change in information gathering is the development of skills that allow novel exploratory strategies (Bushnell & Boudreau, 1993; Gibson, 1988). Of particular interest to the current discussion is the emergence of attention-guided eye movements over the first several postnatal months (e.g., Johnson, 1990, 2005), coinciding in developmental time with the emergence of perceptual completion (Johnson, 2004).

Many saccadic eye movements in the newborn period are reflexive, driven largely by external salient information, and recruit subcortical pathways involving connections from retinal ganglion cells, the lateral geniculate nucleus, and the superior colliculus (Schiller, 1985, 1998). The emergence of voluntary orienting may stem from the development of certain cortical regions (for review, see Johnson, 2005). The frontal eye fields have been implicated in the endogenous control over eye movements. The parietal cortex is engaged in covert shifts of attention. The prefrontal cortex plays a role in endogenous control involving delays, presumably as a function of the requirement to maintain information over the delay period. The development of circuitry involving visual areas V1, V2, V4, parietal cortex, and the frontal eye fields is thought to support saccadic eye movements implicated in active visual inspection (Schiller, 1985, 1998) and to be important for early visual selective attention, which supports the selection of certain stimuli for processing while potentially interfering stimuli are ignored.

Theoretically, even sparse visual scenes have a variety of elements competing for limited processing resources. In the case of the rod-and-box habituation display, the moving aligned rod parts carry important information with respect to unity perception (Juscyk et al., 1999; Kellman & Spelke, 1983). However, the occluder may also be relatively salient, as well as the background texture elements, a grid of white dots that covers the majority of the display. These visually salient display regions are uninformative with respect to the perception of object unity. In principle, continuous voluntary visual attention to the informative moving rod parts necessarily involves suppression of other distracting display regions. The shift from reflexive to voluntary orienting has been found to be involved in infants' ability to resolve the competition between regions in a visual search display (cf. Dannemiller, 2000). Thus, simple reflexive visual orienting, characteristic of the very early postnatal period, would impede effective information gathering about any one element in a complex visual scene. Only with the onset of controlled voluntary orienting should competition between display regions be resolved in the service of structured information gathering.

Visual search tasks have been used extensively with adults to examine sensitivity to competition between parts of a visual scene (Neisser, 1967; Triesman, 1988;

Treisman & Gelade, 1980). Dannemiller (1998, 2000, 2002) first adapted such paradigms to infants, presenting a display in which a moving target was embedded in an array of static red and green distracters that were evenly distributed on the left and right hemifields of a display. Dannemiller hypothesized that sensitivity to the competition between the target and distracters would be related to effects of distracter influence on target detection. He found that competition was greater, and orienting speed was slower, when relatively 'high salience' bars were placed contralateral to the moving target. Salient features, such as static high-contrast bars, divided attention more evenly between hemifields with the net result of weakened target detection. Importantly, this sensitivity to competition must occur in parallel with distracter suppression in instances of accurate target detection. This task captures the interplay between competing display elements and the ability to detect them and guide visual attention to the target. This ability undergoes important developmental change across the first 4–5 months after birth, presumably reflecting cortical development (Dannemiller, 2000).

Amso and Johnson (2006) presented infants with a visual search task wherein a single target bar was embedded in an array of vertical static distracters. Targets could appear in one of eight possible locations, arranged in a circle, equidistant from center fixation. Search task difficulty is a function of the similarity of target and distracter items, with increased similarity resulting in greater competition for attentional resources (e.g., Duncan & Humphreys, 1989). In the *competition* condition (Fig. 9.2), we increased the similarity between the target and distracter elements by delineating the target only by its orientation, tilted away from vertical at one of three possible orientations (30°, 60°, 90°).

Hypothetically, a saccade to the target would require a functional voluntary orienting mechanism in the service of distracter suppression. The *control*

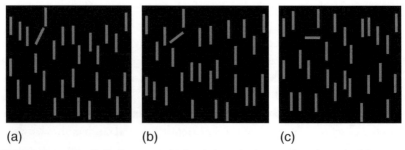

Fig. 9.2 Examples of displays presented to infants in the search task competition condition. (a) Target is oriented 30° from vertical. (b) Target is oriented 60°. (c) Target is oriented 90°. Stimuli from the control task (moving targets) are not shown here.

condition was aimed at indexing reflexive orienting. Here, the target translated laterally at one of three possible speeds (1, 1.5, or 2 Hz) on the otherwise static background of vertical bars. This condition allowed us to test the basic ability to orient to the target reflexively when competition between display elements was low. A group of 3-month-old infants participated in both the rod-and-box habituation as well as this visual search paradigm in the same testing session. A relation between attention-guided visual exploration and perceptual completion across the two paradigms was found. We replicated the finding that infants who provide evidence of perceiving the unity of rod parts show efficient scanning patterns during habituation (Johnson et al., 2004). Importantly, these same infants also provided evidence of visual search behavior indicative of voluntary attention-guided saccadic eye movements. That is, these infants (whom we termed *perceivers*) showed better accuracy for target bar detection relative to nonperceivers. Moreover, perceivers' saccade latencies to targets were slower in the competition condition, presumably reflecting sensitivity to the competition and suppression of distracter elements in favor of better target bar selection (Fig. 9.3), but not in the control condition. Nonperceivers searched the display in a manner more characteristic of reflexive orienting.

These patterns of data suggest utilization of different mechanisms of visual exploration between those who indicated unity perception and those who did not, and provide evidence that oculomotor development, from reflexive to voluntary, has important implications for information gathering and subsequent perception and learning. Evidence for similar changes in information gathering skills comes from the locomotor literature. There is evidence, for example, that infants who engage in active and controlled manual exploration are more capable of segregating an object into its parts than those who engage in less active exploration strategies (Needham, 2000). Similar to oculomotor control, locomotor control shows a pattern of exploratory movement from early spontaneous wiggles or thrashes toward more controlled movements (Adolph et al., 2000).

Findings from the Amso and Johnson (2006) study are also consistent with the concept of active vision with respect to the suggestion that skill in visual exploration develops in parallel with the complexity of object knowledge (Cohen et al., 2002; Haith, 1980; Sandini et al., 1993). This view is consistent with the constructivist approach to cognitive and perceptual development (e.g., Piaget, 1955). Finally, complementary work in machine vision and developmental robotics also holds a prominent place for guided visual exploration prominent in perceptual learning in artificial systems (e.g., Ballard, 1991; Sandini et al., 1993).

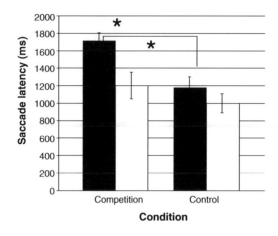

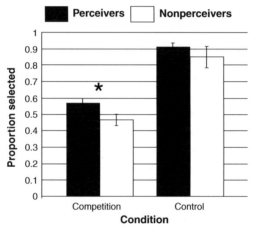

Fig. 9.3 Top panel: Mean saccade latency performance by each group in the competition and control conditions in the search task. Lower panel: Mean proportion selected by each group in the competition and control conditions in Experiment 2. Error bars = SEM. * indicates comparisons statistically significant < .05.

9.3.1 A computational account

We have thus far described changes in the development of cortical pathways involved in visual selection and have linked them to behavioral evidence of attention-guided saccadic eye movements. In this section, we discuss computational modeling work that has examined this assumption explicitly. Schlesinger et al. (2007a, 2007b) used computational modeling to pinpoint the neural mechanisms involved in differences in 3-month-old infants' performance in the visual search paradigm, to formally constrain the circuitry supporting change in visual exploration and object perception in young infants.

The visual search displays (Fig. 9.2) employed by Amso and Johnson (2006) were processed by a multichannel image-filtering model of visual processing originally developed by Itti and Koch (2000) and based on the concept of salience maps (Schlesinger et al., 2007a). The displays were subjected to a series of filters to simulate neural processing in the mammalian visual system. These included decomposition by particular feature dimensions in parallel such as contrast, orientation, motion, retinotopic feature maps, center-surround organization, and competition for attention in a retinotopic salience map (e.g., Kastner & Ungerleider, 2000). Features were weighted for their salience and ultimately recombined into a salience map. Model parameters were varied to simulate the development of neural circuitry at different levels of visual scene processing and to simulate developmental change in neural components of visual selective attention: degree of oculomotor noise, growth of horizontal connections in visual cortex, and duration of recurrent processing in the parietal cortex. The degree of oculomotor noise was varied to test the proposal that 'noisy' behavior may be an adaptive strategy for exploring sensorimotor contingencies, rather than due to immature control systems.

The growth of horizontal connections in V1 provides a second possible constraint on the development of visual selection (e.g., Albright & Stoner, 2002; Hess & Field, 1999). These connections have been suggested to support the perception of contours, particularly in the integration of contours that are interrupted by spatial gaps (e.g., due to occlusion; Albright & Stoner, 2002). Recurrent or sustained activity in the posterior parietal cortex constitutes the third manipulated neural constraint, and is theoretically most consistent with the model of attention-guided eye movement development outlined in the previous section (for review, see Johnson, 2005). The current model was adapted from a recurrent model of parietal activation by Itti and Koch (2000), where sustained competition between salient display regions is associated with recurrent feedback. Of the three parameters, manipulations of both the growth of horizontal connections and recurrent parietal processing parameters approximated differences observed in visual search performance of 3-month-old infants.

In subsequent analyses, real-time visual search performance was simulated with the outcome that increasing recurrent parietal processing increased effective search in the competition condition and also accounted for slower saccade latencies, effectively simulating performance changes on visual search between those infants who perceived object unity (4 loops or more sustained parietal activation or involvement) and those who did not (3 loops). In a second similar model examining performance on the rod-and-box displays, manipulating this same parameter resulted in increases in rod scans and horizontal scans, again approximating performance of 3-month-old unity perceivers (Schlesinger et al., 2007a). Taken together, the computational and infant data point to developments in the posterior parietal cortex and associated connectivity in effective visual search and exploration, and in turn, to complex skills such as object perception. These data support the possibility that developmental changes in visual exploration and associated cortical circuitry bear directly on perception, in this case perceptual completion.

9.4 **Environmental factors supporting object perception**

We have described a series of studies that examines the role of the development of attention-guided eye movements in infants' abilities to construct the visual environment. In a sense, we have described a developing gating mechanism that allows for the sensitivity to a particular stimulus to be increased and for sensitivity to others to be attenuated in a visual scene. The environment often obviates the need for such a mechanism and allows for conditions supporting information uptake even in the absence of voluntary saccadic control. By definition, these conditions must provide the same support as the gating mechanism: that is, there must be very little competition between the most salient element and the rest of the visual scene.

Research into object perception has shed light on the display conditions that support veridical object perception. For example, researchers have examined how differences in the relative size of the occluder, rendering more or less of the rod visible, bear on perceptual completion (Johnson, 2004; Johnson & Aslin, 1995). The thrust behind this work has been to consider possible cues to perceptual completion, rather than to consider the conditions that minimize the competition between information-rich and uninformative display regions. We contend that successful manipulations must do both. Enhancing the salience of the rod parts by reducing the size of the occluder has the effect of increasing the proximity of visible surfaces. However, if these surfaces are not aligned, young infants do not perceive them as connected (Johnson & Aslin, 1996). If they are aligned, even very young infants benefit from the manipulation (Johnson, 2004; Johnson & Aslin, 1995; Smith et al., 2003).

Object properties are relatively stable and constant across a variety of different events. Another example of infants' exploitation of environmental salience in the service of object perception comes from statistical event redundancies. Infants learn about their visual environment by extracting its inherent statistical information (e.g., Kirkham et al., 2003; Kirkham et al., 2007). Although the majority of the research on statistical learning has focused on learning single units, events too feature statistically in the environment and support learning.

Johnson et al. (2003) showed that visual experience with an object event can suffice to bootstrap mature object perception. This study exploited perceptions of object persistence, rather than unity, as a window into object perception. A ball moves back and forth behind an occluder. Consistent anticipations of the ball's emergence from behind the occluder, as indicated by eye movements to the location of reemergence, suggest that the infants represented the ball and its continuous trajectory in the absence of visual evidence of either. In contrast, reactive saccades to the ball after it has reemerged indicate that infants did not represent this information.

Johnson et al. (2003) presented 4- and 6-month-old infants with this paradigm while eye movements were recorded with a corneal reflection eye tracker. Four-month-old infants made mostly reactive eye movements, suggesting that they did not maintain the concept of the object as enduring across space and time. In contrast, 6-month-old infants' pattern of eye movements was more consistent with object representations; they produced reliably more anticipations relative to 4-month-olds. Using the same displays, a different group of 4- and 6-month-old infants were presented with the same object moving along an unoccluded path for 2 minutes before the standard testing (with occluder) took place. Four-month-olds who had the benefit of viewing the unoccluded trajectory event made significantly more anticipations at test, with their anticipation proportions approximating 6-month-olds. Six-month-old infants did not benefit from the training interval, presumably because their performance already indicated robust object representations.

These results provide evidence that repeated exposure to an object event, its continuous trajectory in this case, facilitated the formation of object representations. Interestingly, the repeated presentation of the ball moving behind an occluder did not have the same beneficial results. This work exemplifies the idea that the human system is prepared to benefit from redundancy in the environment. Connectionist models provide mechanistic support for these findings (Mareschal et al., 1999; Munakata et al., 1997), showing that expectations about the trajectory of a moving occluded object can rapidly emerge as a function of strengthening recurrent connections between information across sequential time steps (see Mareschal & Bremner, Chapter 10).

9.5 Short-term learning versus long-term storage

We have discussed the possibility that both neural changes and external environmental conditions can facilitate object perception in infancy. The mechanisms we have highlighted work in the short term, supporting information gathering in real time. A remaining question is how this information becomes integrated into a robust representation of objects and their enduring properties. It may be that these online learning mechanisms support weak representations when considered individually. The additive effects of multiple instances during which infants experience occlusion events, repeated continually across developmental time, may coalesce into long-term storage of the relevant information.

Computational neuroscience approaches are relevant to this possibility (e.g., Rogers & McClelland, 2004). For example, McClelland et al. (1995) considered how an acquired representation can be maintained by the system for subsequent integration and action. Their model makes a distinction between slow or 'neocortical learning' and faster or 'hippocampal' learning. The neocortical learning system retains acquired event information. Maintenance of learned information across time has been associated with the prefrontal cortex, which undergoes considerable change beginning in the postnatal period and into adolescence (Miller & Cohen, 2001). This is complemented by an associative learning hippocampal system, which acquires associations between perceptually distinct properties of objects or events, compared with the stored information. The hippocampus has been found to be functional early in infancy (Chugani & Phelps, 1986). Hence, redundancies strengthen the weights on the existing representation and distinctions are integrated into this representation. For example, object concepts are available before concepts of noncohesive entities (see Rosenberg & Carey, Chapter 7).

Online learning about properties consistent across objects (boundedness and spatiotemporal continuity) encountered across a variety of novel instances may begin to form an enduring representation or concept of 'object' that becomes narrower as instances with both similar and distinct properties are encountered (McClelland et al., 1995). This process will proceed similarly, but necessarily with a slower time course as a function of the relatively fewer instances to integrate over, with substances that violate 'objecthood', such as sand, salt, or liquids. As a consequence, one would expect that the same learning mechanisms may not be as immediately efficient at extracting information when confronted with unfamiliar entities. This should not be interpreted as evidence for core cognition, but rather as an emergent property of the complex interactions between an organizing system and its environment. Infants' learning is complex, involving an interplay between emergent skills and prior information.

9.6 Concluding remarks

We have provided empirical evidence for online learning about objects and their properties, and suggest that these repeated experiences, when maintained by the system, merge into robust and enduring object representations. This approach implicates both visual attention and simple learning mechanisms in the development of object perception and provides a window into how the development of basic skills opens up avenues for building complex percepts. In summary, we argue that optimal object perception involves the interplay between maturation, emergent skills, experience, and available information.

References

Adolph, K. E., Eppler, M. A., Marin, L., Weise, I. B., & Clearfield, M. W. (2000). Exploration in the service of prospective control. *Infant Behavior and Development, 23*, 441–460.

Albright, T. D., & Stoner, G. R. (2002). Contextual influences on visual processing. *Annual Review of Neuroscience, 25*, 339–379.

Amso, D., & Johnson, S. P. (2006). Learning by selection: visual search and object perception in young infants. *Developmental Psychology, 42*(6), 1236–1245.

Ballard, D. H. (1991). Animate vision. *Artificial Intelligence, 48*, 57–86.

Bushnell, E. W., & Boudreau, J. P. (1993). Motor development and the mind: the potential role of motor abilities as a determinant of aspects of perceptual development. *Child Development, 64*, 1005–1021.

Carey, S., & Spelke, E. (1994). Domain-specific knowledge and conceptual change. In L. Hirshfeld, & S. Gelman (Eds.), *Mapping the Mind: Domain Specificity in Cognition and Culture* (pp. 169–200). New York: Cambridge University Press.

Carey, S., & Spelke, E. (1996). Science and core knowledge. *Journal of Philosophy of Science, 63*, 515–533.

Chugani, H. T., & Phelps, M. E. (1986). Maturational changes in cerebral function in infants determined by 18FDG positron emission tomography. *Science, 231*, 840–843.

Cohen, L. B., Chaput, H. H., & Cashon, C. H. (2002). A constructivist model of infant cognitive development. *Cognitive Development, 17*, 1323–1343.

Dannemiller, J. L. (1998). A competition model of exogenous orienting in 3.5-month-old infants. *Journal of Experimental Child Psychology, 68*, 169–201.

Dannemiller, J. L. (2000). Competition in early exogenous orienting between 7 and 21 weeks. *Journal of Experimental Child Psychology, 76*, 253–274.

Dannemiller, J. L. (2002). Relative color contrast drives competition in early exogenous orienting. *Infancy, 3*, 275–301.

Duncan, J., & Humphreys, G. W. (1989). Visual search and stimulus similarity. *Psychological Review, 96*, 433–458.

Gibson, E. J. (1988). Exploratory behavior in the development of perceiving, acting, and acquiring of knowledge. *Annual Review of Psychology, 39*, 1–41.

Gibson, J. J. (1966). *The Senses Considered as Perceptual Systems*. Boston, MA: Houghton-Mifflin.

Haith, M. M. (1980). *Rules That Babies Look by: The Organization of Newborn Visual Activity*. Hillsdale, NJ: Erlbaum.

Hess, R., & Field, D. (1999). Integration of contours: new insights. *Trends in Cognitive Sciences, 12*(3), 480–486.

Itti, L., & Koch, C. (2000). A saliency-based search mechanism for overt and covert shifts of visual attention. *Vision Research, 40,* 1489–1506.

Johnson, M. H. (1990). Cortical maturation and the development of visual attention in infancy. *Journal of Cognitive Neuroscience, 2,* 81–95.

Johnson, M. H. (2005). *Developmental Cognitive Neuroscience,* 2nd edn. London: Blackwell.

Johnson, S. P. (2004). Development of perceptual completion in infancy. *Psychological Science, 15,* 769–775.

Johnson, S. P., & Aslin, R. N. (1995). Perception of object unity in 2-month-old infants. *Developmental Psychology, 31,* 739–745.

Johnson, S. P., & Aslin, R. N. (1996). Perception of object unity in young infants: the roles of motion, depth, and orientation. *Cognitive Development, 11,* 161–180.

Johnson, S. P., Amso, D., & Slemmer, J. A. (2003). Development of object concepts in infancy: evidence for early learning in an eye tracking paradigm. *Proceedings of the National Academy of Sciences (USA), 100,* 10568–10573.

Johnson, S. P., Slemmer, J. A., & Amso, D. (2004). Where infants look determines how they see: eye movements and object perception performance in 3-month-olds. *Infancy, 6,* 185–201.

Jusczyk, P. W., Johnson, S. P., Spelke, E. S., & Kennedy, L. J. (1999). Synchronous change and perception of object unity: evidence from adults and infants. *Cognition, 71,* 257–288.

Kastner, S., & Ungerleider, L. D. (2000). Mechanisms of visual attention in the human cortex. *Annual Review of Neuroscience, 23,* 315–341.

Kellman, P. J., & Spelke, E. S. (1983). Perception of partly occluded objects in infancy. *Cognitive Psychology, 15,* 483–524.

Kirkham, N. Z., Slemmer, J. A., & Johnson, S. P. (2003). Visual statistical learning in infancy: evidence for a domain general learning mechanism. *Cognition, 83,* B35–B42.

Kirkham. N. Z., Slemmer, J. A., Richardson, D. C., & Johnson, S. P. (2007). Location, location, location: development of spatiotemporal sequence learning in infancy. *Child Development, 78,* 1559–1571.

Mareschal, D., Plunkett, K., & Harris, P. (1999). A computational and neuropsychological account of object-oriented behaviors in infancy. *Developmental Science, 2,* 306–317.

McClelland, J. L., McNaughton, B. L., & O'Reilly, R. C. (1995). Why there are complementary learning systems in the hippocampus and neocortex: insights from the successes and failures of connectionist models of learning and memory. *Psychological Review, 102,* 419–457.

Miller, E. K., & Cohen, J. D. (2001). An integrative theory of prefrontal cortex function. *Annual Review of Neuroscience, 24,* 167–202.

Munakata, Y., McClelland, J. L., Johnson, M. J., & Siegler, R. S. (1997). Rethinking infant knowledge: toward an adaptive process account of successes and failures in object permanence tasks. *Psychological Review, 104,* 686–713.

Needham, A. (2000). Improvements in visual exploration skills may facilitate the development of object segregation in early infancy. *Journal of Cognition and Development, 1,* 131–156.

Neisser, R. (1967). *Cognitive Psychology.* New York: Appleton-Century-Crofts.

Piaget, J. (1955). *The Child's Conception of Reality.* London: Routledge and Kegan Paul.

Rogers, T. T., & McClelland, J. R. (2004). *Semantic Cognition: A Parallel Distributed Processing Approach.* Cambridge, MA: MIT Press.

Sandini, G., Gandolfo, F., Grosso, M., & Tistarelli, M. (1993). Vision during action. In Y. Aloimonos (Ed.), *Active Perception* (pp. 151–190). Hillsdale, NJ: Lawrence Erlbaum Associates.

Schiller, P. H. (1985). A model for the generation of visually guided saccadic eye movements. In D. Rose, & V. G. Dobson (Eds.), *Models of the Visual Cortex* (pp. 62–70). New York: John Wiley.

Schiller, P. H. (1998). The neural control of visually eye movements. In J. E Richards (Ed.), *Cognitive Neuroscience of Attention: A Developmental Perspective* (pp. 3–50). Mahwah, NJ: Erlbaum.

Schlesinger, M., Amso, D., & Johnson, S. P. (2007a). The neural basis for visual selective attention in young infants: a computational account. *Adaptive Behavior, 15*(2), 135–148.

Schlesinger, M., Amso, D., & Johnson, S. P. (2007b). Simulating infants' gaze patterns during the development of perceptual completion. In L. Berthouze, C. G. Prince, M. Littman, H. Kozima, & C. Balkenius (Eds.), *Proceedings of the Seventh International Workshop on Epigenetic Robotics: Modeling Cognitive Development in Robotic Systems.* Sweden: Lund University Cognitive Studies.

Slater, A., Johnson, S. P., Brown, E., & Badenoch, M. (1996). Newborn infants' perception of partly occluded objects. *Infant Behavior and Development, 19,* 145–148.

Slater, A., Morison, V., Somers, M., Mattock, A., Brown, E., & Taylor, D. (1990). Newborn and older infants' perception of partly occluded objects. *Infant Behavior and Development, 13,* 33–49.

Smith, W. C., Johnson, S. P., & Spelke, E. S. (2003). Motion and edge sensitivity in perception of object unity. *Cognitive Psychology, 46,* 31–64.

Treisman, A. (1988). Features and objects: the fourteenth Bartlett memorial lecture. *Quarterly Journal of Experimental Psychology, 40,* 210–237.

Triesman, A. M., & Gelade, G. (1980). A feature-integration theory of attention. *Cognitive Psychology, 12,* 97–136.

Chapter 10

Modeling the origins of object knowledge

Denis Mareschal & Andrew J. Bremner

10.1 Computational models of development

10.1.1 Why build computational models?

There are two overarching questions in developmental psychology. The first asks what differences exist between the same individual at different stages of development, and the second is concerned with identifying the causal factors that drive the progression from one stage to another. The second question, which explains how and why behaviors emerge, is the most difficult to answer. The traditional approach has been to describe infant competence across different domains in great detail, in the hope that by establishing the milestones of development a causal explanation will emerge from a synthesis of the data (for an important departure from this approach see Amso & Johnson, Chapter 9). The current chapter, however, presents a very different approach. The alternative approach consists in positing a set of mechanisms, which drive learning (and development), and implementing these mechanisms in a working computer model (a computer program). The model then provides a tool for exploring whether specific behaviors can emerge or be caused by the interaction of this well-defined set of mechanisms with some equally well-defined learning environment (Mareschal & Thomas, 2007).

Computational models can be delineated into two distinct kinds: symbolic processing models and connectionist (or parallel distributed processing models; Boden, 1989). As the name suggests, symbolic models are explicit theories of how cognitive abilities can be instantiated in a set of rule-based algorithms that manipulate symbolic information (Klahr & Wallace, 1976; Marcus, 2001). Connectionist models, on the other hand, are computer models loosely based on the principles of neural information processing (Elman et al., 1996; McLeod et al., 1998; Mareschal et al., 2007; O'Reilly & Munakata, 2000; Rumelhart & McClelland, 1986), and as such attempt to explain cognitive abilities without reference to symbols or rule-based symbolic manipulation.

Although the use of computer modeling in developmental psychology is not new (e.g., Boden, 1980; Klahr & Wallace, 1976; Mareschal & Shultz, 1996; McClelland, 1989; Papert, 1963; Shultz et al., 1995; Simon, 1962; Young, 1976), it has not gained popularity until relatively recently. The last 10 years has seen an increase in the use of computational modeling techniques as tools for understanding cognitive development, especially during infancy. Infancy is a rich period of development in which many behaviors are closely tied to perceptual and motor development. The close link between behavior and perceptual-motor skills makes it easier to posit mechanisms without the need to appeal to poorly defined metacognitive skills.

One particular focus of computational modeling research has been the development of object interactions during infancy. Both symbolic (Luger et al., 1983; Luger et al., 1984; Prazdny, 1980; Simon, 1998) and connectionist (e.g., French et al., 2004; Mareschal & French, 2000; Mareschal et al., 2000; Mareschal et al., 1999; Munakata, 1998; Munakata et al., 1997; Schlesinger, 2006), as well as hybrid (Drescher, 1991) models have been implemented. In this chapter, we will describe a number of computational approaches to understanding the developing object concept, focusing particularly on the contribution of such models to our understanding of the development of representations governing infant–object interactions across the first two years of life. We will argue that connectionist models, in particular, have an important role to play in directing theoretical and empirical research in this area, because they best enable us to understand the causal factors at play in the ontogeny of knowledge about objects and cognition in general (cf. Mareschal et al., 2007). We begin, therefore, with a brief review of connectionist modeling principles.

10.1.2 Why build connectionist computational models?

Connectionist models are computer models loosely based on the principles of neural information processing (Elman et al., 1996; Mareschal et al., 2007; Mareschal & Thomas, 2007; McLeod et al., 1998; O'Reilly & Munakata, 2000; Rumelhart & McClelland, 1986; Shultz, 2003). However, in general, they are not intended to be neural models. Instead, they attempt to strike a balance between importing some of the key ideas from the neurosciences and maintaining sufficiently discrete and definable components to allow questions about behavior to be formulated in terms of high-level computational concepts.

From a developmental perspective, connectionist networks are ideal for modeling because they develop their own internal representations as a result of interacting with an environment (Plunkett & Sinha, 1992). However, these networks are not simply *tabula rasa* empiricist learning machines. The representations they develop can be strongly predetermined by initial constraints.

These constraints can take the form of different associative learning mechanisms attuned to specific information in the environment (e.g., temporal correlation or spatial correlation), or they can take the form of architectural constraints that guide the flow of information in the system. Although connectionist modeling has its roots in associationist learning paradigms, it has inherited the Hebbian rather than the Hullian tradition. That is, the structural constraints placed on what goes on inside the box (inside the network) are as important in determining the overall behavior of the networks across their development as are the correlations between stimuli (sensory inputs) and responses (outputs)

Infant–object interactions are a case in point. As we shall outline later, infants' physical interactions with objects develop to some extent independently within a number of behavioral modalities, such that knowledge of objects is expressed differently within these modalities at a given point in development. Connectionist models offer an ideal opportunity to attempt to understand the mechanistic basis of synergies and dissociations between multiple (simultaneously active) behavioral systems. This is a question of key importance, not just in developmental psychology but also in fields of research tackling the relationship between putative implicit and explicit knowledge in adults (e.g. Cleeremans & McClelland, 1991; Shanks & St. John, 1994).

10.1.3 A primer in connectionist information processing

Connectionist networks are made up of simple processing units (idealized neurons) interconnected via weighted communication lines (idealized synapses). Units are often represented graphically as circles; the weighted communication lines are represented as lines between these circles. Activation flows from unit to unit via these connection weights. Fig. 10.1a shows a generic connectionist network in which activation can flow in any direction. However, most applications of connectionist networks impose constraints on the way activation can flow.

Fig. 10.1b shows a typical feed-forward network. Activation (information) is constrained to move in one direction only. Units through which information enters the network are called input units. Units through which information leaves the network are called output units. Units which interface with neither input nor output are called hidden units. In a feed-forward network, information is first encoded as a pattern of activation across the bank of input units. That activation then filters up through a first layer of weights until it produces a pattern of activation across the band of hidden units. The pattern of activation produced across the hidden units constitutes an internal representation of the information originally presented to the network. The activation at the

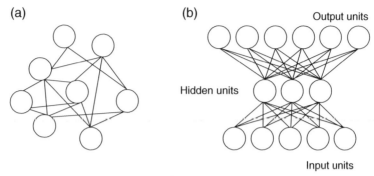

Fig. 10.1 Multidirectional flow versus feed-forward nets.

hidden units continues to flow through the network until it reaches the output unit. The pattern of activation produced at the output units is taken as the network's response to the initial input.

Each unit is a very simple processor that mimics the functioning of an idealized neuron. The unit sums the weighted activation arriving into it. It then sets its own level of activation according to some nonlinear function of that weighted input. The nonlinearity allows the units to respond differentially to different ranges of input values. The key idea of connectionist modeling is that of collective computations. That is, although the behavior of the individual components in the network is simple, the behavior of the network as a whole can be very complex. It is the behavior of the network as a whole that is taken to model different aspects of infant behaviors.

The network's global behavior is determined by the connection weights. As activation flows through the network, it is transformed by the set of connection weights between successive layers in the network. Learning (i.e., adapting one's behavior) is accomplished by tuning the connection weights until some stable behavior is obtained. Supervised networks adjust their weights until the output response (for a given input) matches a target response. That target can come from an active teacher, or passively through observing 'success or failure' in the environment, but it must come from outside the system. Unsupervised networks adjust their weights until some internal constraint is satisfied (e.g., maximally different input must have maximally different internal representations, or associations in input must lead to associations in output). Backpropagation (Rumelhart et al., 1986) is a popular training algorithm for supervised connectionist networks.

Many connectionist network models are very simple and only contain some 100 units. This does not imply that the part of the brain solving the corresponding task uses only 100 neurons. It is important to understand that these models are not neural models, but information-processing models of behavior. The models provide examples of how systems with similar computational properties to the brain can give rise to the behaviors observed in infants. As such, they constitute possible explanations of those behaviors in terms of neurally plausible mechanisms. Sometimes, individual units are taken to represent pools of neurons or cell assemblies rather than single neurons (e.g., Changeux & Dehaene, 1989). According to this interpretation, the activation level of the units corresponds to the proportion of neurons firing in the pool.

As we shall see in the next section, implemented computational models (connectionist or otherwise) render explicit theories of the information processing that occurs in specific tasks.

10.2 Modelling infants' visual interactions with objects

10.2.1 Looking-time paradigms: a window on perception and cognition in infancy

Much of what we know about infants' perceptions and knowledge of objects comes from paradigms that measure infants' looking behavior. Two such paradigms are *Habituation of Looking* (e.g., Bornstein, 1985), and *Violation of Expectation* (VoE; e.g., Baillargeon, 2004). In 'habituation of looking' procedures, infants are presented with a single visual stimulus, or a number of visual stimuli across a series of trials, until they have reached a criterion decline in their visual inspection of such stimuli (Fantz, 1964) or they have inspected the stimuli for a fixed period of time (Slater, 1995). Infants can then be presented with novel and familiar stimuli to examine the degree to which they generalize or exclude such stimuli from the representation they have acquired from the habituation phase. A visual preference for the novel indicates exclusion of that stimulus from the representation they have just acquired. The VoE procedure has a somewhat different rationale. In this paradigm, researchers form a hypothesis about infants' expectations and then present them with visual events that either concur with or violate these expectations. A visual preference for the event that violates the expectation is taken to indicate that the infants possess the hypothesized expectation, and the underlying knowledge that guides it.

In the next sections, we will present computational models that have been constructed to model infants' looking behavior with these paradigms. Firstly, we will describe mechanistic models of the dynamics of habituation–novelty behaviors, using the example of a model of infants' categorizations of visual objects. Secondly, we will describe how models incorporating recurrent connections (subserving a visual short-term memory system) can help shed light on the mechanism underlying infants' ability to form and express, in their visual behavior, expectations regarding events involving objects they can no longer directly perceive.

10.2.2 Autoencoder models of infants' visual habituation behavior

Many infant categorization tasks rely on infants directing more attention to unfamiliar or unexpected stimuli. The standard interpretation of this behavior is that infants are comparing an input stimulus to an internal representation of the same stimulus (e.g., Charlesworth, 1969; Cohen, 1973; Solokov, 1963). As long as there is a discrepancy between the information stored in the internal representation and the visual input, the infant continues to attend to the stimulus. While attending to the stimulus, the infant updates its internal representation. When the information in the internal representation is no longer discrepant with the visual input, attention is directed elsewhere. This process is illustrated in Fig. 10.2a. When a familiar object is presented, there is little or no attending because the infant already has a reliable internal representation of that object. In contrast, when an unfamiliar or unexpected object is presented, there is more attending because an internal representation has to be constructed or adjusted. The degree to which a novel object differs from existing internal representations determines the amount of adjusting that has to be done, and hence, the duration of attention.

Connectionist autoencoder networks have been used to model the relation between sustained attention and representation construction (French et al., 2004; Mareschal & French, 2000; Mareschal et al., 2000; Schafer & Mareschal, 2001).

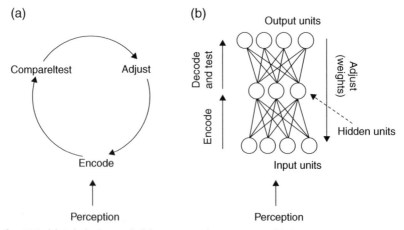

Fig. 10.2 (a) Sokolovian and, (b) Autoencoder accounts of habituation.

An autoencoder is a feed-forward connectionist network with a single layer of hidden units (Fig. 10.2b). It is called an autoencoder because it associates an input with itself. The network learns to reproduce on the output units the pattern of activation across the input units. It relies on a supervised learning algorithm, but because the input signal serves as the training signal for the output units, no teacher other than the environment is hypothesized. In an autoencoder, the number of hidden units is smaller than the number of input or output units. This produces a bottleneck in the flow of information through the network, forcing the network to develop a more compact internal representation of the input (at the hidden unit level) that is sufficiently rich to reproduce all the information in the original input. Information is first compressed into an internal representation and then expanded to reproduce the original input. The successive cycles of training in the autoencoder are an iterative process by which a reliable internal representation of the input is developed. The reliability of the representation is tested by expanding it and comparing the resulting predictions to the actual stimulus being encoded.

This approach to modeling novelty preference assumes that infant looking times are positively correlated with the network error. The greater the error, the longer the looking time, because it takes more training cycles to reduce the error. The degree to which error (looking time) increases on presentation of a novel object depends on the similarity between the novel object and the familiar object. Presenting a series of similar objects leads to a progressive error drop on future similar objects.

Although autoencoder networks have been used to explain habituation behaviors spanning a range of different stimulus domains and modalities (see Sirois, 2004, for a review), we will focus on one particular example in which they have been useful in explaining what was previously a confusing aspect of infant–object interactions. An unusual asymmetry has been observed in infants' formation of natural categories of visual objects (Quinn & Eimas, 1996; Quinn et al., 1993). When 3- to 4-month-olds are initially exposed (habituated) to a series of pictures of cats, they will form a category of cat that excludes dogs. However, when they are exposed to a series of pictures of dogs, they will form a category of dog that does include cats. We used the autoencoder network to explain this behavior. The original cat and dog pictures were measured along 10 dimensions and presented to the networks for categorization. The same presentation procedure was used as with the infants. These networks developed CAT and DOG categories with the same exclusivity asymmetry as the 3- to 4-month-olds. Moreover, the model predicted that learning DOG after CAT would disrupt the prior learning of CAT whereas learning CAT after DOG would not disrupt the prior learning of CATS.

A subsequent study with 3- to 4-month-olds found this to be true of infants as well (Mareschal et al., 2000). The asymmetry was explained in terms of the distribution of cat and dog feature values in the stimuli presented to the infants. Most cat values fell within the range of dog values, but the converse was not true. Thus, for a system that processes the statistical distribution of features of a stimulus, the cats would appear as a subset of the dog category. Further analyses revealed that these networks could parse the world into distinct categories according to the correlation of feature values, as 10-month-olds have been shown to do (Mareschal & French, 2000; Younger, 1985).

Here, we see quite clearly how a particular class of connectionist model (an autoencoder) helped explain confusing behavioral findings by forming an explicit mechanistic theory of that behavior with testable hypotheses. In this case, the model helped demonstrate the bottom-up nature of infants' categories for visual objects, laying down a challenge for theories that explain early categories in terms of phylogenetically provided knowledge (e.g., Fodor, 1980; Marcus, 2001).

10.2.3 Using recurrent connections to model infants' short-term memory for objects

As previously discussed above, the VoE technique is perhaps the best-known behavioral paradigm for assessing knowledge in early infancy. The paradigm was originally developed by Baillargeon and colleagues (e.g., Baillargeon, 1993; Baillargeon et al., 1985) in order to examine one of Piaget's claims concerning the developing object concept: namely, that infants do not have an understanding of object permanence until 7.5–9 months when they become able to successfully reach for an object hidden behind an occluding screen (Piaget, 1952, 1954). In a typical VoE study, infants watch an event in which some physical property of a hidden object is violated (e.g., solidity). Surprise at this violation (as measured by increased visual inspection of the event) is interpreted as showing that the infants know or have the expectation that (a) the hidden object still exists and (b) the hidden object maintains the physical property that was violated (Baillargeon, 1993).

As is well known, the VoE technique has been used to demonstrate that infants have a number of expectations concerning the physical properties of hidden objects, some even by the age of 2.5 months (Baillargeon, 1987; Spelke et al., 1992). Such precocious knowledge in the absence of an ability to manually manipulate objects (especially hidden objects) prompted many researchers to posit a human phylogenetic provision of 'core knowledge' about the continuity or permanence of objects, along with a number of their other characteristics such as solidity (Spelke, 1994; Spelke et al., 1992).

However, in the last 10 years, several connectionist models (Mareschal et al., 1998; Munakata et al., 1997; Schlesinger, 2006) have been developed, which challenge this assumption by showing that representations concerning memory for the location and trajectories of hidden objects can emerge in a 'graded' way commensurate with their experience of the reemergence of an object following its occlusion. These models accomplish this feat by incorporating hidden units that have 'recurrent' connections (Elman, 1990). Feed-forward networks with recurrent connections allow models to associate information at one time step with information presented at subsequent time steps, and as such represent a mechanism for a simplistic short-term memory.

Munakata et al. (1997) developed three models simulating the acquisition of object permanence. We will discuss two of these models here. The first model (Fig. 10.3a) tackles specifically the emergence of visual expectations concerning the spatial location of a briefly occluded object, and models the duration of infants' inspection of possible and impossible visual displays (the VoE paradigm). The third model (Fig. 10.3b), concerning dissociations between looking and reaching behavior (or between Piaget's paradigms and the VoE paradigm), will be discussed in Section 10.3.

Munakata et al.'s models focus on a microworld consisting of objects and an occluder. In this microworld, an occluding screen moves across the stage and temporarily in front of a target object. When this occlusion occurs, the target object disappears, and when the occlusion ends, the target object reappears. This microworld is transduced via a simple retina and learns to predict what the perceptual input at the next time step will be: the model learns to associate the input at time step x with the input at time step $x + 1$. The input retina consists of two rows of seven units (Fig. 10.4). The bottom row codes the position of the moving screen. The position of the screen is coded by turning two units on while all others are set to zero. The top row codes the position of a stationary object by activating one unit and setting all other units to zero. As an event unfolds, the sequence of patterns in Fig. 10.4 codes the progressive movement of the screen from left to right and back again. When the object is occluded, the unit marking that object position is turned off.

The model experiences four kinds of events. In the ball–barrier event, the network sees a stationary ball being occluded by a moving screen. In the barrier-only event, the network sees only a barrier moving across the scene with no ball present. In the ball-only event, the network sees a stationary ball in the same position at all times. Finally, in the nothing event, the network sees nothing throughout the duration of the event. The network's performance is evaluated by comparing its performance in two different conditions. Its ability to predict the object's reappearance when the screen moves away is evaluated

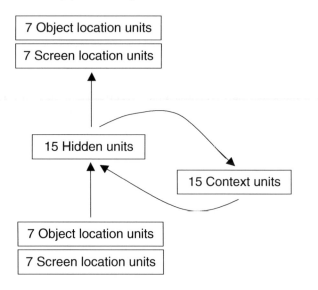

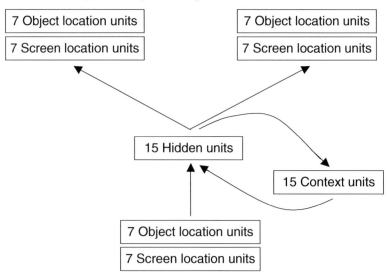

Fig. 10.3 Connectionist models of (a) Visual preference and, (b) reaching (adapted from Munakata et al, 1997).

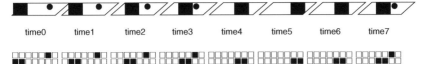

time0   time1   time2   time3   time4   time5   time6   time7

Fig. 10.4 Input patterns (Munakata et al., 1997. Reprinted with permission.)

by reporting the network's sensitivity to a ball. The sensitivity is computed by taking the activation in the unit coding the object's position (top row of units) at the time when the object should reappear in the ball–barrier condition and subtracting the base rate activation for the corresponding time step in the barrier-only condition. The difference is then hypothesized to reflect the network's 'knowledge' or expectation of when an object should reappear (i.e., when it is faced with a ball–barrier event) and when the object should not reappear (i.e., when faced with a barrier-only event). Using this measure of performance, the authors found that the network's object sensitivity increases with increased experience and decreases with increased occlusion duration.

Mareschal et al. (1999) present a model of the acquisition of object permanence incorporating a trajectory prediction module (see Fig. 10.5), which likewise simulates the graded emergence of representations of hidden objects through the strengthening of recurrent connections. Similar to the Munakata et al. model, Mareschal et al.'s model also takes an object–occluder microworld as its input, and is trained to predict input at the next time step on the basis of the current

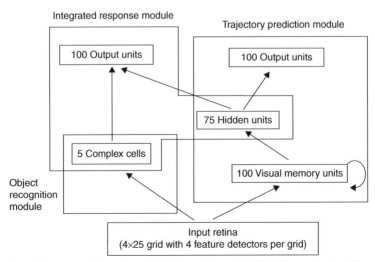

Fig. 10.5 The Mareschal et al. model (Mareschal et al., 1999. Reproduced with permission of the author.)

time step. However, the microworld and the behavior of the object and occluder is somewhat different from that used by Munakata et al. (1997). The retina consists of a 4 × 25 grid, with the object occupying a 2 × 2 location on that grid. The occluder occupies a 4 × 4 location in the center of the grid. Rather than the occluder moving (as in Munakata, et al.), it is the object that moves in the Mareschal et al. model. The model experiences displays in which the object follows either horizontal or vertical trajectories across the grid. On horizontal trajectories, the object becomes fully occluded behind the central screen. In Mareschal et al.'s microworld, four different kinds of objects are presented. For simplicity's sake, we will not discuss this manipulation here, but will return to this in the next section.

Mareschal et al.'s trajectory prediction network quickly learns to predict an object's next position when it is visible. However, the hidden unit representations that are developed persist for some time after the object has disappeared and allow the network to keep track of the object even when it is no longer visible. Fig. 10.6 presents a graphic representation of the network's ability to predict the next position of an occluded object. The left-hand panel shows what is projected onto the retina; the right-hand panel shows the corresponding object position predicted by the trained network. The rows correspond to successive time steps. Note especially step $t = 3$, for which the direct perceptual input available to the network is exactly the same as that at $t = 2$. The network is able to predict the subsequent reappearance of the object, taking into account how long it has been behind the screen.

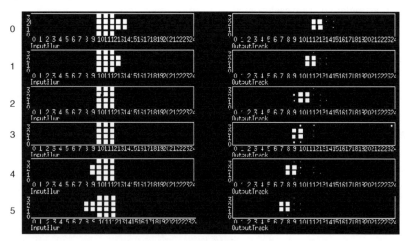

30000 Epochs

Fig. 10.6 Trajectory prediction network (Mareschal et al., 1999. Reproduced with permission of the author). The left-hand column represents the network's perceptual input of an object moving behind an occcluder from right to left, across time. The right-hand column represents the trained network's prediction of where the object will be at the next time step, across time.

Although there are some differences in approach, both of these connectionist models argue that expectations regarding the trajectories of hidden objects emerge from graded, distributed short-term memory representations of objects, facilitated by recurrent connections in the hidden units. Because they are connectionist models, knowledge is also embodied in the interactions between the connection weights of a complex network and the activation that flows through that network. Object representations emerge gradually through experience with an external world.

10.3 Modelling the development of object permanence

10.3.1 Behavioral dissociations in the development of object permanence

The models described in the preceding section demonstrate mechanisms whereby an ability to remember and predict the movements of a hidden object can emerge through the constraints of a neural system and the environment that tutors it. A key contribution in this case is to point out that phylogenetic inheritance need not be invoked to explain early competencies in infants' looking behavior (e.g., Baillargeon, 1993; Baillargeon et al., 1985; Spelke, 1994). Nonetheless, there are still some important questions to answer, both for theories positing innate knowledge of object permanence and for explanations appealing to environmental construction of such knowledge (Mareschal et al., 2007). Concerning the acquisition of the object concept, there is one particular conundrum that has been a sticking point for infancy researchers for over two decades: namely, if very young infants understand the permanence of objects, why can they not act on this knowledge until much later (see also Gjersoe & Hood, Chapter 13; Keen, 2003)? Despite the huge corpus of infant looking-time data attesting to even 2.5-month-old infants' understanding of permanence, Piaget's (1954) original observations of 6-month-olds' inability to manually retrieve hidden objects still stand.

Using manual search to test infants' understanding of hidden objects, Piaget concluded that it was not until 7.5–9 months that infants understand that hidden objects continue to exist, because younger infants do not successfully reach. Researchers are in general accord that the delay cannot be attributed to any motor immaturity (e.g., J. G. Bremner, 1994), and although there is some suggestion that infants do not possess the requisite understanding of means-end relationships to coordinate and subgoal the action of uncovering an object with its eventual retrieval (e.g., Baillargeon et al., 1990; Diamond, 1991; Willatts, 1999), many researchers argue that the delay represents a genuine developmental dissociation between knowledge systems, or qualities of knowledge which subserve separate behavioral modalities.

Various dissociations of knowledge have been invoked. Bower's *Identity Theory* of the developing object concept (Bower, 1982) suggests that knowledge of permanence (as indexed through looking-time tasks) is an early acquisition, and that the failure of manual search can be explained by infants' inability to keep track of the identities of multiple objects (e.g., he argues that infants confuse the hidden object and its occluder.) J. G. Bremner (2000) has argued that looking behavior and manual retrieval tap implicit and explicit forms of infants' knowledge about objects. Indeed, there are some indications that Piaget's account would predict success at visual behavioral tasks well before manual retrieval (see A. J. Bremner & Mareschal, 2004). The exact nature and origins of this developmental lag between understanding the continued existence of a hidden object and searching for it remains a central question of infant cognitive development.

We next describe a number of attempts that have been made to model behavioral dissociations in the development of object permanence. The first three models we describe are symbolic models, and the last two models are connectionist models.

10.3.2 Symbolic models of the development of object permanence

The first two symbolic models are based on some early visual expectation data reported by Bower and colleagues (Bower, 1982). Although these data are no longer considered to be an accurate depiction of infant behaviors, the models can still be evaluated within the context of those data. In addition, they bear some similarities to the 'object file' accounts of infant object knowledge described by other authors in this volume (cf. Flombaum et al., Chapter 6). Prazdny (1980) constructed a model that deals with three levels of representation for objects. The highest level is a conceptual level and the other two are perceptual levels. In this model, object feature and spatiotemporal information are processed separately at the perceptual level (Fig. 10.7). The conceptual level is the only level with access to information from both pathways. An *object description* (OD) is generated at the conceptual level from this information. An OD binds together attributes (e.g., color, size, position, trajectory) into a single structure and labels it with a name. Labeled ODs decay away if no new perceptual information arrives to corroborate them. If perceptual information arrives, which is inconsistent with an existing OD, a second OD is generated. Predictions (expectations) based on both ODs are then tested against new perceptual information in order to select the appropriate description.

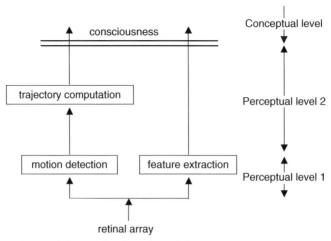

Fig. 10.7 Schema of the Prazdny (1980) model.

The construction of the new OD requires a finite, nonzero time interval. During this interval, behavior is determined by the existing older OD.

Procedural knowledge is stored in the form of IF-THEN rules. If a specific pattern of data is available, then an action is carried out. In particular, IF-ADDED and IF-REMOVED procedures (sensitive to new attributes being added to or removed from an OD) are used to implement expectation behaviors when the state of an object changes (e.g., it disappears after occlusion). No mechanism is implemented for modeling development. However, development is hypothesized to be driven by a streamlining process in which specific rules are combined to produce a single more efficient rule.

Only the conceptual level is actually implemented (i.e., neither of the two perceptual levels are implemented). Raw sensory information enters the system in the form of snapshots of the visual scene coded over a set of attributes. The lowest perceptual level processes these attributes over a single snapshot interval. The second level generates a spatiotemporal representation across a small number of consecutive snapshots. Hence, this level is able to extract simple trajectory information. Part of the infant's behavior is explained in terms of competition between this perceptual level representation of trajectory and the conceptual level representation of the trajectory. Only the conceptual level has access to the features and hence can distinguish between two objects moving on the same trajectory.

This model claims to capture most of Bower's (1982) visual expectation data. By building the model, Prazdny proposes a new theory of how information is processed in order to account for the existing data. In this sense, the model contributes directly to our understanding of infant cognition. Moreover, it attempts to incorporate findings from other fields of psychology (e.g., separate feature and displacement processing). Declarative knowledge is represented as factual assertions about prespecified attributes. Procedural knowledge exists as production rules with predetermined actions.

This model should be admired for trying to incorporate the emerging neuropsychological evidence of a 'what–where' divide in visual processing (Ungerlieder & Mishkin, 1982; Milner & Goodale, 1995) into a process model of object permanence behaviors. Also, the use of rules makes explicit what knowledge is involved in each task and how knowledge is combined to produce the observed behaviors. Unfortunately, the model does not provide a transition mechanism that can account for how one level of performance develops into the next level. In this sense, it is not a developmental model. Moreover, Prazdny only ever implemented the third (conceptual) level of the model. The rest is only hypothetical.

Luger and colleagues (1983, 1984) made a direct attempt to implement Bower's Identity Theory of the developing object concept (Bower, 1982). As outlined in the preceding section, identity theory suggests that rather than studying object permanence, we should be studying the development of object identity. Bower believes that young infants understand that objects continue to exist, but that they have difficulty keeping track of them. Young infants generate a large number of separate object representations for what adults would encode as a single object. The main idea of this model is that infant behaviors can be ascribed to the use of five action rules subsumed under three conceptual rules. Luger et al. describe the three conceptual rules, choosing to remain noncommittal about how the action rules might interact. Hence, the authors believe that there is a complete dissociation between the conceptual level and the response level. The conceptual rules are as follows:

Rule 1: An object is a bounded volume of space in a particular place OR on a particular path of movement.

Rule 2: An object is a bounded volume of space of a certain size, shape, and color, which can move from place to place among trajectories. (Note that this rule now integrates featural information with spatiotemporal information).

Rule 3: Two or more objects cannot be in the same place OR on the same path of movement simultaneously UNLESS they share a common boundary.

These rules are developmentally ordered in that Rule 2 replaces Rule 1 and Rule 3 replaces Rule 2. In accordance with Bower's Identity Theory, infants are assumed to have prior knowledge that objects continue to exist, and of what actions to execute in a given context. The models at different levels set up a different number of separate object representations. The Level 1 models do not rely on featural information to identify an object. Hence, they set up a new object every time there is a change in spatiotemporal information. The Level 2 models only set up a new object token when there are changes in the feature representation. Finally, the Level 3 models do not set up a new object representation when two objects are contiguous. Although no transition mechanism is implemented, it is suggested that development is driven by the acquisition of procedures that lead to more cost-efficient representations.

Luger et al. do not state explicitly what knowledge is available to the system. It is never clear how much (if any) of the knowledge is learned. This reflects the belief that a large part of world knowledge is built-in, and that development consists of the improved control of that knowledge. Not surprisingly, this model captures a wider range of Bower's data than the Prazdny model did.

As with Prazdny model, the use of rules in this model renders explicit the knowledge required for this task and how it is combined to produce the observed behaviors. Also similar to the Prazdny model, this model fails to specify a transition mechanism and is therefore not a developmental model. This model is closely tied to Bower's Identity Theory; in fact, it is an implementation of the theory. It brings more precision, but no new theoretical insight. Hence, once Bower's theory has been refuted, the model becomes obsolete. It does not incorporate domain general principles (such as the 'what-where' visual processing divide that could allow it to be extended to other task domains).

Drescher (1991) constructed a model of object permanence that stands midway between connectionist methods and symbolic methods. Drescher picks up where Piaget left off and suggests a precise mechanism by which object permanence could develop. The mechanism is implemented as part of a simulated organism in a microworld. Knowledge is stored in the form of a three-part action schema. The actions are fixed from the start and represent motor primitives comparable to the abilities of an infant. The context and result parts of the schema are progressively filled in as the organism discovers contingencies in its environment through the execution of an action. What is respectively stored in these registers is a summary of relevant aspects of the world before and after the action has been carried out. The context does not, therefore, describe a necessary set of conditions for the action to be carried out. Rather, it describes a hypothetical state of the world wherein if the action were to be carried out, the result part of the schema would become a true description of the world. Thus, the organism acquires knowledge in the form of counterfactual assertions that link environmental context to potential actions and perceptual consequences.

Drescher splits learning into the two subtasks of identifying the relevant features and then identifying the necessary features for an event to occur. This so-called 'marginal attribution' mechanism is based on detecting significant changes in the probability of occurrence of an event. If the probability of occurrence significantly changes from its base rate, then the environmental context is deemed to be relevant. If several relevant contexts or results are discovered, new sibling schemas are created, each schema corresponding to a distinct context or result.

When an unreliable action schema is found to be locally consistent (in that it gives rise to the same results for a brief period of time), a new synthetic token is created to represent the still unknown feature of the environment that will make the schema reliable. These tokens pick out aspects of the environment that are either independent of perception or that the infant has not yet learned to coordinate in its perceptual and motor schemas. The proliferation and linking of these synthetic tokens supposedly leads to the emergence of a representation of external objects existing independently of perception.

At first sight the results of this modeling are encouraging. The organism builds an intramodal network of sensory actions in each of the visual, tactile, and proprioceptive modes by chaining together action schemas. Moreover, it begins to construct intermodal schemas, thereby learning to coordinate two different sensory modes. However, the system does not progress very far along the Piagetian road of cognitive development (never quite reaching the concept of object), and where it does succeed, it does not seem to have been following the road map described by Piaget.

Even though the simulated microorganism is endowed with a mechanism for recombining its knowledge elements, it fails to generate a more powerful representational system. In fact, it fails to generate a representation of permanent objects precisely because it cannot increase its representational power. Its knowledge remains bound to the perceptual input. This is because it has no means (in its initial state) of representing nonperceptually bound information. Even the synthetic items are perceptually bound in the sense that they are temporary fillers for a not fully understood environmental context. These schemas are replaced by more reliable perceptual schemas when they become available. Thus, the best that this model could hope to achieve is to elaborate a complex network of sensorimotor information.

All three of the models discussed here have their strengths and weaknesses. The symbolic rule-based models (Prazdny, 1980; Luger et al., 1983, 1984) are very clear about the knowledge representations that underlie performance on the different tasks. However, these models do not propose any developmental mechanisms. They are static descriptions of performance at different ages with no account of how performance actually develops. Prazdny is to be commended in trying to incorporate domain-general neuropsychological constraints in his model. Luger et al. tie their models very closely to Bower's Identity Theory. As a result, it is invalidated as soon as Bower's theory is refuted. In contrast, Drescher's model attempts to offer a developmental transition mechanism. Although the mechanism is successful at developing a coherent network of intersensory information for visible objects, it fails to represent hidden objects in any consistent or reliable fashion.

We next describe two full-fledged connectionist models of the development of object permanence. Connectionist models have the advantage of being better suited to the modeling of developmental transitions than symbolic models. Whereas symbolic models often sidestep this question by describing the intact state of a computational system at specific stages of development, connectionist models provide a mechanism by which environmental and organismic constraints can interact (in the training material and the architecture of the model and learning algorithms) to drive developmental shifts in competence from one stage to the next.

10.3.3 Connectionist models of developmental dissociations between knowledge and action

Two of the connectionist approaches to modeling of infants' looking behavior described in Section 10.2 (Mareschal et al., 1999; Munakata et al., 1997) have also sought to model infants' manual retrieval behavior, and the developmental lag between success measured through looking and success measured through reaching. Both models are successful at modeling the lag, but achieve this success through quite different means. Accordingly, the models make different predictions that can be tested in order to evaluate their success.

Munakata et al. modeled the developmental lag by grafting a simple reaching module onto the existing predictive model. The reach module uses the internal representations developed by the predictive module to elicit a response. As is the case with Mareschal et al.'s model, the response module also outputs the predicted next perceptual event. Munakata et al. built constraints into the reaching module that will produce a lag. These constraints involve (1) setting a lower learning rate in the reach module so that development would be slowed down and (2) beginning training of the reach module after the predictive module has developed meaningful representations. Not surprisingly, they then found that the performance of the reach module lags behind that of the predictive module. Although these manipulations do show that two different hypotheses concerning the developmental lag (namely, those related to the delayed maturity of infant reaching and delayed onset of reaching experience) can be implemented in a connectionist model, it does little to further our understanding of the causes of the lag.

Mareschal et al.'s (1999) computational model of the development of object permanence takes a somewhat different approach to modeling the lag between looking and reaching. Their model also incorporates an output system that attempts to model the development of the success in manual retrieval, but the learning rate and the onset of learning are not manipulated in this module. Instead, they examined how the developmental lag might arise as a result of particular patterns of associative learning in the network. The particular constraint they used to achieve this is by building in two streams of learning. This particular architectural constraint is inspired by work on cortical representation of visual object information. Anatomical, neurophysiological, and psychophysical evidence points to the existence of two processing routes for visual object information in the cortex (Goodale, 1993; Milner & Goodale, 1995; Ungerleider & Mishkin, 1982; van Essen et al., 1992;). Although the exact functionality of the two routes remains a hotly debated question, it is generally accepted that they contain radically different kinds of representations. The dorsal (or parietal) route processes spatiotemporal object information, whereas the ventral (or temporal) route processes object featural information.

In Fig. 10.5 discussed previously, each box represents a layer of units and each arrow represents a full set of connections between successive layers. The dotted lines delimit separate modules. Information enters the networks via a simplified retina, which we have already described in Section 10.2. An aspect of the microworld (left undescribed in Section 10.2) is that the objects that followed trajectories across the retina comprised different featural characteristics. All four objects had correlated features (i.e., {−1 1 −1 1}, {−1 1 1 −1}, {1 −1 1 −1}, {1 −1 1 −1}), which remained the same across a full trajectory. Features only changed when a new trajectory was presented to the retina.

The trajectory prediction module already described can be considered to represent the 'dorsal' visual stream projecting into the cortex from the retina. This stream does not encode featural information about the objects, and develops, as described earlier, a spatiotemporal representation of the object (cf. the functions of the dorsal cortical route).

The 'ventral' visual stream is here represented by an *Object Recognition Network* and has quite a different set of constraints to that of the trajectory prediction network. The object recognition network generates a spatially invariant feature-based representation of the object (cf. the functions of the ventral cortical route) by using a modified version of the unsupervised learning algorithm developed by Foldiak (1991). Initially, a bank of five complex cells is fully and randomly connected to all feature detectors. The algorithm exploits the fact that an object tends to be contiguous with itself at successive temporal intervals (i.e., it learns on the basis that two successive images will probably be derived from the same object). At the end of learning, each complex cell becomes associated with a particular feature combination wherever it appears on the retina.

The *Response Integration Network* recruits and coordinates the representations from both streams (a function attributed to the prefrontal cortex; Rao et al., 1997) as and when required by an active, voluntary response. The output of the response integration network corresponds to the infant's ability to coordinate and use the information it has about object positions and object identity. This network integrates the internal representations generated by the other modules (i.e., the feature representation at the complex cell level and the spatiotemporal representation in the hidden unit layer) as required by a retrieval response task. It consists of a single-layered supervised feed-forward network whose task is to output the same next position as the prediction network for two of the objects, and to inhibit any response (all units set to 0.0) for the other two objects. This reflects the fact that infants do not retrieve (e.g., manually uncover) all objects. In general, infants are not asked or rewarded (externally) for search. The experimental setup relies on spontaneous search by the infant. Some objects are desired (e.g., biscuit) whereas others are not (e.g., dummy). Any voluntary retrieval response will necessarily require the processing of featural information (to identify the object as a desired one) as well as trajectory information (to localize the object).

Similar to infants, the model also showed a developmental lag. Active tasks such as retrieval of a desired hidden object required the integration of information across the multiple object representations whereas surprise or dishabituation tasks only required access to one of the representations separately. A developmental lag appeared between retrieval and surprise-based tasks because of the added cognitive demands of accessing two object representations simultaneously in an active response task (see Fig. 10.8). The model predicted that dishabituation tasks that required infants to access two cortically separable representations would also show a developmental lag, compared with tasks that only required access to one cortical representation. This prediction was later confirmed. Mareschal and colleagues (Mareschal & Bremner, 2006; Mareschal & Johnson, 2003) gave infants a habituation display in which spatial arrays of two objects were presented, and then occluded by two screens. 4-month-olds demonstrated an ability to remember the spatial arrangement of objects, and also to remember the featural identity of some objects, but were unable to link spatial and featural information together (they could not remember which object was where).

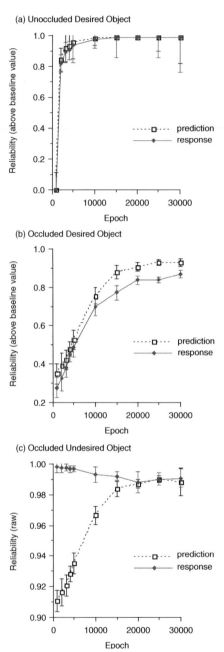

Fig. 10.8 Comparison of model's ability to predict or reach, across development, for (a) a visible desired object across development, (b) an occluded desired object, and (c) an occluded undesired object.

Finally, Mareschal & Bremner (2006) have more recently reported an extension of Mareschal et al.'s (1999) object permanence model, which has begun to explore ways in which the problem of linking information from the dorsal and ventral streams (in other words, linking 'what' an object is to 'where' it is) could be solved in a world where multiple objects exist (a world more similar to our own). More specifically, this model examined the possibility that temporal synchrony could be used as a mechanism for binding and/or retaining the information that is independently processed in the dorsal and ventral streams. Electrophysiological evidence suggests that specifically gamma-band oscillatory synchrony could be used to establish dynamic links between various cortical areas or during short-term memory maintenance tasks (Tallon-Baudry, 2003; Ward 2003) and has been implicated in object memory during infancy (Kaufman et al., 2003; Kaufman et al., 2005). The limitations shown by young infants on object memory tasks could be a result of the immature development of such mechanisms. This project explored how a temporal synchrony binding mechanism interacted with learning (within task adaptation) and development (ontogenetic adaptation).

Some interesting findings have emerged from this model. By interleaving information about different objects on different peaks of oscillatory activity, it can learn to track predictively and respond appropriately to multiple moving objects (as had the original Mareschal et al. model, but with only a single object at a time). This suggests that the gamma-band activity observed infants (Kaufman et al., 2003; Kaufman et al., 2006) may reflect a process of trying to realign neural representations of location and identity with the now-inconsistent perceptual information. Further findings of the model were that although there was an overall improvement in its ability to identify the correct feature-location bindings with increased training, this interacted with the number of objects being tracked and the duration of the occlusion. The more objects present, the more likely the network was to make a binding error. Similarly, the longer the occlusion, the more likely it was that the network made a binding error. It will be interesting to examine whether these behaviors bear out in real infants, and to consider new programs of empirical research, which this particular avenue of modeling can stimulate.

10.3.4 The A-not-B error and competition between active and latent memory

One of the most enduring questions concerning the development of infant–object interactions is why do infants make the A-not-B error?

In the traditional A–B task, designed by Piaget (1954), the infant observes an experimenter hiding an object at two different locations, first at A and then at B. When allowed to search for the object, infants typically search at the hiding place that was used first (A), even when she has seen the object hidden at the other location (B). Piaget originally interpreted this result as being due to infants' incomplete understanding of objects. Piaget's view was that, although infants at this stage search for objects once they are no longer directly visible, the existence of the hidden object is still tied to their action in retrieving it from one location in space, and thus, their object concept is not fully objective. Therefore, when the object's location changes, the infants make errors.

A huge number of studies have been devoted to the investigation of this error through a number of informative manipulations. Researchers have manipulated the number of trials at A which the infant receives (Markovitch & Zelazo, 1999), the distinctiveness of the covers (A. J. Bremner & Bryant, 2001; J. G. Bremner, 1978; Butterworth et al., 1982), and the presence of the object underneath the cover (Smith et al., 1999), to name but a few. Consensus on an explanation is still divided. Recently, Munakata (1998) has attempted to explain the emergence of this strange behavior with a connectionist computational model.

Munakata's (1998) model of the development of performance in the A-not-B task attempts to explain the perseverative response as a result of competition between 'latent' memory for the location of an object (established over a number of trials [reaches] to the object at A), and 'active' memory for the current location of the object (established in the context of the most recent trial). As we shall describe shortly, latent memory is instantiated in weight changes across a number of trials. Active memory is instantiated as residual activation from the input, which is propagated at the hidden units and the output units by virtue of recurrent connections at those nodes. In this model, the A-not-B error results from the success of latent memory for the object at location A established across a number of 'A trials' at the expense of active memory for the object at B on the current trial. The development of eventual success at the task is achieved through a manipulation of the strength of the recurrent connections at the hidden and output layers. Munakata and Stedron (2002) have suggested that this parameter can be regarded as a proxy for the experience-based weight changes demonstrated in the earlier object permanence models put forward by Munakata et al. (1997).

The model's architecture (displayed in Fig. 10.9) comprises three banks of input nodes corresponding to the locations in the tasks, the covers present, and

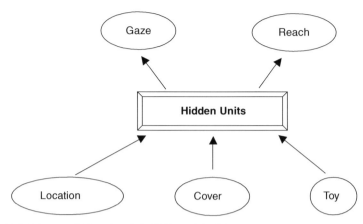

Fig. 10.9 Schema of Munakata's (1998) model of the A-not-B error.

the toys present. Inputs were converged on a hidden layer (an internal representation), within which the units actively compete against each other by virtue of inhibitory connections. The output layer comprises two banks of nodes corresponding to the direction of gaze responses and reaching behaviors. The model was biased with an initial tendency to reach in the direction where the toy had been hidden, such that it would succeed on the first A trial. This bias was justified on the basis that infants also approach the task with this correct bias on A trials. Latent memories (weight changes) were achieved through unsupervised Hebbian learning. The model learned to strengthen its connections that linked input and output (not on the basis of correct performance). Because of the initial bias to respond to the correct location, and the Hebbian learning algorithm, the tendency to respond to A increases across A trials (where both active and latent memory are in agreement). Success on B trials depends on the strength of the active memory (recurrent connections). If the network is young (i.e., the recurrent connections are weak), the latent response to A wins over the active memory for B. If the network is old (i.e., the recurrent connections are strong), the active trace wins, and the network responds correctly.

As well as the standard A–B task, the network also models a number of findings based on variants of the original task, and we will mention some of these here. The model is, similar to infants, generally more accurate at predicting the location of an object on B trials through the gaze response units than through reaching (Ahmed & Ruffman, 1998; Diamond, 1985). This is achieved by allowing the gaze units to update at every time point, in contrast to the reaching system, which was only allowed to update at the end of each trial (i.e., when a reach would be allowed in the context of the task). The model is more accurate on B trials when the object has been hidden under one of two distinctive covers on both A and B trials (Butterworth et al., 1978). In the model, this is a result of the extra input that the models receives when the covers are distinctive. On a distinctive cover variant, the model is presented with input at two cover units rather than one (to simulate the increased salience of two distinctive cover 'features' relative to one). The presence of distinctive covers in the form of additional input on each A trial improves performance on B trials by pulling the associative strength of the input away from the location node A. Lastly, in a simulation of a no-toy variant of the A–B task (where a cover is waved and placed down in front of the infant on each trial; Smith et al., 1999), the network also demonstrates A-not-B errors, as do infants. This is modeled by virtue of the presence of covers being a salient cue to respond.

Munakata (1998) successfully models several findings in the A–B literature, and lays down a strong challenge to a number of alternative interpretations. Her explanation is at odds with Piaget's as it suggests that the dynamics of memories formed within the task are responsible for the error, rather than any immature conception of the way in which hidden objects exist in particular locations (or spatial frameworks). The explanation is also at odds with more current explanations of the error, such as that of Thelen and colleagues (Thelen et al., 2001), who argue that the 'object representations' play no part in the error, and that prior reaching history can be invoked to explain all variants.

However, there are a number of findings that the model has difficulty explaining. One particular problem seems to be that the role of spatially oriented responses has been misconstrued. A number of features are presented to the model on each trial (toys, distinctive covers, etc.), but these are only linked to locations at which they are required to respond through connection weights established within the task setting. Given that we know that even newborn infants can link featural information to direction information (Slater et al., 1991), it seems churlish to propose that they would not use such feature-location bindings in orienting their responses. The only veridical cue to location that Munakata's model is permitted to use is location itself. Indeed, the manipulation of distinctive covers does not reduce errors by virtue of the spatial cues it provides, but by distracting the model from learning about the location at which the object is hidden on A trials. This explanation of the error is at odds with findings that spatial manipulations of the infant's location can increase the effectiveness of distinctive covers (J. G. Bremner, 1978) and that distinctive covers can both increase and decrease performance in different versions of the task, depending on the motivation of the infant to search for a toy (A. J. Bremner & Bryant, 2001).

10.4 **What have computational models contributed to our understanding of developing object knowledge?**

Computational modeling represents a powerful theoretical tool for the formulation of explicit mechanistic accounts of cognitive processing. One aim of this chapter has been to illustrate the strengths and limitations of different approaches used to model object knowledge in infancy. We described a series of symbolic rule-based models developed in the 1980s to model the knowledge available to infants at different ages.

We also have described a number of connectionist models in this chapter that have implemented a range of developing object-directed behaviors. Visual habituation to objects has been modeled using autoencoder models. This class of model has been particularly useful in informing our knowledge of early categorization behaviors. An initially confusing phenomenon (that young infants form asymmetrically exclusive categories of visually presented CATS and DOGS) was explained as being due to the statistical distribution of features on the two classes of objects. French and Mareschal's model made predictions that were tested and upheld, leading to the conclusion that infants' formation of visual categories is largely bottom-up or data-driven, an account which is at odds with putative innate knowledge of natural categories.

We described two models of infants' visual expectations concerning the location of a temporarily hidden object (Mareschal et al., 1999; Munakata et al., 1997). Both demonstrate how aspects of object permanence can be achieved through the strengthening of recurrent connections between representations of information across sequential time steps. Importantly, this demonstration shows that object permanence can emerge through an interaction of experience with a visual environment and a constrained neural architecture, an account which is at odds with both an account of cognitive development resting on active learning in the environment (cf., Piaget, 1952) and those positing innate knowledge of permanence (Spelke et al., 1992).

Connectionist models have also been put forward to explain developmental dissociations in behavioral indices of object permanence. Munakata et al. (1997) model the lag between looking and reaching success by delaying the speed and onset of learning of a reaching system. Mareschal et al. (1999) demonstrate how the dissociation might arise as a result of particular patterns of associative learning in the network. The constraint used to achieve this is by building in two streams of learning. This particular architectural constraint is inspired by work demonstrating separate streams of processing visual information about spatial location and featural identity (e.g., Milner & Goodale, 1995), demonstrating neatly how knowledge of biological constraints can be incorporated into mechanistic models of the development of information processing.

Two further connectionist models that we described incorporate some further biological constraints. Munakata (1998) provides an explicit mechanism for explaining the occurrence of the A-not-B error in infants who have just learned to manually retrieve objects. This model appeals to development of the effectiveness of active (short-term) memory, by introducing a parameter manipulation simulating the maturation of the prefrontal cortex in early infancy. Mareschal and Bremner (2006) describe how neural oscillations can be invoked to explain the emergence of successful tracking of multiple objects across occlusion, while maintaining appropriate feature-location bindings.

There are several key lessons that can be drawn from the material presented throughout this chapter. First, all models, be they connectionist or symbolic, aim to implement some preexisting theory of how object knowledge is represented and acquired. Building a model forces the researcher to be explicit about what they mean by things such as the representational format of knowledge and the possible mechanisms for learning. Such notions are often central to verbal theories of object knowledge, but their exact specification usually is not. Perhaps there is a feeling that such details do not need specifying in high-level theories, but in truth the devil is always in the detail. Indeed, many ideas that seem simple in principle turn out to be difficult or impossible to implement in practice.

Symbolic, connectionist, and hybrid models all have the same aim of clarifying these concepts. A second lesson to draw from this review is that the symbolic and connectionist approaches differ in what they emphasize and hence in what they are best able to capture or explain. Symbolic models emphasize the nature of the knowledge representation. Object knowledge is likened to rules that can be explicitly described and stated, or well-defined symbols that can be compositionally combined with other conceptual symbols, thereby enabling the combinatorial expansion of knowledge. However, these models do not fare well when explaining learning and development. They do not propose any adaptive mechanisms that could successfully capture the way infants' and children's object knowledge changes with age and experience.[1]

---

[1] More recently, Simon (1998) has developed a model of infants' early numerical competence as demonstrated in object permanence tasks that involved occluded objects (Wynn, 1992; Simon et al., 1995). The model is implemented using the ACT-R architecture (Anderson, 1993). It is symbolic in the sense that it has nodes that explicitly represent the existence of an object and its properties. However, it is graded in that nodes had varying levels of activation (reflecting the infants' varying levels of memory for object information). This model was designed to explore the extent to which early numerical competence reflected visual attentional limitations (see Trick & Pylyshyn, 1994) rather than explicit numerical representation.

In contrast, the connectionist models emphasize change and development. An ability to learn from and adapt to environmental experiences is intrinsic to the very nature of these models. This goes hand in hand with the gradual development of graded internal representations of object knowledge that allow connectionist models to acquire object behaviors similar to those observed in the developing infant. The down side of these models is that the representations are not directly available to the modeler, often taking the form of distributed patterns of activity across banks of network units. This requires the modelers to manipulate the representations (such as taking the difference between the states of units under two viewing conditions; see Munakata et al., 1997) in order to try to isolate the component of the representation that might map onto the discrete object knowledge that the researcher is interested in.

Alhough such distributed and context-sensitive representations may be more difficult for the modeler (researcher) to grasp, the fact that these models continue to make predictions of novel infant behaviors that are true of real infants (e.g., Cepeda & Munakata, 2007; Mareschal & Johnson, 2003; Shinskey & Munakata, 2001; Sinskey & Munakata, 2003) suggests that this representational format may in fact be a more accurate depiction of actual object knowledge in infants than discrete compositional symbol-based knowledge formats. Indeed, context dependence and graded representations seem to be a general principle across a broad range of developmental domains (Mareschal et al., 2007). Moreover, such models also provide a conceptual bridge between the cognitive level at which meaningful questions about object knowledge can be formulated and the world of neuroscience in which any such knowledge must ultimately be implemented.

The final lesson to take home from this chapter is one of caution. The last 20 years has seen impressive demonstrations of apparently sophisticated object knowledge in ever-younger infants. This has led some researchers to argue that some core elements of object knowledge are innate (e.g., Spelke, 1994). However, connectionist models demonstrate that even very simple systems can develop representations with relatively little experience that support the kinds of knowledge-based behaviors observed in these young infants. The cautionary note is, therefore, that early competence does not have to imply representational innateness. Just because a 4-month-old can respond to violations of the location of a hidden object it does not mean that they have not acquired the representations necessary to support this behavior over the duration of their very short lives.

Putting aside for the moment the debate of what 'innateness' might mean (see Elman et al., 1997, for a full discussion), what these models demonstrate is the possibility of such development. They do not demonstrate that this is necessarily the case. Indeed, given the constancy of core object properties over the history of the physical world, there is a strong case for arguing that the essential elements of object knowledge (such as continuity, inertia, etc.) might somehow be encoded as part of our phylogenetic heritage. But it is important to note that, even if this is the case, it remains to be shown how information coded in the genome leads to the knowledge representations that are being attributed to the newborn infants (see Marcus, 2004, for an attempt to solve this problem).

The bottom line is that models provide a formal language in which to specify theories. They are not in and of themselves proof or disproof of any empirical questions. Instead, they provide a common language with which researchers can debate their theories of representational content and learning. We believe that many of the debates described in the various chapters within this volume stem in part from miscommunications between the different researchers. It is our view that if each research group attempted to implement their ideas in functioning computer models, it would become much easier to compare the different accounts, identify those self-consistent or precise enough to support predictions, and empirically test the remaining theories.

Acknowledgements

The writing of this work was supported in part by Economic and Social Research Council (UK) grant RES-062-23-0819 and European Commission grant 029088-NEST (ANALOGY). The authors would like to thank the editors of this volume and Amy Proferes for helpful comments on an earlier draft of this chapter.

References

Ahmed, A., & Ruffman, T. (1998). Why do infants make A not B errors in a search task, yet show memory for the location of hidden objects in a non-search task? *Developmental Psychology*, 34, 441–453.

Anderson, J. R. (1993). *Rules of the Mind*. Hillsdale, NJ: Lawrence Erlbaum Associates.

Baillargeon, R. (1987). Object permanence in 3.5- and 4.5-month-old infants. *Developmental Psychology*, 23, 655–664.

Baillargeon, R. (1993). The object concept revisited: new directions in the investigation of infants' physical knowledge. In C. E. Granrud (Ed.), *Visual Perception and Cognition in Infancy* (pp. 265–315). London: Lawrence Erlbaum Associates.

Baillargeon, R. (2004). Infants' reasoning about hidden objects: evidence for event-general and event-specific expectations. *Developmental Science*, 7, 391–414.

Baillargeon, R., Graber, M., DeVos, J., & Black, J. (1990). Why do young infants fail to search for hidden objects? *Cognition*, 36, 255–284.

Baillargeon, R., Spelke, E. S., & Wasserman, S. (1985). Object permanence in 5-month-old infants. *Cognition, 20*, 191–208.

Boden, M. A. (1980). Artificial intelligence and Piagetian theory. In M. Boden (Ed.), *Minds and Mechanisms: Philosophical Psychology and Computational Models* (pp. 236–261). Ithaca, NY: Cornell University Press.

Boden, M. A. (1989). *Computer Models of Mind*. Cambridge: Cambridge University Press.

Bornstein, M. H. (1985). Habituation of attention as a measure of visual information processing in human infants: summary, systematization, and synthesis. In G. Gottlieb, & N.A. Krasnegor (Eds.), *Measurement of Audition and Vision in the First Year of Postnatal Life: A Methodological Overview,* (pp. 253–300). Norwood, NJ: Ablex.

Bower, T. G. R. (1982). *Development in Infancy*, 2nd edn. San Francisco, CA: Freeman.

Bremner, A. J., & Bryant, P. E. (2001). The effect of spatial cues on infants' responses in the AB task, with and without a hidden object. *Developmental Science, 4*, 408–415.

Bremner, A. J., & Mareschal, D. (2004). Reasoning ... what reasoning? *Developmental Science, 7*, 419–421.

Bremner, J. G. (1978). Spatial errors made by infants: Inadequate spatial cues or evidence of egocentrism? *British Journal of Psychology, 69*, 77–84.

Bremner, J. G. (1994). Infancy, 2nd edn. Oxford: Blackwell.

Bremner, J. G. (2000). Developmental relationships between perception and action in infancy. *Infant Behavior and Development, 23*, 567–582.

Butterworth, G., Jarrett, N., & Hicks, L. (1982). Spatiotemporal identity in infancy: Perceptual competence or conceptual deficit? *Developmental Psychology, 18*, 435–449.

Cepeda, N. J., & Munakata, Y. (2007). Why do children perseverate when they seem to know better: Graded working memory, or directed inhibition? *Psychonomic Bulletin and Review, 14*, 1058–1065.

Changeux, J. P., & Dehaene, S. (1989). Neuronal models of cognitive function. *Cognition, 33*, 63–109.

Charlesworth, W. R. (1969). The role of surprise in cognitive development. In D. Elkind, & J. Flavell (Eds.), *Studies in Cognitive Development: Essays in Honor of Jean Piaget* (pp. 257–314). Oxford: Oxford University Press.

Cleeremans, A., & McClelland, J. L. (1991). Learning the structure of event sequences. *Journal of Experimental Psychology: General, 120*, 235–253.

Cohen, L. B. (1973). A two-process model of infant visual attention. *Merrill-Palmer Quarterly, 19*, 157–180.

Diamond, A. (1985). The development of the ability to use recall to guide action, as indicated by infants' performance on A-not-B. *Child Development, 55*, 868–883.

Diamond, A. (1991). Neuropsychological insights into the meaning of object concept development. In S. Carey, & G. Gelman (Eds.), *The Epigenesis of Mind: Essays on Biology and Cognition* (pp. 67–110). Hillsdale, NJ: LEA.

Drescher, G. L. (1991). *Made-up Minds: A Constructivist Approach to Artificial Intelligence*. Cambridge, MA: MIT Press.

Elman, J. L. (1990). Finding structure in time. *Cognitive Science, 14*, 179–211.

Elman, J. L., Bates, E. A., Karmiloff-Smith, A., Johnson, M. H., Parisi, D., & Plunkett, K. (1996). *Rethinking Innateness: Connectionism in a Developmental Framework*. Cambridge, MA: MIT Press.

Fantz, R. L. (1964). Visual experience in infants: decreased attention familiar patterns relative to novel ones. *Science, 146*, 668–670.

Fodor, J. (1980). Fixation of belief and concept acquisition. In M. Piatellim-Palmarini (Ed.), *Language and Learning : The Debate between Chomsky and Piaget* (pp. 142–162). Cambridge, MA; Harvard University Press.

Foldiak, P. (1991). Learning invariance from transformation sequences. *Neural Computation, 3*, 194–200.

French, R. M., Mareschal, D., Mermillod, M., & Quinn, P. C. (2004). The role of bottom-up processing in perceptual categorization by 3- to 4-month-old infants: simulations and data. *Journal of Experimental Psychology: General 133*, 382–397.

Goodale, M. A. (1993). Visual pathways supporting perception and action in the primate cerebral cortex. *Current Opinion in Neurobiology, 3*, 578–585.

Kaufman, J., Csibra, G., & Johnson, M. H. (2003). Representing occluded objects in the human infant brain. *Proceedings of the Royal Society of London, Part B (Suppl): Biology Letters, 270/S2*, 140–143.

Kaufman, J., Csibra, G., & Johnson, M. H. (2005). Oscillatory activity in the infant brain reflects object maintenance. *Proceedings of the National Academy of Sciences, 102*,15271–15274.

Keen, R. (2003). Representation of objects and events: Why do infants look so smart and toddlers look so dumb? *Current Directions in Psychological Science, 12*, 79–83.

Klahr, D., & Wallace, J. G. (1976). *Cognitive Development: An Information Processing View.* Hillsdale, NJ: Lawrence Erlbaum.

Luger, G. F., Bower, T. G. R., & Wishart, J. G. (1983). A model of the development of the early object concept. *Perception, 12*, 21–34.

Luger, G. F., Wishart, J. G., & Bower, T. G. R. (1984). Modelling the stages of the identity theory of object concept development in infancy. *Perception, 13*, 97–115.

Marcus, G. F. (2001). *The Algebraic Mind: Integrating Connectionism and Cognitive Science.* Cambridge, MA: MIT Press.

Marcus, G. F. (2004). *The Birth of The Mind: How a Tiny Number of Genes Creates the Complexities of Human Thought.* New York: Basic Books.

Mareschal, D., & Bremner, A. J. (2006). When do 4-month-olds remember the 'what' and 'where' of hidden objects? In M.H. Johnson, & Y. Munakata (Eds.), *Attention and Performance XXI: Processes of Change in Brain and Cognitive Development.* (pp. 427–447). Oxford: Oxford University Press.

Mareschal, D., & French, R. M. (2000). Mechanisms of categorisation in infancy. *Infancy, 1*, 59–76.

Mareschal, D., French, R. M., & Quinn, P. (2000). A connectionist account of asymmetric category learning in infancy. *Developmental Psychology, 36*, 635–645.

Mareschal, D., & Johnson, M. H. (2003). The 'what' and 'where' of infant object representations. *Cognition, 88*, 259–276.

Mareschal, D., Johnson, M. H., Sirois, S., Spratling, M., Thomas, M., & Westermann, G. (2007). *Neuroconstructivism, Vol. I: How the Brain Constructs Cognition.* Oxford: Oxford University Press.

Mareschal, D., Plunkett, K., & Harris, P. (1999). A computational and neuropsychological account of object-oriented behaviours in infancy. *Developmental Science, 2*, 306–317.

Mareschal, D., & Shultz, T.R. (1996). Generative connectionist networks and constructivist cognitive development. *Cognitive Development, 11*, 571–603.

Mareschal, D., & Thomas, M. S. C. (2007). Computational modeling in developmental psychology. *IEEE Transactions on Evolutionary Computation (Special Issue on Autonomous Mental Development) 11*, 137–150.

Markovitch, S., & Zelazo, P. D. (1999). The A-not-B error: results from a logistic meta-analysis. *Child Development, 70*, 1297–1313.

McClelland, J. L. (1989). Parallel distributed processing: implications for cognition and development. In Morris, R. G. M. (Ed.), *Parallel Distributed Processing: Implications for Psychology and Neurobiology* (pp. 8–45). Oxford: Oxford University Press.

McLeod, P., Plunkett, K., & Rolls, E .T. (1998). *Introduction to Connectionist Modeling of Cognitive Processes*. Oxford: Oxford University Press.

Milner, A. D., & Goodale, M. A. (1995). *The Visual Brain in Action*. Oxford University Press.

Munakata, Y. (1998). Infant perseveration and implications for object permanence theories: a PDP Model of the A-not-B task. *Developmental Science, 1*, 161–184.

Munakata, Y., McClelland, J. L., Johnson, M. J., & Siegler, R. S. (1997). Rethinking infant knowledge: toward an adaptive process account of successes and failures in object permanence tasks. *Psychological Review, 104*, 686–713.

Munakata, Y., & Stedron, J. M. (2002). Memory for hidden objects in early infancy: behavior, theory, and neural network simulation. In J. W. Fagan, & H. Hayne (Eds.), *Progress in Infancy Research, Vol. 2. Mahwah*, NJ: Lawrence Erlbaum.

O'Reilly, R. J., & Munakata, Y. (2000). *Computational Explorations in Cognitive Neuroscience: Understanding the Mind by Simulating the Brain*. Cambridge, MA: MIT Press.

Papert, S. (1963). Intelligence in the child and in the robot. (Note: La filiation the structure translates as 'Structural Lineage' and is the title of the MONOGRAPH which is part of the Etudes d'Epistemologie Genetique series). *Etudes D'Epistemologie Génétiques, 15*, 131–194.

Piaget, J. (1952). *The Origins of Intelligence in the Child*. New York: International Universities Press.

Piaget, J. (1954). *The Construction of Reality in the Child*. New York: Basic Books.

Plunkett, K., & Sinha, C. (1992). Connectionism and developmental theory. *British Journal of Developmental Psychology, 10*, 209–254.

Prazdny, S. (1980). A computational study of a period of infant object-concept development. *Perception, 9*, 125–150.

Quinn, P. C., & Eimas, P. D. (1996). Perceptual organization and categorization in young infants. *Advances in Infancy Research, 10*, 1–36.

Quinn, P. C., Eimas, P. D., & Rosenkrantz, S. L. (1993). Evidence for representations of perceptually similar natural categories by 3-month-old and 4-month-old infants. *Perception, 22*, 463–475.

Rao, S. C., Rainer, G., & Miller, E. (1997). Integration of 'what' and 'where' in the primate prefrontal cortex. *Science, 276*, 821–824.

Rumelhart, D. E., Hinton, G., & Williams, R. (1986) Learning representations by back-propagating errors. *Science, 323*, 533–536.

Rumelhart, D. E., & McClelland, J. L. (1986). *Parallel Distributed Processing: Exploration in the Microstructure of Cognition. (Vol. 1: Foundations)*. Cambridge, MA: MIT Press.

Schafer, G., & Mareschal, D. (2001). Modeling infant speech sound discrimination using simple associative networks. *Infancy*, *2*, 7–28.

Schlesinger, M. (2006). Decomposing infants' object representations: a dual-route processing account. *Connection Science*, *18*, 207–216.

Shanks, D. R., & St. John, M. F. (1994). Characteristics of dissociable human learning systems. *Behavioral and Brain Sciences*, *17*, 367–447.

Shinskey, J. L., & Munakata, Y. (2001). Detecting transparent barriers: clear evidence against the means-end deficit account of search failures. *Infancy*, *2*, 395–404.

Shinskey, J. L., & Munakata, Y. (2003). Are infants in the dark about hidden objects? *Developmental Science*, *6*, 273–282.

Shultz, T. R. (2003). *Computational Developmental Psychology*. Cambridge, MA: MIT Press.

Shultz, T. R., Schmidt, W. C., Buckingham, D., & Mareschal, D. (1995). Modeling cognitive development with a generative connectionist algorithm. In T. Simon, & G. Halford (Eds.), *Developing Cognitive Competence: New Approaches to Process Modeling*, (pp. 347–362). Hillsdale, NJ: Erlbaum.

Simon, H. A. (1962). An information processing theory of intellectual development. *Monograph of the Society for Research in Child Development*, *27*(2, Serial No. 82).

Simon, T. R. (1998). Computational evidence for the foundations of numerical competence. *Developmental Science*, *1*, 71–78.

Simon, T. J., Hespos, S. J., & Rochat, P. (1995). Do infants understand simple arithmetic? A replication of Wynn. *Cognitive Development*, *10*, 253–269.

Sirois, S. (2004). Autoassociator networks and in insights into infancy. *Developmental Science*, *7*, 133–140.

Slater, A. M. (1995). Visual perception and memory at birth. In C. Rovee-Collier, & L. P. Lipsitt (Eds.), *Advances in Infancy Research, Vol. 9*. Ablex, NJ: Norwood.

Slater, A. M., Mattock, A., Brown, E., Burnham, D., & Young, A. W. (1991). Visual processing of stimulus compounds in newborn infants. *Perception*, *20*, 29–33.

Smith, L. B., Thelen, E., Titzer, R., & McLin, D. (1999). Knowing in the context of acting: the task dynamics of the A-not-B error. *Psychological Review*, *106*, 235–260.

Solokov, E. N. (1963). *Perception and the Conditioned Reflex*. Hillsdale, NJ: Laurence Erlbaum.

Spelke, E. S. (1994). Early knowledge: six suggestions, *Cognition*, *50*, 431–445.

Spelke, E. S., Breinlinger, K., Macomber, J., & Jacobsen, K. (1992). Origins of knowledge. *Psychological Review*, *99*, 605–632.

Tallon-Baudry, C. (2003). Oscillatory synchrony and human visual cognition. *Journal of Physiology*, *97*, 355–363.

Thelen, E., Schöner, G., Scheier, C., & Smith, L. B. (2001). The dynamics of embodiment: a field theory of infant perseverative reaching. *Behavioural and Brain Sciences*, *24*, 1–34.

Trick, M., & Pylyshyn, Z. M. (1994). A limited capacity preattentic stage in vision. *Psychological Review*, *101*, 80–102.

Ungerleider, L. G., & Mishkin, M. (1982). *Two cortical visual systems*. In *Analysis of Visual Behavior* (pp. 549–586). Cambridge, MA: MIT Press.

Van Essen, D. C., Anderson, C. H., & Felleman, D. J. (1992). Information processing in the primate visual system: an integrated systems perspective. *Science*, *255*, 419–423.

Ward, L. M. (2003). Synchronous neural oscillations and cognitive processes. *Trends in Cognitive Sciences, 7,* 553–559.

Willatts, P. (1999). Development of means-end behaviour in young infants: pulling a support to retrieve a distant object. *Developmental Psychology, 35,* 651–667.

Wynn, K. (1992). Addition and subtraction in human infants. *Nature, 358,* 749–750.

Young, R. (1976). *Seriation by Children: An Artificial Intelligence Analysis of a Piagetian Task.* Basel, Switzerland: Birkhauser.

Younger, B. A. (1985). The segregation of items into categories by ten-month-old infants. *Child Development, 56,* 1574–1583.

Chapter 11

Induction, overhypotheses, and the shape bias: Some arguments and evidence for rational constructivism

Fei Xu, Kathryn Dewar, & Amy Perfors

11.1 Introduction

A tremendous amount of work has been conducted on infants' representations of physical objects during the last 25 years (see Baillargeon, 2004; Spelke, 1994, for reviews). One particular perceptual dimension, object shape, has received a great deal of attention in both the literature on object representations and generalization (e.g., Baldwin et al., 1993; Rosch et al., 1976; Shutts et al., Chapter 8; Waxman, 1999; Welder & Graham, 2001) and the literature on early word learning, since the initial vocabulary of most infants contains a large number of count nouns that refer to object categories (e.g., Nelson, 1973). This chapter focuses on a case study of how object representations in infants interact with early word learning, in particular the nature of the so-called "shape bias." We will begin with a short review of the controversies in this subfield, and use it to illustrate the two dominant views of cognitive development, which can be roughly classified as nativist or empiricist. We will then present both theoretical arguments and new empirical evidence for a rational constructivist view of cognitive development (see also Xu, 2007a). Our goal is to argue for a new approach to the study of cognitive development, one that is strongly committed to both innate concepts and representations, as well as powerful inductive learning mechanisms. In addition to discussing the shape bias and how it relates to object representations, we will also briefly discuss the generality of the approach.

11.2 Case study: The shape bias in word learning

The debate began with a seminal paper by Landau et al. (1988). They provided the first evidence that 3-year-old children, when taught a new count noun for an object, generalized the word to other objects that shared the same over-all shape as the original object, and ignored variations on other perceptual attributes of the objects such as color, texture, or size. Landau et al. (1988) argued that shape is, perhaps, the most important and salient perceptual dimension that underlies children's rapid learning of count nouns that map onto object categories. Furthermore, these researchers suggested that children could learn that words refer to distinct shapes, based on the correlational information in the input between shape and word usage.

A few years later, Soja et al. (1991) reported a series of experiments providing evidence that the ontological distinction between objects and substances, or individuated versus nonindividuated entities, is of great importance in early word meaning. They showed that 2-year-old children, who have not mastered the count and/or mass syntax of English, generalized novel words for objects based on shape similarity whereas they generalized novel words for substances based on material kind. These researchers argued that early words refer to kinds, not just distinct shapes. Although Soja et al. were not explicit about what they thought the status of the shape bias was, one reading of their work is that children assume that words for objects refer to kinds, and that shape is a particularly salient cue (perhaps even innately given) for kind membership.

Numerous follow-up studies have been conducted in the last two decades, and the debate continues at present—the journal *Developmental Science* devoted a special section on the topic recently (see Markson et al., 2008; Samuelson & Bloom, 2008). Both sides of the debate have conducted ingenious experiments to provide empirical evidence for their point of view. However, neither is convinced by the arguments marshaled by the other side.

Three controversies persist in this debate and they remain unresolved. First, is the shape bias innate or learned? Second, do early words (count nouns) refer to distinct shapes or distinct kinds? Third, what is the mechanism for acquiring the shape bias if it is learned?

Nativists and empiricists give different answers to the first question about innateness. If the shape bias is construed as a solution to the induction problem of word meaning (a la Quine, 1960; Soja et al., 1991), a natural conclusion is that it may have to be innate. That is, if the point of positing the shape bias were to eliminate other hypotheses (e.g., count nouns refer to objects with a shared color; count nouns refer to objects with a shared texture; etc.), then it would be a bit odd to say that the bias itself is learned (although see more discussion in later sections of this chapter). Thus, one version of the shape bias, perhaps the strongest version, is to posit that young children have a bias to pay attention to object shape and to generalize count nouns based on shape similarity. Alternatively, the shape bias may be the product of some learning process. One candidate under consideration is that the shape bias is the result of associating object properties with word usage (e.g., Colunga & Smith, 2005; Samuelson, 2005; Smith et al., 2002).

A careful reading of the literature suggests that nativists, who are particularly concerned with positing biases to solve Quine's induction problem, have mostly claimed that young children assume that 'count nouns refer to object kinds' and have not discussed in great detail the status of the shape bias itself (e.g., Markman, 1989; Soja et al., 1991). However, the notion of kinds is quite abstract and it is not clear how a child is supposed to discover it: What are the perceptual dimensions that signal that objects belong to the same kind? We see two solutions: one is to say that some perceptual dimensions are privileged from the beginning, for instance, shape; the other is to say that the shape bias is learned from the input. Nativists seem to be more sympathetic to the latter view (e.g., Macnamara, 1982; Markson et al., 2008; Soja et al., 1991), *yet* there is no learning mechanism proposed in any of their papers!

Nativists and empiricists also give different answers to the second question: Do early words refer to kinds or distinct shapes? The nativist view suggests that children assume that early words refer to distinct kinds and shape as a cue to kind membership (e.g., Diesendruck & Bloom, 2003; Markson et al., 2008; Soja et al., 1991). This view grants the child some notion of kind that is more abstract than just clusters of perceptual properties such as shape, texture, and color. The reason why the shape bias is important is that shape turns out to be a reliable cue for identifying the kinds in a child's environment. In contrast, the empiricist view suggests that compared to other perceptual dimensions of objects such as texture or color, shape correlates better with word usage. Because the child is trying to figure out how to generalize words, he or she notices this correlation between shape and word usage, and concludes that words (count nouns) refer to objects that share a common shape. Most empiricists would get rid of the notion of kind entirely; for them, the notion of a kind may be reduced to clusters of perceptual properties of objects (e.g., Colunga & Smith, 2005).

Lastly, nativisits and empiricists (unsurprisingly) give different answers to the question of learning. If the shape bias is innate and it provides a solution to the problem of induction in word learning, then no learning mechanism is needed. Curiously, most nativists do not claim that the shape bias is innate (see the following for some possible reasons for this). However, this leaves the nativists in an uncomfortable position of not having a learning story at all. In contrast, the empiricists have provided detailed studies and models of how associative mechanisms may be responsible for the emergence of the shape bias in early word leaning (e.g., Colunga & Smith, 2005; Smith et al., 2002).

Here we take issue with both sides. We will argue that neither view is descriptively or explanatorily adequate. We begin with pointing out a few problems with each of the two standard views.

From the nativist prespective, one thorny problem is that as soon as one looks carefully at the early lexicon, one discovers that the count nouns that refer to object categories vary in terms of the salient perceptual dimension along which they are generalized. For example, for the garden-variety artifact objects, shape is a good indicator for kind membership. However, for animal kinds (which are abundant in the early lexicon), shape is not quite as important and both texture and shape matter for generalization. For food kinds (which are also abundant in the early lexicon), color is perhaps the most important perceptual dimension and shape is not particularly important or salient (e.g., Jones & Smith, 2002). This may be one reason why most nativists do not make the strong claim that the shape bias is innate. However, this leaves the nativists with two problems: one is that we no longer have a solution for the problem of induction in word learning; the other is that nativists offer no mechanisms for how the shape bias is learned. This view now looks neither descriptively nor explanatorily adequate.

The empiricists run into problems as well. Several studies have shown that 2-year-old children take shape to be a heuristic in learning words, but only under some circumstances. Gelman and Ebeling (1998) showed that if a shape is created accidentally, children do not use it as the basis for their word generalization. It is only when a shape is created intentionally that it becomes the basis for word generalization. Similarly, Bloom and Markson (1998) and Diesendruck and Bloom (2003) showed that shape is a proxy for kind and the shape bias is not specific to word learning. In addition, the elegant and impressive training study conducted by Smith et al. (2002) seems to provide evidence *against* a pure associative learning view of the shape bias. In this study, 17-month-old infants were brought into the laboratory once each week for a total of 8 weeks and given a set of training objects with perfect shape regularity while being taught a small number of count nouns. The results showed that the training facilitated the emergence of the shape bias for the novel words they had been exposed to; moreover, the children who were in the experimental condition, and not the ones in the control condition, showed a faster rate of vocabulary acquisition outside of the laboratory! On the one hand, this is a beautiful demonstration that a bias may be trained with a relatively small amount of data; on the other hand, the rapid learning demonstrated by the children calls into question whether associative learning mechanisms, which are often slow and laborious, provide an adequate account for these empirical findings.[1]

Smith et al. (2002) hypothesized that learning the shape bias amounts to making generalizations on two levels. On one level, the child learns that 'cups are cup-shaped, cats are cat-shaped, balls are ball-shaped', and so on. These are the first-order generalizations. On a higher level, the child posits a variable and forms a second-level generalization such as 'Xs are X-shaped'. This is a generalization over all count nouns in the lexicon, not just any particular count noun. By making the second-level generalization, the child is now in a position to apply the shape bias to all new count nouns that he or she might learn in the future. The second-level generalization provides a powerful tool for future learning. The ability to extract a variable, however, is not easily implemented in standard neural network models (see Marcus, 2001, for a critique). Submitting that young learners are capable of extracting variables of this kind is, itself, a concession from the more hardcore empiricist view of learning. Again, this view now looks neither descriptively nor explanatorily adequate.

For the rest of this chapter, we will attempt to characterize a new view—the rational constructivist view—of development (see also Xu, 2007a). This view differs from both of the standard views, and it provides a resolution to the longstanding debate on the nature of the shape bias. In the course of articulating this view, we borrow from two sources: one is the theory of induction explicated by Nelson Goodman (1955), and the other is the machinery of Bayesian inference. We will also report new empirical results that provide support for this view of development.

Most of the studies we see in the literature on the nature of the shape bias have been conducted with 2-, 3-, and 4-year-old children. Recently though, there have been a few studies investigating the importance of shape in property induction, and object categorization and individuation in infants (e.g., Graham et al., 2004; Waxman, 1999; Welder & Graham, 2001; Xu et al., 2004). These studies provide evidence for the privileged role of shape, but mostly they have not focused on word learning per se. We have recently completed several studies to address the three controversies in the shape bias debate systematically in 9- to 12-month-old infants (Dewar & Xu, 2007, 2008, in press; Perfors et al., 2007). These studies investigate the onset of the shape bias, the issue of innateness, and the issue of the learning mechanism.

---

[1] The reader may think that these training studies provide the best evidence for a learned shape bias. However, a possible alternative hypothesis for the effects of training is that perhaps children were more ready for being trained on the dimension of shape, so the laboratory exposure was particularly effective. That is, the training may have served the role of 'triggering' a small but preexisting bias and simply accelerated the rate of development.

11.3 When do we first see some sensitivity to shape in a word learning context?

Analyses of spontaneous language production by young children suggest that the shape bias may emerge as early as 17–24 months (Samuelson & Smith, 2005). What about infants who are at the beginning of word learning: that is, the beginning of comprehending words for object categories? We developed a new method to investigate this question with 9-month-old infants (Dewar & Xu, 2007). In these looking-time experiments, infants watched some events unfold on a puppet stage. We first familiarized the infant with some object pairs. A box was presented on the stage, with the experimenter sitting behind it. After drawing the infant's attention to the box, 'Look, [baby's name]!' the experimenter opened the front panel of the box and revealed a pair of objects sitting side by side inside the box. The object pair consisted of either two identical objects (e.g., two identical toy fish) or two different objects (e.g., a toy frog and a toy dog). The two different objects differed in shape and color (e.g., a toy frog-like animal and a toy dog-like animal). On alternate familiarization trials, the infant saw either an identical pair or a different pair. A total of eight familiarization trials were shown to each infant; the second set of four was a repetition of the first set of four. Thus, we have given each infant some idea as to what to expect inside the box: a pair of identical objects or a pair of different objects.

After the familiarization trials, the test trials began. On each test trial, the same box was presented on the stage, with its front panel closed. The experimenter looked into a top opening of the box and labeled the objects inside. On a two-word trial, she said in infant-directed speech, 'I see a zav! I see a fep!' thrice; on a one-word trial, she said, 'I see a wug! I see a wug!' thrice (Fig. 11.1). The question was whether the infant expected the contents of the box to be predicted by the labeling information. For an adult, hearing two distinct labels will lead to the expectation that the box contains two different objects whereas hearing one label repeated will lead to the expectation that the box contains two identical objects. What about 9-month-old infants? After the labeling information was presented, the experimenter opened the front panel of the box to reveal either two identical objects or two different objects. The experimenter lowered her head and gaze, and the infant's looking times were recorded. If the infant had the same expectations as an adult, she should look longer at the identical objects upon hearing two labels because that was the unexpected outcome. Conversely, the infant should look longer at the different objects upon hearing one label repeated because that was the unexpected outcome. The results were consistent with these predictions—infants' looking times were predicted by the linguistic information provided.

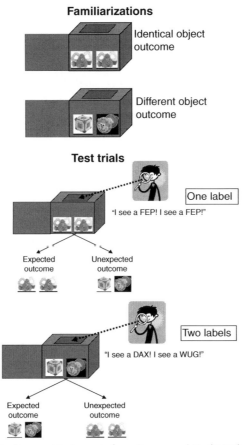

Fig. 11.1 Familiarization and test events from Dewar and Xu (2007).

So far we have only shown that 9-month-old infants expect distinct labels to refer to different-looking objects. In the next two experiments, we used the same methodology but used objects that differed only in shape or only in color. The rationale was that if shape was privileged early on, we might find that infants expect distinct labels to refer to different-shaped objects but not different-colored objects.

In the second experiment, infants were familiarized with pairs of objects that were either identical or differed only in shape. On the test trials, either two distinct labels or one repeated label were provided. The box was then opened to reveal its contents and looking times were recorded. We found that infants looked longer at the identical object pair upon hearing two distinct labels whereas they looked longer at the different-shaped object pair upon hearing one label repeated.

In the third experiment, infants were familiarized with pairs of objects that were either identical or differed only in color. Again, either two distinct labels or one repeated label were provided on the test trials. We found that infants' looking times were not predicted by the number of labels; they looked longer at the different-colored object pair on all trials.

Taken together, the results of these three experiments suggest that at as young as 9 months of age, infants expect distinct labels to refer to different-shaped, but not different-colored, objects. The sensitivity to the perceptual dimension of shape appears to emerge at the very beginning of word learning (Dewar & Xu, 2007).[2]

Is the sensitivity to shape innately given or learned? The studies we have described so far do not address this question. With older children, both corpus analyses and word-learning experiments suggest that names for different domains of objects—animals, artifacts, food objects—have different perceptual correlates. Shape is a very salient and reliable cue for artifact categories whereas both shape and texture matter for animal categories. For food objects, color and texture are more reliable cues for category membership than shape (e.g., Jones & Smith, 2002). What about for infants? It is conceivable that infants start off considering shape as the most important perceptual dimension for word meaning, and later on they start to use different perceptual dimensions for different domains given the input.

To investigate the origin of the shape bias, we conducted another series of experiments with food objects. The general methodology was the same as Dewar and Xu (2007), but we used objects that looked like food objects. The objects were made out of Fema (a material similar to play dough that, once baked, becomes solid) and they were made to look like a slice of watermelon or a bunch of grapes, and so on. Before the experiment started, the experimenter picked up each of the food object and pretended to eat it. The rest of the experiment used the same procedure as Dewar and Xu (2007). In each of two experiments, the object pairs differed only in shape or only in color. With 9-month-old infants, we found no sensitivity to shape: their looking times were not predicted by the labeling information. With 9-month-old girls, but not boys, we found some sensitivity to color: the girls' looking times were predicted by the labeling information when they were presented with different-colored food objects (Dewar & Xu, 2008). Preliminary results from

---

[2] The reader may think that these experiments contradict the results of the Smith et al. (2002) training studies. However, in Dewar and Xu (2007), no specific mapping between a word and an object was required. All the infants had to do was the use the number of labels to predict which two objects should be revealed inside the box. Thus, the information-processing demand was lower in these experiments, and that might account for the early sensitivity to shape we have found.

12-month-old infants suggest color sensitivity for the whole age group when given labeling information. We are currently investigating if shape also emerges as a reliable cue for category membership with food objects by 12 months.

The results of this second series of experiments show that shape is not a privileged perceptual dimension for all object categories. As early as we can test, infants show differential sensitivity to shape or color depending on the domain of objects under consideration. It was remarkable and surprising to find sensitivity to color as early as 9 months, albeit only in girls. These two sets of studies strongly indicate a *learned* shape bias that is driven by environmental input.

11.4 **Do early words refer to kinds or shapes?**

Have we settled the disagreements between the nativists and the empiricists vis a vis the origin and the nature of the shape bias? Not yet. The empirical results we just described indicate a *learned* bias, but we still do not know if early words and/or count nouns refer to distinct shapes or distinct kinds. On the latter view, shape is a reliable cue to kind membership and infants observe this regularity from the input quite early on.

Several studies with 2- to 4-year-old children show that shape is a proxy for kind membership. For example, Gelman & Ebeling (1998) showed 2- and 3-year-old children line drawings roughly shaped like various namable objects. For half the participants, each line drawing was described as depicting a shape that was created intentionally (e.g., someone painted a picture). For the remaining participants, each drawing was described as depicting a shape that was created accidentally (e.g., someone spilled some paint). Participants were asked to name each picture. The findings suggest that children used shape as the basis of naming primarily when the shapes were intentional. Although shape does play an important role in children's early naming, other factors are also important, including the mental state of the picture's creator.

Similarly, Bloom and Markson (1998) found that when a picture was ambiguous (e.g., resembling both a balloon and a lollipop), 3- and 4-year-olds named the picture based on the creative intent of the artist. These results demonstrate that the sameness of shape is not sufficient in determining children's naming preferences: something can be shaped like a lollipop, but not called 'a lollipop'. These studies suggest that for young children, labels for objects (and pictorial representations of those objects) are not wholly determined by shape similarity; shape may be a proxy for kind membership (see also Cimpian & Markman, 2005). A recent study provides evidence that infants as young as 18 months take into account both perceptual and conceptual knowledge when extending a novel word. Booth et al. (2005) found that when targets were described as artifacts, infants extended on the basis of shape; however, when targets were described as animates, infants extended on the basis of both shape and texture. These findings suggest that shape is being used as a cue for kind membership in children's naming (see also Shutts et al., Chapter 8).

By 18 months of age, children expect words for object categories to refer to kinds. However, it remains an open question whether infants who are at the beginning of word learning hold the same expectations. It may be the case that infants expect words to refer to distinct shapes and, later in development, they realize that shape is correlated with kind membership.

How can we get at the question of kind versus shape in infants? In a recent study, we borrowed an idea from previous studies with preschoolers, and developed a methodology that could be used to test much younger infants: a group of 10-month-olds. One way to distinguish between shape versus kind is by investigating infants' expectations about nonobvious properties (Baldwin et al., 1993; Graham et al., 2004; Welder & Graham, 2001). The notion of kind implies that members of the same kind share deep, internal, nonobvious properties, and their shared surface perceptual properties are caused by the shared deeper causal properties, a la psychological essentialism (Gelman, 2003; Medin & Ortony, 1989). If early count nouns refer to distinct shapes, we should see no effects of nonobvious properties. If, on the other hand, early count nouns refer to kinds, we may expect to see labeling predict internal, nonobvious properties of objects.

We therefore designed a study that pitted perceptual similarity against labeling, and we asked if 10-month-old infants would use the labeling information to predict internal, nonobvious properties, in this case, sound properties (Dewar & Xu, in press). We used a between-subject design: half of the infants were familiarized with identical object pairs, and the other half of the infants were familiarized with different-looking object pairs (see Fig. 11.2). On the familiarization trials, infants were shown one pair of objects (identical or different) that made the same sound when shaken and one pair of objects (identical or different) that made different sounds when shaken. On the test trials, pairs of objects were placed on the stage. The experimenter picked up each of the two objects and labeled it with either the same label or two distinct labels. The objects were then shaken to demonstrate their sound properties. The objects then sat stationery and silent on the stage and the infant's looking times were recorded.

We analyzed the effects of object appearance (identical or different), the number of labels (1 vs. 2), and the sound properties (identical or different). The analysis of variance revealed a two-way interaction between the number of labels and the sound properties, and no other main effects or interactions.

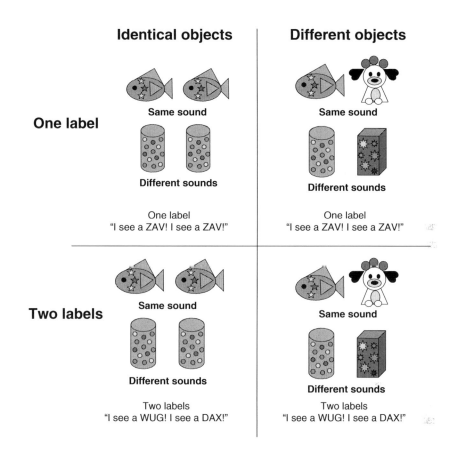

Fig. 11.2 Test trials for all four conditions (identical vs. different objects; one vs. two labels) from Dewar and Xu (in press). See colour plates.

Thus, regardless of object appearance, infants expected the object pair to make the same sound if one label was provided for both objects, and regardless of object appearance, infants expected the object pair to make different sounds if two distinct labels were provided. This was a surprising and striking result. For infants who live in contemporary society (at least in the United States or Canada), they are constantly exposed to toys that make different sounds; our impression is that there may not be a particular good correlation between object appearance and sound properties. Nevertheless, 10-month-old infants expected labeling to be predictive of an internal, nonobvious property, and they were willing to override perceptual similarity in favor of labeling information.

11.5 **What is the mechanism of learning?**

The previous three studies provide evidence that (1) the shape bias is learned and (2) shape is a proxy for kind membership. If the shape bias is learned, how is it learned? What is the mechanism of learning such that even 9-month-old infants have acquired the bias? One prominent proposal in the literature is that the shape bias is learned through associative mechanisms, often instantiated in neural network and/or connectionist models (e.g., Colunga & Smith, 2005; Samuelson, 2005). An alternative account, which we will argue for, is a hierarchical Bayesian model that captures the idea of overhypothesis formation in general.

Kemp et al. (2007) presented the basics of a Bayesian model of overhypothesis formation, and one of their chosen case studies was the shape bias. They (and we) borrowed the idea of an overhypothesis from the philosopher Nelson Goodman, whose well-known book *Fact, Fiction, and Forecast* (1955) is considered a classic on induction. One widely cited example that Goodman uses to illustrate the idea is the following:

> Suppose I show you a bunch of bags that are all identical. From the first bag I pull out a few marbles and they are all white. From the second bag I pull out a handful of marbles and they are all red. From the third bag I pull out some marbles and they are all green. If I ask you what you think the color of the next marble would be from the first, second, or the third bag, presumably you will answer with a high degree of confidence that the next marble will be white, red, and green, respectively. Now suppose I show you a new bag, and I pull out one marble that is blue. What do you think the color of the next marble will be from this new bag? Again, I think you will answer with a high degree of confidence that it is going to be blue (Fig. 11.3).

Goodman suggests, and we concur, that the learner is making both a first-order and a second-order generalization in this case, and perhaps with equal levels of confidence. In other words, the learner has formed an overhypothesis— 'Bagfuls of marbles are uniform in color'—and this second-order generalization allows the learner to make predictions about a brand new bag with new marble colors she has never seen before.

Several researchers have applied this general idea to address the problem of how children acquire the shape bias (e.g., Smith et al., 2002; Samuelson, 2005; Kemp et al. 2007). Smith et al. (2002) hypothesized that first, children acquire count nouns that refer to object categories, e.g., 'cat' refers to cats, 'horse' refers to horses, and 'chair' refers to chairs, etc. For each word and each category, children may form a first-order generalization, e.g., the word 'cat' refers to objects that are cat-shaped, the word 'horse' refers to objects that are horse-shaped, and the word 'chair' refers to objects that are chair-shaped, etc. Once a number of individual words and categories are learned, the child

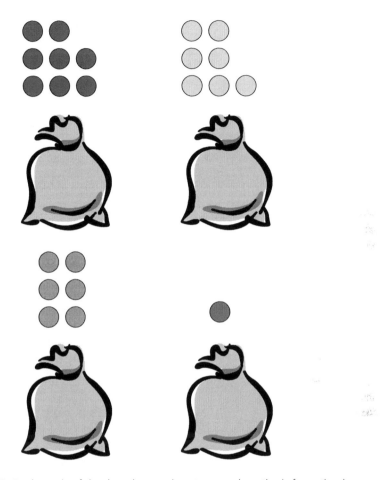

Fig. 11.3 A schematic of the thought experiment on overhypothesis formation by Goodman (1955). See colour plates.

may form a second-order generalization—that is, an overhypothesis—that 'Noun X refers to objects that are X-shaped'. This mechanism allows the child to go beyond the specific words and categories they have learned and to make a principled generalization about all count nouns that refer to object categories. In a set of elegant training studies, Smith et al. (2002) found that laboratory exposure to shape regularity and word usage with 17-month-old infants induced the shape bias and subsequently allowed these children to learn words faster outside of the laboratory.

The new studies we described earlier in this chapter suggest that the shape bias emerges earlier than 17 months, at least when the infants are not required to map specific words to specific objects (Dewar & Xu, 2007, 2008). If the

shape bias is indeed learned through a mechanism of overhypothesis formation, we will need evidence from much younger infants. To date, two studies
provide preliminary evidence that 8- to 12-month-old infants are able to form
overhypotheses based on either shape or color after fairly limited exposure
(Dewar & Xu, in preparation; Perfors et al. 2007).

In one experiment, we taught 8- to 12-month-old infants a visual rule: if
two objects that collide have the same shape, an explosion effect occurs (i.e.,
interesting sounds playing and sparkles flying). If two objects that collide have
the same color and texture, no effect occurs (see Fig. 11.4). During the training phase, the infants were shown combinations of five different shapes, five
different colors, five different textures, and five different effects. Each habituation trial consisted of a continuous string of collision events, randomly chosen
from the whole set. The habituation phase ended when the infants' looking
times dropped to 50% or less of the initial level.

On the test trials, infants were shown two test events alternately: an expected
event when two objects that shared a novel shape collided and a new effect
occurred, and an unexpected event when two objects that shared a novel color
and texture collided and a new effect occurred. If the infants had formed an

Fig. 11.4 Sample event from habituation trial. (a) When the objects match in shape,
there is a sparkly effect when they collide. (b) When the objects do not match in
shape, there is no effect.

overhypothesis about how a shape match predicts an effect, they should look longer at the unexpected event than the expected event, even though both involved new objects and new effects. These were the results we found. When we divided up our sample into younger and older infants (8:15 to 10:15 and 10:16 to 12:15), we found no differences in looking times between the two age groups. Thus, at both 9 and 11 months, infants were readily able to form an overhypothesis based on shape. (For various technical reasons, these results are preliminary and they need to be replicated.)

Given these findings, however, one might still argue that perhaps shape is special—it may be more salient and therefore it may be easier to form an over-hypothesis over this dimension. In the second study, we used a different experimental paradigm and conducted a version of the bags-of-marbles experiment a la Goodman (Dewar & Xu, in preparation). In the experimental condition, the experimenter began by bringing out a rectangular box. She pulled out four ping-pong balls from the box and placed them into a small transparent container in front of the box; all four balls were white. Next, the experimenter brought out another box and set it beside the first box. She pulled out four yellow ping-pong balls and placed them in front of the second box. The experimenter repeated the sequence with a third box and four pink ping-pong balls. Then, she brought out a fourth box and pulled out three black ping-pong balls plus a white ping-pong ball—this was the unexpected outcome. The ping-pong balls were placed into the small container and looking time was recorded. Adults watching this event found the last draw surprising, because they have formed an overhypothesis about how each box contained uniformly colored ping-pong balls. For the expected outcome, the experimenter did exactly the same thing up until the last draw from the fourth box: instead of pulling the white ping-pong ball from the fourth box, she pulled it out of the first box, which in fact contained all white ping-pong balls. Thus, the outcomes of the expected and unexpected events were identical so as to rule out any intrinsic preferences for one outcome versus the other. We found that 9-month-old infants looked longer at the unexpected outcome than the expected outcome in the experimental condition.

In the control condition, the ping-pong balls placed into the first three boxes were drawn from all boxes (e.g., the first and the fourth white balls were drawn from the first box, the second white ball from the third box, and the third white ball from the second box), so the final display of three containers with four ping-pong balls of one color was the same as before but there was no overhypothesis to be formed about how 'boxes contain uniformly colored ping-pong balls'. The fourth box was brought out and the four ping-pong balls were drawn as in the expected and unexpected outcomes of the experimental condition. Results showed that infants looked about equally at the two outcomes, suggesting that it was not the perceptual grouping or simply forming a first-order generalization with the last box that drove the effect in the experimental condition.

With very minimal exposure, infants seem to be willing to form an overhypothesis quickly, and this overhypothesis guides their inductive inference immediately. Which overhypothesis has been formed in these studies? At least two overhypotheses are consistent with the data we have collected so far: one is Goodman's 'bagfuls of marbles are uniform in color' (or our equivalent 'boxes of ping-pong balls are uniform in color', but they may vary on other dimensions); the other is 'bagfuls of marbles are identical within each bag'. Studies are underway to tease these apart. Are shape, color, and texture equally good candidate perceptual dimensions for forming overhypotheses? These are still open questions and studies are currently being conducted in our laboratory to address these issues.

In the hierarchical Bayesian model for overhypothesis learning presented by Kemp et al. (2007), a small number of perceptual dimensions (e.g., shape, texture, and color) are assigned a uniform prior probability. The inferential mechanism (i.e., Bayesian belief updating or estimation of the posterior probability given the data) updates all these hypotheses simultaneously given the data. In addition, it estimates two second-level parameters, one corresponding to how uniform a particular feature is within a category and the other corresponding to how that feature is distributed across categories. The uniform prior assumption is an important one: it states that no perceptual dimension is privileged at the beginning. The input statistics will push the model to consider one or another perceptual dimension as a reliable cue for word meaning, for example, for artifact objects, shape will receive a greater posterior; whereas for food objects, color will receive a greater posterior given the data. This model ensures rapid inductive learning in part because every item contributes to the second-order inference, whereas a more bottom-up or associative learner would require many items before forming even first-order generalizations. This sort of rapid learning is one of the characteristics that distinguish a Bayesian model from a standard neural network model (e.g., Colunga & Smith, 2005).

How do we know which hypotheses children assign initial high prior probability to? We can think of two possible empirical tests. One is to show that given roughly the same amount of data, overhypotheses over *shape* or *color* (or a few other perceptual dimensions) can be formed fairly quickly and easily; the other is to investigate whether certain features, such as *being placed on the left side of the table*, are also subject to overhypothesis formation.

	Learned or innate?	Kinds vs. shapes?	Mechanism of learning
Standard nativist	innate	kinds	N/A
Standard empiricist	learned	shapes	associative learning
Rational constructivist	**learned**	**kinds**	**overhypothesis formation**

Fig. 11.5 Three views of the development of the shape bias.

The rational constructivist view differs from both the nativist and the empiricist view of cognitive development. Using the shape bias in word learning as an example, the rational constructivist view is committed to this bias being learned, being subject to object domain effects, and to be learned via domain-general inferential mechanisms such as overhypothesis formation (this is the non-nativist part). At the same time, this view accepts that early count nouns for objects map onto kinds, and that shape is a proxy for kind membership. Furthermore, the mechanisms we suggest are not 'dumb' correlation detectors but rather complex rational learning mechanisms (this is the non-empiricist part) (see Fig. 11.5 of the various views).

11.6 **Generality of the approach: other learned biases in language and cognition**

Other word-learning biases may be acquired in a similar way. We briefly describe three cases in this section. Some researchers have argued that the basic-level bias is learned (e.g., Callanan, 1989; Callanan et al., 1994; Xu & Tenenbaum, 2007). One possible learning mechanism for this bias is overhypothesis formation. The child learns early on that words for object categories tend to refer to objects that have high within-category perceptual similarity and low between-category similarity, i.e., the basic level, then she expects other count nouns for objects to work the same way. For example, all dogs share a basic shape, but we also have subordinate-level count nouns such as *poodle*, *terrier*, *Chihuahua*, and *German Shepard*. This learning story suggests that if most of the count nouns a child was exposed to referred to subordinate-level categories, the child might instead arrive at the generalization that count nouns tend to refer to subordinate-level categories. Thus, an overhypothesis about the level of category specificity to which count nouns tend to refer may be formed to guide future word learning.

In another line of research, we have charted the development of sortal concepts in infants, and suggested that word learning may be an important causal factor in acquiring sortal concepts, which are a subset of our concepts that provide criteria for individuation and identity (see Xu, 2007b, for a review). Some of our empirical work suggests that at 9 months infants can use the presence of two distinct count noun labels to help them make the inference that two objects are behind an occluder in an object individuation task. By 12 months, online verbal labeling is not needed in the same task, at least for different-shaped objects, suggesting that by the end of the first year, infants may have formed a general rule of thumb about whether particular perceptual differences provide sufficient evidence for positing a second object in the event. One possible learning mechanism is that the younger infants learn piecemeal that certain perceptual features matter for object identity and hearing linguistic labels provide strong evidence for that. By tracking word usage and object features over time, the infants may form an overhypothesis about which perceptual features may be important for object identity. Once that overhypothesis is formed, infants no longer need explicit labeling for object individuation.

Lastly, biases for other aspects of language can be acquired via overhypothesis as well. Wonnacott et al. (2007) present evidence from adults learning the word order of an artificial language that adults not only learn the specific frequency distribution of individual verbs (i.e., whether they appear in a Verb-Subject-Object order or a VOS-particle order) but also track the overall distribution of verb types (e.g., if majority of the verbs allow the alternation, then they generate novel alternations for other verbs in the language.) Again, the general idea of an overhypothesis applies: what the adults may have learned by tracking verb-type information is that they entertain the hypothesis 'in this language, word order is flexible' if enough verb types support it (see Perfors, 2008, for a Bayesian model that captures these phenomena).

Overhypothesis formation is presumably a domain-general mechanism, not specific to word learning, or to language. Shipley (1993) was probably the first psychologist to draw our attention to Goodman's work (1955) and to apply it to developmental psychology. She points out that a child learning about animal species may acquire knowledge about specific animal kinds, and then form an overhypothesis about all animal kinds. For example, children may learn that cows eat grass, rabbits eat carrots, and monkeys eat bananas. They may also learn that fish live in water, goats live on mountains, and dogs often live in people's homes. From these data, children may form the overhypothesis that animal kinds have characteristic diets and they have characteristic habitats. Once this second-order generalization is formed, children would expect new animal kinds they encounter to have these properties, and this may give them pointers when seeking new knowledge. We have followed up on these studies in the laboratory to address the issue of how domain-general these learning mechanisms are.

11.7 Conclusions: the basic commitments of rational constructivism

The case study on the shape bias is meant to illustrate the basic ideas behind a rational constructivist approach to studying development. On the one hand, we are committed to a representational view of the mind, and we submit that certain conceptual primitives such as OBJECT, AGENT, NUMBER, and KIND may be innately given (or learned very early), and they provide the foundation for later development. At the same time, we suggest that specific biases such as the shape bias or the basic-level bias are learned, and we provide some suggestions and evidence for the existence of powerful, domain-general inductive learning mechanisms such as overhypothesis formation and probabilistic reasoning (e.g., Girotto & Gonzalez, 2007; Gopnik et al., 2004; Kushnir et al., in press; Schlottman, 2001; Teglas et al., 2007; Xu & Garcia, 2008; Xu & Tenenbaum, 2007). Our hope is that the existence of these inductive learning mechanisms, perhaps best instantiated as computational models within a Bayesian framework, gives us the tools we need to avoid ascribing very specific, innately given biases to the young human learner. Furthermore, these mechanisms themselves need to be discovered and studied in a great deal more detail. In each case, a detailed learning story may be in sight, one that meets the challenges of human inductive learning—making meaningful and principled generalizations based on limited amount of data.

Acknowledgment

We thank Susan Carey, Stephanie Denison, Charles Kemp, Mijke Rhemtulla, Joshua Tenenbaum, and Henny Yeung for helpful discussions. This research was supported by grants from NSERC and SSHRC Canada to F. Xu.

References

Baillargeon, R. (2004). Infants' physical world. *Current Directions in Psychological Science, 3*, 89–94.

Baldwin, D., Markman, E. M., & Melartin, R. L. (1993). Infants' ability to draw inferences about nonobvious object properties: evidence from exploratory play. *Child Development, 64*, 711–728.

Bloom, P., & Markson, L. (1998). Intention and analogy in children's naming of pictorial representations. *Psychological Science, 9*, 200–204.

Booth, A. E., Waxman, S. R., & Huang, Y. T. (2005). Conceptual information permeates word learning in infancy. *Developmental psychology, 41*, 491–505.

Callanan, M. A. (1989). Development of object categories and inclusion relations: pre-schoolers' hypotheses about word meanings. *Developmental Psychology, 25*, 207–216.

Callanan, M. A., Repp, A. M., McCarthy, M. G., & Latzke, M .A. (1994). Children's hypotheses about word meanings: Is there a basic level constraint? *Journal of Experimental Child Psychology, 57*, 108–138.

Cimpian, A., & Markman, E. M. (2005). The absence of a shape bias in children's word learning. *Developmental Psychology, 41*, 1003–1019.

Colunga, E., & Smith, L. B. (2005). From the lexicon to expectations about kinds: a role for associative learning. *Psychological Review, 112*, 347–382.

Dewar, K. & Xu, F. (in preparation) Overhypothesis formation in 9-month-old infants. Manuscript in preparation.

Dewar, K. & Xu, F. (in press) Do early nouns refer to kinds or distinct shapes? Evidence from 10-month-old infants. *Psychological Science.*

Dewar, K., & Xu, F. (2007) Do 9-month-old infants expect distinct words to refer to kinds? *Developmental Psychology, 43*, 1227–1238.

Dewar, K. & Xu, F. (2008) Do 9-month-old infants expect distinct labels to refer to kinds: the effect of domain. Poster presented at the 16th Biennial International Conference on Infant Studies, Vancouver, Canada.

Diesendruck, G., & Bloom, P. (2003) How specific is the shape bias? *Child Development, 74*, 168–178.

Gelman, S. A. (2003). The *Essential Child*. Oxford: Oxford University Press.

Gelman, S. A., & Ebeling, K. S. (1998). Shape and representational status in children's early naming. *Cognition, 66*, B35–B47.

Girotto, V., & Gonzalez, M. (2007). Children's understanding of posterior probability. *Cognition, 106*, 325–344.

Goodman, N. (1955). *Fact, Fiction, and Forecast*. Cambridge, MA: Harvard University Press.

Gopnik, A., Glymore, C., Sobel, D. M., Schulz, L. E., Kushnir, T., & Danks, D. (2004). A theory of causal learning in children: causal maps and Bayes nets. *Psychological Review, 111*, 3–32.

Graham, S. A., Kilbreath, C. S., & Welder, A. N. (2004). 13-month-olds rely on shared labels and shape similarity for inductive inferences. *Child Development, 75*, 409–427.

Jones, S. S., & Smith, L. B. (2002). How children know the relevant properties for generalizing object names. *Developmental Science, 5*, 219–232.

Kemp, C., Perfors, A., & Tenenbaum, J.B. (2007). Learning overhypotheses with hierarchical Bayesian models. *Developmental Science, 10*, 307–321.

Kushnir, T., Xu, F. & Wellman, H. (2008) Preschoolers use statistical sampling information to infer the preferences of others. In V. Sloutsky, B. Love, & K. MacRae (Eds.) *Proceedings of the 30th Annual Conference of the Cognitive Science Society.*

Landau, B., Smith, L. B., & Jones, S. S. (1988). The importance of shape in early lexical learning. *Cognitive Development, 3*, 299–321.

Macnamara, J. (1982). *Names for Things: A Study of Human Learning*. Cambridge, MA: MIT Press.

Marcus, G. (2001). *The Algebraic Mind*. Cambridge, MA: MIT Press.

Markman, E. M. (1989). *Categorization and Naming in Children*. Cambridge, MA: MIT Press.

Markson, L., Diesendruck, G., & Bloom, P. (2008). The shape of thought. *Developmental Science, 11*, 204–208.

Medin, D., & Ortony, A. (1989). Psychological essentialism. In S. Vosniadou, & A. Ortony (Eds.), *Similarity and Analogical Reasoning* (pp. 179–195). New York: Cambridge University Press.

Nelson, K. (1973). Structure and strategy in learning to talk. *Monographs of the Society for Research in Child Development, 38*.

Perfors, A. (2008). *Learnability, Representation, and Language: A Bayesian Approach.* Unpublished doctoral dissertation, Massachusetts Institute of Technology.

Perfors, A., Kemp, C., Tenenbaum, J. B., & Xu, F. (2007) Learning inductive constraints. Talk presented at the Biennial Meeting of the Society for Research in Child Development, March 29–April 1, Boston, MA.

Quine, W. V. O. (1960). *Word and Object.* Cambridge, MA: MIT Press.

Rosch, E., Mervis, C. B., Gray, W., Johnson, D., & Boyes-Braem, P. (1976). Basic objects in natural categories. *Cognitive Psychology, 8*, 382–439.

Samuelson, L. K. (2005). Statistical regularities in vocabulary guide language acquisition in connectionist models and 15–20 month olds. *Developmental Psychology, 38*, 1016–1037.

Samuelson, L. K., & Bloom, P. (2008). The shape controversy: What counts as an explanation of development? Introduction to the special section. *Developmental Science, 11*, 183–184.

Samuelson, L. K., & Smith, L. B. (2005). They call it like they see it: spontaneous naming and attention to shape. *Developmental Science, 8*, 182–198.

Schlottman, A. (2001). Children's probability intuitions: understanding the expected value of complex gambles. *Child Development, 72*, 103–122.

Shipley, E. (1993). Categories, hierarchies, and induction. *The Psychology of Learning and Motivation, 30*, 265–301.

Smith, L. B., Jones, S. S., Landau, B., Gershkoff-Stowe, L., & Samuelson, L. (2002). Object name learning provides on-the-job training for attention. *Psychological Science, 13*, 13–19.

Soja, N. N., Carey, S., & Spelke, E. S. (1991). Ontological categories guide young children's inductions of word meaning: object terms and substance terms. *Cognition, 38*, 179–211.

Spelke, E. S. (1994). Initial knowledge: six suggestions. *Cognition, 50*, 431–445.

Teglas, E., Girotto, V., Gonzalez, M., & Bonatti, L. (2007) Intuitions of probabilities shape expectations about the future at 12 months and beyond. *Proceedings of the National Academy of Sciences of the United States of America, 104*, 19156–19159.

Waxman, S. R. (1999). Specifying the scope of 13-month-olds' expectations for novel words. *Cognition, 70*, B35–B50.

Welder, A. N., & Graham, A. (2001). The influence of shape similarity and shared labels on infants' inductive inferences about nonobvious object properties. *Child Development, 72*, 1653–1673.

Wonnacott, E., Newport, E. L., & Tenenhaus, M. K. (2007) Acquiring and processing verb argument structure: distributional learning in a miniature language. *Cognitive Psychology, 56*, 165–209.

Xu, F. (2007a). Rational statistical inference and cognitive development. In P. Carruthers, S. Laurence, & S. Stich (Eds.), *The Innate Mind: Foundations and the Future*, vol. 3 (pp. 199–215). Oxford University Press.

Xu, F. (2007b). Sortal concepts, object individuation, and language. *Trends in Cognitive Sciences, 11*, 400–406.

Xu, F., Carey, S., & Quint, N. (2004). The emergence of kind-based object individuation in infancy. *Cognitive Psychology, 49*, 155–190.

Xu, F., & Garcia, V. (2008). Intuitive statistics by 8-month-old infants. *Proceedings of the National Academy of Sciences of the United States of America, 105*, 5012–5015.

Xu, F., & Tenenbaum, J. B. (2007). Word learning as Bayesian inference. *Psychological Review, 114*, 245–272.

Chapter 12

Young infants' expectations about self-propelled objects

Renée Baillargeon, Di Wu, Sylvia Yuan, Jie Li, & Yuyan Luo

12.1 Introduction

Investigations of the development of infants' physical reasoning over the past 20 years have revealed that even young infants possess expectations about physical events (for recent reviews, see Baillargeon et al., 2006; Baillargeon et al., 2009). These findings, which come increasingly from both violation-of-expectation tasks (e.g., Aguiar & Baillargeon, 1999, 2002; Hespos & Baillargeon, 2001b; Lécuyer & Durand, 1998; Luo & Baillargeon, 2005b; Spelke et al., 1992; Wang et al., 2005; Wilcox et al., 1996) and action tasks (e.g., Goubet & Clifton, 1998; Hespos & Baillargeon, 2006, 2008; Hofstadter & Reznick, 1996; Hood & Willatts, 1986; Kochukhova & Gredeback, 2007; Ruffman et al., 2005; von Hofsten et al., 2007), support the notion that infants are born with an abstract, unconscious, physical-reasoning system, which provides them with a shallow causal framework for making sense of the displacements and interactions of objects and other physical entities (e.g., Baillargeon et al., 2009; Carey & Spelke, 1994; Gelman, 1990; Keil, 1995; Leslie, 1994; Premack & Premack, 1995; Spelke, 1994; Wellman & S. A. Gelman, 1997).

Gelman (1990; Gelman & Spelke, 1981; Gelman et al., 1995; Subrahmanyam et al., 2002) and Leslie (1984a, 1994, 1995; Leslie & Keeble, 1987) have suggested that part of the skeletal causal framework infants bring to bear when interpreting physical events is a fundamental distinction between inert and self-propelled objects. When watching a novel object begin to move or change direction, infants' physical-reasoning system attempts to determine whether the change in the object's motion state is caused by forces internal or external to the object. According to Leslie (1994), 'the more an object changes motion state by itself and not as a result of external impact, the more evidence it provides, the more likely it is, that it is [self-propelled]' (p. 133). An object that is judged to be self-propelled is endowed with *an internal source of energy*. A self-propelled object can use its internal energy directly to control its own motion and indirectly (through the application of force) to control the motion of other objects.

Do young infants distinguish between inert and self-propelled objects? Do they endow self-propelled objects with internal energy? One way to address these questions empirically is to examine whether young infants hold different expectations for physical events involving inert and self-propelled objects. Upon observing that a novel object begins to move on its own, or changes direction on its own, do infants hold different expectations about how the object might behave in various physical events? Are these expectations causally consistent with the notion that the object possesses internal energy it can use to control its motion or that of other objects?

This chapter is organized into two sections. In the first, longer section, we summarize the results of several series of experiments from our laboratory that compared the responses of 2.5- to 6.5-month-old infants to various physical events involving an inert or a self-propelled object. To control for extraneous factors, the inert and the self-propelled object used in each experiment was typically the *same novel object*. During familiarization, half the infants were given evidence that the object was self-propelled (e.g., it initiated its motion in plain view); the other infants were given no such evidence and so presumably categorized the object as inert. During test, the infants saw new physical events involving the object. The experiments tested whether infants (1) would view the outcomes of some events as surprising when they categorized the object as inert but *not* when they categorized it as self-propelled, because in the latter case they could infer that the object had used its internal energy to bring about the observed outcomes; and (2) would view the outcomes of other events as surprising whether they categorized the object as inert *or* as self-propelled, because they realized that no application of internal energy could have brought about the observed outcomes.

In the second, shorter section of the chapter, we consider what might be the links between the concept of self-propelled object explored here and other key concepts. Are young infants who see a novel object initiate its own motion likely to view it *only* as a self-propelled object endowed with internal energy— or are they likely to view it as something more? For example, could infants view the object as an *agent* that can detect its environment and move intentionally in pursuit of goals, or as an *animal* composed of biological matter? We discuss various characterizations and consider their implications for infants' construal of the novel self-propelled objects studied in this chapter (for additional discussion of these issues, see Shutts et al., Chapter 8).

12.2 **Infants' expectations about self-propelled objects**

To our knowledge, the first experiment that directly compared infants' responses to physical events involving inert and self-propelled objects was conducted by Woodward and her colleagues (Spelke, Phillips et al., 1995; Woodward et al., 1993). This experiment examined whether 7-month-old infants believe that (1) a self-propelled object can initiate its own motion, whereas an inert object cannot, and (2) an inert object can be set into motion only through contact with (and the application of force by) another physical entity. The infants were assigned to an inert or a self-propelled condition. Infants in the *inert* condition were habituated to a videotaped event involving two different, large (human-sized), wheeled pillars. To start, one pillar stood partly visible at the right edge of a large occluder at the center of the television monitor (events in this and in all other experiments in this chapter are described from the infants' perspective). The second pillar moved into view on the left side of the monitor and disappeared behind the left edge of the occluder; after an appropriate interval, the first pillar moved to the right and disappeared on the right side of the monitor. The entire event sequence was then repeated in reverse. Following habituation, the occluder was removed, and the infants saw two test events in which the pillars moved as before; the only difference between the events had to do with what happened during the previously occluded portion of the pillars' trajectories. In one event (contact event), the moving pillar collided with the stationary pillar and set it in motion; in the other event (no-contact event), the moving pillar stopped short of the stationary pillar, which then set off on its own. Infants in the *self-propelled* condition saw identical events except that the two pillars were replaced with a man and a woman who walked along the same path as the pillars.

The infants in the inert condition looked reliably longer at the no-contact than at the contact event, whereas those in the self-propelled condition tended to look equally at the two events. These and control results suggested three conclusions. First, because there was no clear indication that the pillars were self-propelled during the habituation trials (it was unclear what caused them to roll into view on either side of the television monitor), the infants categorized them as inert; infants thus appear to hold the default assumption that a novel object is inert unless given unambiguous evidence that it is not. Second, the infants believed that inert objects can be set in motion only through contact with (and the application of force by) other physical entities, and thus, they inferred that one pillar must be colliding with the other behind the occluder. Third, the infants realized that humans are self-propelled objects, and thus, they understood that each human could move on its own or as a result of an application of force by the other human.

The preceding results suggest that, by 7 months of age, infants hold different expectations for at least some physical events involving inert and self-propelled objects. As alluded to earlier, our own experiments attempted to extend these results in several directions. First, they asked whether infants younger than 7 months might also hold such differential expectations. Second, our experiments compared infants' responses to events involving the same novel object, presented as either inert or self-propelled. One limitation of the results described in the preceding paragraph is that, because the events involving the pillars and humans were so different, it is difficult to determine what role perceptual differences or prior experiences with humans might have played in the infants' responses. Our approach, in essence, was to compare infants' responses to events involving only pillars (and other similar objects such as boxes, cylinders, and balls), to determine what additional expectations infants might hold simply from observing that a pillar was inert or self-propelled. Third, our experiments explored a wide range of physical events. In choosing these events, we considered specific ways in which a self-propelled object might use its internal energy to control its motion or that of other objects. Thus, as described in the following sections, we asked whether young infants would believe that a self-propelled object might use its internal energy (1) to alter the direction of its motion, (2) to change location when out of sight, (3) to change the orientation or position of its parts when out of sight, (4) to remain stationary when hit, (5) to remain stable when released without adequate external support, and finally (6) to 'hold' an inert object so as to prevent it from falling.

12.2.1 Can a self-propelled object alter the direction of its motion?

The results of Woodward and her colleagues (Spelke, Phillips et al., 1995; Woodward et al., 1993) suggested that infants realize that a self-propelled object can initiate its own motion, whereas an inert object cannot (see also Kosugi & Fujita, 2002; Kosugi et al., 2003; Kotovsky & Baillargeon, 2000; Saxe et al., 2005; Saxe et al., 2007). Our first experiment asked whether 5-month-old infants hold different expectations not only for the *onset* of inert and self-propelled objects' motion but also for the *path* they follow once in motion (Luo et al., in press). As adults, we expect an inert object traveling on a horizontal plane to follow a smooth path, without abrupt changes in direction;[1] in contrast, we recognize

---

[1] The expectation that an inert object traveling on a horizontal plane will follow a smooth path, with no abrupt change in direction, is consistent with, though considerably weaker than, the Newtonian principle of inertia. According to this principle, 'if no external forces act on a body, it moves uniformly, that is, always with the same velocity along a straight line' (Einstein & Infeld, 1960, p. 8). In everyday life, however, uniform motion can 'never

that a self-propelled object may use its internal energy to change direction at will. Thus, we would be surprised if a ball rolling on a table changed direction as it reached each corner so as to follow the perimeter of the table: for inert objects, abrupt changes in direction cannot be achieved without external impact. Experiment 1 (Luo et al., in press) thus asked whether 5-month-old infants would expect an inert but not a self-propelled object to follow a smooth path, with no abrupt change in direction.

Previous research suggested that young infants are in fact *not* surprised when an inert object abruptly deviates from its initial path. Spelke et al. (1994) habituated 4- and 6-month-old infants to an event in which a ball rested in the front right corner of a large table; a horizontal screen hid the left half of the table. An experimenter's hand hit the ball, which then rolled diagonally across the table until it disappeared under the screen at the center of the table. Next, the screen was removed to reveal the ball resting in the back left corner of the table, further along its pre-occlusion trajectory. Following habituation, the infants saw a linear and a nonlinear test event. The linear event was similar to the habituation event, except that the ball started from the back right corner of the table; it rolled diagonally across the table until it disappeared under the screen, and was revealed resting in the front left corner of the table, as expected. In the nonlinear event, the ball again started from the back right corner of the table and rolled diagonally across the table; however, when the screen was removed, the ball rested in the same back left corner as in the habituation event, as though it had performed a 90° turn when under the screen. The infants did not look longer at the nonlinear than at the linear event, and Spelke and her colleagues concluded that young infants do not expect an inert object, once in motion, to follow a smooth path, with no abrupt change in direction.

However, other interpretations of these negative results were possible. Because of limitations in the apparatus used to implement the experimental design, the infants were actually presented with a more subtle violation than is suggested by the preceding description. In reality, most of the left side of the table was filled with a large insert with a central indentation in its right edge; the ball came to rest in the front or back corner of this indentation. Thus, rather than seeing the ball at rest in the front or back left corner of the table at the end of the test events (a large and salient absolute difference), the infants

be realized; a stone thrown from a tower, a cart pushed along road can never move absolutely uniformly because we cannot eliminate the influence of external forces' (Einstein & Infeld, 1960, p. 8). Not surprisingly, as the principle of inertia is derived from scientific reasoning rather than from immediate observation, it was not understood for many centuries, until the discoveries of Galileo and Newton, and it plays little role in adults' everyday physical reasoning (e.g., Einstein & Infeld, 1960; McCloskey, 1983; Spelke et al., 1994).

saw the ball at rest in the front or back corner of the indentation (a smaller and perhaps less salient absolute difference). This arrangement might have made it difficult for the infants to determine whether or how far the ball had deviated from its pre-occlusion trajectory. Keeping in mind that young infants might be limited in their ability to detect path deviations, we presented the infants in Experiment 1 with a very salient violation: a full reversal, in plain view.

The infants were assigned to an inert or a self-propelled condition (see Fig. 12.1) and sat in front of a large apparatus whose right side was occluded by a large screen. A small box (5 cm high, 19.5 cm wide, 17 cm deep) was visible on the left side of the apparatus; this box was covered with red felt and had a 'skirt' made of white lace that reached the apparatus floor and hid the motorized system that controlled the box's motion back and forth across the apparatus. In the inert condition, an experimenter's gloved hand activated this system by simultaneously hitting the box and a microswitch located next to the box, so that it appeared as though the hand caused the box to move. In the self-propelled condition, the experimenter activated the system by depressing a button on a control panel located under the apparatus floor, so that it appeared as though the box began to move on its own. The box's motion back and forth across the apparatus was accompanied by noise from the motorized system; this noise was identical in the inert and self-propelled conditions.

In the familiarization events shown in the *inert* condition, the gloved hand hit the box, which then moved to the right until it disappeared behind the left edge of the screen. After a few seconds, the box reappeared from behind the same edge of the screen and returned to its starting position to begin a new event cycle (in all experiments in this chapter, unless otherwise noted, events were repeated until the trial ended). Following familiarization, the screen was removed, and the infants watched a near- and a far-wall test event (here and in all other pertinent experiments in this chapter, order of presentation was counterbalanced). In the near-wall event, the hand again hit the box, which moved to the right until it hit a wall partition at the right end of the apparatus; the box then reversed direction and returned to its starting position (although the box appeared to hit the partition and 'bounce back', in actuality only its lace skirt contacted the partition; a reverse-switch under the apparatus caused the box to reverse direction). In the far-wall event, the wall partition was placed farther to the right; because the box moved exactly as before, it no longer hit the partition and thus appeared to reverse direction on its own. As the partition changed position in the near- and far-wall test events, it was also placed in the same two positions on alternate familiarization trials; however, because the screen was in place during these trials, only the very top of the partition was visible above the screen (see Fig. 12.1).

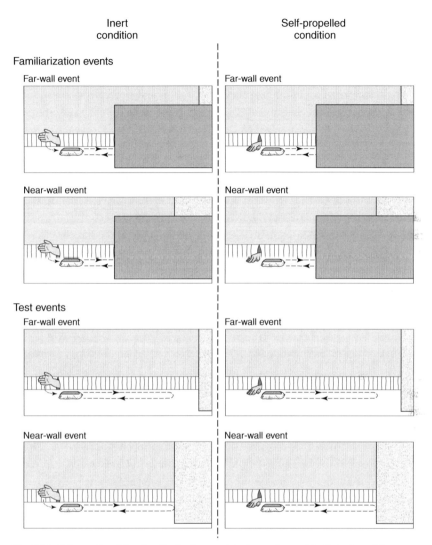

Fig. 12.1 Schematic of the familiarization and test events used in Experiment 1 (Luo et al., in press).

The infants in the *self-propelled* condition saw identical near- and far-wall familiarization and test events, except that the box initiated its own motion; the hand remained stationary on the apparatus floor.

Our reasoning was as follows. If at 5 months infants tend to view an object as inert unless given unambiguous evidence that it is not (e.g., Leslie, 1994, 1995; Luo & Baillargeon, 2005a; Spelke, Phillips et al., 1995; Woodward et al., 1993), then the infants in the inert condition should categorize the box as inert during the familiarization trials because (1) they saw the hand set it in motion and (2) they had no evidence as to what caused its reversal behind the screen. In contrast, the infants in the self-propelled condition should categorize the box as self-propelled, because they saw it initiate its own motion in plain view.

Furthermore, if at 5 months infants (1) endow self-propelled but not inert objects with internal energy and (2) expect an object to follow a smooth path unless a force—either internal or external to the object—intervenes to bring about an abrupt change, then the infants in the inert and self-propelled conditions should respond differently to the test events. In the inert condition, the infants should be surprised when the box appeared to reverse direction spontaneously, but not when it reversed direction after hitting the wall partition: this impact provided an external cause for the abrupt change in its trajectory. The infants should thus look reliably longer at the far- than at the near-wall event. In the self-propelled condition, in contrast, the infants should not be surprised when the box reversed direction either spontaneously—it could use its internal energy to do so—or after hitting the wall partition. The infants should thus look about equally, and equally short, at the far- and near-wall events.

Results were as predicted: the infants in the inert condition looked reliably longer at the far- than at the near-wall event, whereas those in the self-propelled condition tended to look equally, and equally short, at the two events. These results suggested that the infants in the inert condition (1) categorized the box as an inert object because they received no evidence to the contrary; (2) expected the box to follow a smooth path, with no abrupt deviation, in the absence of external impact; and hence (3) were surprised when it spontaneously reversed direction. In contrast, the infants in the self-propelled condition (1) categorized the box as self-propelled because it initiated its own motion, (2) understood that the box could use its internal energy to alter its path, and hence (3) were not surprised when it spontaneously reversed direction.

12.2.1.1 Links to other findings: predictive tracking and reaching

The results of the *inert* condition in Experiment 1 help reconcile previously discrepant findings in the infancy literature. In contrast to the violation-of-expectation findings of Spelke et al. (1994) described in Section 12.2.1, experiments using action tasks such as predictive reaching (for visible objects) and predictive tracking (for occluded objects) have found that young infants do expect objects to follow a smooth path, with no abrupt change in direction (e.g., Kochukhova & Gredeback, 2007; Spelke & von Hofsten, 2001; von Hofsten et al., 1998; von Hofsten et al., 2007). These contrastive results have sometimes been taken to point to the existence of a dissociation between the physical knowledge underlying infants' responses in violation-of-expectation and action tasks (e.g., von Hofsten et al., 1998). However, the positive results of the inert condition in Experiment 1 suggest that the design used by Spelke et al. was perhaps less than optimal and that young infants can demonstrate an expectation that objects follow a smooth path in both violation-of-expectation and action tasks.

To give an example of such an action task, Kochukhova and Gredebäck (2007) showed 6-month-old infants computer-animated events in which a self-propelled object approached and then disappeared behind an occluder; while behind the occluder, the object effected a 90° turn (e.g., the object disappeared behind the left edge of the occluder and reappeared at its bottom edge). Analyses of the infants' anticipatory responses using an eye tracker revealed that, on the initial trials, the infants expected the object to reappear further along its pre-occlusion trajectory, on the opposite side of the occluder (e.g., at the occluder's right edge). After two or three trials, however, the infants began to anticipate the object's reappearance on the correct side of the occluder (e g , at the occluder's bottom edge). One interpretation of these results, consistent with those of Experiment 1, is that when watching a self-propelled object move behind an occluder, young infants initially hold the default assumption that the object will follow a smooth path, with no abrupt change in direction, just as they do for an inert object. However, if this expectation is violated, infants conclude that the object is using its internal energy to alter its trajectory when behind the occluder, and they then allow their prior observations (about where the object has reappeared on previous trials) to guide their future anticipations.

Finally, the results of the *self-propelled* condition in Experiment 1 are consistent with a plethora of violation-of-expectation experiments over the past 20 years that have presented young infants with a self-propelled object moving back and forth across an apparatus, with or without occluders at the center of the apparatus (e.g., Aguiar & Baillargeon, 1999, 2002; Baillargeon & DeVos, 1991; Baillargeon & Graber, 1987; Bremner et al., 2005; S. P. Johnson, 2004; S. P. Johnson et al., 2003; Kellman & Spelke, 1983; Luo & Baillargeon, 2005a, 2005b; Luo et al., 2003; Slater et al., 1996; Spelke, Kestenbaum et al., 1995; Wilcox, 1999; Wilcox & Baillargeon, 1998b; Wilcox & Schweinle, 2003). Although this issue was typically not examined directly, there was no empirical reason to suspect that the infants in these experiments were surprised when the object reversed direction at either end of its trajectory, and the present data support this interpretation.

12.2.1.2 Control findings

One possible objection to our interpretation of the results of the self-propelled condition in Experiment 1 and in Woodward et al. (1993; see also Spelke, Phillips et al., 1995) was the following: perhaps the infants were merely confused by the test events they were shown and hence held no specific expectations about their outcomes. This interpretation seemed unlikely: as was just mentioned in the last section, numerous experiments over the past 20 years have presented infants with events involving self-propelled objects; had infants found these objects confusing, the results of the experiments would have been consistently negative, and they were not. Nevertheless, Experiment 2 (Luo et al., in press) was conducted to rule out this alternative interpretation.

A large body of evidence suggests that young infants interpret physical events in accord with a principle of *persistence* (e.g., Baillargeon, 2008; Baillargeon et al., 2009), which states that objects persist, as they are, through time and space. An important corollary of this principle is the *solidity* principle, which states that, for two objects to each persist in time and space, the two cannot occupy the same space at the same time. Numerous investigations have shown that infants aged 2.5 months and older recognize that an object, whether self-propelled or not, cannot pass through space occupied by another object (e.g., Aguiar & Baillargeon, 1998, 2003; Baillargeon, 1986, 1987, 1991; Baillargeon et al., 1985; Baillargeon et al., 1990; Baillargeon & DeVos, 1991; Hespos & Baillargeon, 2001a, 2001b; Luo et al., 2003; Saxe et al., 2006; Sitskoorn & Smitsman, 1995; Spelke et al., 1992; Wang et al., 2004; Wang et al., 2005). Experiment 2 therefore examined whether 5-month-old infants would recognize that an object, whether self-propelled or not, cannot pass through another object.

The infants were assigned to an inert or a self-propelled condition (see Fig. 12.2) and received familiarization trials identical to those shown in the inert and self-propelled conditions of Experiment 1, respectively, with one exception: in these trials, as in all other trials of Experiment 2, the wall partition was always in the far position (with the large screen occluding the right side of the apparatus, the infants in the inert condition could not determine just how far the box traveled behind the screen or what caused it to reverse direction.) Next, the familiarization screen was removed, and the infants received two orientation trials in which they were introduced to a large table (table orientation event) and a large block (block orientation event); each rested across the box's path, directly in front of the infants, and was briefly rotated upward to make clear that it extended from the front to the back of the apparatus. Finally, the infants were shown a table and a block test event.

In the table event shown in the *self-propelled* condition, the box began to move to the right, passed under the table, reversed direction, passed under the table once more, and finally returned to its starting position. The block event was similar except that the table was replaced with the block; the box appeared

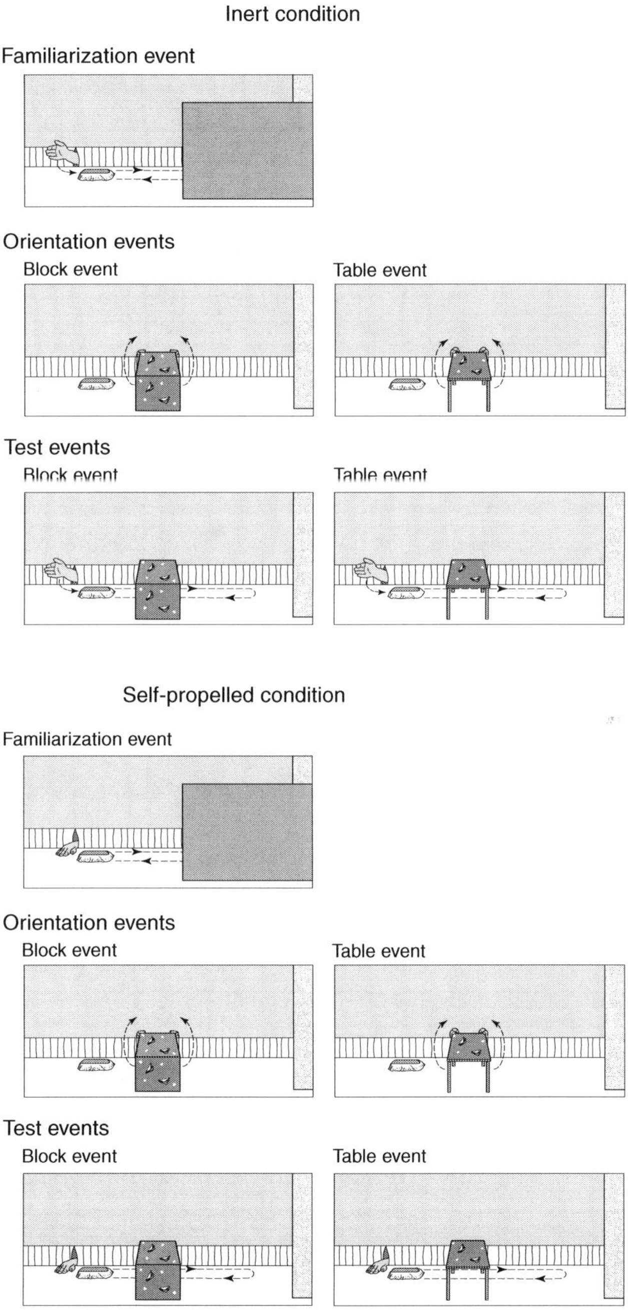

Inert condition

Familiarization event

Orientation events

Block event   Table event

Test events

Block event   Table event

Self-propelled condition

Familiarization event

Orientation events

Block event   Table event

Test events

Block event   Table event

Fig. 12.2 Schematic of the familiarization, orientation, and test events used in Experiment 2 (Luo et al., in press).

to pass through the block once as it traveled to the right and once more after it reversed direction to return to its starting position (the block used in the block test event had a small tunnel that allowed the box to pass through; because the infants sat centered in front of the block, they could not see the opening of the tunnel on either side of the block). The infants in the *inert* condition saw the same test events except that the box did not initiate its motion: as in the familiarization trials, the box began to move only after it was hit by the experimenter's gloved hand.

We reasoned that if the infants in the self-propelled condition of Experiment 1 looked about equally at the test events because they were confused by our self-propelled box, then the infants in the self-propelled condition of Experiment 2 should also be confused and hence should also look about equally at the test events. However, if the infants in the self-propelled condition of Experiment 1 looked about equally at the test events because they realized that the box could reverse its motion either spontaneously or following impact with the wall partition, then the infants in Experiment 2 should respond differentially to the block and table test events. Because even young infants realize that an object, whether self-propelled or not, cannot pass through another object, the infants should be surprised when the box appeared to pass through the block but not under the table. The infants should thus look reliably longer at the block than at the table event. In contrast, the infants in the inert condition should find both test events surprising: the table event, because the box appeared to reverse direction spontaneously (as in the far-wall test event of Experiment 1), and the block event, because the box appeared to reverse direction spontaneously and to pass through the block. The infants should tend to look equally, and equally long, at the block and table events.[2]

Results were as predicted: the infants in the self-propelled condition looked reliably longer at the block than at the table event, whereas those in the inert condition looked about equally, and equally long, at the two events. These results, together with those of Experiment 1, supported the proposal that young infants endow self-propelled objects with an internal source of energy. On the one hand, infants are *not* surprised when a self-propelled object spontaneously initiates or reverses its motion, because they realize that the object can use its internal energy to do so; on the other hand, infants *are* surprised

---

[2] Readers might wonder why we did not predict that the infants in the inert condition would look reliably longer at the block than at the table test event, becasue the block event was, in a sense, doubly surprising: the box not only reversed on its own but also passed through the block. The reason we did not is that in our experience the violation-of-expectation method is a categorical rather than a proportional measure: it tells us whether infants view an event as unexpected, not how unexpected it appears to them.

when a self-propelled object passes through an obstacle, because they realize that no application of internal energy could allow the object to do so. Infants' expectations about self-propelled objects are thus neither undefined nor arbitrary but appear causally consistent with the notion that self-propelled objects use their internal energy to control their motion.

12.2.2 Can a self-propelled object change location when out of sight?

If young infants realize that self-propelled objects can initiate their motion at will, could they posit hidden displacements to make sense of events that would otherwise seem impossible? In particular, could infants infer that a self-propelled object had moved to another hiding location when out of sight, to make sense of a disappearance that would otherwise seem inexplicable? Our next experiment examined this question, and built on two bodies of experimental findings.

One body concerned another corollary of the principle of persistence, the *continuity* principle, which states that objects exist and move continuously in time and space. Numerous experiments have shown that infants aged 2.5 months and older recognize that an object, whether inert or self-propelled, cannot magically appear or disappear, nor can it magically move from one location to another without traveling the distance between them (e.g., Aguiar & Baillargeon, 1999, 2002; Ahmed & Ruffman, 1998; Baillargeon et al., 1989; Baillargeon & Graber, 1988; Luo & Baillargeon, 2005b; Spelke, Kestenbaum et al., 1995; Wilcox et al., 1996; Xu & Carey, 1996). The other body of findings involved experiments showing that, when confronted with events that seem to violate the continuity principle, infants are sometimes able to generate explanations for these violations, typically by inferring the presence of additional objects in the events (e.g., Aguiar & Baillargeon, 2002; Spelke, Kestenbaum et al., 1995; Xu & Carey, 1996). For example, when a self-propelled toy mouse disappears at one edge of a screen and reappears at the other edge without appearing in a large opening at the bottom of the screen, 3.5-month-old infants assume that two mice are involved in the event, one traveling to the left and one to the right of the screen (Aguiar & Baillargeon, 2002).

In Experiment 3 (Luo et al., in press), we presented young infants with an apparent continuity violation: an inert or a self-propelled object magically disappeared when behind a screen. We asked whether infants might infer that the self-propelled object had used its internal energy to move to a different hiding location when the physical layout of the apparatus made such an invisible displacement possible. Experiment 3 thus examined whether 6-month-old infants would be surprised (1) if an inert but *not* a self-propelled object disappeared from behind a screen, when the self-propelled object could have moved to an alternative hiding place, and (2) if an inert *or* a self-propelled object disappeared from behind a screen, when no alternative hiding place was available.

The infants were assigned to an inert or a self-propelled condition and saw novel familiarization events suggested by the results of Experiments 1 and 2. At the start of the familiarization event in the *self-propelled* condition, the wall partition was in its far position, and the box rested in its usual starting position at the left end of the apparatus; however, the box was now hidden by a large screen. During the event, the box emerged to the right of the screen, traveled to the right a short distance, reversed direction on its own (at its usual reversal point), and returned behind the screen. The familiarization event in the *inert* condition was similar except that the wall partition was in its near position: the box thus hit the wall partition before reversing direction and returning behind the screen. The familiarization event in the self-propelled condition thus offered unambiguous evidence that the box was self-propelled, because it reversed direction spontaneously. In contrast, the familiarization event shown in the inert condition offered no such evidence, because (1) it was unclear what caused the box to emerge from behind the screen and (2) the box reversed direction as a result of external impact, after hitting the wall partition.

During test, half of the infants in each condition saw a one-screen event (see Fig. 12.3), and half saw a two-screen event (see Fig. 12.4).

In both events, the box rested on the apparatus floor, and a gloved hand pointed to its top surface; the hand reached into the apparatus through a window in the left wall. Next, a screen was raised and then lowered to reveal that the box had disappeared; the hand pointed to the space previously occupied by the box. Finally, the screen was again raised and lowered to reveal that the box had reappeared, beginning a new event cycle (because the gloved hand rested on the apparatus floor between the screen and the window when the screen was lifted and lowered, it was clear that it could not have surreptitiously removed and replaced the box). The only difference between the one- and two-screen events was that in the latter event a second screen stood to the right of the box. When raised, the first screen occluded the left edge of the second screen, making it possible for the self-propelled box to surreptitiously move behind it.

Results were as expected: in the self-propelled condition, the infants who saw the one-screen event looked reliably longer than those who saw the two-screen event; in the inert condition, the infants tended to look equally, and equally long, at both events. These results suggested two conclusions. First, the infants attended to the box's reversal during the familiarization trials, and they categorized the box as self-propelled when it reversed direction spontaneously

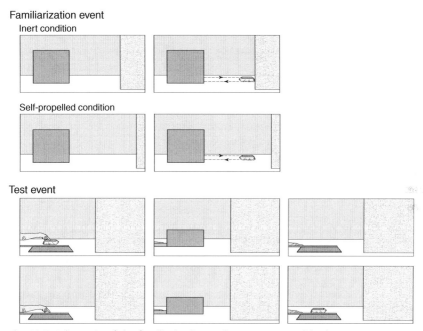

Fig. 12.3 Schematic of the familiarization and test events used in the one-screen condition of Experiment 3 (Luo et al., in press).

and as inert when it reversed direction only after hitting the wall partition. Second, during the test trials, the infants in the inert condition detected the continuity violation in the one- and two-screen events: in each case, they were surprised that the box inexplicably disappeared and reappeared. In contrast, the infants in the self-propelled condition found the one- but not the two-screen event surprising, because they were able to generate an explanation for the latter event: they inferred that the box used its internal energy to move behind the second screen when it 'disappeared', and to return from behind the second screen when it 'reappeared'.

12.2.2.1 Test with younger infants

Would infants younger than 6 months also invoke invisible displacements to make sense of continuity violations involving self-propelled but not inert objects? Experiment 4 (Wu et al., 2006) attempted to address this question and tested 4-month-old infants using a new experimental design. We reasoned that positive findings would suggest that infants as young as 4 months of age already hold different expectations for at least some physical events involving inert and self-propelled objects.

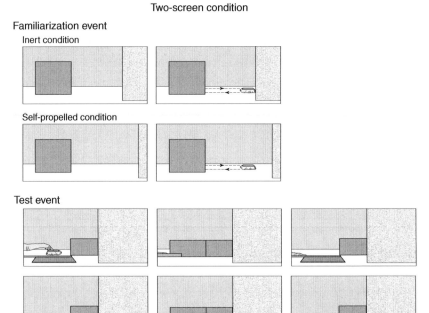

Fig. 12.4 Schematic of the familiarization and test events used in the two-screen condition of Experiment 3 (Luo et al., in press).

The infants were assigned to an inert or a self-propelled condition (see Fig. 12.5). The infants in the *inert* condition faced a wide screen with two closed windows located a short distance apart. In the familiarization trial, an experimenter's gloved hand (which reached into the apparatus through a fringe curtain in the back wall) lifted a red column above the screen, between the two windows. The hand gently tilted the column to the left and right twice, and then lowered it back behind the screen, in the same location as before. Next, the hand performed exactly the same actions with a black ball. Infants in the *self-propelled* condition saw a similar occlusion event except that the objects now appeared to move by themselves. Each object had a thin stick at its back that protruded through a slit in a cardboard inserted behind the fringe curtain; the experimenter used the stick, out of the infants' view, to move the column and ball as in the inert condition.

Following the familiarization trial, all the infants saw the same one- and two-window test events. In the two-window event, the gloved hand opened the right window in the screen (by pulling a handle that protruded above the screen) to reveal the column, and then closed the window; next, the hand opened the left window to reveal the ball, and then again closed the window.

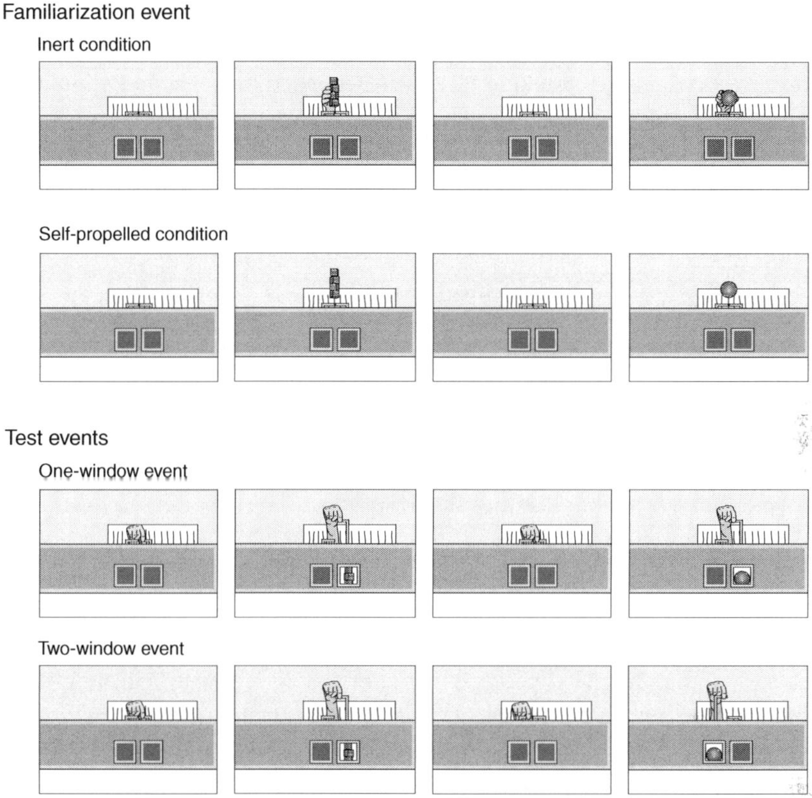

Familiarization event

Inert condition

Self-propelled condition

Test events

One-window event

Two-window event

Fig. 12.5 Schematic of the familiarization and test events used in Experiment 4 (Wu et al., 2006).

In the one-window event, the hand again opened the right window to reveal the column, but then opened the *same* window to reveal the ball. The two objects thus appeared in different windows in the two-window event, but in the same window, in alternation, in the one-window event.

Our reasoning was as follows. Prior research on infants' physical reasoning suggests that, by 4 months of age, infants have identified height, width, and shape as occlusion variables, and thus typically include such information in their representations of occlusion events (e.g., Baillargeon & DeVos, 1991; Wang et al., 2004; Wilcox, 1999). Thus, we expected that the infants in Experiment 4 would attend to the differences in height, width, and shape between the column and the ball, and would conclude that two different objects were involved in the familiarization event, even though the objects followed exactly the same path when moving above the screen. Furthermore, given the results of Experiments 1 to 3, we expected that the infants in the inert condition would categorize the objects as inert, because they received no evidence to the contrary, and that the infants in the self-propelled condition would categorize the objects as self-propelled, because they spontaneously altered their motions in plain sight (recall that the objects rose above the screen and then tilted left and right twice before returning behind the screen.) Finally, we reasoned that the infants in the inert condition should find the one- but not the two-window test event surprising: whereas the two-window event was consistent with there being two inert objects, a column and a ball, occupying two distinct locations behind the screen, the one-window event involved a continuity violation, because the two objects appeared to magically exchange locations behind the screen. On the other hand, if infants as young as 4 months of age recognize that self-propelled objects can move at will, then the infants in the self-propelled condition might not view either test event surprising: when faced with the one-window event, the infants could infer that the objects surreptitiously exchanged locations when out of sight.

As predicted, the infants in the inert condition looked reliably longer at the one- than at the two-window event, whereas those in the self-propelled condition looked about equally, and equally short, at the events. These results suggested that infants as young as 4 months of age (1) distinguish between inert and self-propelled objects, (2) endow self-propelled objects with internal energy, and (3) infer that self-propelled objects are engaging in invisible displacements to make sense of occlusion events that would otherwise violate the principle of continuity.

Experiment 5 (Wu et al., in preparation) was designed to provide converging evidence for our interpretation of the results of the self-propelled condition. The experiment examined whether 4-month-old infants would infer that two self-propelled objects (now a multicolored column made of Lego blocks and a green ball) exchanged locations out of view when it was physically possible for the objects to do so, but not otherwise.

The infants faced a wooden vertical frame; each end of the frame was hidden by a screen. Each screen had a tab at its outer top corner, which was held by an experimenter's gloved hand (the experimenter stood behind a window filled with a fringed curtain in the back wall of the apparatus and held the left screen's tab in her right hand and the right screen's tab in her left hand.) Each tab could be used to lower the screen to the apparatus floor, in the manner of a drawbridge. The area between the two screens was either closed by a cardboard insert (closed condition) or open (open condition). The infants in the *closed* condition (see Fig. 12.6) first saw a one- and a two-screen orientation event designed to introduce them to the motion of the screens.

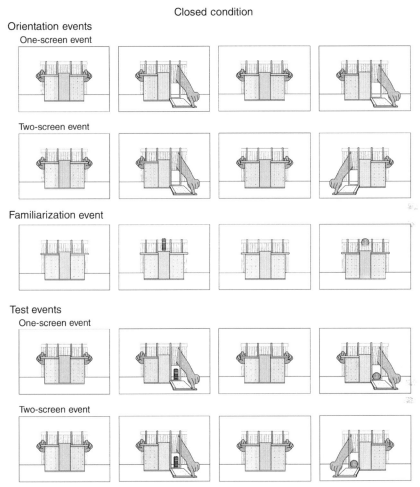

Fig. 12.6 Schematic of the orientation, familiarization, and test events used in the closed condition of Experiment 5 (Wu et al., in preparation).

In the two-screen event, the experimenter lowered the right screen to the apparatus floor (to reveal empty space behind it), and then raised it again; next, the experimenter performed the same actions on the left screen (again to reveal empty space). The one-screen event was identical except that the experimenter lowered and raised only the right screen. Next, as in the self-propelled condition of Experiment 4, the infants saw a familiarization event in which the column and ball rose (one at a time) above the center of the frame, tilted gently to the left and right twice, and then returned behind the frame. Finally, the infants saw two test events identical to the one- and two-screen orientation

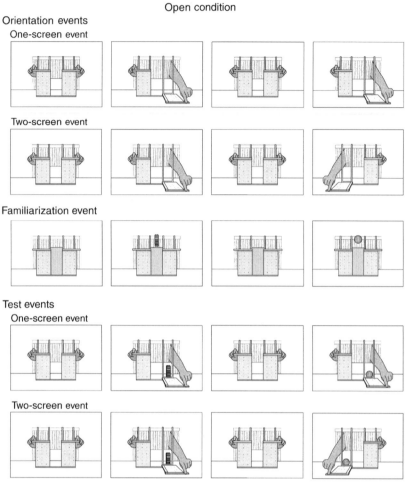

Fig. 12.7 Schematic of the orientation, familiarization, and test events used in the open condition of Experiment 5 (Wu et al., in preparation).

events except that the column and ball were now present. In the two-screen event, the column was revealed behind the right screen and the ball behind the left screen; in the one-screen event, the two objects were revealed behind the right screen, in alternation. The infants in the *open* condition (see Fig. 12.7) were tested using the same procedure except that the area between the two screens was open in the orientation and test events (it was closed in the familiarization event, when the column and ball rose above the frame.)

Although the one-screen test event was possible in the closed condition (the infants could infer that the column and ball exchanged locations when the two screens were raised), it was not possible in the open condition, where the area between the screens remained visible and empty, making it clear that the objects did not exchange locations.

As predicted, the infants in the open condition looked reliably longer at the one- than at the two-screen event, whereas those in the closed condition looked about equally, and equally short, at the events. Together, these results suggested that the infants (1) categorized the column and ball as self-propelled during the familiarization trial; (2) did *not* find the one-screen event surprising when the area between the screens was closed, because they could then infer that the objects exchanged locations out of sight; but (3) *did* find the one-screen event surprising when the area between the screens was open, because such an explanation was then not possible; the objects appeared to magically exchange locations, which constituted a continuity violation.

Together, the results of Experiments 3 to 5 suggest that infants aged 4 months and older believe that self-propelled objects can use their internal energy to move to new locations when out of view. However, these invisible displacements are expected to be constrained by the continuity principle: similar to inert objects, self-propelled objects cannot magically disappear, nor can they magically move from one location to another without traveling the distance between them.

12.2.2.2 Links to other findings: are humans subject to the continuity principle?

Kuhlmeier et al. (2004) reported data (collected with a design adapted from Spelke, Kestenbaum et al., 1995) that might be taken to challenge the notion that infants expect *all* objects, whether inert or self-propelled, to move continuously through time and space, in accordance with the continuity principle. In one condition (box condition), 5-month-old infants were habituated to a videotaped event in which a self-propelled box slid back and forth across a room, briefly passing behind two door-sized screens placed some distance apart; the box never appeared in the gap between the screens. During test, the screens were removed, and the infants saw two test events: in one, a single box moved back and forth across the room (one-object event); in the other, two boxes moved back and forth, in a manner consistent with the habituation event (two-object event). Infants in another condition (human condition) saw similar habituation and test events, except that the self-propelled box was replaced with a woman walking across the room; the woman and her twin, in identical clothes, were involved in the two-object event. The results of these and other conditions suggested that infants in the box condition viewed the one-object event as surprising, whereas infants in the human condition viewed neither event as surprising. The authors concluded that at 5 months of age infants apply the continuity principle to nonhuman but not to human self-propelled objects, suggesting perhaps that they do not view humans as physical entities.

However, the results of Experiments 3 to 5 suggest another interpretation of the human condition data (for other interpretations, see Rakison & Cicchino, 2004). If young infants can posit invisible displacements to make sense of apparent continuity violations, then the habituation event in the human condition was open to two different explanations (which could have been generated by the same or by different infants). One explanation, as in the box condition, was that two different women were involved in the event. The other explanation was that a single woman left and reentered the room through hidden doorways in the wall behind the screens. After all, infants have a great deal of experience watching adults (although not self-propelled boxes) leave and enter rooms through doors that are open or ajar; the fact that the screens were door-sized may have helped remind the infants of these familiar experiences, leading them to posit invisible displacements. In this view, the infants in the human condition thus looked equally at the one- and two-object test events because both events were consistent with possible explanations for the habituation event.

12.2.3 Can a self-propelled object move or change its parts when out of sight?

Research on object segregation indicates that young infants view contiguous surfaces that move together as connected surfaces that belong to a single object; furthermore, this conclusion holds whether the surfaces are similar or dissimilar in shape, pattern, and color (e.g., Kestenbaum et al., 1987; Needham, 1998, 1999, 2000; Spelke, 1988). This research suggested that young infants who saw a novel box with distinct parts move across an apparatus floor would perceive the box and its parts as a single, connected object.

Our next experiments (Wu & Baillargeon, 2006, 2007a, 2008) examined infants' responses to events in which one or more parts of a box moved while the box was briefly hidden. In designing these experiments, we considered three different ways in which parts might move; for ease of communication, we refer to these as changes in location, position, and orientation. A *location* change is one in which a part moves from one side of the object to another; a *position* change is one in which a part remains on the same side of the object, but moves up or down; and finally, an *orientation* change is one in which a part preserves its location and position on the object but changes its orientation.

Evidence that infants might discriminate between at least some of these changes came from research by Slaughter and Heron (2004). In one experiment, 12-month-old infants were habituated to pictures of a novel three-dimensional 'geobody', which consisted of a large cylindrical red 'torso' with two cylindrical blue 'legs', two cylindrical green 'arms', and a square yellow 'head'. Across pictures, the geobody was shown with its arms and legs in different orientations. During the test, the infants were shown scrambled geobodies with their arms and legs either disconnected or moved to different locations (e.g., one arm and one leg were now attached to a different side of the torso, or both arms were attached to the head.) The infants dishabituated to these scrambled geobodies, suggesting that they (1) represented which parts were located where on the habituation geobody and (2) discriminated between the orientation changes shown in habituation and the location changes shown in test.

In the following, we describe our experiments on orientation, position, and location changes, and conclude with an experiment on appearance changes.

12.2.3.1 Orientation changes

In Experiment 6 (Wu & Baillargeon, 2006), 5.5-month-old infants were shown an inert or a self-propelled box with two salient parts; during test, while the box was briefly hidden, the orientation of its parts was changed. Our experiments examined whether the infants would view this change as surprising when the box was inert but not when it was self-propelled, because in the latter case they could infer that the box had used its internal energy to reorient its parts (e.g., in the same way that a man might change the orientation of his arms while out of sight).

The infants were assigned to an inert or a self-propelled condition (see Fig. 12.8) and were shown events involving a blue box with two large rectangular flaps. The flaps were attached to the upper left and right edges of the box and rested against each other at the top, above the box (similar to two large 'ears' touching each other at the top). The interior and exterior surfaces of the flaps and the top of the box were red and decorated with bright yellow dots. The familiarization trials were modeled after those in Experiment 3 and used the same apparatus.

In the *self-propelled* condition, the wall partition at the right of the apparatus was in its far position; the box emerged to the right of the large screen, traveled to the right a short distance, and then reversed direction on its own to return behind the screen. In the *inert* condition, the wall partition was in its near position; the box moved as before but now hit the wall partition before reversing direction and returning behind the screen. Following the familiarization trials, all of the infants received a single test trial in which they saw either a *no-change* or a *change* event. At the start of each event, the box stood behind

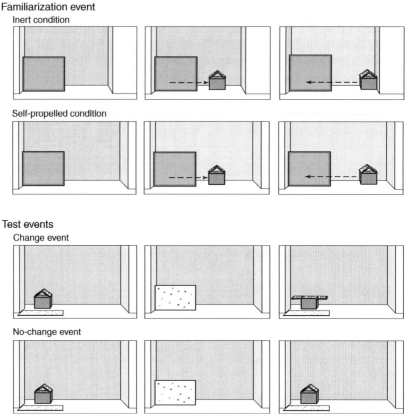

Fig. 12.8 Schematic of the familiarization and test events used in Experiment 6 (Wu & Baillargeon, 2006).

a small screen laying flat on the apparatus floor, near the left wall. The screen was rotated upward to hide the box and, after a pause, was rotated back down again. When revealed, the box was either the same as before (no-change event) or was altered: its flaps had moved apart and now extended on either side of its top surface, parallel to the apparatus floor (change event). The screen was then rotated again, to begin a new event cycle; the box always had its flaps together in the no-change event and had its flaps alternately together and apart in the change event.

In the inert condition, the infants who saw the change event looked reliably longer than those who saw the no-change event; in the self-propelled condition, in contrast, the infants tended to look equally at the two events. Together, these results suggested that 5.5-month-old infants realize that a self-propelled object can use its internal energy not only to control its motion through space, as we saw in previous sections, but also to alter the orientation of its parts. Additional support for this interpretation came from another experiment (Experiment 7) that used a new blue box with a single, jagged flap extending from its upper left edge, parallel to the apparatus floor (see Fig. 12.9). The lower portion of the flap was red and was decorated with yellow dots; its upper portion consisted of three yellow, triangular projections. In the change test event, the flap was flipped upward to hang above the box (similar to a large 'tail' extending either behind or above the back of an animal). The results of Experiment 7 were identical to those of Experiment 6, and confirmed that young infants are surprised when the parts of an inert but not a self-propelled object spontaneously change orientation.

12.2.3.2 Position changes

Our next experiment (Wu & Baillargeon, 2008) examined infants' responses to events in which the parts of a box changed position, rather than orientation, when the box was briefly hidden. As mentioned earlier, by a position change we mean a change in the place where a part is connected to the box: the part remains on the same side of the box but moves up or down. We speculated that, as with orientation changes, young infants might view position changes as surprising for an inert but not a self-propelled box. To young infants with a limited understanding of how connections are made or of how far they can stretch or shift in any direction, it might seem possible for a self-propelled box to use its internal energy to move its parts up or down (e.g., perhaps in the same way that a man can move his shoulders, or his eyebrows, up or down.)

Experiment 8 used the same design as Experiments 6 and 7, with a new red box that was decorated with two blue stripes at the bottom and that sported a yellow rectangular flap on either side, parallel to the apparatus floor (see Fig. 12.9). For half the infants, the flaps were even with the top of the box in the familiarization and the no-change test events and were positioned lower (just above the blue stripes) in the change test event; for the other infants, the reverse was true. Results were identical to those in Experiments 6 and 7: in the inert condition, the infants who saw the change event looked reliably longer than those who saw the no-change event, whereas in the self-propelled condition, the infants looked about equally at the two events. The infants were thus surprised when the inert but not the self-propelled box changed the position of its flaps up or down.

12.2.3.3 Location changes

As was mentioned earlier, location changes refer to changes in which a part moves to a different side of a box. We speculated that such changes, unlike

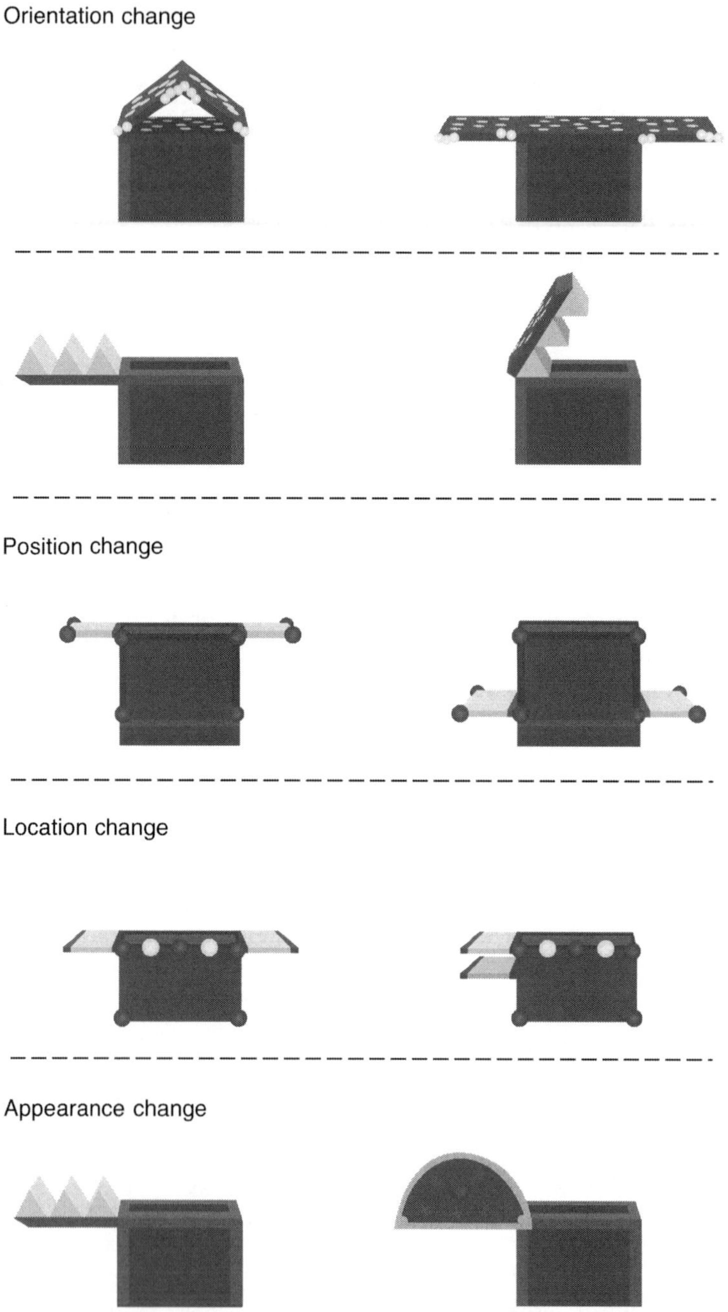

Orientation change

Position change

Location change

Appearance change

Fig. 12.9 Boxes used to investigate infants' sensitivity to an orientation change (Experiments 6 and 7; Wu & Baillargeon, 2006), a position change (Experiment 8; Wu & Baillargeon, 2008), a location change (Experiment 9; Wu & Baillargeon, 2008), and an appearance change (Experiment 10; Wu & Baillargeon, 2007a).

orientation and position changes, might seem surprising to infants even for a self-propelled box. If infants interpreted a location change as indicating that a part had become disconnected from its initial location on the box and had become reconnected at the new location, then such a change would violate two corollaries of the principle of persistence: the *cohesion* and *boundedness* principles (e.g., Spelke, 1990, 1994; Spelke, Phillips et al., 1995). These principles state that objects are connected and bounded entities: they cannot spontaneously fragment as they move (cohesion) or fuse with other objects (boundedness). Numerous experiments have shown that infants aged 3 months and older detect violations when objects spontaneously break apart or become connected to other objects (e.g., Kestenbaum et al., 1987; Needham, 1999, 2000; Needham & Baillargeon, 1997; Spelke, 1988; Spelke et al., 1993).

In Experiment 9 (Wu & Baillargeon, 2008), 5.5-month-old infants were tested with the same procedure as in the self-propelled condition of Experiments 6 to 8, using a new red box with two rectangular yellow flaps (see Fig. 12.9). For half the infants, the flaps were on opposite sides of the box, flush with its top, in the familiarization and the no-change test events, and the right flap moved to a new location a short distance below the left one in the change test event; for the other infants, the reverse was true. Results indicated that the infants who saw the change event looked reliably longer than those who saw the no-change event. For the first time in this series of experiments, infants viewed the change introduced—a part moving from one side of a self-propelled box to the other—as unexpected, as though they realized that no application of internal energy could result in a part becoming disconnected from one location and reconnected at another location.

The results of Experiment 9 extend the results of Slaughter and Heron (2004) mentioned earlier in several ways. First, they suggest that, when shown a simple self-propelled object with two parts, infants as young as 5.5 months of age detect when one of the parts changes location. Second, the results indicate that infants' ability to detect location changes does not depend on the parts being symmetrically distributed; similar results were obtained in Experiment 9 whether the two parts were initially on the same side or on opposite sides of the box. Finally, the results suggest that infants not only detect location changes but view them as unexpected. Infants in Experiments 6 to 9 looked reliably longer at the change event when the parts of the self-propelled box changed location behind the screen, but not when they simply changed orientation or position. These results suggest that the infants realized that no application of energy could allow a self-propelled object to disconnect a part (a cohesion violation) and reconnect it elsewhere (a boundedness violation).

12.2.3.4 Appearance changes

Experiment 10 (Wu & Baillargeon, 2007a) examined 5.5-month-old infants' responses to events in which a part of a self-propelled box preserved its orientation, position, and location but changed its appearance (i.e., its size, shape, pattern, and color) while the box was occluded by a screen. We expected that infants would find such a change surprising. According to the principle of persistence (e.g., Baillargeon, 2008; Baillargeon et al., 2009), an object, whether inert or self-propelled, cannot magically change its appearance: apples cannot change into bananas, and frogs (no matter what the fairy tales say) cannot change into princes. Whether infants detect an appearance change in an event depends on (1) whether they have identified the relevant variables (e.g., size, shape, pattern, and color) for the event category involved, and hence (2) whether they include information about these variables in their physical representation of the event (e.g., Wang & Baillargeon, 2006, 2008). Prior research indicates that, by 4.5 months of age, infants have identified height, width, and shape as occlusion variables (e.g., Baillargeon & DeVos, 1991; Wang & Baillargeon, 2006; Wang et al., 2004; Wilcox, 1999) and thus detect appearance changes involving these variables in occlusion events. For example, Wilcox (1999; Wilcox & Baillargeon, 1998a, 1998b) found that infants aged 4.5 months and older are surprised if a self-propelled box changes into a self-propelled ball when passing behind a screen too narrow to hide both objects at once. Experiment 10 built on these results and asked whether infants would realize that not even a *part* of a self-propelled box could change its appearance while the box was briefly occluded.

Infants were tested with the same procedure as in the self-propelled condition of Experiments 6 to 8. For half the infants, the box used in the familiarization and the no-change test events was the blue box with the yellow jagged flap from Experiment 7, and the box used in the change test event was a similar blue box with a new flap consisting of a red half circle outlined with light green tape and decorated with dark green stars (see Fig. 12.9); for the other infants, the reverse was true. In either case, infants who saw the change event looked reliably longer than those who saw the no-change event, indicating that by 5.5 months of age infants recognize that a self-propelled box cannot change the appearance of a part. (Because at 5.5 months infants have identified size and shape but not yet pattern and color as occlusion variables, we suspect that the infants in Experiment 10 responded primarily to the impossible change in the size and shape of the box's flap; Wilcox, 1999.)

12.2.3.5 Persistence revisited

One important theme to emerge from the research reported in this and the preceding sections is that even young infants recognize that the principle of persistence applies somewhat differently to self-propelled and inert objects. Infants recognize that, when behind a screen, a self-propelled object may use its internal energy to move to an alternative hiding place (Experiments 3 to 5), to change a part's orientation (Experiments 6 and 7), or to change a part's position (Experiment 8). At the same time, infants view as impossible other changes that cannot be explained by an application of internal energy, such as disappearing into thin air (Experiment 3), changing a part's location (Experiment 9), or changing a part's appearance (Experiment 10). For inert objects, in contrast, infants construe *all* of the changes listed here as impossible.

These findings suggest two conclusions. First, when it comes to distinguishing between possible and impossible changes, what the principle of persistence essentially states is that objects can undergo no *uncaused* change. Because a self-propelled object can use its internal energy to change the orientation of its parts, such a change is deemed possible; because an inert object cannot spontaneously reorient its parts, such a change is deemed impossible and is flagged as a persistence violation. Second, infants adopt a *conservative* stance in judging what changes might be caused or uncaused in the world. If the handle of a teacup changes orientation behind a screen, infants do not assume that some causal process unknown to them must have effected the change; only when they possess some hint about the causal process that could have produced a change (e.g., an application of internal energy) do they view the change as possible. Of course, because of their limited physical knowledge, infants are very often wrong about the nature, operation, or details of these causal processes; we return to this point in a later section.

12.2.3.6 Links to further results: expecting self-propelled objects to move

In all of the experiments discussed so far, infants aged 4–6 months categorized the novel object they were shown as self-propelled based on what might be called *behavioral* information: the object either initiated its motion in plain view or reversed direction on its own. Prior research suggests that infants aged 7 months and older can also use *featural* information to determine which objects are likely to be self-propelled and which are not (e.g., Golinkoff et al., 1984; Johnson et al., 1998; Markson & Spelke, 2006; Poulin-Dubois et al., 1996; Poulin-Dubois & Shultz, 1988, 1990; Rakison, 2003; Rakison & Poulin-Dubois, 2001, 2002; Spelke, Phillips et al., 1995; Traeuble et al., 2006; Woodward et al., 1993). Indeed, we have already discussed evidence to this effect: recall that the 7-month-old infants tested by Woodward and her colleagues (Spelke, Phillips et al., 1995; Woodward et al., 1993) viewed the man and woman who walked back and forth behind the occluder as self-propelled. Additional evidence comes from research by Traeuble et al. (2006). In one experiment, 7-month-old infants first received a trial in which they saw two objects standing apart and motionless on an apparatus floor: a ball and a novel toy animal with a face and a furry body. In the next trial, the ball and animal were intertwined and moved together in a self-propelled manner. In the final trial, the two objects again stood apart and motionless. The infants looked reliably longer at the animal on the last than on the first trial, suggesting that they (1) believed that the animal was more likely than the ball to be self-propelled, (2) assumed that the animal was the cause of the two objects' joint motions, and (3) anticipated that the animal might move again.

These results give rise to an interesting question concerning some of the experiments discussed in previous sections. To see why, consider the infants in Experiments 6 to 8 who saw the no-change event in the test trial. Given the results of Traeuble et al. (2006), we might ask whether the infants who believed the box was self-propelled tended to look longer than those who believed the box was inert, because they expected the box to move again. Of course, such a prediction might not hold in our experiments, for two reasons: first, the screen in front of the box was continually raised and lowered throughout the trial, so that the infants might have been preoccupied with other aspects of the event; second, the effect observed by Traeuble et al. might be found primarily in situations where infants are presented with two objects standing side by side, one inert and one self-propelled. Nevertheless, to get at this question, we pooled the data from Experiments 6 to 8 and compared the responses to the no-change test event of the infants in the inert and self-propelled conditions. No reliable difference was found, suggesting that our experiments did not create an appropriate context to observe the effect reported by Traeuble and her colleagues.

Markson and Spelke (2006) reported findings that might at first appear consistent with those of Traeuble et al. (2006) but inconsistent with our own. In a series of experiments, 7-month-old infants saw two familiarization events in which they were presented with two different windup toys from the same category (e.g., two animals, two vehicles, or two amorphous shapes consisting of the toy animals covered with various materials). In one event, an experimenter's hand held one object (e.g., a bear) and moved it across the apparatus (inert event). In the other event, the hand held a different object (e.g., a rabbit) and released it; the object then moved across the apparatus until it was stopped by the hand (self-propelled event). During the test trials, the two objects stood apart and motionless on the apparatus floor, and the infants' looking time at each object was measured. Analysis of the test data revealed two findings. First, as in Traeuble et al., the infants looked reliably longer at the self-propelled object, as though anticipating that it would move again. Second, this last result was obtained when the two objects were animals but not when they were vehicles or shapes. Markson and Spelke concluded that the infants could 'reliably learn the property of self-propelled motion only for animate objects' (p. 67).

This conclusion is surprising in light of the results of the many experiments reported in this chapter where infants readily learned whether the objects shown in the familiarization trials were self-propelled or not. However, Shutts et al. (Chapter 8) recently suggested that extraneous factors might have contributed to the different results Markson and Spelke (2006) obtained with their animals, vehicles, and shapes. Specifically, when released by the hand, the animals moved in a way that clearly suggested they were self-propelled, because they had various parts that moved independently (e.g., a mouth that opened or a head that bobbed up and down); in contrast, the vehicles and shapes moved rigidly across the apparatus, leaving open the possibility that the hand had set them in motion when releasing them. According to this interpretation, the infants failed to learn which object in each pair of vehicles or shapes was self-propelled simply because they received no clear evidence that either object was in fact self-propelled. To test their interpretation, Shutts et al. conducted experiments with vehicles and other objects that gave unambiguous evidence of self-propulsion (e.g., a truck that had independently moving parts and periodically changed direction, a shape that flipped over backwards several times). As predicted, and consistent with the findings reported in this chapter, infants now readily learned which object was inert and which was self-propelled in all pairs of objects.

12.2.4 Can a self-propelled object remain stationary when hit?

The evidence reviewed in the previous sections suggests that young infants believe that a self-propelled object can use its internal energy to spontaneously *move* itself or its parts, either in or out of view. In this section and the next, we examine whether young infants also believe that a self-propelled object can use its internal energy to *resist* moving.

The point of departure for Experiment 11 (Luo et al., in press) came from investigations of infants' responses to collision events. Prior research with *inert* objects (e.g., Baillargeon, 1995; Kotovsky & Baillargeon, 1998, 2000; Wang et al., 2003) suggests that, when a first object hits a second object, infants as young as 2.5 months of age expect the second object to be displaced and are surprised if it is not. By 5.5 to 6.5 months, infants take into account the size (or weight) of the first object, and they expect the second object to be displaced farther when hit by a larger (or heavier) as opposed to a smaller (or lighter) object. Finally, by about 9 months, infants begin to take into account the size (weight) of the second object, and now they expect a very large (heavy) object to remain stationary when hit by a small (light) object. Prior research with *self-propelled* objects (e.g., Leslie, 1982, 1984b; Leslie & Keeble, 1987; Oakes, 1994), however, paints a different picture: in particular, it suggests that young infants may *not* expect a self-propelled object to be displaced when hit.

In a seminal experiment, Leslie and Keeble (1987) habituated 6-month-old infants to one of two filmed events; both events involved two self-propelled objects, a red and a green brick.[3] In one event (launching event), one brick began to move toward the other brick and collided with it; the second brick then immediately moved off. In the other event (delayed-reaction event), the second brick moved off only after a 0.5-s delay. During test, the infants watched the same event they had seen during habituation, now shown in reverse. The infants habituated to the launching event showed greater recovery of attention than those habituated to the delayed-reaction event, suggesting that the infants attributed a causal role to the first brick only in the launching event: they assumed that the first brick caused the second one to move in the habituation trials, and they looked reliably longer when the bricks' causal roles were reversed in the test trials.

From the present perspective, the results of the habituation trials were just as interesting: the infants tended to look equally whether they were shown the launching or the delayed-reaction event (see also Leslie, 1982, 1984b; Oakes, 1994). This finding suggested that the infants were not surprised when the second brick did not move off *immediately* when hit. As such, this finding gave rise to the possibility that infants also might not be surprised if a self-propelled object did not move off *at all* when hit. Experiment 11 examined this possibility: it asked whether 6-month-old infants would be surprised when an inert but not a self-propelled object remained stationary when hit.

The infants were assigned to an inert or a self-propelled condition and received familiarization trials identical to those in Experiment 3 (see Fig. 12.10): a box emerged from behind a large screen, traveled to the right, and then reversed direction either spontaneously (self-propelled condition) or after hitting a wall partition at the right end of the apparatus (inert condition). Next, all of the infants saw the same test event, on two successive trials: an experimenter's gloved hand hit the box, which remained stationary.

---

[3] Because the first brick always initiated its motion in plain view, and the two bricks differed only in color, we assume that the infants viewed not only the first brick but both bricks as self-propelled.

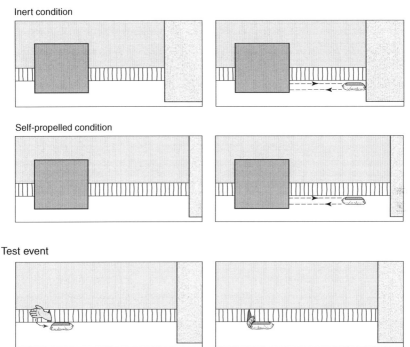

Fig. 12.10 Schematic of the familiarization and test events used in Experiment 11 (Luo et al., in press).

In line with the research summarized in the preceding paragraphs, we predicted that the infants in the inert condition would expect the box to move when hit and would be surprised that it did not; in contrast, the infants in the self-propelled condition would *not* be surprised that the box did not move when hit, because they could infer that the box was using its internal energy to counteract the hand's impact. We thus predicted that the infants in the inert condition would look reliably longer during the test trials than would the infants in the self-propelled condition.

Results indicated that, although the infants in both conditions looked equally during the familiarization trials, infants in the inert condition looked reliably longer than those in the self-propelled condition during the test trials. Similar results were obtained in another experiment in which the gloved hand pulled on a strap attached to the left side of the box; as in Experiment 11, the box remained stationary when acted upon.

Together, these results suggest that, by 6 months of age, infants assume that a self-propelled object can use its internal energy to resist or counteract efforts to move it. As such, these results are consistent with the evidence reviewed earlier that infants are not surprised when a self-propelled object does not move immediately upon being hit (e.g., Leslie, 1982, 1984b; Leslie & Keeble, 1987; Oakes, 1994). When a self-propelled object is hit, infants apparently assume that (1) it can elect to go along with the efforts to move it (recall that the infants tested by Leslie and Keeble (1987) assumed that the first brick caused the second one to move; and the infants tested by Woodward et al. (1993) may also have assumed that the first human caused the other human to move in the contact test event); or (2) it can elect to resist these efforts, in which case it may choose to move after a delay, or not at all.

12.2.5 Can a self-propelled object remain stable in midair?

If young infants believe that a self-propelled object can use its internal energy to *resist moving* when hit, do they also believe that it can also use its internal energy to *resist falling* when released in midair? Experiment 12 (Luo et al., in press) was designed to examine this question.

The point of departure for this experiment came from investigations of infants' responses to support events. We have suggested (Li et al., in preparation; Yuan & Baillargeon, 2008, 2009) that infants are born with the intuitive understanding that each object has a *weight*, which causes it to fall; furthermore, the heavier the object, the greater its tendency to fall. As infants learn about support, they learn about the ways and means by which an object's tendency to fall can be checked: either (1) by the application of a *force* (as when a person's hand holds an object; the heavier the object, the greater the force needed to hold it in place) or (2) by the introduction of a *surface* in the path of the object, blocking its fall.

Consistent with this analysis, prior research with *inert* objects (e.g., Baillargeon, 1995; Baillargeon et al., 1992; Hespos & Baillargeon, 2008; Li et al., 2006, under review; Needham & Baillargeon, 1993; Yuan & Baillargeon, 2008, in preparation) suggests that, by 2.5–3.5 months of age, infants (1) expect an object to fall when released in midair, (2) expect an object to be stable when held by a hand, and (3) have no clear expectation as to whether an object should be stable or fall when released in contact with another object. By about 4.5–5.5 months of age, infants identify a first support variable, *type-of-contact*: they now expect an object to be stable when released on top of, but not against the side of, another object. By about 6.5 months of age, infants identify another support variable, *proportion-of-contact*: they now expect an object to be stable when released on another object only if half or more of the supported object's bottom surface rests on the supporting object.

In contrast to these findings, prior research with *self-propelled* objects (e.g., Leslie, 1984a) suggests that young infants may not expect a self-propelled object to fall when in midair. In one experiment, Leslie (1984a) habituated 7-month-old infants to one of several different filmed events. At the start of one event, a hand grasped a doll resting on a table; the hand lifted the doll and carried it off screen, exiting at the top left corner of the television screen. In another event, the hand was separated from the doll by a short gap. Other events were similar to the first two, except that the hand was replaced with a box. For present purposes, the key finding was that the infants looked about equally at all of the events during the habituation trials, suggesting that they were not surprised to see a self-propelled object move in midair.

This conclusion is consistent with findings from myriad experiments in the infancy literature—on object completion, object individuation, and physical reasoning, in particular—that have presented infants, for reasons of methodological convenience, with events involving self-propelled objects moving in midair (e.g., Bremner et al., 2005; S. P. Johnson, 2004; S. P. Johnson et al., 2003; Kellman & Spelke, 1983; Kochukhova & Gredebäck, 2007; Slater et al., 1996; Spelke, Kestenbaum et al., 1995; see also Experiments 4 and 5). Had the infants in these experiments been surprised or confused to see the objects move in this manner, the results of the experiments would have been consistently negative; the fact that they were not suggests that young infants believe that self-propelled objects require no external support to move in midair. Experiment 12 examined this issue more directly, and asked whether 6.5-month-old infants would expect an inert but not a self-propelled box to fall when released in midair.

The infants were assigned to an inert or a self-propelled condition and were given the same familiarization trials as in Experiment 11. Next, all of the infants saw the same test event, on two successive trials: to start, an experimenter's gloved hand held the box in midair; after a pause, the hand released the box, which remained stationary (see Fig. 12.11).

In line with the research summarized in the preceding, we predicted that infants in the inert condition would expect the box to fall when released and would be surprised that it did not; in contrast, infants in the self-propelled condition would *not* be surprised that the box did not fall, because they could infer that the box was using its internal energy to counteract its own weight and thus in effect to resist falling. We thus predicted that infants in the inert condition would look reliably longer during the test trials than would infants in the self-propelled condition.

Results indicated that, although the infants in the two conditions looked equally during the familiarization trials, infants in the inert condition looked

Familiarization event

Inert condition

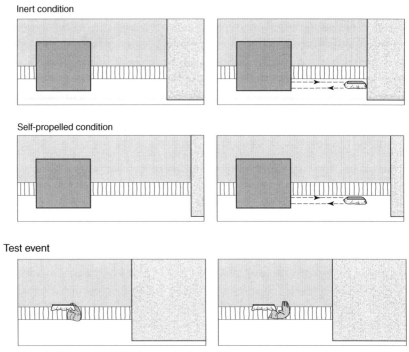

Self-propelled condition

Test event

Fig. 12.11 Schematic of the familiarization and test events used in Experiment 12 (Luo et al., in press).

reliably longer than those in the self-propelled condition during the test trials. Similar results were obtained in another experiment in which the box, instead of being released in midair, was released with only 1/6 or 1/3 of its bottom surface supported on a platform; as before, the box remained stationary when released. Infants in the inert condition realized that the box was released without adequate support and should fall (recall that infants this age have already identified proportion-of-contact as a support variable); in contrast, infants in the self-propelled condition recognized that the box could remain stable because it could use its internal energy to keep itself in place.

12.2.5.1 Tests with younger infants

We have suggested that infants are born with an intuitive understanding that each object has a weight which causes it to fall unless this weight is counteracted (1) by a force, which may be either external to the object (e.g., a hand holding a cup) or internal to the object (e.g., a hummingbird hovering near a flower), or (2) by a surface blocking the object's path. If infants are born with

Inert condition

Test events

Unsupported event

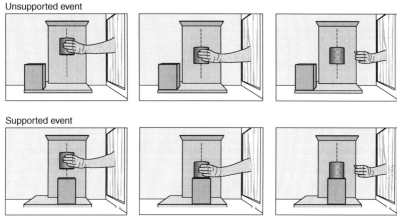

Supported event

Self-propelled condition

Test events

Unsupported event

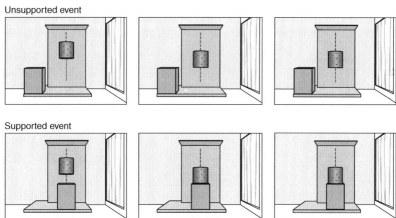

Supported event

Fig. 12.12 Schematic of the test events used in Experiment 13 (Yuan & Baillargeon, 2008).

this causal knowledge, they should be able to demonstrate it at a very early age. Experiment 13 (Yuan & Baillargeon, 2008) examined this question, with infants aged 2.5–3 months.

The infants were assigned to an inert or a self-propelled condition (see Fig. 12.12) and saw a supported and an unsupported test event.

In the supported event shown in the *inert* condition, an experimenter's gloved hand held a red cylinder in midair, lowered it onto a platform, released it for a few seconds, and then lifted it back to its starting position. In the unsupported event, the hand performed the same actions but the platform now stood to the side so that the cylinder was released and remained stable in midair. The infants in the *self-propelled* condition saw similar test events except that the hand was absent and the cylinder moved by itself.

As predicted, the infants in the inert condition looked reliably longer at the unsupported than at the supported event (this result was replicated in another experiment conducted with a slightly different procedure); in contrast, the infants in the self-propelled condition looked about equally at the two test events. These results suggested that, by 2.5–3 months of age, infants already hold different expectations about the support of novel inert and self-propelled objects.

However, an alternative interpretation of the results of the self-propelled condition was that the infants were merely confused by the self-propelled cylinder and held no expectation about its behavior. Experiment 14 (Yuan & Baillargeon, 2008) was designed to address this alternative interpretation and also to confirm the results of the self-propelled condition in Experiment 13 (see Fig. 12.13).

The infants first received a familiarization trial. To start, the infants faced a small table with a scalloped front edge that hid its top surface. An experimenter's gloved hands grasped the two right legs of the table and rotated it forward so that the infants could inspect its top surface. For half the infants, this surface was closed (closed condition); for the other infants, the surface had a large opening in its center (open condition). Next, all of the infants saw the same test event, on two successive trials. At the start of the event, the table stood upright, and a self-propelled cylinder stood stationary in midair above it. The cylinder then moved down, passing through the table until it was visible beneath it, and then returned to its starting position.

Although the infants in the two conditions tended to look equally during the familiarization trial, the infants in the closed condition looked reliably longer during the test trials than did the infants in the open condition. These results suggested two conclusions. First, consistent with the solidity principle discussed in Experiment 2, the infants realized that the self-propelled cylinder could not pass through the closed table; this result in turn suggested that the infants were not, in fact, confused by the cylinder and unable to reason about its displacements. Second, consistent with the results of Experiment 13, the infants were not surprised to see the cylinder travel up and down through the open table, presumably because they inferred that the cylinder was using its internal energy to initiate its motion and counteract its weight so as to resist falling.

Familiarization event

Closed condition

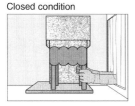 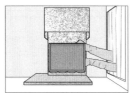

Open condition

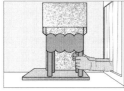 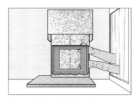

Test event

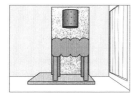 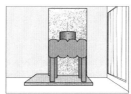 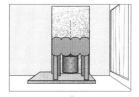

Fig. 12.13 Schematic of the familiarization and test events used in Experiment 14 (Yuan & Baillargeon, 2008).

12.2.5.2 Kinds of explanations

To adults, the results of Experiments 12 to 14 (see also Experiments 4 and 5) may appear particularly surprising: why would infants believe that a novel self-propelled object can move through the air or can remain stable in midair? However, a moment's reflection is sufficient to realize that from this perspective we are not so very different from infants. If we were watching an unfamiliar insect crawl on a table and saw it suddenly fly to a plant and hover near it, we would not be astounded: if the insect flies and hovers, then it follows that it *can* fly and hover, and we would take these actions to be part of its behavioral repertoire.

Of course, as adults we know a great deal more than infants do about what physical structures and processes might allow an insect—or any other self-propelled object, such as a bird, butterfly, helicopter, or plane—to move through the air. Infants' reasoning in our experiments is no doubt highly abstract and divorced of most mechanistic details: although infants may believe that a self-propelled object can use its internal energy to move through the air, they can have no conception at all of the particular mechanism that allows it to do so.

This notion is strongly reminiscent of Keil's (1995) claim that our concepts are 'embedded in theory-like structures which owe their origins to a small but diverse set of fundamental modes of construal ... one key part of these early modes of construal may be more general expectations ... [that] exist before any specific explanation or detailed intuitive theory, and thus indicate kinds of explanations rather than any particular explanation' (pp. 260–261). In line with Keil's claim, we would argue that the infants in our experiments are offering *kinds of explanations*, rather than specific or particular explanations, for the actions of our self-propelled objects.

12.2.6 Can a self-propelled object act on an inert object?

Do young infants believe that a novel self-propelled object can use its internal energy to control not only its own motion, but also that of other objects? In particular, do they believe that a novel self-propelled object can set an inert object into motion, or prevent it from falling, through the application of force? We discuss each question in turn.

12.2.6.1 Setting an inert object into motion

If infants believe that (1) an inert object cannot initiate its own motion and (2) a self-propelled object can use its internal energy to exert a force on an inert object and set it in motion, then the following prediction should hold: if infants see an inert object emerge from behind an occluder and are asked which of two stationary targets, one inert and one self-propelled, could have set it in motion, they should select the self-propelled target. Of course, infants realize that an inert object, once in motion, can cause another inert object to move (e.g., Kotovsky & Baillargeon, 1998, 2000; Wang et al., 2003; Woodward et al., 1993). However, when confronted with two stationary targets, as in the situation described above, infants should correctly infer that only the self-propelled target could have initiated its own motion out of view and acted on the inert object to set it in motion.

A number of researchers have recently examined infants' ability to draw inferences about the likely cause of an inert object's motion (e.g., Kosugi et al., 2003; Saxe et al., 2005, 2007). For example, in an experiment by Saxe et al. (2007), 7-month-old infants saw two boxes standing left and right of midline on an apparatus floor; each box had no top and no back. During the habituation event, a beanbag was thrown out of one of the boxes (right box for half of the infants, left box for the others) and landed on the apparatus floor between the boxes. Next, the infants saw two test events similar to the habituation event except that, after the beanbag came to rest on the apparatus floor, the fronts of the boxes were lowered. In the same-side event, the infants saw a stationary human hand in the box from which the beanbag had been thrown (the hand emerged from a curtain at the back of the apparatus), and a block in the other box. In the different-side event, the positions of the hand and block were reversed. The infants looked reliably longer at the different- than at the same-side event, suggesting that they (1) categorized the hand as a self-propelled object (they no doubt recognized it as a human body part) and the beanbag and block as inert objects (they had no evidence to the contrary); (2) understood that the beanbag could not initiate its own motion; and (3) realized that the hand could have set the beanbag into motion, but the block could not.

The research reported in this chapter suggests that infants should look equally at the different- and same-side events if they saw the block move by itself prior to the test trials so that they categorized it as self-propelled. Evidence for this suggestion comes from another experiment conducted by Saxe et al. (2007) with 9.5-month-old infants. Prior to the experiment, the infants were given evidence that a small furry puppet was self-propelled: it jumped slowly across the apparatus floor (it was controlled by invisible threads). At the start of each test event, two screens stood on the apparatus floor on either side of midline. The screens were lowered to reveal two stationary objects: the puppet on one side and a toy train on the other. Next, the screens were raised, and a beanbag was thrown from behind one of the screens to land on the apparatus floor. The infants looked reliably longer when the beanbag emerged from the screen with the train than from the screen with the puppet, suggesting that they judged that the puppet could have set the beanbag in motion, but the train could not. Because the puppet had no arms and was about the same size as the beanbag, the infants' responses seemed to reflect an abstract inference that the puppet could have used its internal energy to act on the beanbag rather than a specific belief in the puppet's ability to throw or kick objects. This conclusion is consistent with our claim in the last section that infants are producing abstract kinds of explanations, divorced of all mechanistic details, for the actions of self-propelled objects (Keil, 1995).

12.2.6.2 Preventing an inert object from falling

We saw earlier that infants expect an inert object to fall unless a surface blocks its path or an external force counteracts its weight (e.g., Baillargeon, 1995; Li et al., under review; Needham & Baillargeon, 1993; Yuan & Baillargeon, 2008). This research gave rise to the following question: would infants believe that a novel self-propelled object could use its internal energy to exert a force on an inert object and prevent it from falling (e.g., in the same manner that a hand might hold a cup in midair)? To address this question, we conducted experiments with 4.5- to 5.5-month-old infants (Li et al., 2009a).

Baseline condition

Test events
Unsupported event

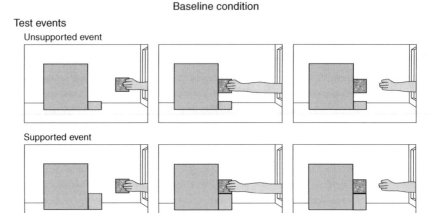

Supported event

Fig. 12.14 Schematic of the test events used in the baseline condition of Li et al. (2006).

Our research built on prior experiments that tested whether 4.5-month-old infants have identified the variable type-of-contact in support events and thus realize that an object can be stable when released on top of, but not against, another object (Li et al., 2006). In a baseline condition, infants were shown a supported and an unsupported test event (see Fig. 12.14).

At the start of each event, a large yellow platform stood on the apparatus floor, and a yellow box rested at the bottom of the platform's right wall. In both test events, an experimenter's gloved hand placed a small green box against the center of the platform's right wall and then released it. In the supported event, the yellow box was sufficiently tall that the green box rested on it; in the unsupported event, the yellow box was much shorter so that the green box rested well above it. The experiment thus asked whether the green box could be stable when resting against the right wall of the platform, with no surface immediately under it. Results indicated that 4.5-month-old female infants looked reliably longer at the unsupported than at the supported event, whereas male infants looked about equally at the two events. Additional results indicated that (1) male infants aged 5–5.5 months looked reliably longer at the unsupported than at the supported event and (2) female infants aged 3.5–4 months tended to look equally at the two events. These and control results (in which the hand never released the green box) suggested that the variable type-of-contact is identified a few weeks earlier in female than in male infants, most likely because of female infants' superior depth perception at this stage of development (e.g., Bauer et al., 1986; Gwiazda et al., 1989a, 1989b). (In order to learn that objects

Familiarization event

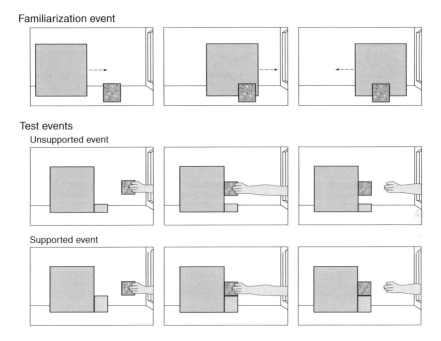

Test events
Unsupported event

Supported event

Fig. 12.15 Schematic of the familiarization and test events used in Experiment 15 (Li et al., in preparation).

typically fall when released against the side of a platform, infants have to be able to determine whether the objects are released against the platform or in midair next to it; infants would expect the objects to fall when released in midair.)

Experiment 15 (Li et al., in preparation) built on the preceding results and asked whether infants would respond differently to the supported and unsupported test events if first shown that the yellow platform was self-propelled (see Fig. 12.15). Would infants then conclude that the unsupported event was in fact possible because the platform could use its internal energy to 'hold' the green box in place? Participants were 4.5-month-old females and 5.5-month-old males. Prior to seeing the test events, they received two familiarization trials in which they saw the yellow platform move back and forth across the apparatus floor; the small green box stood stationary at the front of the apparatus (to make it clear to the infants that the green box was inert). Unlike infants in the baseline experiment, those in Experiment 15 tended to look equally at the supported and unsupported events, suggesting that they believed that the self-propelled platform could use its internal energy to 'hold' the green box against its midsection.

Familiarization event

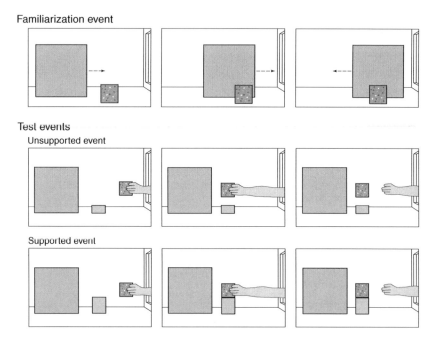

Test events
Unsupported event

Supported event

Fig. 12.16 Schematic of the familiarization and test events used in Experiment 16 (Li et al., in preparation).

Of course, another possible interpretation was that the infants were simply confused by the self-propelled platform and thus had no expectation about the outcomes of the subsequent events. To examine this alternative interpretation, in Experiment 16 (Li et al., in preparation; see Fig. 12.16), 4.5-month-old females and 5.5-month-old males saw the same familiarization and test events as in Experiment 15, with one exception: in the test events, the platform was now shifted 10 cm to the left. The tall and short yellow boxes stood in the same position as before, and the gloved hand performed the same actions as before. Thus, in the supported event, the hand placed the green box on the tall yellow box; in the unsupported event, the hand placed the green box in the same position above the short yellow box, so that the green box appeared to float or hover in midair above it. The infants now looked reliably longer at the unsupported than at the supported event, suggesting that (1) they were not confused by the self-propelled platform and (2) they believed that the self-propelled platform could use its internal energy to 'hold' the green box in place when the two were in direct contact, but not when they were separated by a short distance. Infants in Experiment 16 could generate no explanation for why the green box remained stable when released above the short yellow box, and they were thus surprised by this event.

The results of Experiments 15 and 16 are consistent with prior results from collision experiments with inert objects, which suggest that infants as young as 2.5 months of age realize that a force can only be applied through direct contact (e.g., Kotovsky & Baillargeon, in Baillargeon, 1995; Kotovsky & Baillargeon, 2000). These experiments showed that, although infants expect a wheeled toy bug to be displaced when hit by a rolling cylinder, they also expect the bug *not* to be displaced when a small obstacle prevents the cylinder from coming into direct contact with the bug. In the same manner, infants in Experiments 15 and 16 apparently understood that the platform could 'hold' the green box only through direct contact.

Readers might be puzzled by the results of Experiment 15. How could the infants believe that the yellow platform prevented the green box from falling by exerting a force upon it? The platform could not grip the green box, so how could it 'hold' it in place? How could the platform exert a force on the green box directly through its right wall? Here again, following Keil (1995), we believe that infants are generating only an abstract kind of explanation divorced from all specific mechanistic details: they assume that the platform is exerting a force on the green box to 'hold' it in place, but they have no idea at all of the mechanism by which this feat is accomplished.

As adults, we too might occasionally find ourselves in the same position as the infants in Experiment 15. Consider the following situation: we are watching a science-fiction movie and see a box-shaped alien creature fly to an inert object on a planet's surface (e.g., a rock filled with kryptonite), make contact with the object, and fly off with it. We would assume that the alien had used its internal energy to somehow seize and carry off the object—just as the infants in Experiment 15 assumed that the self-propelled platform was using its internal energy to somehow 'hold' the green box against its midsection.

12.2.7 Summary

The evidence reviewed in this section suggests that, from a very young age, infants distinguish between inert and self-propelled objects. Furthermore, infants seem to endow self-propelled objects with an internal source of energy. On the one hand, infants are *not* surprised when shown events that can be explained by assuming that a self-propelled object used its internal energy to control its motion or that of other objects. Thus, infants are not surprised when a self-propelled object initiates its own motion, alters the direction of its motion, moves to a different location when out of sight, changes the orientation or position of a part when out of sight, remains stationary when hit or pulled, remains stable when released without adequate external support, and sets an inert object into motion or 'holds' it to prevent it from falling. On the other hand, infants *are* surprised when shown events that cannot be explained by appealing to a self-propelled object's internal energy. Thus, infants are surprised when a self-propelled object passes through a solid obstacle, magically disappears and reappears out of thin air, changes the location or appearance of a part, and perhaps sets an inert object into motion or 'holds' it in place without direct contact (infants may construe these last events without reference to the self-propelled object and simply assume that the inert object is behaving in an inexplicable fashion.)

12.3 **How do infants characterize self-propelled objects?**

In Section 12.2, we have provided evidence that infants distinguish between inert and self-propelled objects and attribute to the latter an internal source of energy. But is this really how infants construe self-propelled objects? Perhaps infants view objects that spontaneously initiate or alter their motion as objects that possess a rich constellation of properties, only one of which is self-propulsion. Humans, for example, are not only self-propelled objects: they are also *agents* that can pursue goals and *animals* that are composed of biological matter and that can undergo biological transformations such as growth. Is it possible that the infants in our experiments viewed the self-propelled boxes, balls, columns, and cylinders we showed them not merely as self-propelled objects but as agents or animals? We discuss each possibility in turn.

12.3.1 **Do infants distinguish between self-propelled objects and agents?**

When infants see a novel object move by itself across an apparatus, do they tend to view it as an agent that does so because it wants to do so? Recent research (reviewed in the following section) suggests that infants do not in fact equate self-propulsion and agency: a self-propelled object is not necessarily an agent, and an agent is not necessarily self-propelled.

In order to be categorized as an agent, an object must demonstrate that it possesses at least two essential properties: first, its behavior must appear to be autonomous or self-generated, and second, its behavior must appear to be intentional or guided by mental states such as perceptions, dispositions, and goals. For ease of communication, we refer to the first property as *autonomy* and to the second as *intention*; each property is discussed in turn.

12.3.2 **Autonomy**

In a seminal series of experiments, Woodward (1998, 1999) tested 5- to 12-month-old infants' ability to reason about a human agent's motivational states.

The infants first received habituation trials in which they faced two toys: object A, on the left, and object B, on the right. In each trial, a human agent's left hand reached into the apparatus and grasped object A. During test, the two toys' positions were reversed, and the agent grasped either object A (old-object event) or object B (new-object event). Across experiments, the infants consistently looked longer at the new- than at the old-object event. We take these results to suggest three conclusions: (1) during habituation, the infants attributed to the agent a particular disposition, a preference for object A over object B; (2) during test, the infants expected the agent to maintain this preference and hence to form the goal of reaching for object A in its new position; and hence (3) during test, the infants were surprised when the agent grasped object B instead of object A. These results provided the first experimental demonstration that infants as young as 5 months of age can already attribute motivational states—such as dispositions and goals—to agents.

In additional experiments, Woodward (1998) found that infants did not look reliably longer at the new- than at the old-object event when the human agent was replaced with a flat occluder shaped like an arm and hand, a rod tipped with a sponge, or a mechanical claw. Woodward concluded that infants initially attribute goals to human but not to nonhuman agents. However, there was another possible interpretation for the negative findings of the occluder, rod, and claw experiments: because each object extended from the right side of the apparatus, its right end was hidden from view, making it unclear whether its actions were externally or internally caused. If an object must appear to be acting *autonomously* to be construed as an agent, then perhaps the infants did not attribute motivational states to the occluder, rod, and claw simply because the available information did not clearly mark them as agents. This interpretation predicted that 5-month-olds might attribute such states to a nonhuman agent if given unambiguous evidence that they were faced with an autonomous agent.

Experiment 17 (see Fig. 12.17) examined this prediction (Luo & Baillargeon, 2005a), with 5-month-old infants. The experiment included orientation, familiarization, display, and test trials. During the orientation trials, a small green box moved back and forth across the central portion of the apparatus. During the familiarization trials, a cylinder and cone were placed on either side of the box near the left and right walls of the apparatus, respectively. In each trial, the box moved toward and rested against the cone. During the display trial, the positions of the cone and cylinder were reversed. Finally, during the test trials, the box approached and rested against either the cone (old-object event), as before, or the cylinder (new-object event). As in Woodward's (1998, 1999) experiments, the infants looked reliably longer at the new- than at the old-object event suggesting that (1) they viewed the box as an agent;

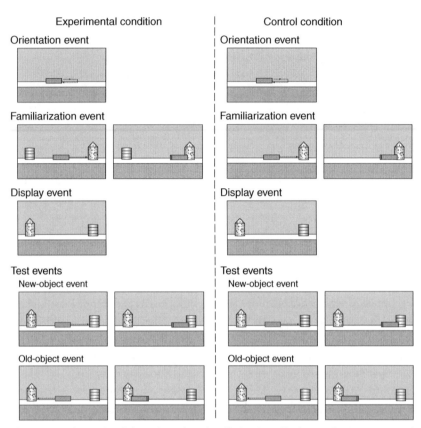

Fig. 12.17 Schematic of the orientation, familiarization, display, and test events used in Experiment 17 (Luo & Baillargeon, 2005a).

(2) during familiarization, they attributed to the box a preference for the cone over the cylinder; and (3) during test, they expected the box to maintain this preference and hence to approach the cone in its new position. Support for these conclusions came from a control condition (see Fig. 12.17) identical to the experimental condition just described, with one exception: during the familiarization trials, only the cone was present. Although the infants in this condition could view the actions of the box during the familiarization trials as directed toward the goal of contacting the cone, they had no information as to whether the box would prefer the cone or the cylinder when both objects were present in test. As a result, the infants tended to look equally at the new- and old-object test events.

The results of Experiment 17 indicated that infants as young as 5 months of age can attribute motivational states to nonhuman agents. As such, these results

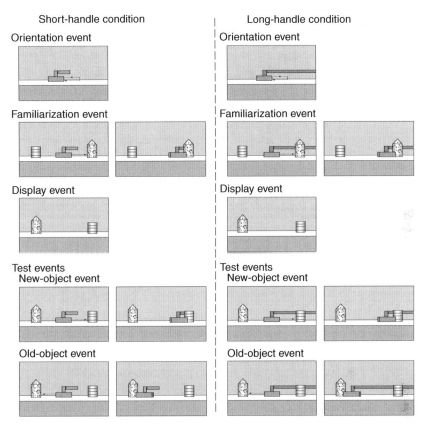

Fig. 12.18 Schematic of the orientation, familiarization, display, and test events used in Experiment 18 (Luo & Baillargeon, 2005a).

provided support for the hypothesis that the infants in Woodward's (1998) experiment failed to attribute motivational states to the occluder, rod, and claw because it was unclear whether these objects were acting autonomously. To provide additional evidence for this interpretation, in Experiment 18 (see Fig. 12.18), infants were tested with the same procedure as in the experimental condition of Experiment 17, except that a handle was attached to the box (Luo & Baillargeon, 2005a). When the handle was long and protruded from the right side of the apparatus (long-handle condition), making it unclear whether the box was acting autonomously, infants looked about equally at the new- and old-object test events. In contrast, when the handle was short so that the box appeared to be acting on its own (short-handle condition), as in Experiment 17, then infants again looked reliably longer at the new- than at the old-object event.

Together, the results of Experiments 17 and 18 provided evidence for two conclusions. First, infants as young as 5 months of age attribute motivational states not only to human but also to nonhuman agents. Second, and most relevant to the present discussion, infants do not view an object as an agent if it does not clearly appear to be acting on its own. A rod, claw, or long-handled box that protrudes from one side of an apparatus and consistently approaches object A over object B is not seen as an agent exhibiting a preference for object A because it is unclear whether its behavior is self-generated or is caused by some external force.[4]

12.3.3 Intention

In light of the results of Experiments 17 and 18, should we conclude that the infants in the experiments reviewed in Section 12.2 of this chapter viewed the self-propelled objects they were shown (e.g., the boxes, balls, columns, cylinders, etc.) as agents? After all, the objects appeared to be acting on their own, with no visible handles guiding them to and fro. However, recent research by Johnson, Csibra, and their colleagues (e.g., Csibra, 2008; Johnson et al., 2007; Shimizu & Johnson, 2004) suggests that autonomous action alone is not sufficient for infants to view a self-propelled object as an agent: the object must also provide evidence that it is acting intentionally; perceptions, dispositions, goals, and/or other mental states inside the object must be causing its actions.

In this view, an object that follows the same fixed path over and over again (think of a ceiling fan going round and round, or of the sun following the same arc daily across the sky), or an object whose behavior appears random (think of a tree branch swaying in the wind), is unlikely to be viewed as an agent. Only objects whose actions appear to be intentional, or guided by mental states, can be agents. As we will see, infants seem to be sensitive to several types of evidence for intention, from taking turns in a conversation with a partner to modifying one's behavior in order to achieve a goal, to selecting different means at different times to achieve the same goal. Interestingly, all of these examples involve goal-directed actions, suggesting that intention may be easiest to detect in the context of communicative or other goals, as agents detect and act on or react to external stimuli.

In a seminal series of experiments, Johnson and her collaborators (Johnson et al., 2007; Shimizu & Johnson, 2004) tested 12-month-old infants in a task

---

[4] Recent research suggests that, if provided with sufficient cues, infants may view the actions of a rod or claw that protrudes from one side of an apparatus as goal-directed in the sense that they construe the rod or claw as a mechanical device or tool manipulated by an unseen agent to achieve a certain goal (e.g., Biro & Leslie, 2007; Hofer et al., 2005).

modeled after that of Woodward (1998). As in Experiments 17 and 18, the human agent was replaced with a nonhuman self-propelled object, an oval-shaped 'blob' covered with bright green fiberfill. The blob was placed near the front of the apparatus; at the back of the apparatus were two toys, object A on the left and object B on the right. During each habituation trial, the blob approached and stopped against object A. During the test trials, the toys' positions were reversed, and the blob approached either object A (old-object event) or object B (new-object event). At the start of each habituation and test trial, the blob's front-to-back axis was aligned with the object it approached during the trial. The infants tended to look equally at the new- and old-object events. This negative result suggested that the infants viewed the blob as a self-propelled object—because it initiated its motion in plain sight—but *not* as an agent: although the blob appeared to move autonomously, it followed the same fixed path on every habituation trial and thus gave no clear evidence that it was acting intentionally.

To borrow an analogy from Section 12.2 of this chapter, consider an object that emerges from behind a screen and comes to a stop. The object could be self-propelled—but it could also be an inert object set in motion by some external force behind the screen. We saw that in such cases infants typically select the second, weaker interpretation: they do not view an object as self-propelled unless it gives (what they construe as) clear evidence that it possesses an internal source of energy. In the same way, a blob that repeatedly approaches and contacts object A could be pursuing the goal of approaching its preferred toy—but it could also be a self-propelled object moving on a fixed path that happens to intersect with object A. These results suggest that infants again select the second, weaker interpretation: they do not view an object as an agent unless it gives (what they construe as) clear evidence that it possesses mental states.

Support for this interpretation comes from additional results by Johnson and her colleagues (Johnson et al., 2007; Shimizu & Johnson, 2004). Infants looked reliably longer at the new- than at the old-object event in two key conditions. In one, instead of being aligned with object A at the start of each habituation trial, the blob faced a position midway between the two toys and turned toward object A—as though making a choice—before approaching it. In the other condition, the blob participated in a scripted 'conversation' with an experimenter prior to the habituation trials; the experimenter spoke English and the blob responded with a varying series of beeps. The positive results obtained in each condition suggested that the infants now viewed the blob as an agent: they interpreted its behavior in habituation as revealing a preference for object A, they expected this preference to be maintained in test, and they thus looked reliably longer when the blob approached object B instead. Interestingly, negative results were obtained (1) if the blob remained silent when the experimenter spoke (suggesting that it was not merely seeing the experimenter talk to the blob that led the infants to view it as an agent) or (2) if the blob beeped as before but the experimenter remained silent and stared at the floor (suggesting that it was not merely observing that the box could produce varying beeps that led the infants to view it as an agent; apparently, variable self-generated behavior, if it appears random, does not constitute evidence of agency).

Not surprisingly, positive results were also obtained when the experimenter and the blob conversed at the start of the test session *and* the blob turned toward object A at the start of each habituation trial: because each factor alone led to an attribution of agency, both factors together naturally did so as well (Shimizu & Johnson, 2004). Finally, in converging experiments using a 'gaze-following' measure, Johnson and her colleagues (e.g., Johnson, 2003; Johnson et al., 1998, 2008) found that, after observing the blob turn toward one of two targets, 14- to 15-month-old infants tended to turn in the same direction if the blob first participated in a conversation with an experimenter (agent condition), but not if it beeped and the experimenter remained silent (nonagent condition).

Together, these results suggest that (1) infants view an object as an agent if its actions appear not only autonomous but also intentional or guided by mental states and (2) infants are sensitive to several types of evidence for intention. A blob that beeps contingently in a conversation with an experimenter gives evidence of intention because it appears to be detecting and responding to the utterances of the experimenter (a blob that beeps on its own could be beeping randomly). Similarly, a blob that first rotates toward and then approaches a toy gives evidence of intention because it appears to be adjusting its behavior so as to achieve a particular goal: namely, contacting its preferred toy. The same could be said of the self-propelled box in Experiments 17 and 18 (short-handle condition): although the box moved back and forth across the center of the apparatus in the orientation trials, it approached and stopped against the cone in the familiarization trials, suggesting that it was modifying its behavior so as to contact its preferred object.

Recent work by Csibra (2008) points to yet another type of evidence for intention: choosing different means to achieve the same goal across trials. This research built on work by Kamewari et al. (2005), which itself was designed to extend earlier work by Csibra, Gergely, and their colleagues (e.g., Csibra et al., 1999; Gergely et al., 1995). Kamewari et al. habituated 6.5-month-old infants to a videotaped event in which an agent moved around an obstacle to reach a target. The agent was either a human, a human-like robot, or a self-propelled box. In test, the obstacle was removed, and the agent either moved in a straight line to the target (new-path event) or followed the same path as before (old-path event). Infants looked reliably longer at the new- than at the old-path event when the agent was the human or the robot, but not when it was the self-propelled box. Csibra (2008) replicated this last, negative result and suggested that, because the novel self-propelled box followed the same fixed path in every habituation trial, infants were not certain whether it was an agent; it was clearly acting autonomously, but there was perhaps insufficient evidence that its actions were intentional.

To test this idea, Csibra (2008) again habituated 6.5-month-old infants to events in which a self-propelled box moved around an obstacle to reach a target; however, the box now moved around the right *or* the left end of the obstacle on alternate habituation trials. Results were now positive, suggesting that this slight variation in means was sufficient to lead the infants to conclude that the box's behavior was intentional. They attributed to the box the goal of reaching the target, and they expected it to do so efficiently in every trial. Thus, when the obstacle was removed in test, they expected the box to now move directly toward the target, and they were surprised when it did not.

Together, the results summarized here suggest that for infants a self-propelled object is an agent if it gives evidence that it possesses mental states such as perceptions, dispositions, and goals. To return to the question raised at the start of this section (i.e., did the infants in the experiments reviewed in Section 12.2 of this chapter view the novel self-propelled objects they were shown as agents?), we suspect that in at least some cases the answer was no. For example, the infants in Experiments 1 and 2 would have had little basis to view the box as an agent because it followed the same fixed path in every trial as it moved back and forth across the apparatus.

12.3.4 **Inert agents**

The research on autonomy and intention leads to a strong prediction: infants might view an *inert* object as an agent if it gave evidence that (1) it could produce some behavior on its own and (2) this behavior was guided by mental states. Think, for example, of the Magical Mirror in the fairy tale 'Snow White', who always responds accurately when asked for the name of the fairest woman in the kingdom. Most adults would agree that the Magical Mirror is an inert agent: although it cannot initiate its own motion, its communicative behavior is self-generated and intentional.

Experiments 19 and 20 (Wu & Baillargeon, 2007b) were designed to examine whether 14-month-old infants could view an object as an inert agent.

Inspired by the work of Johnson and her colleagues (Johnson et al., 2007, 2008; Shimizu & Johnson, 2004), we used a beeping box as our agent.

In Experiment 19 (see Fig. 12.19), we first asked whether infants would view a box that responded with beeps in a conversation with an experimenter, but otherwise remained stationary, as inert. Alternative possibilities were that infants might expect any object capable of self-generated behavior (such as beeping) to be self-propelled, or that they might view any agent as self-propelled. To test whether the infants would view the box as inert, we built on the results of Experiments 12 to 14 and examined whether infants would expect the box to fall when released in midair.

The infants were assigned to an inert or a self-propelled condition. The only difference between the two conditions involved the first, orientation trial: the box either remained stationary (inert condition) or moved back and forth a short distance (self-propelled condition). Next, in a conversation trial, all infants observed an experimenter (with bare hands) participate in a scripted conversation with the box. The experimenter sat at window in the left side of the apparatus and spoke English; the box responded with varying series of beeps. Following the conversation (which lasted about 47 s), the experimenter closed the curtain in the window and the box remained stationary and silent until the trial ended. In the next, familiarization trial, the box was held above the apparatus floor by a gloved hand that reached through a fringed curtain in the window. Finally, in the test trial, the hand released the box, which remained stationary in midair.

Although the infants in the self-propelled condition looked reliably longer than those in the inert condition during the orientation trial (not surprisingly, the box was more interesting when it moved than when it remained stationary), the infants in both conditions tended to look equally during the conversation and familiarization trials. During the test trial, however, the infants in the inert condition looked reliably longer than those in the self-propelled condition. Together, these results suggested that the infants in the inert condition viewed the box as an inert agent: although it beeped in response to the experimenter in the conversation trial, it never moved on its own and hence possessed no internal energy that could allow it to resist falling when released in midair.

Experiment 20 was designed to provide additional support for the notion that the infants in the inert condition viewed the box as an inert agent (see Fig. 12.20).

Similar to Experiments 17 and 18, and the experiments of Johnson and her colleagues (Johnson et al., 2007; Shimizu & Johnson, 2004), Experiment 20 was modeled after Woodward's (1998) work and asked whether infants would attribute to a box that beeped only when one of two toys was revealed

Orientation event

Inert condition

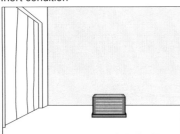

Self-propelled condition

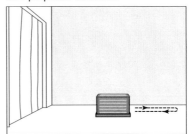

Conversation event

Familiarization event

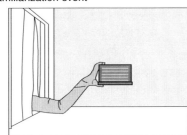

Test event

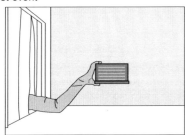

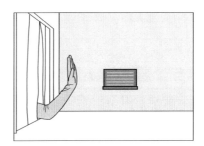

Fig. 12.19 Schematic of the orientation, conversation, familiarization, and test events used in Experiment 19 (Wu & Baillargeon, 2007b).

Orientation event

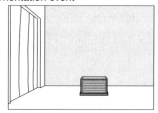

Conversation event

Familiarization event

 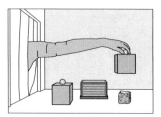

Test events
New-object event

 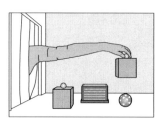

Old-object event

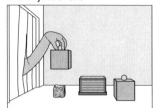 

Fig. 12.20 Schematic of the orientation, familiarization, display, and test events used in Experiment 20 (Wu & Baillargeon, 2007b).

a preference for that toy over the other toy. The infants first received the same orientation and conversation trials as in the inert condition of Experiment 19. Next, the infants received familiarization trials in which the box stood centered and behind two small covers. Hidden under the covers were two toys, a ball and a block; toy position (left or right cover) was counterbalanced across infants. A gloved hand lifted and lowered the left cover and then the right cover; the box beeped when the left cover was lifted to reveal object A, but not when the right cover was lifted to reveal object B. Next, the infants received a display trial in which the box was absent and the hand lifted and lowered each cover in turn to show that the toys' positions had been reversed. Finally, in the test trials, the box stood in its original position, the hand lifted and lowered the left and right covers in turn, and the box beeped when object B but not object A was revealed (new-object event), or when object A but not object B was revealed (old-object event).

Results indicated that the infants looked reliably longer at the new- than at the old-object event, suggesting that they (1) viewed the box as an agent based on its behavior in the conversation trial, (2) attributed to the box a preference for object A over object B during the familiarization trials, and (3) expected this preference to be maintained in the test trials and were therefore surprised in the new-object event when the box beeped to object B instead of object A. This interpretation was supported by the results of a control condition similar to that in Experiment 17: when only one toy was present in the familiarization trials, the infants tended to look equally at the new- and old-object test events, because they had no information as to which toy the box would prefer when both toys were present in test.

12.3.2 Do infants distinguish between self-propelled objects and animals?

In the previous section, we asked whether the infants in the experiments reviewed in Section 12.2 might have viewed the self-propelled objects they were shown as agents. In this section, we ask whether the infants might have viewed the objects as *animals*. As might be expected, how one answers this question depends on how one characterizes infants' concept of animal; here we consider two possible characterizations.

12.3.2.1 Animals as self-propelled agents

In a recent chapter, Mandler (in press) suggested that infants 'divide the world of objects into animals and nonanimals' (p. 5), and that their concept of animals is composed of two conceptual primitives: objects 'that start motion by themselves' and objects 'that interact contingently with other objects from a distance' (p. 13). According to Mandler, conceptual primitives are 'innate, in the sense that they are activated by innate attentional proclivities' (p. 22); they correspond to 'pieces of spatial information, especially movements in space' (p. 7); and they are used by a Perceptual Meaning Analysis mechanism to redescribe (reduce and recode) perceptual patterns into global and skeletal concepts such as that of animal.

As may be clear from the evidence and arguments presented in previous sections of this chapter, our position differs from that of Mandler (in press) on several counts. First, although we also emphasize the central importance of the concepts self-propelled object and agent for infants, we see each of these concepts as embedded in a causal framework—the concept of self-propelled object (with its link to internal energy) in the causal framework that makes possible infants' physical reasoning (e.g., Baillargeon et al., 2006, 2009; Gelman et al., 1995; Leslie, 1994; Spelke, 1994) and the concept of agent (with its link to mental states) in the causal framework that makes possible infants' psychological reasoning (e.g., Gergely & Csibra, 2003; Johnson, 2003; Luo & Baillargeon, 2007; Premack, 1990; Scott & Baillargeon, 2009; Song et al., 2008). Second, infants appear to realize that self-propelled objects may not be agents, and that agents may not be self-propelled, suggesting that they recognize that the world of objects is not simply composed of inert objects and self-propelled agents.

Despite these differences, we can still adopt Mandler's (in press) suggestion that, for infants, animals are essentially self-propelled agents. If this hypothesis is correct, then it is likely that the infants in the experiments reported in Section 12.2 did not view the novel self-propelled objects they were shown as animals: as was discussed earlier, there was typically little or no evidence that the objects were agents.

12.3.2.2 Animals as self-propelled biological agents

Subrahmanyam et al. (2002) reviewed evidence that young children distinguish between animals, moving machines, sentient machines, and inert objects. According to these authors, for an object to be classified as an animal, it is not sufficient that it be self-propelled and an agent: it must also be composed of the 'right kind of stuff': namely, 'biological stuff' (p. 347). This is because young children's reasoning about animate objects is informed by domain-specific causal principles allowing them to appreciate 'the connection between biological matter and animate motion' (p. 346). As the authors point out, 'although all objects obey the laws of physics, animate objects also obey biochemical ones ... the cause of animate motion and change comes from the channeled release of internally stored chemical energy that is characteristic of biological entities' (p. 346). Although young children do not possess an adult-like biological theory (e.g., their attribution of animate properties to animals is highly selective; see also Carey, 1985), their concept of animal still has fundamental biological properties. Thus, when asked which objects can move by themselves and which cannot, children typically justify their answers with 'relevant comments about their material composition and the inside of these objects' (p. 369).

What are the implications of the research and theoretical views of Subrahmanyam et al. (2002) for infants' reasoning about animals? There are at least two developmental possibilities. One is that infants attribute internal energy to self-propelled agents without distinguishing between biological and nonbiological energy. In this view, as in Mandler's (in press) view, animals are initially self-propelled agents. In the course of development, children would come to recognize that (1) certain self-propelled agents—animals—are made of 'biological stuff' and (2) animals' energy emanates from the very stuff they are made of. Such expectations appear to be in place by at least 4 years of age: for example, Gottfried and S. A. Gelman (2005) found that 4-year-olds who were interviewed about unfamiliar animals and machines were reliably more likely to answer yes when asked if the animals, as opposed to the machines, used their 'own energy' to move and grow (see also Massey & Gelman, 1988; S. A. Gelman & Gottfried, 1996; Morris et al., 2000).

Another developmental possibility is that infants possess expectations about self-propelled agents that go beyond their separate properties of being self-propelled and agents and that might be characterized as biological. One such expectation has to do with the notion of *insides*. Previous research suggests that by 3–5 years of age children already expect animals and artifacts to have *different* insides (e.g., Gelman, 1990; S. A. Gelman & Gottfried, 1996; Gottfried & S. A. Gelman, 2005; Simons & Keil, 1995). Here we are focusing on the simpler question of whether infants expect certain objects to *have* insides. If infants expect self-propelled agents to have insides (but have no clear expectations about the insides of self-propelled objects that are not agents or about the insides of agents that are not self-propelled), then it might suggest that infants' concept of animal is not reducible to that of self-propelled agent. We are beginning experiments to explore this possibility.

12.4 **Conclusions**

The evidence reviewed in this chapter suggests three broad conclusions. First, from a very early age, infants distinguish between inert and self-propelled objects and endow self-propelled objects with an internal source of energy. A self-propelled object can use its internal energy either directly to control its own motion (e.g., to alter the direction of its motion, to move to a new location, to change the orientation or position of its parts, to resist moving when hit, or to resist falling when released in midair) or indirectly to control the motion of other objects, through the application of force (e.g., to set another object in motion or to prevent it from falling).

Second, just as infants do not view an object as self-propelled unless it provides (what they construe as) unambiguous evidence that it can move itself and thus has internal energy, infants do not view a self-propelled object as an agent unless it provides (what they construe as) unambiguous evidence that it can act intentionally and thus has mental states. Infants thus appear to hold separate concepts of self-propelled object and agent, the first rooted in the causal framework that makes possible their physical reasoning and the second rooted in the causal framework that makes possible their psychological reasoning. Whether infants possess separate concepts of self-propelled agent and of animal is at present unclear.

Finally, infants' concepts of self-propelled object and agent function as abstract 'kinds of explanations' (Keil, 1995; Wilson & Keil, 2000) that are devoid of all mechanistic details but still make possible rich inferences about objects' actions in new contexts. Thus, infants who endow a box that initiates its own motion with internal energy may not understand exactly how this internal energy works or where it comes from, but they recognize that the box can also use its energy to counteract a force exerted by another object (e.g., to remain stationary when hit) or to exert a force of its own (e.g., to hold objects so as to prevent them from falling).

Together, these various lines of evidence are thus helping us to better understand the conceptual basis of infants' cognitive development.

Acknowledgments

The research reported in this chapter was supported by a grant from the National Institute of Child Health and Human Development (HD-21104) to R. Baillargeon. We thank Jerry DeJong for helpful discussions, Amélie Bernard for helpful comments and suggestions, the staff of the University of Illinois Infant Cognition Laboratory for their help with the data collection, and the parents and infants who participated in the research.

References

Aguiar, A., & Baillargeon, R. (1998). Eight-and-a-half-month-old-infants' reasoning about containment events. *Child Development, 69*, 636–653.

Aguiar, A., & Baillargeon, R. (1999). 2.5-month-old infants' reasoning about when objects should and should not be occluded. *Cognitive Psychology, 39*, 116–157.

Aguiar, A., & Baillargeon, R. (2002). Developments in young infants' reasoning about occluded objects. *Cognitive Psychology, 45,* 267–336.

Aguiar, A., & Baillargeon, R. (2003). Perseverative responding in a violation-of-expectation task in 6.5-month-old infants. *Cognition, 88,* 277–316.

Ahmed, A., & Ruffman, T. (1998). Why do infants make A not B errors in a search task, yet show memory for the location of hidden objects in a non-search task? *Developmental Psychology, 34,* 441–453.

Baillargeon, R. (1986). Representing the existence and the location of hidden objects: object permanence in 6- and 8-month-old infants. *Cognition, 23,* 21–41.

Baillargeon, R. (1987). Object permanence in 3.5- and 4.5-month-old infants. *Developmental Psychology, 23,* 655–664.

Baillargeon, R. (1991). Reasoning about the height and location of a hidden object in 4.5- and 6.5-month-old infants. *Cognition, 38,* 13–42.

Baillargeon, R. (1995). A model of physical reasoning in infancy. In C. Rovee-Collier, & L. P. Lipsitt (Eds.), *Advances in Infancy Research,* Vol. 9 (pp. 305–371). Norwood, NJ: Ablex.

Baillargeon, R. (2008). Innate ideas revisited: for a principle of persistence in infants' physical reasoning. *Perspectives on Psychological Science, 3,* 2–13.

Baillargeon, R., & DeVos, J. (1991). Object permanence in young infants: further evidence. *Child Development, 62,* 1227–1246.

Baillargeon, R., DeVos, J., & Graber, M. (1989). Location memory in 8-month-old infants in a non-search AB task: Further evidence. *Cognitive Development, 4,* 345–367.

Baillargeon, R., & Graber, M. (1987). Where's the rabbit? 5.5-month-old infants' representation of the height of a hidden object. *Cognitive Development, 2,* 375–392.

Baillargeon, R., & Graber, M. (1988). Evidence of location memory in 8-month-old infants in a non-search AB task. *Developmental Psychology, 24,* 502–511.

Baillargeon, R., Graber, M., DeVos, J., & Black, J. (1990). Why do young infants fail to search for hidden objects? *Cognition, 36,* 225–284.

Baillargeon, R., Li, J., Luo, Y., & Wang, S. (2006). Under what conditions do infants detect continuity violations? In Y. Munakata, & M. H. Johnson (Eds.), *Processes of Change in Brain and Cognitive Development* (Attention and Performance XXI, pp. 163–188). New York: Oxford University Press.

Baillargeon, R., Li, J., Ng, W., & Yuan, S. (2009). An account of infants' physical reasoning. In A. Woodward, & A. Needham (Eds.), *Learning and the Infant Mind,* (pp. 66–116). New York: Oxford University Press.

Baillargeon, R., Needham, A., & DeVos, J. (1992). The development of young infants' intuitions about support. *Early Development and Parenting, 1,* 69–78.

Baillargeon, R., Spelke, E. S., & Wasserman, S. (1985). Object permanence in 5-month-old infants. *Cognition, 20,* 191–208.

Bauer, J., Shimojo, S., Gwiazda, J., & Held, R. (1986). Sex differences in the development of binocularity in human infants. *Investigative Ophtalmology and Visual Science (Supplement), 27,* 265.

Bíro, S., & Leslie. A. M. (2007). Infants' perception of goal-directed actions: development through cue-based bootstrapping. *Developmental Science, 10,* 379–398.

Bremner, J. G., Johnson, S. P., Slater, A. M., et al. (2005). Conditions for young infants' perception of object trajectories. *Child Development, 74,* 1029–1043.

Carey, S. (1985). *Conceptual Development in Childhood*. Cambridge, MA: MIT Press.

Carey, S., & Spelke, E. S. (1994). Domain-specific knowledge and conceptual change. In L. A. Hirschfeld, & S. A. Gelman (Eds.), *Mapping the Mind: Domain Specificity in Cognition and Culture* (pp. 169–200). New York: Cambridge University Press.

Csibra, G. (2008). Goal attribution to inanimate agents by 6.5-month-old infants. *Cognition, 107,* 705–717.

Csibra, G., Gergely, G., Biro, S., Koos, O., & Brockbank, M. (1999) Goal attribution without agency cues: the perception of 'pure reason' in infancy. *Cognition, 72,* 237–267.

Einstein, A., & Infeld, L. (1960). *The evolution of physics: From early concepts to relativity and quanta,* 2nd edn. New York: Simon and Schuster.

Gelman, R. (1990). First principles organize attention to and learning about relevant data: number and the animate-inanimate distinction as examples. *Cognitive Science, 14,* 79–106.

Gelman, R., Durgin, F., & Kaufman, L. (1995). Distinguishing between animates and inanimates: not by motion alone. In D. Sperber, D. Premack, & A. J. Premack (Eds.), *Causal Cognition: A Multidisciplinary Debate* (pp. 150–184). Oxford: Clarendon Press.

Gelman, R., & Spelke, E. S. (1981). The development of thoughts about animate and inanimate objects: implications for research on social cognition. In J. H. Flavell & L. Ross (Eds.), *Social Cognitive Development: Frontiers and Possible Futures* (pp. 43–66). Cambridge: Cambridge University Press.

Gelman, S. A., & Gottfried, G. M. (1996). Children's causal explanations of animate and inanimate motion. *Child Development, 67,* 1970–1987.

Gergely, G., & Csibra, G. (2003). Teleological reasoning in infancy: the naïve theory of rational action. *Trends in Cognitive Science, 7,* 287–292.

Gergely, G., Nádasdy, Z., Csibra, G., & Bíró, S. (1995). Taking the intentional stance at 12 months of age. *Cognition, 56,* 165–193.

Golinkoff, R., Harding, C., Carlson, V., & Sexton, M. E. (1984). The infants' perception of causal events: the distinction between animate and inanimate objects. In L. P. Lipsitt, & C. Rovee-Collier (Eds.), *Advances in Infancy Research,* Vol. 3 (pp. 145–151). Norwood, NJ: Ablex.

Gottfried, G. M., & Gelman, S. A. (2005). Developing domain-specific causal-explanatory frameworks: the role of insides and immanence. *Cognitive Development, 20,* 137–158.

Goubet, N., & Clifton, R. K. (1998). Object and event representation in 6.5-month-old infants. *Developmental Psychology, 34,* 63–76.

Gwiazda, J., Bauer, J., & Held, R. (1989a). Binocular function in human infants: correlation of stereoptic and fusion-rivalry discriminations. *Journal of Pediatric Ophthalmology and Strabismus, 43,* 109–120.

Gwiazda, J., Bauer, J., & Held, R. (1989b). From visual acuity to hyperacuity: a 10-year update. *Canadian Journal of Psychology, 43,* 109–120.

Hespos, S. J., & Baillargeon, R. (2001a). Infants' knowledge about occlusion and containment events: a surprising discrepancy. *Psychological Science, 12,* 140–147.

Hespos, S. J., & Baillargeon, R. (2001b). Knowledge about containment events in very young infants. *Cognition, 78,* 204–245.

Hespos, S. J., & Baillargeon, R. (2006). Décalage in infants' knowledge about occlusion and containment events: Converging evidence from action tasks. *Cognition, 99,* B31–B41.

Hespos, S. J., & Baillargeon, R. (2008). Young infants' actions reveal their developing knowledge of support variables: converging evidence for violation-of-expectation findings. *Cognition, 107,* 304–316.

Hofer, T., Hauf, P., & Aschersleben, G. (2005). Infants' perception of goal-directed actions performed by a mechanical device. *Infant Behavior and Development, 28,* 466–480.

Hofstadter, M., & Reznick, J. S. (1996). Response modality affects human infant delayed-response performance. *Child Development, 67,* 646–658.

Hood, B., & Willatts, P. (1986). Reaching in the dark to an object's remembered position: evidence of object permanence in 5-month-old infants. *British Journal of Developmental Psychology, 4,* 57–65.

Johnson, S. C. (2003). Detecting agents. *Philosophical Transactions of the Royal Society of London, Series B, 358,* 549–599.

Johnson, S. C., Bolz, M., Carter, E., Mandsanger, J., Teichner, A., & Zettler, P. (2008). Calculating the attentional orientation of an unfamiliar agent in infancy. *Cognitive Development, 23,* 24–37.

Johnson, S. C., Shimizu, Y. A., & Ok, S-J. (2007). Actors and actions: the role of agent behavior in infants' attribution of goals. *Cognitive Development, 22,* 310–322.

Johnson, S. C., Slaughter, V., & Carey, S. (1998). Whose gaze will infants follow? The elicitation of gaze-following in 12-month-olds. *Developmental Science, 1,* 233–238.

Johnson, S. P. (2004). Development of perceptual completion in infancy. *Psychological Science, 15,* 769–775.

Johnson, S. P., Amso, D., & Slemmer, J. A. (2003). Development of object concepts in infancy: evidence for early learning in an eye-tracking paradigm. *Proceedings of the National Academy of Sciences (USA), 100,* 10568–10573.

Kamerawi, K., Kato, M., Kanda, T., Ishiguro, H., & Hiraki, K. (2005). Six-and-a-half-month-old children positively attribute goals to human action and to humanoid-robot motion. *Cognitive Development, 20,* 303–320.

Keil, F. (1995). The growth of causal understandings of natural kinds. In D. Sperber, D. Premack, & A. J. Premack (Eds.), *Causal Cognition: A Multiplinary Debate* (pp. 234–267). Oxford: Clarendon Press.

Kellman, P. J., & Spelke, E. S. (1983). Perception of partly occluded objects in infancy. *Cognitive Psychology, 15,* 483–524.

Kestenbaum, R., Termine, N., & Spelke, E. S. (1987). Perception of objects and object boundaries by 3-month-old infants. *British Journal of Developmental Psychology, 5,* 367–383.

Kochukhova, O., & Gredeback, G. (2007). Learning about occlusion: Initial assumptions and rapid adjustments. *Cognition, 105,* 26–46.

Kosugi, D., & Fujita, K. (2002). How do 8-month-old infants recognize causality in object motion and that in human action? *Japanese Psychological Research, 44,* 66–78.

Kosugi, D., Ishida, H., & Fujita, K. (2003). 10-month-old infants' inference of invisible agent: distinction in causality between object motion and human action. *Japanese Psychological Research, 45,* 15–24.

Kotovsky, L., & Baillargeon, R. (1998). The development of calibration-based reasoning about collision events in young infants. *Cognition, 67,* 311–351.

Kotovsky, L., & Baillargeon, R. (2000). Reasoning about collision events involving inert objects in 7.5-month-old infants. *Developmental Science, 3,* 344–359.

Kuhlmeier, V. A., Bloom, P., & Wynn, K. (2004). Do 5-month-old infants see humans as material objects? *Cognition, 94,* 95–103.

Lécuyer, R., & Durand, K. (1998). Bi-dimensional representations of the third dimension and their perception by infants. *Perception, 27,* 465–472.

Leslie, A. M. (1982). The perception of causality of infants. *Perception, 11,* 173–186.

Leslie, A. M. (1984a). Infant perception of a manual pick-up event. *British Journal of Developmental Psychology, 2,* 19–32.

Leslie, A. M. (1984b). Spatiotemporal continuity and the perception of causality in infants. *Perception, 13,* 287–305.

Leslie, A. M. (1994). ToMM, ToBY, and Agency: core architecture and domain specificity. In L. A. Hirschfeld, & S. A. Gelman (Eds.), *Mapping the Mind: Domain Specificity in Cognition and Culture* (pp. 119–148). New York: Cambridge University Press.

Leslie, A. M. (1995). A theory of agency. In D. Sperber, D. Premack, & A. J. Premack (Eds.), *Causal Cognition: A Multidisciplinary Debate* (pp. 121–141). Oxford: Clarendon Press.

Leslie, A. M., & Keeble, S. (1987). Do six-month-old infants perceive causality? *Cognition, 25,* 165–288.

Li, J., Baillargeon, R., & Needham, A. (2006). When is an object released in contact with another object stable? Learning about support events in young infants. Paper presented at the Biennial International Conference on Infant Studies, Kyoto, Japan.

Li., J., Baillargeon, R., & Needham, A. (in preparation). Learning about support events in young infants.

Li, J., Yuan, S., Needham, A., & Baillargeon, R. (under review). 3-month-old infants except an object to fall when unsupported.

Luo, Y., & Baillargeon, R. (2005a). Can a self-propelled box have a goal? Psychological reasoning in 5-month-old infants. *Psychological Science, 16,* 601–608.

Luo, Y., & Baillargeon, R. (2005b). When the ordinary seems unexpected: evidence for incremental physical knowledge in young infants. *Cognition, 95,* 297–328.

Luo, Y., & Baillargeon, R. (2007). Do 12.5-month-old infants consider what objects others can see when interpreting their actions? *Cognition, 105,* 489–512.

Luo, Y., Baillargeon, R., Brueckner, L., & Munakata, Y. (2003). Reasoning about a hidden object after a delay: Evidence from robust representations in 5-month-old infants. *Cognition, 88,* B23–B32.

Luo, Y., Kaufman, L., & Baillargeon, R. (in press). Young infants' reasoning about physical events involving inert and self-propelled objects. *Cognitive Psychology.*

Mandler, J. M. (in press). In the beginning. In J. Snedeker, & S. Niyogi (Eds.), *Responses to Fodor's Problem of Concept Acquisition.* Cambridge, MA: MIT Press.

Markson, L., & Spelke, E. S. (2006). Infants' rapid learning about self-propelled objects. *Infancy, 9,* 45–71.

Massey, C. M., & Gelman, R. (1988). Preschoolers' ability to decide whether a photographed unfamiliar object can move itself. *Developmental Psychology, 24,* 307–317.

McCloskey, M. (1983). Naive theories of motion. In D. Gentner, & A. L. Stevens (Eds.), *Mental Models* (pp. 299–324). Hillsdale, NJ: Erlbaum.

Morris, S. C., Taplin, J. E., & Gelman, S. A. (2000). Vitalism in naive biological thinking. *Developmental Psychology, 36,* 582–595.

Needham, A. (1998). Infants' use of featural information in the segregation of stationary objects. *Infant Behavior and Development, 21*, 47–76.

Needham, A. (1999). The role of shape in 4-month-old infants' segregation of adjacent objects. *Infant Behavior and Development, 22*, 161–178.

Needham, A. (2000). Improvements in object exploration skills may facilitate the development of object segregation in early infancy. *Journal of Cognition and Development, 1*, 131–156.

Needham, A., & Baillargeon, R. (1993). Intuitions about support in 4.5-month-old infants. *Cognition, 47*, 121–148.

Needham, A., & Baillargeon, R. (1997). Object segregation in 8-month-old infants. *Cognition, 62*, 121–149.

Oakes, L. M. (1994). The development of infants' use of continuity cues in their perception of causality. *Developmental Psychology, 30*, 869–879.

Poulin-Dubois, D., Lepage, A., & Ferland, D. (1996). Infants' concept of animacy. *Cognitive Development, 11*, 19–36.

Poulin Dubois, D., & Shultz, T. R. (1988). The development of understanding of human behavior: from agency to intentionality. In J. W. Astington, P. L., Harris, & D. R. Olson (Eds.), *Developing Theories of Mind* (pp. 109–125). Cambridge: Cambridge University Press.

Poulin-Dubois, D., & Shultz, T. R. (1990). The infant's concept of agency: the distinction between social and nonsocial objects. *Journal of Genetic Psychology, 151*, 77–90.

Premack, D. (1990). The infant's theory of self-propelled objects. *Cognition, 36*, 1–16.

Premack, D., & Premack, A. J., (1995) Origins of human social competence. In M. S. Gazzaniga (Eds), *The Cognitive Neurosciences* (pp. 205–218). Cambridge, MA: MIT Press.

Rakison, D. H. (2003). Parts, motion, and the develpment of the animate-inanimate distinction in infancy. In D.H. Rakison, & L. M. Oakes (Eds.), *Early Category and Concept Development: Making Sense of the Blooming, Buzzing Confusion* (pp. 159–192). New York: Oxford University Press.

Rakison, D. H., & Cicchino, D. H. (2004). Is an infant a people person? *Cognition, 94*, 104–107.

Rakison, D. H., & Poulin-Dubois, D. (2001) Developmental origin of the animate-inanimate distinction. *Psychological Bulletin, 127*, 209–228.

Rakison, D. H., & Poulin-Dubois, D. (2002). You go this way and I'll go that way: developmental changes in infants' attention to correlations among dynamic features in motion events. *Child Development, 73*, 682–699.

Ruffman, T., Slade, L., & Redman, J. (2005). Young infants' expectations about hidden objects. *Cognition, 97*, B35–B43.

Saxe, R., Tenenbaum, J., & Carey, S. (2005). Secret agents: 10- and 12-month-old infants' inferences about hidden causes. *Psychological Science, 16*, 995–1001.

Saxe, R., Tzelnic, T., & Carey, S. (2006). Five-month-old infants know humans are solid, like inanimate objects. *Cognition, 101*, B1–B8.

Saxe, R., Tzelnic, T., & Carey, S. (2007). Knowing who-dunnit: infants identify the causal agent in an unseen causal interaction. *Developmental Psychology, 43*, 149–158.

Scott, R. M., & Baillargeon, R. (in press). Which penguin is this? Attributing false beliefs about object identity at 18 months. *Child Development*.

Shimizu, Y. A., & Johnson, S. C. (2004). Infants' attribution of a goal to a morphologically unfamiliar agent. *Developmental Science, 7*, 425–430.

Sitskoorn, S. M., & Smitsman, A. W. (1995). Infants' perception of dynamic relations between objects: passing through or support? *Developmental Psychology, 31*, 437–447.

Simons, D. J., & Keil, F. (1995). An abstract to concrete shift in the development of biological thought: the insides story. *Cognition, 56*, 129–163.

Slater, A., Johnson, S. P., Brown, E., & Badenoch, M. (1996). Newborn infant's perception of partly occluded objects. *Infant Behavior and Development, 19*, 145–148.

Slaughter, V., & Heron, M. (2004). Origins and early development of human body knowledge. *Monographs of the Society for Research in Child Development, 69*(2 Serial no. 276).

Song, H., Onishi, K. H., Baillargeon, R., & Fisher, C. (2008). Can an agent's false belief be corrected by an appropriate communication? Psychological reasoning in 18-month-old infants. *Cognition, 109*, 295–315.

Spelke, E. S. (1988). Where perceiving ends and thinking begins: the apprehension of objects in infancy. In A. Yonas (Ed.), *Perceptual Development in Infancy* (pp. 187–234). Hillsdale, NJ: Erlbaum.

Spelke, E. S. (1990). Principles of object perception. *Cognitive Science, 14*, 29–56.

Spelke, E. S. (1994). Initial knowledge: six suggestions. *Cognition, 50*, 431–445.

Spelke, E. S., Breinlinger, K., Jacobson, K., & Phillips, A. (1993). Gestalt relations and object perception: a developmental study. *Perception, 22*, 1483–1501.

Spelke, E. S., Breinlinger, K., Macomber, J., & Jacobson, K. (1992). Origins of knowledge. *Psychological Review, 99*, 605–632.

Spelke, E. S., Katz, G., Purcell, S. E., Ehrlich, S. M., & Breinlinger, K. (1994). Early knowledge of object motion: continuity and inertia. *Cognition, 51*, 131–176.

Spelke, E. S., Kestenbaum, R., Simons, D. J., & Wein, D. (1995). Spatiotemporal continuity, smoothness of motion, and object identity in infancy. *British Journal of Developmental Psychology, 13*, 1–30.

Spelke, E. S., Phillips, A., & Woodward, A. L. (1995). Infants' knowledge of object motion and human action. In D. Sperber, D. Premack, & A. J. Premack (Eds.), *Causal Cognition: A Multidisciplinary Debate* (pp. 44–78). Oxford: Clarendon Press.

Spelke, E. S., & von Hofsten, C. (2001). Predictive reaching for occluded objects by 6-month-old infants. *Journal of Cognition and Development, 2*, 261–281.

Subrahmanyam, K., Gelman, R., & Lafosse, A. (2002). Animate and other separably moveable objects. In E. Fordes, & G. Humphreys (Eds.), *Category Specificity in Brain and Mind* (pp. 341–373). London: Psychology Press.

Traeuble, B., Pauen, S., Schott, S., & Charalampidu, A. (2006). Do 7-month-old infants pay attention to causality in ambiguous dynamic events? Paper presented at the Biennial Internal Conference on Infant Studies, Kyoto, Japan.

Von Hofsten, C., Kochukova, O., & Rosander, K. (2007). Predictive tracking over occlusions by 4-month-old infants. *Developmental Science, 10*, 625–640.

Von Hofsten, C., Vishton, P., Spelke, E. S., Feng, Q., & Rosander, K. (1998). Predictive action in infancy: tracking and reaching for moving objects. *Cognition, 67*, 255–285.

Wang, S., & Baillargeon, R. (2006). Infants' physical knowledge affects their change detection. *Developmental Science, 9*, 173–181.

Wang, S., & Baillargeon, R. (2008). Can infants be 'taught' to attend to a new physical variable in an event category? The case of height in covering events. *Cognitive Psychology*, *56*, 284–326.

Wang, S., Baillargeon, R., & Brueckner, L. (2004). Young infants' reasoning about hidden objects: evidence from violation-of-expectation tasks with test trials only. *Cognition*, *93*, 167–198.

Wang, S., Baillargeon, R., & Paterson, S. (2005). Detecting continuity and solidity violations in infancy: a new account and new evidence from covering events. *Cognition*, *95*, 129–173.

Wang, S., Kaufman, L., & Baillargeon, R. (2003). Should all stationary objects move when hit? Developments in infants' causal and statistical expectations about collision events. *Infant Behavior and Development (Special Issue)*, *26*, 529–568.

Wellman, H. M., & Gelman, S. A. (1997). Knowledge acquisition in foundational domains. In W. Damon (Series Ed.), & D. Kuhn & R. Siegler (Vol. Eds.), *Handbook of Child Psychology: Vol. 2. Cognition, Perception, and Language*, 5th edn. (pp. 523–573). New York: Wiley.

Wilcox, T. (1999). Object individuation: infants' use of shape, size, pattern, and color. *Cognition*, *72*, 125–166.

Wilcox, T., & Baillargeon, R. (1998a). Object individuation in infancy: the use of featural information in reasoning about occlusion events. *Cognitive Psychology*, *37*, 97–155.

Wilcox, T., & Baillargeon, R. (1998b). Object individuation in young infants: further evidence with an event monitoring task. *Developmental Science*, *1*, 127–142.

Wilcox, T., Nadel, L., & Rosser, R. (1996). Location memory in healthy preterm and full-term infants. *Infant Behavior and Development*, *19*, 309–323.

Wilcox, T., & Schweinle, A. (2003). Infants' use of speed information to individuate objects in occlusion events. *Infant Behavior and Development*, *26*, 253–282.

Wilson, R. A., & Keil, F. C. (2000). The shadows and shallows of explanation. In F. C. Keil, & R.A. Wilson (Eds.), *Explanation and Cognition* (pp. 87–114). Cambridge, MA: MIT Press.

Woodward, A. L. (1998). Infants selectively encode the goal object of an actor's reach. *Cognition*, *69*, 1–34.

Woodward, A. L. (1999). Infants' ability to distinguish between purposeful and non-purposeful behaviors, *Infant Behavior and Development*, *22*, 145–160.

Woodward, A. L., Phillips, A., & Spelke, E. S. (1993). Infants' expectations about the motion of animate versus inanimate objects. *Proceedings of the Fifteenth Annual Meeting of the Cognitive Science Society* (pp. 1087–1091). Hillsdale, NJ: Erlbaum.

Wu, D., & Baillargeon, R. (2006). Can a self-propelled object rearrange its parts? 6-month-old infants' reasoning about possible object transformations. Paper presented at the Biennial International Conference on Infant Studies, Kyoto, Japan.

Wu, D., & Baillargeon, R. (2007a). Can a self-propelled object change its parts without constraints? 5-month-olds' detection of impossible object transformations. Paper presented at the Biennial Meeting of the Society for Research in Child Development, Boston, MA.

Wu, D., & Baillargeon, R. (2007b). Can an agent be inert? 14-month-old infants' reasoning about agency without motion cues. Paper presented at the Biennial Meeting of the Society for Research in Child Development, Boston, MA.

Wu, D., & Baillargeon, R. (2008). Can a self-propelled object change the position of its parts? Paper presented at the Biennial International Conference on Infant Studies, Vancouver, Canada.

Wu, D., Luo, Y., & Baillargeon, R. (2006). What object should appear in the window? 4-month-old infants' reasoning about inert and self-moving objects. Paper presented at the Biennial International Conference on Infant Studies, Kyoto, Japan.

Wu, D., Luo, Y., & Baillargeon, R. (in preparation). 4-month-old infants' reasoning about inert and self-propelled objects.

Xu, F., & Carey, S. (1996). Infants' metaphysics: the case of numerical identity. *Cognitive Psychology, 30,* 111–153.

Yuan, S., & Baillargeon, R. (2008). 2.5-month-olds hold different expectations about the support of inert and self-propelled objects. Paper presented at the Biennial International Conference on Infant Studies, Vancouver, Canada.

Yuan, S., & Baillargeon, R. (in preparation) Exposure to weight information primes 11-month-old infants to detect support violations.

Chapter 13

Clever eyes and stupid hands: Current thoughts on why dissociations of apparent knowledge occur on solidity tasks

Nathalia L. Gjersoe & Bruce M. Hood

13.1 Introduction

Researchers studying cognitive development in very young children cannot rely on verbal reports to investigate knowledge, and so have to use other indirect measures. After all, the word *infant* comes from the Latin for 'one unable to speak'. Even if verbal reports were readily available, they are not immune to higher-level biases and production constraints that frequently mask underlying representational capability or lead to conflicting results, especially in young children. This raises serious questions about the context in which behavior is measured, which behavior to measure, and the different factors that limit or constrain behavior. This chapter will outline some of the major theoretical standpoints for why dissociations between different measures occur in developing populations. As a case-study, core knowledge regarding the solidity of objects will be discussed as this is an area that has received a great deal of empirical attention which, over the years, has iteratively addressed a number of different assumptions and critiques regarding developing 'knowledge'.

Piaget (1954) pioneered the behavioral response approach as a barometer of underlying conceptual mechanisms in infants. He identified consistent and universal patterns of performance operating throughout early childhood that he interpreted to generate his theoretical model of stage-like progression toward increasingly more sophisticated mental representational capacity. However, this reliance on behavioral measures remains a source of criticism and confusion regarding Piaget's conclusions—to what extent do changes in behavioral performance signal conceptual development or simply changes in the child's ability to respond to the task demands? Rather than assuming that failure on the performance measure implies that the child does not have an appropriate representation of the event, it may be that the child is simply unable to act on that representation until later in development. This issue has become known as the competence-performance distinction and has highlighted the dual imperatives of developmental psychology: namely, to understand cognitive development not only in terms of *when* significant change occurs but also *why*.

The competence-performance distinction really rose to prominence in infant cognitive development research during the mid 1980s when a new technique revealed evidence of mental representation much earlier and more sophisticated than the account proposed by Piaget with his behavioral methods. This technique was based on the principle that reasoning about the world produces intuitive frameworks that lead to expectations about properties in different domains. When these expectations are violated, the infant registers an anomaly and responds by increasing the allocation of attention toward such events. The rationale of the technique was that, similar to adults, infants tended to look longer at events that did not meet with their expectations and spent longer looking at novel displays than they did at displays they had already seen a number of times before.

Spelke and colleagues capitalized on this phenomenon by conducting a series of experiments that manipulated the physical properties of object movement and measured the extent to which very young infants' expectations were violated when objects seemed to behave in impossible ways. For example, infants look longer when a solid object appears to travel through another solid object (Spelke et al., 1992), when two objects move in unison but are not joined (Kellman & Spelke, 1983; van de Walle & Spelke, 1996), and when objects appear to dematerialize at one location and rematerialize at another (Spelke et al., 1995).

Spelke (1994) concluded that infants from at least 2.5 months of age (and possibly birth) applied three constraints to their reasoning about object movement—notions of solidity (solid objects do not pass through each other), cohesion (objects remain bounded entities as they move through time and space), and continuity (objects do not spring in and out of existence). She referred to these three constraints as *core knowledge* upon which further learning about objects was built; hence, they were 'core' because they were central to reasoning about objects and the principles were unchanging over the course of development.

Crucially, these studies show that infants can not only represent hidden objects long before they are acting on them in Piaget's (1954) search experiments but also have a range of sophisticated expectations about the properties of those objects while out of sight. These findings are corroborated by a wealth of further studies that demonstrate that infants look longer at events in which some aspect of an object (e.g., number, location, volume, trajectory, shape, size, or surface features) is violated while occluded. Notably, they do not regard similar violations involving noncohesive substances as anomalous (Huntley-Fenner, 2001; Huntley-Fenner et al., 2002; see also Rosenberg & Carey, Chapter 7).

13.2 **Physical reasoning on the wall task**

Why then do toddlers fail to search accurately if the prerequisite object is present? As an example of the difficulties resolving this competence-performance distinction, we focus here on the case of developing knowledge about the core principle of solidity. For example, understanding that a ball cannot pass through a wall. By Piaget's (1954) estimations, infants should not reliably predict how a solid ball and wall should interact if the event is obscured from view because they lack object permanence to represent the continued independent existence of the wall and ball as well as sufficient physical knowledge that solid objects should be impenetrable. Nevertheless, Spelke et al. (1992) showed that even very young infants had expectations about the end state of such a display when measured via looking-time responses.

Spelke et al. (1992, Experiment 3) habituated 2.5-month-olds to a ball rolling behind a screen, its path impeded by a far wall situated behind the screen but visible above it (as depicted in Fig. 13.1). Following habituation, another near wall, again visible over the top of the screen, was placed in front of the far wall. The ball was launched and on consistent trials came to a stop by the near wall but on inconsistent trials came to a stop in front of the far wall again, appearing to have travelled through the near wall. Despite the end state being the same as on habituation trials, infants looked longer at the inconsistent events, suggesting that the ball having apparently travelled through the solid obstacle was in some way anomalous with their expectations. These findings, among others addressing similar spatiotemporal properties of objects, led Spelke to conclude that infants at this age could not only represent objects that were out of sight but also maintain expectations about their position and physical properties that constrain predictions and responses. She argued that infant failures to succeed in Piagetian search tasks arose as a result of motor difficulties in translating representations into actions rather than any difficulties in conceptualizing the continued existence of the object or the nature of solidity.

Given Spelke's assertion that this early developing solidity knowledge constitutes a core constraint of physical reasoning about the world, it was to be expected that older children should also possess the same awareness

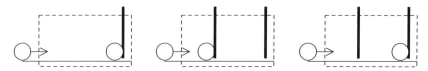

Fig. 13.1 Diagram of the wall study used in Experiment 3 of Spelke et al.'s (1992) studies. On the left is an example of a habituation trial where the infant sees the ball roll behind the screen that is then removed to show the ball resting against the far wall. In the test event, infants either witness a consistent event where the ball is revealed at the near wall or they see the ball resting against the far wall in the inconsistent outcome.

to guide their predictions and actions. Furthermore, as older children are not constrained by the performance limitations operating in infants, they should be expected to use core principles to search appropriately for objects. However, the prediction that older children would exhibit core knowledge on search measures was somewhat premature. A number of studies adapted from the range of Spelke's solidity task measures (e.g., Spelke et al., 1992) were used to explore the extent to which young children were able to represent hidden object interactions and utilize these representations to guide their search (e.g., Berthier, Bertenthal, Seaks, Sylvia, Johnson & Clifton, 2001; Hood, 1994; Hood et al., 2000). For example, one paradigm adapted Spelke's infant looking-time study and presented 2-year-olds with a panel of four doors, a ramp passing behind them, and a moveable, partially visible barrier wall. This four-door solidity apparatus is illustrated in Fig. 13.2.

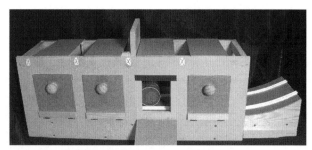

Fig. 13.2 The four-door solidity apparatus. This image illustrates the four-door apparatus showing the four doors, the partially visible wall, and an object rolling down the ramp. See colour plates.

A toy inside a tin can was rolled down the ramp where it was stopped by a barrier wall and the child was asked to retrieve it from one of the doors. If toddlers really understood the solidity constraint and could use that understanding to guide action, then they should have no difficulty with this task.

If children failed to search appropriately, however, it would suggest that the core principles demonstrated in infancy were not sufficient to constrain the search behavior of older children. Under these conditions, 2- and 2.5-year-olds consistently failed to search at the correct location, and it was not until around 3–3.5 years of age that they began to reliably pass the task (e.g., Berthier et al., 2000; Hood et al., 2000; Hood et al., 2003; Kloos & Keen, 2005; Kloos et al., 2006; Shutts et al., 2006), much later than would have been predicted on the core knowledge hypothesis. Critically, Hood et al. (2003) and Mash et al. (2003) conducted an equivalent looking-time study with toddlers and found that children in the same age group would look longer at an impossible event in which the ball appeared to have travelled through the barrier wall but would also search in the wrong location when asked to retrieve it. Thus, dissociations occur between gaze and search measures even within the same participant group. This shows that, at the very least, toddlers maintain a representation of the solidity constraint equivalent to that exhibited by the infants, but that this is insufficient to guide their real-world search. It remains unclear, however, why toddlers appear to show one level of knowledge when measured via gaze but a different level of knowledge when measured via search.

These issues have also emerged in the comparative studies mentioned earlier in the book (Santos & Hood, Chapter 1). Similar dissociations between gaze and search behavior occur in nonhuman primate populations on solidity tasks. Rhesus macaques were shown two cups, one resting on top of a shelf and one resting beneath it. A screen was raised, a piece of food dropped straight down, and the screen removed to reveal the outcome. Under these circumstances, the rhesus macaques looked longer if the food was retrieved from the lower cup, indicating that it had fallen through the table (Hauser, 2001). This suggests that the monkeys had an expectation that hidden solid objects could not pass through each other and so were surprised when this expectation was violated. However, when the screen was raised and the macaques were allowed to come and search for the food, they repeatedly searched in the lower cup, suggesting that the knowledge revealed by looking time does not support successful search (Santos & Hauser, 2002). These findings are echoed under the same conditions in the developmental literature—2-year-olds repeatedly search under a solid shelf for a dropped object when allowed to approach a similar setup (Hood, 1994; Hood et al., 2000).

13.3 Dissociations: methodological interpretations

In order to explain the apparent dissociation between knowledge shown on the looking-time studies and ignorance on equivalent search studies, some researchers claim that the results of the looking-time studies have been over-interpreted and that longer looking is not sufficient to indicate appropriate representation. For instance, Haith (1998) argued that the looking-time technique addressed only perceptual analysis of events. In other words, we may look longer at an event that violates some law but not be aware what the nature of the violation is (Hood, 2004). Other researchers claim that the looking-time and search experiments cannot be compared because they differ in the extent to which they require the child to predict the end state of the display (Meltzoff & Moore, 1998).

There is evidence that the prediction-postdiction distinction may contribute to children's difficulty on these tasks. While the looking-time studies require only that participants must notice that 'something is amiss' after the event (Diamond, 1998), the search tasks require the participant to predict where the object is going to land and the interaction between the object and the wall, before seeing the final state of the display. Similar dissociations have been found in other tasks comparing prediction and postdiction. For example, Kyeong and Spelke (1999) found that 2-year-olds asked to predict what trajectory a ball would take if launched off a cliff answered incorrectly by predicting a straight down path. And yet, when shown the outcome events, the same children looked much longer at this movement event compared with the normal parabolic curve. This dissociation has also been found in adults (McClosky, 1983; Kaiser et al., 1985).

Alternatively, Keen and colleagues propose that dissociations occur because in the predictive search task, participants must do the far more difficult task of integrating their representations of the different elements of the display — ball, wall, track and door — to determine where the object has stopped (Keen, 2003; Mash et al., 2003). Several studies have shown that children in this age range have difficulty with spatial integration of cues. For instance, DeLoache (1986) showed that 27-month-olds, but not 21-month-olds, could determine which of four identical containers an object was hidden in if there was a cue on the target. To pass this task, the toddlers had to integrate the cue with the hiding container, a task that was difficult for younger children. Shutts and colleagues (Shutts et al., 2006) extended the cue-integration proposal by referring to the adult visual attention literature. They hypothesized that factors that impair adults' attentive tracking of objects may account for children's search errors. Studies on object-based attention in adults suggest that attention is spread in a gradient-type fashion within an object and that cue proximity is only vital when the cue is part of the same object (known as the *same object advantage*; Egly et al., 1994).

In children's studies, Shutts et al. (2006) found that a tall pompom attached to the car and continuously visible as the car rolled behind the occluder was an insufficient cue to improve 2-year-olds' search performance. And yet, when a shorter pompom was attached and appeared in a window just above the location where the hidden toy had stopped, children's performance improved dramatically. They suggest that having the cue in closer proximity, and attached to, the moving object enables children's attention to more easily spread from the visible part to the hidden body. In this way, children's ability to form representations of the location of the toy following invisible displacement and interaction with the wall conforms to the same constraints as adult visual processes and thus can be explained in terms of the same models of mid-level object-directed attention (e.g., Scholl, 2001; Scholl & Pylyshyn, 1999; Treisman, 1998).

13.4 **Responses to methodological critiques**

Conversely, there have been a number of studies suggesting that neither prediction nor cue integration are the main limiting factors in success on the four-door task. First, 2-year-olds still perform poorly on the task if they observe the ball roll down the ramp and stop against the wall, then watch as the occluder is inserted afterwards (Mash et al., 2003). Here, there is no prediction and the child simply has to remember the last seen position of the ball. Even the visible portion of the wall extended over the screen fails to aid memory. Most dramatically, Kloos and Keen (2005) showed that 2.5-year-olds would correctly place a doll at the location in front of the wall where the ball would land once rolled. Thus, the children could integrate the relevant aspects of the task and predict the end state given the location of the barrier wall. If the display was occluded, then this predictive ability was lost. Thus, children know that the occluded object and wall continue to exist and can predict the effect of a wall on a moving object, yet they seem unable to use that knowledge to constrain their search.

To determine whether the dissociations between the search and gaze results could be explained by the need to predict outcomes in one but not the other on the four-door solidity task, we filmed toddlers' predictive gaze behavior before they got up to search (Gjersoe & Hood, 2005). This equated the level of prediction necessary on the gaze and search tasks while keeping the other parameters, such as number of available cues, constant. Under these conditions, a significant number of 2.5-year-olds gazed at the correct door but subsequently searched at the wrong location. Thus, children of this age will look at the correct door from among the array, fixating it first and longest while waiting to be asked to search but then will approach the apparatus and open an incorrect door. Clearly, when measured by gaze, these children are holding a sufficiently strong representation of the ball's hidden trajectory and its interaction with the partially visible wall and are capable of integrating those aspects of the display with their view of the panel of doors in order to determine where the ball will stop. Yet, something about the process of getting up to search disrupts this representation sufficiently for them to consistently fail at the task when endeavoring to utilize it for directed action.

Moreover, children exhibit this knowledge via a relatively complicated action response. Further preliminary evidence of this ability was found by Wilson et al. (2007) who showed that 2.5-year-olds would answer appropriately if the experimenter pointed to each of the doors and the child responded with a 'yes' or 'no' to directed questions about whether the toy was behind a particular door or not. This ability to express their knowledge verbally goes beyond the predictions of the traditional implicit-explicit accounts as declaring one's knowledge in an explicit verbal response is thought to require stronger representations than search alone (e.g., Karmiloff-Smith, 1992).

These findings suggest that the dissociations in knowledge found in infants, toddlers and non-human primates tested on different measures arise as a result of more than just methodological confounds. Which in turn raises the question of whether knowledge exhibited on gaze-measures alone is even interesting. Philosophers have questioned whether constructs such as 'knowledge' and 'mental representation' can exist independently of contexts (Churchland & Sejnowski, 1992; Rorty, 1979) and Mother Nature seems to select for clever actions, not good ideas (Hood, 2004). On the other hand, dissociations that occur in developing populations may provide fundamental insights into the manner in which knowledge is represented in the mind. By exploring how different modes of thought become integrated through development, researchers can better understand these individual processes before they become inextricably linked in the developed system. This reasoning has led a number of cognitive scientists to propose theories for why dissociations between gaze and search occur.

13.5 Dual processing pathways for object knowledge

The difference between looking and reaching has been interpreted as evidence for two separable systems: a fast, automatic perceptual one and a slower action system open to higher-level processing (Milner & Goodale, 1995). Drawing primarily from a range of evidence based on adult and animal studies, it is recognized that there is specialization within the visual processing architecture such that information regarding features (e.g., color, faces, some aspects of shape and size) is processed in the ventral stream of the brain, separately from information appropriate for action (e.g., location, motion, size, and crude shape for grasping), which is processed in the dorsal stream (e.g., Glover, 2002; Grossberg et al., 1993; Hu & Goodale, 2000; Jeannerod, 1988; Milner & Goodale, 1995; Rizzolatti et al., 1994; Ungerleider & Mishkin, 1982). Critically, it is believed that the two streams of information emerging from the dorsal and ventral pathways are integrated in the frontal and parietal lobes, areas that have maturation periods that extend throughout early childhood. Mareschal and Johnson (2003) attributed dissociations in infants' performance to the fact that gaze responses could be directed by representations on either stream but action responses required integration of information from both of the streams to recognize and locate the object and to plan and conduct appropriate actions upon it (see Mareschal & Bremner, Chapter 10).

The dual-path theory is more usually applied to search errors that occur in young infancy, before 7.5 months of age (e.g., Bertenthal, 1996; Mareschal & Johnson, 2003; Newman et al., 2001), but have also been used to explain dissociations in preschoolers' performance. For instance, DeLoache et al. (2004) showed that children between 18 and 30 months of age frequently make scale errors—trying to get into tiny cars and sit on tiny chairs. Whereas the perception of an object and the organization of actions upon it are normally seamlessly integrated in adults, DeLoache et al. suggested that scale errors occurred in young children because of a failure of inhibitory control combined with the use of visual information for planning versus controlling their actions. Specifically, they suggested that scale errors occurred when the identity of an object, processed by the ventral stream, was not integrated with information about its size, processed by the dorsal stream. This, in turn, resulted in inappropriate action sequences that were not inhibited by the immature prefrontal cortex. Thus, by this reasoning, errors in toddlers' responses could have occurred because multiple representations of a display, processed in separate parts of the brain, failed to integrate in a manner that appropriately guided object-directed actions. So, although the perceptual systems of children may appropriately integrate the available cues in the four-door solidity task, as evident from the gaze studies, that information is unavailable to the immature action-planning system.

13.6 **Spatiotemporal versus contact mechanical knowledge**

Another possibility is that dissociations of the type of knowledge exhibited via different measures are most evident on specifically those tasks that measure understanding of object interactions. Researchers analyzing the results in terms of object-file theories have found a divide between children's perform-ance on tasks that require representation of object mechanics (how objects interact in space and time) compared with spatiotemporal constraints (how object move through space and time) to guide their expectations about hidden entities (Leslie, 1994; Scholl & Leslie, 1999; Santos, 2004). Contact-mechanical tasks include those tests that explore understanding about solidity and per-sistence (Baillargeon et al., 1985; Baillargeon & DeVos, 1991; Spelke et al., 1992), physical causality (Cohen & Oakes, 1993; Leslie, 1984; Leslie & Keeble, 1987), collision (Baillargeon, 1995), containment, and support (Aguiar & Baillargeon, 1998 ; Baillargeon et al., 1992; Needham & Baillargeon, 1993) whereas spatiotemporal tasks explore understanding about such things as con-tinuous motion (Spelke et al., 1992, 1995), number, and extent (Wynn, 1992; Feigenson et al., 2002).

There is a paucity of empirical research that directly compares the develop-ment of children's spatiotemporal and contact-mechanical knowledge, but this theoretical stand-point has been addressed in a number of reviews of the field (Leslie, 1988, 1994; Scholl & Leslie, 1999; Santos, 2004; Santos & Hauser, 2002; Santos et al., 2006), and the most compelling within group studies have come from the comparative psychology literature. Santos (2004) showed that adult rhesus macaques, similar to toddlers, consistently fail to search at the correct location for a treat that has been rolled behind an occluder and stopped by a par-tially visible wall (a contact-mechanical task). However, the same monkeys can pass the task if smaller screens are placed in front of each possible search location and the object's trajectory is visible (a spatiotemporal task). Santos concludes that dissociations in the results of human infants', toddlers', and nonhuman primates' object-gaze and object-search tasks may be attributable to different systems for processing spatiotemporal compared to contact-mechanical events. She also points out that processing requirements for the two tasks were differ-ent; whereas spatiotemporal tasks required reasoning about how things move in time and space, contact-mechanical tasks necessitated the additional step of understanding that objects continue to exist as bounded entities even when occluded.

Leslie's (1994) dual-systems account of this divide in the results argues that spatiotemporal understanding can feasibly grow directly out of visual proc-esses from tracking objects through time and space and that these processes may be early developing, hard-wired, and remain fundamentally unchanged throughout the lifespan. Conversely, he suggests that the nature of knowledge about contact-mechanical interactions is more in keeping with traditional definitions of core cognitive architectures in that it is theory-based and prin-ciple-driven. Leslie's dual-systems account is inconsistent with Spelke's core knowledge theory that argues that a single system of knowledge underlies the perception of object motion and object reasoning.

If the dual-systems theory is correct, it suggests that different cognitive and neural architectures may underlie each mechanism. There is some evidence for this hypothesis already as perception of spatiotemporal constraints appears inevitable regardless of top-down processing (as in visual illusions) whereas perception of contact-mechanical events can be influenced by prior experience with the objects. For instance, Baillargeon (1991) showed that infants from 8 months of age would look longer if a rotating screen appeared to pass through a solid block but did not look longer if they have been shown beforehand that the block was compressible. Santos (2004, Santos et al., 2006) proposes that the spatiotemporal processing mechanism is unlikely to be disrupted by outside influences and thus results in robust responses across tasks, ages, and populations. Conversely, the results suggest that the contact-mechanical system could be more easily disrupted by outside influences, which may include perseverative biases, naive theories, or difficulties with task demands. Consequently, understanding how children's knowledge in each domain is developing may require a more sensitive approach to experimental design that considers the architecture of each system and the extent to which it may be interrupted by outside influences.

13.7 Competition and inhibition in search

One implication of this theory is that infants and children may be forming appropriate representations of the event but that these are competing with equally strong (but contextually inappropriate) representations or action responses formed by the task setup that must be inhibited in order to succeed. This idea builds on the theory that infants' improvement on search tasks is linked not only to developing memory capacity but also to the ability to inhibit prepotent responses (e.g., Bell & Fox, 1992; Diamond, 1991, 1998; Diamond & Doar, 1989; Matthews et al., 1996; Piaget, 1954).

Perseveration is the repetition of a particular response, often launched by a triggering stimulus without conscious intervention. As such, these responses can be activated even when they are incompatible with the current goals and visible cues (Simpson & Riggs, 2007). For instance, Butterworth (1977) has shown that infants will make perseverative errors to reach for a previously correct location even when they can see the target object through an adjacent transparent cover. Importantly, many researchers (e.g., Diamond, 1990; Diamond & Gilbert, 1989) have shown that lack of inhibition can get in the way of demonstrating what you already know. Irrational biases in children's successful performance on another naïve physics task—avoiding a ball dropped down a deviated tube—have also been explained by inhibitory processing (Freeman, Hood & Meehan, 2004). A general capacity for inhibitory control has been shown to improve steadily between 3 and 5 years of age (Gerstadt et al., 1994; Jones et al., 2003; Simpson & Riggs, 2005), and this has been linked to a corresponding maturation of the prefrontal cortex.

Disruption or damage to this region can generate perseverative responding on a variety of tasks in otherwise healthy humans and animals, indicating its role as a site where inhibitory control is somehow regulated (for review, see Passingham, 1993). There is therefore good reason to believe that it may still be a factor in preschoolers' performance on the four-door task. The increased prefrontal lobe function between the ages of 2 and 3 years may reflect an increased inhibitory capacity that enables the older children to succeed whereas the knowledge of the younger toddlers is masked by perseverative responses elicited by the complexity of the task.

Hauser (1999) makes a distinction between different types of inhibition that occur at an 'affective' action level (e.g., prepotent reaching for a visible object) compared with a 'paradigmatic' level in which the perseverative response is in relation to a dominant 'theory' rather than a dominant action. He suggests that an example of the latter type of perseverative responding occurs on the shelf study described earlier (Section 13.2). Although children and macaques are aware that solid objects do not pass through each other, Hood (1995) and Hauser (2003) suggest that they simultaneously hold a theory—the 'gravity bias'—that all things must drop straight down to the ground, which could be innately endowed or constructed through multiple incidences throughout very early development. Thus, the solidity constraint is sufficient to guide their gaze responses but, when asked to come and search for the object, the gravity bias takes over and controls their action responses.

By this explanation, success on the search task is dependent on the development of the frontal lobes throughout early childhood to inhibit this dominant theory and enable the child to become sensitive to alternative representations and the available cues in the display. Dissociations, by this explanation, occur in children's responses when different modalities are compared because the task constraints quickly establish a dominant action response or they come to the task with preconceived representations of how objects should behave and these biases are difficult to overcome motorically without mature frontal lobe functioning. Thus, constantly reaching for an object directly below the location where it was dropped regardless of the shelf occurs as a result of paradigmatic perseveration—the naive theory that all objects must fall straight down to the ground interrupts the representation of the object having been stopped by the shelf. Conversely, constantly reaching to the location where the object was previously placed (Butterworth, 1977) occurs due to affective perseveration—the action response of reaching to that location interrupts the representation of the object at the new location.

13.8 **Perseverative search**

One way to determine the extent and type of perseverative biases in the four-door solidity experiment is to examine the types of errors that children make. Analysis of this type has revealed that the majority of errors in children under the age of 3 years can be attributed to perseverative action responses—such as returning repeatedly to the same door—or perseverative theories—such as searching on the wrong side of the wall (Berthier et al., 2000; Gjersoe & Hood, 2005; Hood et al., 2003). Interestingly, the pattern of errors in younger children tends more toward perseverative action responses whereas older children seem to more frequently be responding in relation to an alternative 'theory' (Gjersoe & Hood, 2005; Hauser, 2003).

For instance, one of the dominant perseverative error patterns in younger children (2–2.6 years of age) is to return to a door that was correct on the previous trial. This search error is often seen in infant studies (e.g., Ahmed & Ruffman, 1998; Hofstadter & Reznick, 1996) and is attributed to immature frontal lobe function (Diamond, 1998). Interestingly, older children (3–3.6 years of age) perform this error pattern significantly less than chance, suggesting that they may be inhibiting this perseverative strategy in order to search at the correct location. Indeed, a further study deliberately biased children to search at one door by having the ball land there repeatedly. The wall was then moved and the children were asked to go to a door where there was no ball (this paradigm in which the correct location is avoided was based on Leslie & Polizzi, 1998). Thus the children had three equally correct options - to go to the previously biased door or to the two unbiased locations. Under these circumstances, 3 year olds went to the biased location significantly less often than either of the other two options (Gjersoe & Hood, 2005). A similar response bias known as 'inhibition of return' has also been observed in the visual search literature that shows that it is harder to return to a previously attended location than to a novel, unattended location. This is thought to aid search through a number of targets by inhibiting return to those targets that have already been checked (Klein, 1988). Thus, the toddlers' tendency not to go back to the location that was correct on the previous trial suggests that this may be a perseverative action response that they are inhibiting in order to succeed at the task. The perseverative compulsion seems to fade as children get older, however, as the pattern does not persist in 4 year olds who go to all three locations with equal regularity. As compared to the 2 year olds, 3 and 4 year olds tended to make more errors in which they searched on the wrong side of the wall, indicating an associative or theoretical strategy being over-applied. These findings suggest that eventual success may arise through a combination of inhibiting perseverative action responses and maintaining the correct strategy.

13.9 **Conclusion**

Although the wealth of looking-time studies suggest much earlier and more sophisticated object knowledge than Piaget attributed to children, at the root of the performance-competence distinction is a lack of agreement as to where to set the threshold for what we consider as knowledge. Is it sufficient for knowledge to be revealed after an event as a violation of expectations, or is it the ability to put those expectations into action before an event that is a marker for true knowledge? By pulling apart the dissociations and contradictions prevalent throughout the cognitive development literature, a richer picture of how knowledge is constructed and the different levels at which biases can occur has been revealed. Dissociations between gaze and search measures can no longer be attributed solely to methodological confounds nor to age-related differences.

Yet, an empirical chasm remains in determining why different levels of knowledge are evident via different modalities. It remains to be seen whether children's difficulty on traditional search tasks arises at the level of building appropriate representations, using those representations for action, or inhibiting alternative, inappropriate representations. The prevalence of dissociations highlights the importance of careful experimental design that simultaneously measures knowledge from a variety of modalities. Further, it is important that interpretations of results in relation to levels of knowledge be carefully modulated by an understanding that multiple representations may coexist at any one time. Studying dissociations over different concurrent modalities enables us to constrain our theories as to the manner in which cognitive development occurs and build a richer picture of how it is that children are representing the world, how multiple representations are maintained, and how these processes may have evolved.

Acknowledgments

The work reported in this chapter was supported by grants from the Economic and Social Research Council (UK) awarded to the second author. We thank Alice Wilson and Josie Waskett for assistance in collecting data and all the families who took part in studies at the Bristol Cognitive Development Centre.

References

Aguiar, A. & Baillargeon, R. (1998). 8.5-month-old infants' reasoning about containment events. *Child Development, 69*, 636–653.

Ahmed, A., & Ruffman, T. (1998). Why do infants make A-not-B errors in a search task, yet show memory for the location of hidden objects in a non-search task? *Developmental Psychology, 34*, 441–453.

Baillargeon, R. (1995). A model of physical reasoning in infancy. *Advances in Infancy Research*, vol. 9 (pp. 306–371). Norwood, NJ: Ablex.

Baillargeon, R., & DeVos, J. (1991). Object permanence in young infants: further evidence. *Child Development, 62*, 1227–1246.

Baillargeon, R., Graber, M., DeVos, J., & Black, J. C. (1990). Why do young infants fail to search for hidden objects? *Cognition, 36*, pp. 255–284.

Baillargeon, R., Needham, A., & DeVos, J. (1992). The development of young infants' intuitions about support. *Early Development and Parenting, 1*, 69–78.

Baillargeon, R., Spelke, E. S., & Wasserman, S. (1985). Object permanence in five-month-old infants. *Cognition, 20*, 191–208.

Bell, M. A., & Fox, N. A. (1992). The relations between frontal brain electrical activity and cognitive development during infancy. *Child Development, 23*, 1142–1163.

Bertenthal, B. I. (1996). Origins and early development of perception, action, and representation. *Annual Review of Psychology, 47*, 431–459.

Berthier, N. E., Bertenthal, B. I., Seaks, J. D., Sylvia, M., Johnson, R., & Clifton, R. K. (2001). Using object knowledge in visual tracking and reaching. *Infancy, 2*, 257–284.

Berthier, N., DeBlois, S., Poirier, C. R., Novak, M. A., & Clifton, R. K. (2000). Where's the ball? Two and three year olds reason about unseen events. *Developmental Psychology, 36*, 394–401.

Butterworth, G. E. (1977). Object disappearance and error in Piaget's stage IV task. *Journal of Experimental Child Psychology, 23*, 391–401.

Cohen, L. B., & Oakes, L. M. (1993). How infants perceive a simple causal event. *Developmental Psychology, 29*, 421–433.

Churchland, P. S., & Sejnowski, T. J. (1992). *The Computational Brain*. Cambridge, MA: MIT Press.

DeLoache, J. (1986). Symbolic functioning in very young children: understanding of pictures and models. *Child Development, 62*, 736–752.

DeLaoche, J. S., Uttal, D. H., & Rosengren, K. S. (2004). Scale errors offer evidence for a perception-action dissociation early in life. *Science, 304*, 1027–1029.

Diamond, A. (1990). Developmental time course in human infants and infant monkeys, and the neural bases of inhibitory control in reaching. *Annals of the New York Academy of Sciences, 608*, 637–676.

Diamond, A. (1991). Neuropsychological insights into the meaning of object concept development. In S. Carey, & R. Gelman (Eds.), *The Epigenesis of Mind: Essays on Biology and Cognition* (pp. 67–110). Hillsdale, NJ: Erlbaum.

Diamond, A. (1998). Understanding the A-not-B error: working memory vs. reinforced response, or active trace vs. latent trace. *Developmental Science, 1*, 185–189.

Diamond, A., & Doar, B. (1989). The performance of human infants on a measure of frontal cortex function, the delayed response task. *Developmental Psychobiology, 22*, 271–294.

Diamond, A., & Gilbert, J. (1989). Development as progressive inhibitory control of action: retrieval of a contiguous object. *Cognitive Development, 4*, 223–249.

Egly, R., Driver, J., & Rafal, R. (1994). Shifting visual attention between objects and locations: evidence for normal and parietal lesion subjects. *Journal of Experimental Psychology: General, 123*, 161–177.

Feigenson, L., Carey, S., & Spelke, E. S. (2002). The representations underlying infants' choice of more: object-files versus analog magnitudes. *Psychological Science, 13*, 150–156.

Freeman, N. H., Hood, B. M., & Meehan, C. (2004).Young children who abandon error behaviourally still have to free themselves mentally: a retrospective test for inhibition in intuitive physics. *Developmental Science, 7*, 277–282.

Gerstadt, C., Hong, Y., & Diamond, A. (1994). The relationship between cognition and action: performance of 3-7 year old children on a Stroop-like day-night test. *Cognitive Development, 53*, 129–153.

Gjersoe, N. G. & Hood, B. M. (2005). The development of object knowledge dissociations in toddlers. Paper presented at the Economic and Social Research Council Symposium: Comparative Issues in Object Representation, Yale University.

Glover, S. (2002). Visual illusions affect planning but not control. *Trends in Cognitive Sciences, 6*, 288–292.

Grossberg, S., Guenther, F., Bullock, D., & Greve, D. (1993). Neural representations for sensory-motor control, II: learning a head-centered visuomotor representation of 3-D target position. *Neural Networks, 6*, 43–67.

Haith, M. M. (1998). Who put the cog in infant cognition? Is rich interpretation too costly? *Infant Behavior and Development, 21*, 167–79.

Hauser , M. D. (1999). Perseveration, inhibition and the prefrontal cortex: a new look. *Current Opinion in Neurobiology, 9*, 214–222.

Hauser, M. D. (2001). Searching for food in the wild: a non-human primate's expectations about invisible displacement. *Developmental Science, 4*, 84–93.

Hauser, M. D. (2003). Knowing about knowing: dissociations between perception and actions systems over evolution and in development. *Annual New York Academy of Sciences, 1*, 1–25.

Hofstadter, M., & Reznick, J. S. (1996). Response modality affects human infant delayed-response performance. *Developmental Psychology, 67*, 646–658.

Hood, B. M. (1994). Searching for falling objects in 2-year-olds is different from watching them fall in 4-month-olds. Poster presented at the 9th Biennial International Conference for Infant Studies, Paris, France.

Hood, B.M. (1995). Gravity rules for 2- to 4-year olds? *Cognitive Development, 10*, 577–598.

Hood, B. M. (2004). Is looking good enough or does it beggar belief? *Developmental Science, 7*, 415–417.

Hood, B. M., Carey, S., & Prasada, S. (2000). Predicting the outcomes of physical events. *Child Development, 71*, 1540–1554.

Hood, B. M., Cole-Davies, V., & Dias, M. (2003). Looking and searching measures of object knowledge in preschool children. *Developmental Psychology, 39*, 61–70.

Huntley-Fenner, G. (2001). Why count stuff? Young preschoolers do not use number for measurement in continuous dimensions. *Developmental Science, 4*, 456–462.

Huntley-Fenner, G., Carey, S., & Solimando, A. (2002). Objects are individuals but stuff doesn't count: perceived rigidity and cohesiveness influence infants' representations of small groups of discrete entities. *Cognition, 85*, 203–221.

Hu, Y., & Goodale, M. A. (2000). Grasping after a delay shifts size-scaling from absolute to relative metrics. *Journal of Cognitive Neuroscience, 12*, 856–868.

Jeannerod, M. (1988). *The Neural and Behavioral Organization of Goal-Directed Movements*. Oxford: Oxford University Press.

Jones, L. B., Rothbart, M. K., & Posner, M. I. (2003). Development of executive attention in preschool children. *Developmental Science, 6*, 498–504.

Kaiser, M. K., Proffitt, D. R., & McCloskey, M. (1985). The development of beliefs about falling objects. *Perception & Psychophysics, 38*, 533–539.

Karmiloff-Smith, A. (1992). *Beyond Modularity*. Cambridge, MA: MIT Press.

Keen, R. (2003). Representation of objects and events: Why do infants look so smart and toddlers look so dumb? *Current directions in Psychological Science, 12*, 79–83.

Kellman, P. J., & Spelke, E. S. (1983). Perception of partly occluded objects in infancy. *Cognitive Psychology, 15*, 483–524.

Kim, I. K., & Spelke, E. S. (1999). Perception and understanding of effects of gravity and inertia on object motion. *Developmental Science, 2*, 339–362.

Klein, R. (1988). Inhibitory tagging system facilitates visual search. *Nature, 334*, 430–431.

Kloos, H., Haddad, J. M., & Keen, R. (2006). Which measures are available to 24-motnh-olds? Evidence from point-of-gaze measures during search. *Infant Behavior and Development, 29*, 243–250.

Kloos, H., & Keen, R. (2005). An exploration of toddlers' problems in a search task. *Infancy, 7*, 7–34.

Leslie, A. M. (1984). Spatiotemporal continuity and the perception of causality in infants. *Perception, 13*, 287–305.

Leslie, A. M. (1988). The necessity of illusion: perception and thought in infancy. In L Weiskrantz (Ed.), *Thought Without Language* (pp. 185–210). Oxford: Clarendon.

Leslie, A. M. (1994). ToMM, ToBy, and agency: core architecture and domain specificity. In L. A. Hirschfeld, & S. A. Gelman (Eds.), *Mapping the Mind: Domain Specificity in Cognition and Culture* (pp. 119–148). Cambridge: Cambridge University Press.

Leslie, A. M., & Keeble, S. (1987). Do six-month-old infants perceive causality? *Cognition, 25*, 265–288.

Leslie, A. M., & Polizzi, P. (1998). Inhibitory processing in the false belief task: two conjectures. *Developmental Science, 1*, 247–253.

Leslie, A. M., German, T. P., & Polizzi, P. (2005). Belief-desire reasoning as a process of selection. *Cognitive Psychology, 50*, 45–85.

Mareschal, D., & Johnson, M. H. (2003). The 'what' and 'where' of object representations in infancy. *Cognition, 88*, 259–276.

Mash, C., Keen, R., & Berthier, N. E. (2003). Visual access and attention in two-year-olds' event reasoning and object search. *Infancy, 4*, 371–388.

Matthews, A., Ellis, A. E., & Nelson, C. A. (1996). Development of preterm and full-term infant ability on AB, recall memory, transparent barrier detour and means-end tasks. *Child Development, 67*, 2658–2676.

McCloskey, M. (1983). Intuitive physics. *Scientific American, 248*, 122–130.

Meltzoff, A. N., & Moore, M. K. (1998). Objects representation, identity and the paradox of early performance. *Infant Behavior and Development, 21*, 201–236.

Milner, A. D., & Goodale, M. A. (1995). *The Visual Brain in Action*. Oxford: Oxford University Press.

Munakata, Y. (1997). Perseverative reaching in infancy: the roles of hidden toys and motor history in the A-not-B task. *Infant Behavior and Development, 20*, 405–416.

Munakata, Y., McClelland, J. L., Johnson, M. H., & Siegler, R. (1997). Rethinking infant knowledge: toward an adaptive process account of successes and failures in object permanence tasks. *Psychological Review, 104*, 686–713.

Munakata, Y., Santos, L. R., Spelke, E. S., Hauser, M. D., & O'Reilly, R. C. (2001). Visual representation in the wild: how rhesus monkeys parse objects. *Journal of Cognitive Neuroscience, 13*, 44–58.

Needham, A., & Baillargeon, R. (1993). Intuitions about support in 4.5-month-old infants. *Cognition, 47*, 121–148.

Newman, C., Atkinson, J., & Braddick, O. (2001). The development of reaching and looking preferences in infants to objects of different sizes. *Developmental Psychology, 37*, 561–572.

Passingham, R. (1993). *The Frontal Lobes and Voluntary Action*. Oxford: Oxford University Press.

Piaget, J. (1954). *The Construction of Reality in the Child*. New York: Basic Books.

Rorty, R. (1979). *Philosophy and the Mirror of Nature*. Princeton, NJ: Princeton University Press.

Rizzolatti, G., Riggio, L., & Sheliga, B. M. (1994). Space and selectiveattention. In C. Umiltà, & M. Moskovitch (Eds.), *Attention and Performance XV* (pp. 231–265). Cambridge, MA: MIT Press.

Santos, L. R. (2004). Core knowledges: a dissociations between spatiotemporal knowledge and contact-mechanics in a non-human primate? *Developmental Science, 7*, 167–174.

Santos, L. R., & Hauser, M. D. (2002). Monkey see monkey do? Dissociations between looking and action in a non-human primate. *Developmental Science, 5*, F1–F7.

Santos, L. R., Seelig, D., & Hauser, M. D. (2006). Cotton-top tamarins' (*Saguinus oedipus*) expectations about occluded objects: a dissociation between looking and reaching tasks. *Infancy, 9*, 133–146.

Scholl, B. J. (2001). Object and attention: the state of the art. *Cognition, 80*, 1–46.

Scholl, B. J., & Leslie, A. M. (1999). Explaining the infant's object concept: beyond the perception/cognition dichotomy. In E. Lepore, & Z. Pylyshyn (Eds.), *What is Cognitive Science?* (pp. 26–73). Oxford: Blackwell.

Scholl, B. J., & Pylyshyn, Z. W. (1999). Tracking multiple items through occlusion: clues to visual objecthood. *Cognitive Psychology*, 259–290.

Shutts, K., Keen, R., & Spelke, E. S. (2006). Object boundaries influence toddlers' performance on a search task. *Developmental Science, 9*, 97–107.

Simpson, A. & Riggs, K. J. (2005). Factors responsible for performance on the day-night task: response set or semantics? *Developmental Science, 8*, 360–71.

Simpson, A., & Riggs, K. J. (2007). Under what conditions do young children have difficulty inhibiting manual actions? *Developmental Psychology, 43*, 417–428.

Spelke, E. S. (1994). Initial knowledge: six suggestions. *Cognition, 50*, 431–445.

Spelke, E. S., Breinlinger, K., Macomber, J., & Jacobson, K. (1992). Origins of knowledge. *Psychological Review, 99*, 605–632.

Spelke, E. S., Kestenbaum, R., Simons, D. J., & Wein, D. (1995). Spatiotemporal continuity, smoothness of motion and object identity in infancy. *British Journal of Developmental Psychology, 13*, 113–142.

Treisman, A. (1998). Feature binding, attention and object perception. *Philosophical Transactions of the Royal Society, 353*, 1295–1306.

Ungerleider, L. G., & Mishkin, M. (1982). Two cortical visual systems. In M. A. Goodale, & R. J. W. Mansfield (Eds.), *Analysis of Visual Behavior* . Cambridge, MA: MIT Press.

van de Walle, G. & Spelke, E. S. (1996). Spatiotemporal integration of object perception in infancy. *Child Development, 67*, 2621–2640.

Wilson, A., Gjersoe, N. L., & Hood, B. M. (2007). Serial and parallel inhibitory control on successful search? Poster presented at the biannual symposium of the Society for Research into Cognitive Development, Boston, Massachusetts.

Wynn, K. (1992). Addition and subtraction by human infants. *Nature, 358*, 749–750.

Index

accumulator 85, 99–100
active memory 249–52
active vision 214–18
amodal completion 137, 138
amodal integration 137–41
animals
  autonomous movement 193–7
  categorization of 190–2
  generalization of learning
    on color 202–4
    on shape 202
  numerical cognition 53–5
    cross-modal representations 65–9
    selective pressure for 63–4
    vs humans 58–63
  object representation 7–8
animate motion 207
A-not-B error 3–4, 14–15, 249–52
apparent motion 141–4
  repetition blindness 143, 144
appearance changes 312
areas of interest 214
arithmetic 100–1
artifacts 190, 205, 207
autoencoder models 232–4
autonomous motion
  animals 193–7
  nonsense objects 198–9
  vehicles 197–8
  see also self-propelled objects
autonomy 330–4

back propagation 230
Balint syndrome 145
Bayesian learning 185
behavioral dissociation 239–40
behavioral information 313
Berkeley, George 3
bias
  gravity 364
  learned 279–81
  shape
    development of 268–71, 279
    in word learning 263–81

binding problem 144
bootstrapping 97
boundedness 354

catastrophic forgetting 30, 37–46
categorization
  of animals 190–1
  of vehicles 190, 191
caused motion 207
change detection task 37
Clever Hans 54
cognition
  infant 109–10
    occlusion vs implosion 116–20
    simple splitting events 124–7
    spatiotemporal priority 146–8
  visual 110–12
cognitive science, objects in 17–18
cohesion 6, 7, 107–29, 143, 311, 354
  violations of 120–7
    adult perception 121–4
    infant research 120–1
    simple splitting events 124–7
cohesive entities 165–70
coincidences, avoidance of 156–7
color 204–5
  learning generalization on 202–4
competence-performance distinction 354
competition 363–5
computational modeling 227–31
  connectionist 227, 228–31
    autoencoder networks 232–4
    connection weights 230
    feed-forward network 229–30
    information processing 229–31
    multidirectional flow 230
    object permanence 245–9, 253–5
    reasons for building 228–9
    violation of expectation 236
  constraints 228–9
  symbolic 227
    object permanence 240–5
conceptual heterogeneity 40–6
connectionist algorithms 185

connectionist models 227, 228–31
  autoencoder networks 232–4
  connection weights 230
  feed-forward network 229–30
  information processing 229–31
  multidirectional flow 230
  object permanence 245–9, 253–5
    Mareschal model 246–8
    Munakata model 245–6
  reasons for building 228–9
  violation of expectation 236
contact 6, 8
contact mechanical knowledge 361–3
continuity 6, 7, 94, 107–29, 207, 305–6
  self-propelled objects 297–306
  through occlusion 113–20
continuous amounts 91–2
core cognition/knowledge hypothesis 6–9,
    107, 120, 148, 165, 177–8, 211, 234,
    353, 354, 356
  noncohesive entities 177–8, 179
  object recognition 4–9
correspondence 153

declarative knowledge 242
discrete quantities 86–8, 93–102
  integers 100–2
  mental magnitudes/accumulator
    99–100
  object indexing 93–5
  sets 95–9
dishabituation 66–8, 86–7
displacement 297–306
  tests with younger infants 299–305
dissociations 357–9
domain-specific learning mechanisms 165
dorsal lateral prefrontal cortex 15
dual processing pathways 360–1

element integrity principle 143
empiricism 265–6
enriched parallel individuation 97
entity detector 182–4
entity files 171, 172
enumeration 10, 12–13
event files 95
expectancy violation 7–8, 168, 231
    234–9, 285
  connectionism models 236
  looking-reaching dissociation
    model 236
  trajectory prediction model 237–8

falling, resistance to 318–24
  explanations 323–4
  tests with younger infants 320–3
familiarization 199–201
featural information 313

files
  entity 171, 172
  event 95
  object 94, 110, 122, 153
flash-lag illusion 157
form face area 150

gaze behavior 359–60
generalization of learning 201–4
  animals
    on color 202–4
    on shape 202
  mechanisms 204–5
grasping 180–2
gravity bias 364

habituation
  autoencoder models 232–4
  Sokolovian 232
habituation of looking paradigm 231
Hebbian learning 251
hippocampal learning 222

identification 10
identity theory of Bower 240, 242, 243
illusory conjunctions 144–6
impletion 154
implosion 116–20
inanimate motion 207
individuals, recognition of see individuation
individuation 9–13
  in infants 9–13, 33, 148
  parallel 95–6
    enriched 97
  property/kind 10–12
inert objects 285, 286
  action of self-propelled objects on
    324–9
  as agents 337–41
  prevention from falling 325–9
  resistance to falling 318
  resistance to movement 315–16
  setting in motion 324–5
infants
  A not B error 3–4, 14–15, 249–52
  categorization by 191–2
  cognition 109–10
    occlusion vs implosion 116–20
    simple splitting events 124–7
    spatiotemporal priority 146–8
  expectations about self-propelled objects
    287–330
  forgetting 37–46
    catastrophic 30, 38
  individuation in 9–13, 33, 148
  looking 5–6
  means-end coordination 5
  multiple object tracking 85–102

numerical cognition 66–8
object competence 3–4
object interaction 229
reaching and grasping 180–2
representations of material entities
    165–86
working memory
    capacity 27–31
    complexity 32–7
    exceeding capacity 38–46
information
    behavioral 313
    featural 313
    processing 229–31
    spatiotemporal 12
inhibition 363–5
    of return 365
input analyzers 165, 167
integers 100–2
intention 334–7
intraparietal sulcus 27, 32, 74, 75

knowledge
    contact mechanical 361–3
    core 6–9, 107, 120, 148, 177–8, 234, 353,
        354, 356
    declarative 242
    procedural 241, 242
    spatiotemporal 361–3

language
    and individuation 10–12
    learned bias 279–81
latent memory 249–52
lateral intraparietal area 76, 77
learning 185–6, 189
    Bayesian 185
    generalization of 201–4
        animals 202–4
        mechanisms 204–5
    Hebbian 251
    hippocampal 222
    mechanism of 274–9
    neocortical 222
    short-term 221–2
    words, shape bias in 263–81
lexical heterogeneity 40–6
location changes 306, 309–11
Locke, John 3
long-term storage 221–2
looking 5–6
looking-reaching dissociation model
    16, 236
looking-time paradigms 231–2, 358

material entities
    cohesive vs noncohesive 166–70
    representations of 165–86

means-end coordination 5
memory
    active 249–52
    latent 249–52
    working see working memory
mental magnitudes 99–100
metaphysics 3
mid-level vision 110
modularity 165
motion
    apparent 141–4
        repetition blindness 143, 144
    autonomous 193–7
        nonsense object 198–9
        vehicles 197–8
    direction of 288–92
    expectance of 313–15
    inanimate 207
    resistance to 315–18
multiple object tracking 12, 85–102, 111,
    121–2
    confounds 88
    continuous quantities 86–8, 91–2
    controlling for stuff 89–91
    discrete quantities 86–8, 93–102
        integers 100–2
        mental magnitudes/accumulator
            99–100
        object indexing 93–5
        sets 95–9

nativism 265–6
nearest neighbor principle 143, 154
neocortical learning 222
neurobiology 73–6
next number concept 97, 98, 101
noncohesion 165–70
    disruption of representations 170–7
    lack of core cognition 177–8, 179
    as projectable property 178–9
    sensitivity to 182
nonobjects 178
nonsense objects, autonomously moving
    198–9
nonverbal representation of numbers
    55–8, 69
numbers
    analog magnitude representations
        69–73
    nonverbal representation 55–8, 69
    ratio dependence 55–7
    representation of 53–5
    subitizing 69, 71, 72
numerical cognition 53–78
    animals vs humans 58–63
    cross-modal representations 65–9
    infants 66–8, 86–7
    as last-resort strategy 63–5

numerical cognition (*cont.*)
 neurobiology 73–6
 selective pressure for 63–4
numerical identity 96

objects
 in cognitive science 17–18
 as entities to be acted upon 13–17
 as external entities 2–4
 inert 285, 286
  action of self-propelled objects on 324–9
  as agents 337–41
  prevention from falling 325–9
  resistance to falling 318
  resistance to movement 315–16
  setting in motion 324–5
 permanence 3, 9
 self-propelled 190
  animals 104–7
  attention to 199–201
  infants' learning about 193–9
  nonsense objects 198–9
  vehicles 197–8
 tracking 12–13
object categorization 189–208
object concepts 190
 development of 205–8
object files 94, 110, 122, 153
object indexing 8–9, 93–5
object interactions 229
object perception 211–23, 231–9
 active vision 214–18
 areas of interest 214
 computational modeling 218–20, 227–56
  connectionism 227, 228–31
  constraints 228–9
  symbolic processing 227
 dual processing pathways 360–1
 environmental factors 220–1
 habituation 232–4
 looking-time paradigms 231–2
 violation of expectancy 168, 231,
   234–9
 visual exploration 212–13
object permanence 147
 A-not-B error 3–4, 14–15, 249–52
 behavioral dissociation 239–40
 connectionist models 245–9, 253–5
  Mareschal model 246–8
  Munakata model 245–6
 models of development 239–52
 symbolic models
  Drescher model 243–4
  Luger model 242–3
  Prazdny model 240–2, 243
  symbolic 240–5
object persistence 107, 108–13
 in adult visual cognition 110–12

 in infant cognition 109–10
 spatiotemporal cues 150–2
 see also spatiotemporal priority
object recognition 1–24
 core knowledge theories 4–9
 objects as permanent entities 2–4
object recognition network 246
object representation 94, 165–6, 184–5
 in animals 7–8
object review 110, 111, 123, 155
object-specific preview benefit 111,
  123, 155
object unity 212–13
occlusion 113–20
 adult perception 114–16
 infant research 113–14
 vs implosion 116–20
orientation changes 306, 307–9, 310
overhypothesis, Bayesian model 274–9

parallel individuation 95–6
 enriched 97
parietal cortex 74
 ventral 75
perceivers 217
perception
 cohesion violations 121–4
 spatiotemporal continuity 114–16
perseverative search 365–6
persistence 136–7, 294
 self-propelled objects 312–13
 see also continuity; object permanence
persons 190
Piagetian tradition 95, 100
Piaget, Jean 3–4, 146
position changes 306, 309
prefrontal cortex 70
procedural knowledge 241, 242
property/kind individuation 10–12
proportion-of-contact 318
Pylyshyn, Zenon 170

ratio dependence 55–7
rational constructivism 263–81
reaching 180–2
 dissociation from looking 16, 236
 predictive 292–3
reacquiring of objects 117–18
reflectance 159
regular-random numerosity illusion 59
relative velocity principle 143, 154
repetition attenuation 150
repetition blindness 143, 144
representations
 analog magnitude 69–73
 cross-modal 65–9
 material entities 165–86
 noncohesive entities 170–7

non-verbal 55–8, 69
numbers 53–5
objects 7–8, 94, 165–6
response integration network 247
reviewing 154
rhesus monkeys, tunnel effect in 149
    numerical cognition 54–5
    object representation by 7–8
    search errors 17

saccadic eye movements 214–18
salience maps 219
same object advantage 358
searching
    competition and inhibition 363–5
    perseverative 365–6
    random 16
selective attention 26
self-motion 207
self-propelled objects 190, 285–344
    action on inert objects 324–9
    altering direction of motion 288–92
    animals 194–7, 341–3
        as agents 341–2
        as biological agents 342–3
    appearance changes 312
    attention to 199–201
    characterization of 330–43
        autonomy 330–4
        inert agents 337–41
        intention 334–7
        self-propelled objects vs agents 330
    displacement out of sight 297–306
        tests with younger infants 299–305
    expectance of movement 313–15
    infants' expectations about 287–330
    learning about 193–9, 201–4
        generalization 201–4
    location changes 306, 309–11
    nonsense objects 198–9
    orientation changes 306, 307–9, 310
    persistence 312–13
    position changes 306, 309
    resistance to falling 318–24
        explanations 323–4
        tests with younger infants 320–3
    resistance to movement 315–18
    vehicles 197–8
semantic congruity 59–60
sets 95–9
set-based quantification 96
set-size limitation 87–8, 94
shape 204–5
    learning generalization on 202
    vs kind 271–3
shape bias
    development of 268–71, 279
    in word learning 263–7

Sokolovian habituation 232
solidarity 354
    wall task 355–7
solidity 8, 294
spatiotemporal continuity see continuity
spatiotemporal cues 150–2
spatiotemporal information 12
spatiotemporal knowledge 361–3
spatiotemporal priority 112, 135–59
    evolution of 148–9
    explanation of 152–9
        functional 156–9
        mechanistic 153–6
    infant object cognition 146–8
    ontogenetic origins 146–9
    phylogenetic origins 146–9
    visual cognition 137–46
        amodal completion 137
        amodal integration and tunnel effect 137–41
        apparent motion 141–4
        illusory conjunctions 144–6
stimulus differences 38–9
subitizing 69, 71, 72
substance tracking 122
surface features 158–9
surviving occlusion 112
symbolic models 227
    object permanence 240–5
        Drescher model 243–4
        Luger model 242–3
        Prazdny model 240–2, 243

tracking, predictive 292–3
trajectory prediction model 237–8
tunnel effect 137–41
    rhesus monkeys 149
type-of-contact 318

updating 135

vehicles
    autonomously moving 197–8
    categorization of 190, 191
violation of expectancy see expectancy
    violation
visual cognition 110–12, 137–46
    amodal completion 137
    amodal integration and tunnel effect
        137–41
    apparent motion 141–4
    illusory conjunctions 144–6
visual expectation model 236
visual exploration 212–13
visual memory 141
visual object interactions 231–9
    habituation 232–4
    looking-time paradigms 231–2
    violation of expectation 168, 231, 234–9

wall task 355–7
Weber fraction 91
Weber's Law 57, 59, 99
words
  kinds vs shapes 271–3
  learning, shape bias in 263–71
working memory 25–47, 98
  capacity
    adults 26–7

    flexibility of 31–2
    infants 27–31
  complexity vs capacity 31–7
    adults 31–2
    infants 32–7
  exceeding capacity 37–46
  forgetting 37–46
    adults 37–8
    infants 37–46

Printed and bound by CPI Group (UK) Ltd, Croydon, CR0 4YY